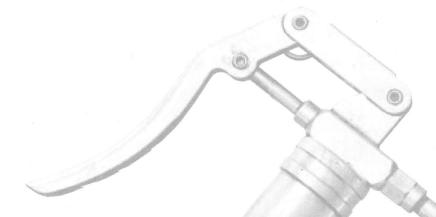

DESIGNING MICROSOFT®
ASP.NET
APPLICATIONS

Microsoft®
.net

Douglas J. Reilly

PUBLISHED BY
Microsoft Press
A Division of Microsoft Corporation
One Microsoft Way
Redmond, Washington 98052-6399

Library of Congress Cataloging-in-Publication Data
Reilly, Douglas J.
    Designing Microsoft ASP.NET Applications / Douglas J. Reilly.
       p. cm.
    Includes index.
    ISBN 0-7356-1348-6
    1. Internet programming. 2. Active server pages. 3. Web servers. I. Title.

  QA76.625 .R45 2001
  005.2'76--dc21   2001051310

Printed and bound in the United States of America.

3 4 5 6 7 8 9   QWE   6 5 4 3 2

Distributed in Canada by Penguin Books Canada Limited.

A CIP catalogue record for this book is available from the British Library.

Microsoft Press books are available through booksellers and distributors worldwide. For further information about international editions, contact your local Microsoft Corporation office or contact Microsoft Press International directly at fax (425) 936-7329. Visit our Web site at www.microsoft.com/mspress. Send comments to *mspinput@microsoft.com*.

ActiveX, JScript, Microsoft, Microsoft Press, MS-DOS, Visual Basic, Visual C++, Visual Studio, Windows, and Windows NT are either registered trademarks or trademarks of Microsoft Corporation in the United States and/or other countries. Other product and company names mentioned herein may be the trademarks of their respective owners.

The example companies, organizations, products, domain names, e-mail addresses, logos, people, places, and events depicted herein are fictitious. No association with any real company, organization, product, domain name, e-mail address, logo, person, place, or event is intended or should be inferred.

Acquisitions Editor: David Clark
Project Editor: Sally Stickney
Manuscript Editor: Jennifer Harris

Body Part No. X08-06257

For Jean, Tim, and Erin—
I owe my life to the people I love.

Table of Contents

Acknowledgments

I'm one of a relatively small group of people: long-term survivors of liver cancer. As I was writing my last book, I was diagnosed with and treated for liver cancer. That I am here to write about it almost four years later is a testament to good fortune, good technology, and good people. First among the good people who got me this far is Dr. Hans Gerdes at Memorial Sloan Kettering Cancer Center, who, along with his office assistant, Joanne Booth-Pezantez, didn't take "We don't know what that spot on Doug's liver is" for an answer. Dr. Gerdes is more than a doctor; he has become someone I trust for advice and support for all the chaos caused by Familial Adenomatous Polyposis, the disease at the root of my family's health problems. For more information on this and other hereditary colon cancers, see *http://www.hereditarycc.org*.

I must mention the "Freds" (Fred Stodolak and Fred Paliani), Jim Hoffman, Rich Iavarone, Tara O'Neill, and Jason Nadal at Golf Society of the U.S. The Freds provided a work environment that allowed me to use neat technology while not requiring me to dress up. They also kindly allowed me to use a couple of the articles from the Golf Society of the U.S. Web site (*http://www.golfsociety.com*) for an example in Chapter 10. Jim was the best boss a guy could have, especially a guy like me who likes to hole up in the basement and play with computers. Jim has looked at some of the chapters, and his honest assessment of what makes sense and what doesn't has helped me a great deal. Rich and Jason have given me a hand on occasion with JavaScript questions. Tara worked some magic on my picture for use in the author bio page. Trust me, she didn't have much to work with! Thanks, all.

In my spare time, I do a great deal of work for the St. Barnabas Healthcare System (SBHCS). Kathy Collins and Rich Wheatley have allowed me to continue working on cool projects in the four years or so since I left full-time employment there. SBHCS has provided a wonderful environment for creating cool systems that work on one of the largest intranets in the state. In addition to Rich and Kathy, I also work closely with Darcy Kindred (an interface goddess), Ryan Grim, and Joanne Gibson, among others. Thanks for your patience while I was writing this book. A special thanks to the folks in the SBHCS Behavioral Health Call Center, who have put up with delays in making changes to their system due to my too busy schedule during the writing of this book.

Susan Warren at Microsoft was an amazing help, answering more than one frazzled e-mail when I was late delivering a chapter and the examples just wouldn't work. Her patience in pointing out my mistakes and her willingness to dig in to get to the bottom of things when there was a real problem helped immensely. Susan, along with Scott Guthrie and Rob Howard, also provided great support for me and all the ASP.NET authors, starting what seems like a lifetime ago, back at the first ASP.NET author's summit.

At that first ASP.NET author's summit, I happened to get teamed up with G. Andrew Duthie of Graymad Enterprises for a hands-on exercise. Since then, we have corresponded and commiserated through e-mail and in person at various conferences. Andrew's book on ASP.NET should be finished "real soon now," and I encourage you to take a look at it when it hits the shelves. Andrew is perhaps the most outspoken proponent of Microsoft technology that I know, and he uses that technology to do some neat things. Others who I trust for technical feedback and just plain advice include Ed Colosi, Tom Dignan, Michael Zaccardi, and Sue Shaw. Claudette Moore, my agent, worked harder on this book than she might on some others. Thank you for getting in there and helping me organize my thoughts.

Writing a book for Microsoft Press is different than most other book-writing experiences. But writing this book was different than even the normal Microsoft Press experience. This is not exactly the book I had initially planned, due in part to the huge success of ASP.NET, even in beta. Because of this unexpected success, it was important to get the book out there, even if that meant some last-minute changes. My editor, Sally Stickney; Jennifer Harris, the manuscript editor; David Clark, the acquisitions editor; and Robert Lyon, the technical editor, have all been amazing even in the face of seemingly unreasonable deadlines, the normal beta software weirdness, and my constantly remembering one more great thing I needed to add. Robert especially has saved me from myself on more than one occasion. Thanks!

Of course, living with an author while he or she is writing a book can be quite an experience as well. Erin, my daughter, has ensured that I continue to be involved in some of the finer things in life, such as Ani DiFranco's music. I can't wait for that concert coming up! My son, Tim, reminded me all summer how important exercise is, and I really did listen. Thanks for the walks and the bike rides!

Jean, my wife of 23 years, has long been the rock that grounds our family. While I may drift off on this or that tangent, Jean is the one who makes sure everything that needs to be done gets done. In the case of our family, that includes almost daily dealings with one health insurance company or another. For that alone, she has earned a seat in heaven. Of course, there's much more than that. You know that whole, "In sickness and in health, for better or worse" agreement? Jean really meant it! There has been more *health* than *sickness*, and more *better* than *worse*, but you really know someone will be there for you when they are there for you at the worst time of your life and show no signs of giving up on you. Jean, may we spend forever together, with 100-year extensions!

Introduction

When I look down, I miss all the good stuff.
And when I look up, I just trip over things.

—Ani DiFranco

When I first heard about ASP.NET at a Microsoft author's conference over a year ago, I thought it might just be too good to be true. I can now create Web pages that are based on compiled code, in one of many *very* cool, object-oriented languages? I can use *real* variables with types and all? I can create server-side components using the .NET languages that will allow me to encapsulate all kinds of functionality that my applications need, and I don't have to worry about deploying COM components? I can use special validator components to magically test values entered on the client *and* the server? As I said, it sounded too good to be true.

In fact, ASP.NET lets you do all that and more. ASP.NET has quite simply changed the way I build Web applications. While doing some heavy-duty Active Server Pages (ASP) programming, I always tried to move any functionality I could into the database because the deployment issues in the database were much easier to deal with than the deployment issues with ASP files spread over a cluster of machines. I no longer have to do that, and neither will you!

Of course, with the new abilities comes some additional complexity. The only thing harder than working with all this new Microsoft .NET Framework complexity is trying to describe it. While working on many of the chapters in this book, I felt like the writer quoted above. Dealing with all the nitty-gritty details might hide the total coolness of what I was doing, yet just looking at the cool results without seeing the details can trip you up.

I've tried to give you the details you need to know to get the job done, but the entire .NET Framework is *huge*. There are literally thousands of classes. In many places, I've referred you to the MSDN documentation included with the .NET Framework, and I encourage you to use it. If you need to do something with strings, look up the *System.String* class on MSDN. If file access is important, look at the *System.IO* namespace. I've tried to refrain from reproducing the same information that the MSDN documentation offers, except in areas in which exhaustive reference source, and this book is more of a tutorial that, after some basics are covered, will take you through real-world problems and solutions. Both types of information sources have their place.

Who Should Read This Book?

ASP.NET provides an opportunity for developers currently working with ASP to create more powerful and scalable Web applications. At the same time, ASP.NET provides developers who haven't previously been involved with Web development with a new opportunity to begin developing Web applications. Because of the two likely audiences for this book, I don't assume that all readers will have tremendous experience with Web development. That said, if you don't understand HTML at all, you need to make sure you know at least what's covered in Appendix B.

Because you can use both Microsoft Visual Basic .NET and C# with ASP.NET, I don't focus on one language to the exclusion of the other. A Visual Basic programmer or a C++ programmer new to ASP.NET should be able to follow the samples. The samples alternate between Visual Basic .NET and C#. In the few cases in which the programming language matters, I've shown the samples in both languages or, more frequently, pointed out the differences between the languages. Learning the .NET Framework is the better part of the work required to learn to use ASP.NET.

Overview of the Book

Chapter 1 introduces you to ASP.NET development. To help you better understand ASP.NET, I go through the earlier alternatives to ASP.NET. If you don't have extensive Web development experience, this chapter will be very important. Chapter 2 introduces managed code and the common language runtime. Developing .NET applications is very different from developing traditional Win32 applications. If you're new to .NET development (and virtually everyone is at this point), this chapter will bring you up to speed.

The bane of many Visual Basic and C++ developers (and especially those who work in both languages) is the lack of common types. For Visual Basic developers, the inability to easily get to *all* the Win32 API is an additional problem. The .NET Framework, which addresses both of these issues, is covered in Chapter 3. In Chapter 4, I dig into ASP.NET development, showing samples in both Visual Basic .NET and C#. I show you how to create ASP.NET applications in Visual Studio .NET. Visual Studio .NET provides a very convenient environment for developing ASP.NET applications, but it is different than developing using simpler tools such as a text editor.

Chapter 5 looks at ASP.NET Web Forms. At the heart of all ASP.NET applications are Web Forms. Developers new to ASP.NET but experienced with ASP need to know that the development patterns used in ASP.NET are different than those used in ASP. Visual Basic developers need to understand the many ways that Web Forms differ from the forms they're used to. Chapter 5 covers these differences.

Chapter 6 introduces you to a new way of developing components. In addition to creating user controls, ASP.NET developers can create components entirely in the same languages that their Web Forms use. Or they can create components in a different language the .NET Framework supports, if that better suits their needs. Chapter 7 demonstrates how to create components that mix and match client and server functionality. Sometimes it makes sense to do a task on the client, and sometimes it makes sense to do it on the server. Chapter 7 walks you through creating components that allow you to do the work of the component (the client, the server, or a combination of both) wherever it makes sense.

Chapter 8 introduces ADO.NET. No introduction to ADO.NET would be complete without some discussion of XML, and you'll find that there as well. Chapter 9 combines ADO.NET with some of the ASP.NET server controls that allow you to create data grids and tables more easily than you might think possible. In addition, I use an example database to show you how to create a form that allows the user to add, edit, and delete records.

Finally, Chapter 10 uses the same example database to allow information to be shared using XML Web services. XML Web services are a new way to share functionality across the enterprise or across the world.

About the Companion CD

All the sample code is on the companion CD that accompanies this book. The code has been tested using post–Beta 2 builds of Microsoft Visual Studio .NET. The primary test configuration has been Microsoft Windows 2000 Server with Service Pack 2 and Information Internet Services (IIS) installed. Chapters 8, 9, and 10 demonstrate database access and require Microsoft SQL Server 2000 to be installed. Chapters 9 and 10 use a SQL Server 2000 database named GolfArticles that is provided on the CD.

Each sample folder has a Readme file that describes how to set up and test the sample. Be sure to review these Readme files when testing the samples.

I could add value to what's there. The MSDN documentation is an amazing, System Requirements
You'll need the following software to run the samples included on the companion CD:

- Microsoft Visual Studio .NET Beta 2 or later

- Microsoft Windows 2000 or Microsoft Windows XP

- Microsoft SQL Server 2000 (for samples in Chapters 8, 9, and 10)

Do You Have Any Questions?

Every effort has been made to ensure the accuracy of this book and the contents of the companion CD. Should you run into any problems or issues, refer to the following resources.

Author

In the end, in spite of all the help from the folks at Microsoft and Microsoft Press, any errors or omissions are mine. ASP.NET is a new technology, and it was still in flux as I wrote this book. On more than one occasion, Robert Lyon, the technical editor of this book, found that what was clear and unambiguously presented in one build of the .NET documentation would be either completely wrong or unclear in a later build. Such are the challenges of writing books on Beta software. Recent builds have been much more stable, and the documentation has settled down, with new builds very rarely changing a behavior, and much more often expanding on a topic, making it clearer.

That said, I fear that you may find something here and there that doesn't quite jive with the final build, or certain topics that require clarification. If you do, please feel free to let me know. Future editions can be better as a result, and in any event, I intend to create a page on my Web site that will allow you to see any changes or corrections. Thank you for reading the book!

Douglas Reilly
doug@ProgrammingASP.NET
http://www.ProgrammingASP.NET

Microsoft Press

Microsoft Press provides corrections for books through the World Wide Web at:

http://www.microsoft.com/mspress/support/

If you have comments, questions, or ideas regarding this book or the companion CD, please send them to Microsoft Press using either of the following methods:

E-mail:

mspinput@microsoft.com

Postal Mail:

Microsoft Press
Attn: Designing Microsoft ASP.NET Applications Editor
One Microsoft Way
Redmond, WA 98052-6399

Please note that product support is not offered through the above addresses.

1

Introduction to ASP.NET Development

Although this book is about ASP.NET, you can't fully appreciate this new technology unless you understand how Web development has evolved over the last few years. In this first chapter, I'll provide you with a brief history of the various ways in which Web applications have traditionally been developed. I'll start with HTML and then go quickly through the Common Gateway Interface (CGI), the Internet Server Application Programming Interface (ISAPI), and Active Server Pages (ASP). Although these historical alternatives are all perfectly acceptable ways to create Web applications, ASP.NET has many capabilities that make it easier for Web developers to create scalable, dynamic Web applications.

In the beginning, there was Hypertext Markup Language (HTML). And it was good. In fact, it was—and still is—very good. HTML is a *markup language*—that is, a language used to describe the presentation of text and graphics. HTML documents contain *tags* that control *elements* within an HTML document. Tags are keywords, often with attributes, enclosed within less than and greater than signs (<>) (also called angle brackets). For example, the *<BODY>* tag describes the body of a document. Most (though not all) tags have an end tag that contains the element name prefixed with a slash (/)—for example, *</BODY>*. Tags used to break lines and start paragraphs (*
* for line breaks and *<P>* for paragraphs) typically are not matched with end tags. For those of you who want to know more about HTML, see Appendix B, which is a short HTML primer.

For static content that rarely changes and isn't customized for each viewer, HTML as it stands is reasonable, and for years after the introduction of HTML, this static content was good enough. Think back to the early 1990s and the difficulty involved with sharing documents. Back then, if you had a word processing document, it might be in WordPerfect format, or perhaps in WordStar or Microsoft Word format. Documents from one program were almost universally inaccessible to users of the other programs, and the lingua franca of the day, plain ASCII, might convey the actual content but at the cost of all formatting.

HTML allowed documents to be viewed by users who not only did not have the same word processing application but who also might not even use the same type of computer, and in any event, might be thousands of miles apart. To this day, one common use for HTML is to publish documents on the Internet or local intranets in a format that virtually all users can access.

HTML and the protocol that serves it across the Web, Hypertext Transfer Protocol (HTTP), had some additional advantages when they were first introduced. HTTP is a lightweight protocol, and made very efficient use of the extremely limited bandwidth available at the time. I now communicate with the Web over a very fast cable modem, but for many years, I accessed Web pages over a 28.8 or 56 Kbps modem. Although I enjoy the greater bandwidth of today, I was still able to access HTML documents at the slower modem speeds. In addition to HTTP's modest use of network bandwidth, serving static HTML pages didn't seriously stress the server, the machine that hosted the HTML content.

The Problem: Developing Dynamic Web Applications

Eventually, folks realized that in addition to mere page viewing, HTTP could be used for dynamic content. Note that by *dynamic content,* I do *not* mean the animated icons and dancing farm animals that are visible on many Web pages. Generally, these sorts of animations are created using client-side JavaScript within the user's browser. What I do mean by *dynamic content* is content tailored to the individual user for a particular visit. Dynamic content allows communication in both directions. Using a form on a Web page, a user can send requests for customized content. For instance, by entering a package tracking number, a user can retrieve details about the status of a particular shipment. Of course, the communications between the user and the server include more than just forms and customized content—*cookies,* or small bits of information, might be saved on the user's machine to help identify the user either later in the session or on his or her next visit to the Web site.

> **Note**   Client-side programming using JavaScript or another scripting language usually isn't enough to create fully dynamic Web pages. For sure, it can be useful for more than just animated icons. A particularly effective use is providing client-side validation without requiring a round-trip to the server. ASP.NET makes using client-side validation code remarkably easy. In Chapter 5, I'll cover some of the standard validation routines, and in Chapter 6, I'll explain how to create your own components that can use client-side and server-side code together to provide an efficient and reliable application.

In the mid-1990s, many companies were under increasing pressure to lower total cost of ownership. Traditional "fat client" applications, with dueling dynamic-link libraries (DLLs) and registry settings, were becoming an increasingly large part of this cost. Many companies saw Web-based applications as a way to quickly deploy mission-critical applications across the enterprise with minimal impact on the client machines. For example, as I'm writing this, I'm working on several applications that are deployed via e-mail, giving the user the Uniform Resource Locator (URL) as well as some initial details required for operation of the system. An administrator registering a new user on the system triggers these automatic e-mail notices, minimizing the work required to deploy an application.

Managing all this dynamic content became much more of a challenge than simply placing static HTML documents in an appropriate directory and allowing users to read it. There are several ways to provide this dynamic content. In the sections that follow, I'll describe the various techniques for creating dynamic content. Each technique has its pros and cons, and each was specifically designed to provide dynamic content.

One Solution: Common Gateway Interface

An early solution for providing dynamic Web content, and still extremely popular in the UNIX world, is the Common Gateway Interface (CGI) specification. CGI applications are executable programs that can run on a Web server and can be used to create dynamic Web content. For instance, Listing 1-1 is a simple CGI console application that displays "Hello CGI World" in a browser.

```
// SayHelloCGI.cpp: A simple CGI application
//

#include "stdafx.h"
#include <stdio.h>

int main(int argc, char* argv[])
{

    printf("HTTP/1.0 200 OK\r\nContent-Type: text/html\r\n\r\n");
    printf("<HTML>\r\n<HEAD>");
    printf("<TITLE>Hello CGI World</TITLE></HEAD>\r\n");
    printf("<BODY>\r\n<CENTER><H3>Hello CGI World</H3></CENTER>");
    printf("<BR>\r\n</BODY>\r\n");
    printf("</HTML>\r\n");
    return 0;
}
```

Listing 1-1 A simple CGI application

This very simple CGI program prints both the header information and the HTML that produces the page shown in Figure 1-1. The first *printf* function sends out the minimum headers required. The first header gives the HTTP version (*HTTP/1.0*) as well as a code indicating success (*200 OK*). The next line gives the content type—in this case, *text/html*. The content type tells the browser how to interpret the content. For instance, if we used *application/msword* instead of *text/html*, the browser would expect the balance of the content to be a Microsoft Word or Rich Text Format (RTF) file rather than HTML. Following the last header are two carriage return/line feed pairs, signaling the end of the headers. After that comes the normal HTML content.

Figure 1-1 The browser screen produced by the program in Listing 1-1

About Console Applications

Although the program in Listing 1-1 can be compiled as a standard 16-bit MS-DOS application, I've compiled it as a full 32-bit console application. When run, this application looks like an old-fashioned MS-DOS text-mode application, as shown below, but it truly is a full 32-bit application, able to call virtually all the Win32 functions, load DLLs, and so on. There are usually better ways to create quick-and-dirty applications these days, but some applications—notably command-line tools—are really more appropriate as console applications. *Service applications*—applications that run even when no user is logged on—are console applications that call a couple of special application programming interface (API) functions to allow them to run as services.

In most typical console applications, *standard input* refers to the input the program will get from the keyboard. *Standard output* is normally written to the screen. A CGI application reads from standard input and writes to standard output. In most operating systems, standard input and standard output can be redirected, and that is exactly what happens to a program run as a CGI program.

The Good News About CGI

A CGI program can do virtually anything you can imagine. You can use a CGI program to access databases, read files, work with the registry, and everything else that a Win32 program can normally do.

The example application in Listing 1-1 uses C/C++, but there's nothing to prevent you from using any other programming language or development environment to create a console application that can read from standard input and write to standard output. PERL is often used in the UNIX world to create CGI programs, and in the Win32 world, Borland's Delphi offers explicit support for

CGI applications, providing classes to manage reading from and writing to standard input and standard output.

If you teach a group of programmers who are experienced in creating text-mode programs a little bit about HTML, it's likely that they will be able to create halfway decent CGI programs. CGI programs are easy to test, and the code/test/debug cycle is straightforward. You can simply have the compiler deposit the executable file in the correct directory, test the application in the browser, and then go back to the editor to make changes, repeating the process as necessary.

The Bad News About CGI

To understand the drawbacks of CGI, you have to consider exactly what's happening when a CGI program is executed. For example, to call the application in Listing 1-1, I might use a URL like this:

http://localhost/sayhellocgi/sayhellocgi.exe

In Microsoft Internet Information Services (IIS), this URL will do one of two things. It will either offer to download the program SayHelloCGI.exe from the sayhellocgi virtual directory to the local machine, or it will execute the program. We obviously want the program executed in this case, and to allow that to happen, you must allow execute permissions for the virtual directory in question. (See Appendix A for details on how to set these permissions.)

If execute permissions is allowed, when this URL is entered, SayHelloCGI.exe will be executed, with information about the request available via standard input and with whatever is sent to standard output sent to the browser. If the headers aren't properly formed—for example, if you don't place the second carriage return/line feed pair after the last of the headers—some browsers will simply ignore the text, whereas others will display an error message along with the text written to standard output. Once the CGI program completes its task, it exits.

The CGI model is good because once the program has been run and it exits, you can modify or remove the CGI program just as you can any other program; however, the ability to do this is at the heart of the problem with CGI. When a CGI program is executed, it is loaded into memory, and when the program finishes, it is then completely removed from memory. A lot of work is associated with creating and destroying processes. Creating a process is a relatively expensive operation compared to, say, simply reading an HTML file. This creation and destruction of processes for each request eventually leads to performance problems. Also, an issue related to resources is involved. If there are 100 clients accessing the same CGI program, there will be 100 instances of that program in memory. This can quickly eat up resources on a Web server and cause scalability problems. As Web sites evolved from mere conveniences to large mission-critical e-commerce organizations, it became apparent that a solution that addressed problems with CGI was needed.

Another Solution: Internet Server Application Programming Interface

To overcome the performance and scalability problems that CGI brings, Microsoft developed a new way for developers to build scalable applications. This high-performance alternative is called the Internet Server Application Programming Interface (ISAPI). Instead of housing functionality in executable files, ISAPI uses DLLs. Using DLLs instead of executable programs has some definite performance and scalability advantages.

There are two distinct types of ISAPI DLLs: *ISAPI extensions* and *ISAPI filters*. ISAPI extensions are explicitly called in a URL sent to the IIS server, as shown here:

http://localhost/sayhelloisapi/sayhelloisapi.dll

The ISAPI extension could also be called with arguments that will allow a single ISAPI extension to perform multiple tasks. Just as in the CGI example, the directory must have execute permissions enabled, or the DLL will be downloaded to the client rather than run on the server. ISAPI extensions are typically used to process client requests and output a response as HTML, which is very similar to the way CGI programs are used.

ISAPI filters perform a function that can't be directly duplicated with CGI applications. ISAPI filters are never explicitly called; instead, they are called by IIS in response to certain events in the life of a request. The developer can request that an ISAPI filter be called whenever any of the following events occur:

- When the server has preprocessed the client headers

- When the server authenticates the client

- When the server is mapping a logical URL to a physical URL

- Before raw data is sent from the client to the server

- After raw data is sent from the client to the server but before the server processes it

- When the server logs information

- When the session is ending

As with any filter, ISAPI filters should request only the notifications it requires and process them as quickly as possible. One of the more common uses of ISAPI filters is to provide custom authentication. Another use is to modify the HTML that will be sent to the client. For example, an ISAPI filter could be used to change the background color of each page. Because ISAPI filters aren't nearly as common as ISAPI extensions, I won't cover them any further in this book. If you want to learn more about ISAPI extensions, you can check out my book *Inside Server-Based Applications* (Microsoft Press, 1999).

ISAPI specifies several entry-point functions that must be exported from the DLL. Using these entry points, IIS can load the DLL; call the functions that it implements, passing in parameters as required; and receive the data to write back to the browser. ISAPI requires only two entry-point functions to be implemented (*GetExtensionVersion* and *HTTPExtensionProc*).

ISAPI extensions are often created using the Microsoft Foundation Class Library (MFC) ISAPI classes. Using these MFC classes can make developing your ISAPI extensions a lot easier. For example, if you select the ISAPI Extension Wizard in the New Projects dialog box in Microsoft Visual C++ 6.0, the first screen of the wizard will appear, as shown in Figure 1-2. If you're creating only an ISAPI extension, this is the only step required. Click Finish, and the ISAPI Extension Wizard will create the files needed to create an ISAPI extension. In this example, the ISAPI extension is named SayHelloISAPI.

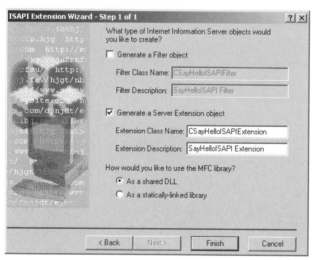

Figure 1-2 The first step in creating an ISAPI extension in Visual C++ 6.0

One of the functions created by the ISAPI Extension Wizard is named *Default*. To duplicate the functionality of the CGI program in Listing 1-1, I've modified the wizard-provided implementation of *Default*, as shown in Listing 1-2.

```
////////////////////////////////////////////////////////////////////////
// CSayHelloISAPIExtension command handlers

void CSayHelloISAPIExtension::Default(CHttpServerContext* pCtxt)
{
    StartContent(pCtxt);
    WriteTitle(pCtxt);

    *pCtxt <<
        _T("<CENTER><H3>Hello ISAPI World</H3></CENTER>");
    *pCtxt << _T(" \r\n");

    EndContent(pCtxt);
}
```

Listing 1-2 *Default* function in a simple ISAPI extension

Notice that in this example, all that is being explicitly written is the actual content that appears in the browser window. The default implementation of *StartContent* writes the start *<BODY>* and *<HTML>* tags. The default implementation of *WriteTitle* calls *GetTitle* and then writes that title within the *<TITLE> </TITLE>* tags. In this case, I wanted to replace the default implementation of *GetTitle* so that I could provide my own title, as in the CGI example in Listing 1-1. The following code fragment does exactly that:

```
LPCTSTR CSayHelloISAPIExtension::GetTitle() const
{
    return "Hello ISAPI World";
}
```

EndContent writes the ending *</BODY>* and *</HTML>* tags.

After compiling the ISAPI extension DLL and setting up the appropriate virtual directory in IIS, the ISAPI DLL can be copied to the directory and run by entering the correct URL. The browser will display a screen similar to the one shown in Figure 1-3.

Figure 1-3 The browser screen created by the SayHelloISAPI example

The Good News About ISAPI

ISAPI addresses many of the weaknesses of CGI applications. Unlike CGI applications, which create and destroy processes with each request, the code of an ISAPI extension is generally loaded once for the lifetime of the server (unless the memory is needed for other purposes—in practice, not a very common event). As an added bonus, the ISAPI application generally runs within the process space of IIS, allowing the ISAPI extension to have better communication with IIS. Recent versions of IIS have given the administrator greater control over which memory space each application runs within. Commonly, new or distrusted applications are run in a process separate from the IIS server itself. Running in an existing process space and remaining in memory offers significant advantages in both performance and scalability.

Like a CGI application, a single ISAPI application can perform multiple tasks by accepting parameters passed in the URL. One difference in ISAPI is that the MFC classes hide many of the parameter-cracking details from the ISAPI extension developer. Using *parse maps* (preprocessor macros that are common throughout MFC applications), requests are transparently mapped to member functions of the main class of the ISAPI extension, a descendant of the *CHttpServer* class. Even better for people who aren't MFC fans, the ISAPI extensions can run using only the ISAPI-related classes, leaving behind the bulk of the MFC class structure. In a lightweight, server-based application, this lack of baggage can be a significant advantage.

The Bad News About ISAPI

The problems with ISAPI are almost all associated with ISAPI application development. First and foremost, the ISAPI extensions developer isn't your average developer. Developing an ISAPI application requires a developer who is at least familiar with C++ and MFC as well as HTML. To say that these two skill sets are not related is an understatement. Although a fair number of developers are familiar with MFC and a large number of developers are familiar with HTML, the intersection of these two skill sets just isn't that common; MFC developers have likely been working on traditional Windows applications, where HTML knowledge isn't a requirement. Unlike some of the other Internet development technologies we'll look at in this chapter, ISAPI development can't be easily divided between the core of the application and the details of presentation. ISAPI has a single, monolithic DLL, and without providing your own, homegrown scripting, there's no easy way for the HTML user interface designer and the core business logic designer to independently perform their tasks.

The second problem with developing ISAPI applications once you've found appropriate development staff occurs when testing builds of your DLL. As I was generating the simple SayHelloISAPI application, I first called the URL and then, while getting ready to shoot the screen for Figure 1-3, realized that I had forgotten to center the text in the browser, as I had in the CGI example. I recompiled the example and tried to copy it back to the appropriate directory, only to be reminded of another limitation of ISAPI applications: by default, the ISAPI application is loaded in memory and held there until the World Wide Web Publishing service is stopped. Thus, until the service was stopped, I couldn't replace the ISAPI application. It's possible to request that ISAPI applications not be cached by IIS. On a development machine, that's generally what I would do. However, before you release an ISAPI extension, you *must* test the application with caching turned off to verify that you don't have bugs hidden by variables always being initialized because the DLL is loaded with each request.

Beyond the problem of actually replacing your ISAPI DLL on a running server, problems arise when you're trying to debug the DLL. MFC developers in particular, and Visual C++ developers in general, are used to the convenient debugging provided by the Visual C++ integrated development environment (IDE) when creating standard applications. Although it isn't impossible to debug an ISAPI application using the Visual C++ IDE, it isn't easy.

> **Note**   ASP.NET programmers who still need some of the power and flexibility that ISAPI applications and filters offer can use HTTPhandlers and HTTPmodules.

A Better Solution: Active Server Pages

If you're wondering why we've dwelt on the alternatives to ASP.NET in a book about programming ASP.NET, the answer lies in the details of the implementation of ASP.NET and its predecessor, Active Server Pages (ASP). Understanding ISAPI is required for a deeper understanding of ASP and thus ASP.NET.

During the beta of IIS 2.0, which became part of Windows NT 4.0, Microsoft introduced a new technology initially codenamed "Denali." This was during Microsoft's "Active" period, and so the technology was eventually named Active

Server Pages, or ASP. Several versions of ASP have been released, most notably the versions included with Windows NT 4.0 Option Pack (ASP 2.0 and IIS 4.0) and Windows 2000 (ASP 3.0 and IIS 5.0). For the purposes of this discussion, I'll consider ASP as a whole, without referring to version differences.

How Does ASP Work?

The more inquisitive among you may be wondering, "How does ASP convert scripts into HTML?" The short answer is ISAPI. Let me explain.

If you dig deep into IIS, you'll find the Application Configuration dialog box, shown here. This dialog box controls what is done when each of a dozen or so file extensions are passed in a URL. Notice that for URLs with an .asp extension, ASP.dll is specified.

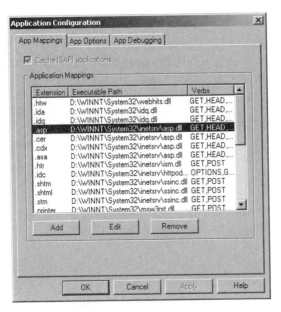

The following screen shot shows the Dependency Walker tool included with Visual C++. The middle pane on the right side shows the functions that are exported from ASP.dll. Interestingly, two of the functions exported are *GetExtensionVersion* and *HttpExtensionProc*, functions required for ISAPI extensions. There's also an optional function, *TerminateExtension*, that ISAPI extensions may support.

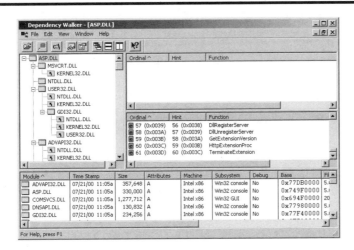

You might expect that ASP would be implemented as an ISAPI filter, but as you can see in this investigation of the ASP.dll included with IIS 5.0, ASP is implemented using an ISAPI extension. It's surprisingly simple to create your own ASP-like system. Simply register an extension you want to process and add it to the Application Configuration dialog box. Next create an ISAPI DLL that will be called when a file with the specified extension is included in a URL. When a URL with the specified file extension is requested, the *HttpExtensionProc* function in the ISAPI DLL is called. ISAPI DLLs have access to callback functions to allow them to get all the information they need to process requests.

Why might you create your own ISAPI DLL and map it to a specific file extension? If you have very specialized scripting requirements, this might be a reasonable solution if no other reasonable scripting alternative is available. Or you might want to create an ASP-like scripting engine in a language not currently available. With the advent of ASP.NET, there's very little reason to implement a different language in exactly this way. ASP.NET provides a much more convenient and powerful way to include of new languages.

ASP is a different type of development environment. First, ASP is a scripting environment. You simply edit the page, place it in a properly configured directory with the proper permissions assigned, and call it from a browser. Second, and something that was originally quite impressive but would later become a significant obstacle to development, ASP code can be mixed with standard HTML.

> **Note**   Active Server Pages, long known as ASP, has unfortunately become a victim of a name collision: *ASP* is also used to refer to Application Service Providers. To avoid confusion, throughout this book, *ASP* refers to Active Server Pages. I'll refer to Application Service Providers as Application Service Providers rather than the using the abbreviation *ASP*.

ASP code is generally written in Microsoft Visual Basic Scripting Edition (VBScript), but Microsoft JScript is also available. Listing 1-3 is a sample ASP application, SayHelloASP, written in VBScript.

```
<% Option Explicit %>
<HTML>
<HEAD>
<TITLE>Hello ASP World</TITLE>
</HEAD>
<BODY>
<CENTER>
<%
Dim x
For x=1 to 5
    Response.Write("<FONT size=" & x)
    Response.Write(">Hello ASP World</FONT><BR>" & vbCrLf)
Next
%>
</CENTER>
</BODY>
</HTML>
```

Listing 1-3 The SayHelloASP sample application

The SayHelloASP application's output is shown in Figure 1-4.

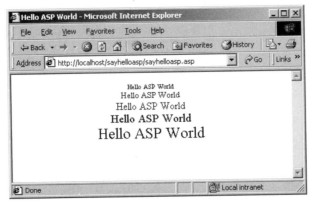

Figure 1-4 The output from the SayHelloASP sample in Listing 1-3

The SayHelloASP example is a little grander than the previous SayHelloCGI and SayHelloISAPI examples, to show you some of the power of ASP. Rather than simply displaying "Hello ASP World" a single time, here the text is displayed in a loop, with the text gradually increasing in size. The first line in Listing 1-3 is a directive to the VBScript engine, *Option Explicit*. This directive instructs VBScript to insist that all variables be explicitly declared. (I'll elaborate on that directive and its implications in the section "The Bad News About ASP" later in this chapter.) The directive is enclosed within a <% and %> character pair. This character pair represents the start and end delimiters for scripting within an ASP page. Scripting to be executed on the client can be enclosed within the *<SCRIPT></SCRIPT>* tags.

What follows in the next six lines is standard HTML code, just like you would see in a typical HTML file. After these six lines, the code enters another section of script (denoted by the <% delimiter). A variable named *x* is declared, but notice that the variable isn't declared as any particular type of variable. A *For* loop increments *x* from 1 through 5, and within the loop, the *Write* method of the *Response* object is used. The *Response* object is made available to all ASP pages, along with several other objects, including *Request*, *Server*, *Session*, and *Application* objects. At the end of the loop, the script section is terminated using a %> delimiter, and then I finish up with a few lines of standard HTML.

The *For* loop could also be written as follows:

```
<%
Dim x
For x = 1 To 5
%>
    <FONT size=<%=x %>>Hello ASP World</FONT><BR>
<%
Next
%>
```

In this version, the loop doesn't use the *Response.Write* method to write out the five versions of the "Hello ASP World" line. Instead, the font tag and the text are written directly, with one special string, *<%=x %>*. Within HTML code on an ASP page, using <%= followed by a variable and an end delimiter (%>) is a shortcut for using *Response.Write* to write a variable to the HTML stream.

Note   Using the <%=variable%> syntax has some debugging implications. If you receive an error message related to, for example, the variable not being declared, the message might refer to *Response.Write(*variable*)* rather than the actual syntax used. If you receive an error message referring to code you don't actually have in your script, you should look at these kinds of script shortcuts.

The Good News About ASP

ASP became an instant hit, in large part because it made something that was difficult (create dynamic Web content) relatively easy. Creating CGI applications and ISAPI applications wasn't terribly difficult, but using ASP was much simpler.

By default, ASP uses VBScript. Literally millions of developers are at least somewhat familiar with Visual Basic, Visual Basic for Applications (VBA), or VBScript. For these developers, ASP was *the* way to enter the Internet age. Certainly the developers could have learned a new programming language, but they didn't have to with ASP. Partly because of its use of VBScript, ASP became a viable way to build Web applications.

Just as important was the relatively easy access to databases allowed through Microsoft ActiveX Data Objects (ADO). When you need to generate dynamic content, that dynamic content obviously needs to come from somewhere, and ADO made it easy to get at that data.

Finally, and perhaps most important, the ASP development model allowed developers to essentially write code and run it. There was no need to perform compilation or elaborate installation steps. As you'll see in Chapter 4, the ASP.NET architects were careful to capture this same development model, even though what's going on under the covers is quite a bit different.

The Bad News About ASP

ASP is a powerful tool for Web developers who need to build large, scalable Web applications. Web sites such as *www.microsoft.com* and *www.dell.com* and many other sites large and small have used ASP with great success. I have no experience on such massive Web sites, but I've done a fair amount of work with ASP on a moderate-size site for SportSoft Golf, *www.golfsocietyonline.com*. Much of my experience with real-world Internet application scalability comes from working with this site, which I think is fairly representative of such moderate-size sites.

The first thing I looked into when considering ASP on sites larger than single-server intranet sites was the overhead of interpreting the VBScript or JScript code on each request. To my great surprise, with just a few notable exceptions, ASP was almost always fast enough.

On most moderate-size ASP sites, more bottlenecks are caused by database access and updates than by the ASP scripting engine. Later versions of ASP have become increasingly efficient in serving up pages, even pages with somewhat complex scripting.

Why Is VBScript String Manipulation So Slow?

My background is very heavy on C and C++, much lighter on Visual Basic, VBA, and VBScript. One of my greatest complaints about Visual Basic in general, and VBScript in particular, was the seemingly abysmal string handling performance. For instance, to use a silly example, try to append 50,000 *A*'s to a string in Visual Basic, like so:

```
Private Sub GoSlow_Click()
    Dim tstr As String
    Dim tloop As Long

    For tloop = 1 To 50000
        tstr = tstr & "A"
    Next
    MsgBox "Done"
End Sub
```

On my 400 MHz Dual Pentium machine, this code takes about 12 seconds to run. This is an extreme example, of course, but it surely shouldn't take that long to append characters to a string, even 50,000 of them.

Bob Snyder, active in the Microsoft Access and Visual Basic communities, showed me a better way to achieve the same results in a much more efficient manner, as shown here:

```
Private Sub GoFast_Click()
    Dim tstr As String
    Dim tloop As Long

    tstr = Space(50000)
    For tloop = 1 To 50000
        Mid(tstr, tloop, 1) = "A"
    Next
    MsgBox "Done"
End Sub
```

On the same machine, the previous code took 12 seconds to append 50,000 *A*'s to a string; with this code, inserting 50,000 *A*'s into a previously allocated string is instantaneous! Clearly, the issue isn't string handling per se but the allocation of strings. In the *GoSlow_Click* subroutine, each of the 50,000 times that *tstr = tstr & "A"* is called, *tstr* is reallocated.

The problem with this solution for ASP developers is that VBScript provides a *Mid* function, *not* a *Mid* statement, which would be required for use on the left side of the equals sign.

ASP.NET will have similar performance when manipulating strings in the same way, but ASP.NET does allow you to use the new *StringBuilder* class as an alternative. The *StringBuilder* class has better performance when manipulating lots of strings.

What ASP doesn't provide is a flexible, powerful, and truly scalable programming environment. For example, in Listing 1-3, when declaring the variable *x*, I don't specify a type. I can't, because all variables in VBScript are the *Variant* data type, able to hold any data, but not permanently a particular type. For instance, I could have said *x* = *"duck"* and then followed that with *x* = *7* and that would be perfectly valid code. The lack of strongly typed variables makes VBScript prone to all sorts of errors not seen in strongly typed languages.

Recall that the first line in the SayHelloASP example in Listing 1-3 is an *Option Explicit* directive. Without this directive, VBScript will happily create a variable the first time it's used. Thus, if you have a variable named *x1* and you mistype it as *xl* (*x* and the letter *l*, not *x* and the numeral *1*), VBScript will happily create a new variable *xl* with no value. Not needing to declare variables seems convenient. In fact, a review of scripting languages even gave points to ASP and another scripting environment for not requiring variables to be declared, but this isn't appropriate for professional developers creating reliable, scalable sites.

Another problem is the ability to mix and match standard HTML and scripting. More to the point, the problem is the *necessity* to intersperse code directives within HTML. In addition to hurting performance by requiring a context change each time a script section is entered and exited, this intermixing code into raw HTML makes it extremely difficult to separate the presentation from the core of the application.

A concrete example of this is the difficulty I have when working with SportSoft Golf to create content for syndication. Syndication relies on a business model very much like that of an Application Service Provider. SportSoft Golf provides the content. Their customers link the SportSoft Golf site to their own sites. The actual location of the content—whether it's on the customer's site or on the SportSoft Golf site—should be transparent to the ultimate consumer of the content. To accomplish that, the content provided by SportSoft Golf must look like the content of each of its customer's sites.

To perform this magic of creating content that looks and feels like the home sites of many different customers requires a separation between presentation and content. Although this can be done using ASP, it is painfully difficult. One common solution is to use a complex set of include files that allow content to be included separately. Using include files alone isn't sufficient, but it can work in combination with a complex set of variables that allow presentation details, such as the colors for tables, to work their way into the content.

Maintaining multiple include files and allowing the unstructured sharing of presentation details between the files defining the content and the files defining the presentation is a daunting task. This, combined with the real and perceived weaknesses of VBScript, has served to limit acceptance of ASP within many areas of the development community, especially C/C++ programmers.

A New Solution: ASP.NET

When version 3.0 of ASP was released along with Windows 2000, it became clearer that the future of software development was closely tied to the future of the Web. As part of its .NET initiative, Microsoft has introduced ASP.NET, a new version of ASP that retains the model of development ASP developers have come to know and love: you can create the code and place it in the correct directory with the proper permissions, and it will just work. ASP.NET also introduces innovations that allow easier separation of the development of the core of an application and its presentation.

ASP.NET adds many features to and enhances many of the capabilities in classic ASP. ASP.NET isn't merely an incremental improvement to ASP; it's really a completely new product, albeit a new product designed to allow the same development experience that ASP developers have enjoyed. Here are some of the notable features of ASP.NET:

- **.NET Framework**   The .NET Framework is an architecture that makes it easier to design Web and traditional applications. (Chapter 2 provides an overview of the .NET Framework.)

- **Common language runtime**   The common language runtime provides a set of services for all ASP.NET languages. If you're an ASP developer who has had to combine ASP scripting with COM objects, you'll appreciate the beauty of a common set of types across many languages. (The common language runtime is discussed in Chapter 2.)

- **Compiled languages**   ASP.NET provides enhanced performance through the use of compiled languages. Compiled languages allow the developer to verify that code is at least syntactically correct. ASP doesn't provide any such facility, so simple syntax errors might not be caught until the first time the code is executed. (Chapter 2 describes the compilation process and managed code.)

- **Cool new languages**   Visual Basic .NET is a completely new version of Visual Basic that provides a new, cleaner syntax. C# (pronounced "C sharp") is a new language designed to look and feel a lot like C++, but without some of the unsafe features that make C++ difficult to use to create reliable applications. These two languages are available out of the box, but other languages will be available from third parties as well. As of this writing, COBOL and Eiffel implementations should be available for Visual Studio .NET as well. (Visual Basic .NET and C# are discussed in Chapters 3 and 4.)

- **Visual Studio .NET**   Visual Studio .NET is a cool new development environment that brings rapid application development (RAD) to the server. (Visual Studio .NET is introduced in Chapter 4.)

- **Improved components**   The .NET Framework supports the use of new types of components that can be conveniently replaced in a running application. (Creating components for ASP.NET is discussed in Chapters 6 and 7.)

- **Web Forms**   Web Forms allow Visual Basic–like development, with event handlers for common HTML widgets. (Web Forms are discussed in Chapter 5.)

- **XML Web services**   XML Web services enable developers to create services and then make them available using industry standard protocols. (Web services are discussed in Chapter 10.)

- **ADO.NET**   ADO for the .NET Framework is a new version of the technology that allows ASP.NET applications to more conveniently get at data residing in relational databases and in other formats, such as Extensible Markup Language (XML.) (XML and ADO.NET are discussed in Chapters 8 and 9.)

Conclusion

This brief history of Web development should provide you with a foundation as you continue reading about ASP.NET. Learning a programming language or development environment is much like learning a human language. Although books that cover the syntax and vocabulary are helpful, it's often just as useful to understand the history of the people who use the language.

If you're an ASP developer, much of this chapter might be a review for you, but I hope that you've added something to your understanding of the history of ASP. If you're new to ASP and ASP.NET, understanding the history of ASP and what came before it will be useful as you begin to explore the exciting new technologies that make up ASP.NET.

2

Managed Code and the Common Language Runtime

As you'll recall from Chapter 1, with Active Server Pages (ASP), the two scripting language choices were Visual Basic Scripting Edition (VBScript) and JScript. ASP pages were placed in directories with the proper Internet Information Services (IIS) permissions, and when a client requested a page, any script code on the page was interpreted and the finished HTML for the page was returned to the client. This provided a convenient development model even for nonprogrammers. Unlike with Internet Server Application Programming Interface (ISAPI) or COM+ components, the code on an ASP page could be changed as needed. Barring client-side caching of a page, any change was immediately visible to clients.

One of the most significant improvements that ASP.NET offers is the way code is used at runtime. As mentioned in Chapter 1, although the ASP.NET and ASP development models are similar, the two technologies differ quite a bit behind the scenes. Instead of interpreting the page source each time a client requests a page, ASP.NET seamlessly compiles the page to Microsoft intermediate language (MSIL) code the first time the page is requested. Once the page is compiled in MSIL, the just-in-time (JIT) compiler converts the MSIL to native code.

> **Note**   Rather than wait for an ASP.NET page to be compiled in MSIL on first use, it's also possible to force all pages in a site to be compiled in MSIL at one time, thus catching syntax errors and other compile-time errors in a single step. The easiest way to compile all files at once is to build the application using Microsoft Visual Studio .NET.

In this chapter, I'll first introduce you to the .NET Framework, and then we'll look more closely at MSIL and the JIT compiler. Once you're familiar with MSIL code, I'll explain how the JIT compiler enables ASP.NET to use the same development model as ASP. Next we'll look at managed code and data, including some of the benefits and costs of using managed code. Finally, I'll talk about unsafe code, code that exists outside the managed runtime.

Overview of the .NET Framework

The .NET Framework is designed from the ground up to allow developers of both Web and traditional applications to build their applications more efficiently and enable them to work more flexibly. One of the most significant features of the .NET Framework is that it enables code written in multiple languages to work together seamlessly. Figure 2-1 shows the structure of the .NET Framework at a very high level.

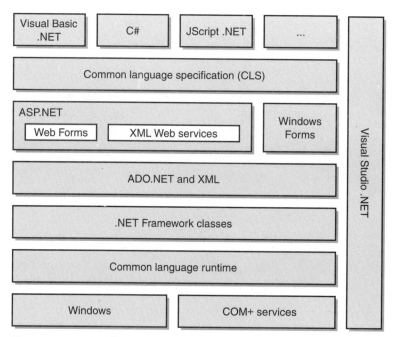

Figure 2-1 The .NET Framework architecture

Underlying the entire framework are system services. In the current implementation, this base is the Win32 API and COM+ services, although the abstraction would allow any operating system to provide the services, in theory if not in practice. Traditionally, applications have called the operating system's API directly. In the Win32 programming world, this model is difficult for Visual Basic programmers because some APIs require using data structures that are convenient for C/C++ programmers but much less convenient for Visual Basic programmers.

Layered on top of the system services is the common language runtime. The runtime loads and runs code written in any language that targets the runtime. Code targeted to the runtime is called *managed code*. (I'll describe managed code in detail later in this chapter.) The runtime also provides integrated, pervasive security. Previous Win32 environments provided security only for file systems and network resources, if at all. For example, file security on Microsoft Windows NT and Microsoft Windows 2000 is available only for volumes formatted using NTFS. The runtime provides code access security that allows developers to specify the permissions required to run the code. At load time and as methods are called, the runtime can determine whether the code can be granted the access required. Developers can also explicitly specify limited permissions, meaning that code designed to do something simple and not very dangerous can seek the minimal permissions. Compare this situation to today's VBScript-enabled mail readers, such as Microsoft Outlook, that have been targeted by virus developers. Even on a secure system, if a user with Administrator rights opens a VBScript virus, the script can do whatever the administrator can do. The role-based security that the runtime provides allows permissions to be set based on the user on whose behalf the code is running.

Relying on the runtime are the .NET Framework classes. The .NET Framework classes provide classes that can be called from any .NET-enabled programming language. The classes follow a coherent set of naming and design guidelines in mind, making it easier for developers to learn the classes quickly. We'll introduce the class libraries in Chapter 3; they cover virtually all the areas a developer would expect, from data access services to threading and networking.

On the top of the .NET Framework class library is ADO.NET and XML data. ADO.NET is a set of classes that provide data access support for the .NET Framework. ADO.NET is based on ADO but is designed to work with XML and to work in a disconnected environment.

On top of ADO.NET and XML lies specific support for two different types of applications. One is the traditional client application that uses Windows Forms, a combination of what Visual Basic and the Microsoft Foundation Class Library (MFC) had to offer. The other type of application available is ASP.NET, including Web Forms, and XML Web services.

On top of ASP.NET and the Windows Forms is the common language specification (CLS) and the languages that follow the CLS. The CLS is a set of rules that a CLS-compliant language needs to follow, ensuring that each language has a common set of features.

Introduction to Microsoft Intermediate Language

Although this description of the workings of ASP.NET and the .NET Framework might sound a lot like a description of the way a Java Virtual Machine (JVM) works, ASP.NET and JVM are different. A Java compiler creates byte code, and that byte code is passed through the JVM at runtime. This approach is slightly different than using an intermediate language to generate native code at runtime, but that slight difference has enormous implications with respect to performance.

Java's use of byte code is really nothing new. Long ago, other environments used this same structure and generally failed, partly because the hardware wasn't up to the task and partly just because the Internet didn't exist. What the .NET Framework offers that is genuinely different is code that isn't interpreted at runtime but rather becomes native code that is executed directly. One of Java's strengths (and also something that can drive developers crazy at times) is the tight security the Java/JVM model provides. The .NET Framework provides the same level of security, along with the ability to run native code, provided the user has the proper security clearance.

One significant advantage that the .NET Framework offers over Java and the JVM is the choice of programming language. If you target the JVM, you must use Java. Java is a perfectly fine programming language, but it's just one language. Developers comfortable with Visual Basic or C++ would have to spend time learning how to use the Java/JVM model. The .NET Framework allows developers to work in whatever language they're most comfortable with, from Visual Basic and C# to Eiffel and COBOL.

Let's take a look at the world's simplest Visual Basic .NET program:

```
Public Module modmain
    Sub Main()
        System.Console.WriteLine("Hello .NET World!")
    End Sub
End Module
```

For a moment, ignore anything you don't recognize here from earlier versions of Visual Basic. The intent of this program should be clear—it simply writes the string "Hello .NET World!" to the console. The details of this program are unimportant for now; it's the output we're interested in. This program, when compiled on a machine with the .NET Framework installed, will compile when the following command line is executed:

```
vbc HelloDotNet.vb /out:HelloDotNet.exe
```

> **Note**   Knowing how to use the command-line compiler isn't essential for an ASP.NET programmer, especially one who is planning to use Visual Studio .NET. At times, however, knowing how to compile from the command line can give you a better understanding of what is happening in Visual Studio .NET, as well as automate tasks.

The resulting executable file is about 3 KB, and when run, it does indeed print "Hello .NET World!" to the console, as advertised. The executable file consists of two parts: the first part is MSIL code that is used to generate the native code. The second part is metadata, which is information about the code and other elements that is required by the runtime. The .NET Framework includes a program named MSIL Disassembler (Ildasm.exe). Running the MSIL Disassembler and passing in the name of the executable file we just created results in the output shown in Figure 2-2.

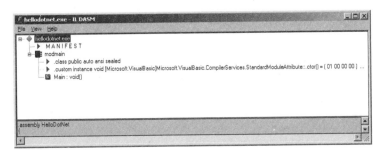

Figure 2-2 The Ildasm.exe window when HelloDotNet.exe is examined

For our purposes, the significant part of the output is the last item in the tree: *Main : void()*. C/C++ veterans will recognize the reference to *void*. In this case, it confirms that this is a section of code that doesn't return any value. A function that returns *void* in C/C++ is the same as a Visual Basic *Sub* function. When you double-click on this item, a window containing the following code appears:

```
.method public static void  Main() cil managed
{
  .entrypoint
  .custom instance void [mscorlib]System.STAThreadAttribute::.ctor() =
    ( 01 00 00 00 )
  // Code size       11 (0xb)
  .maxstack  8
  IL_0000:  ldstr      "Hello .NET World!"
  IL_0005:  call       void [mscorlib]System.Console::WriteLine(string)
  IL_000a:  ret
} // end of method modmain::Main
```

Even without the source code for this simple routine, and knowing nothing about MSIL, it's not too difficult to figure out what's going on. Line *IL_0000* is loading the constant string "Hello .NET World!". The next line is calling another *void* function, *System.Console::WriteLine*. This function expects a string. Notice also the reference to *mscorlib*—for now, you can take it on faith that this is a major library in the .NET Framework.

Pressing Ctrl+M displays a window containing the metadata for HelloDotNet.exe, shown in Listing 2-1.

```
ScopeName : HelloDotNet.exe
MVID      : {D9382B73-AF72-4778-8184-38EEA6400342}
================================================================
Global functions
------------------------------------------------------------


Global fields
------------------------------------------------------------


Global MemberRefs
------------------------------------------------------------


TypeDef #1
------------------------------------------------------------
    TypDefName: modmain  (02000002)
    Flags     : [Public] [AutoLayout] [Class] [Sealed] [AnsiClass]  (00000101)
    Extends   : 01000001 [TypeRef] System.Object
    Method #1 [ENTRYPOINT]
    ------------------------------------------------------------
        MethodName: Main (06000001)
        Flags     : [Public] [Static] [ReuseSlot]  (00000016)
        RVA       : 0x00002050
        ImplFlags : [IL] [Managed]  (00000000)
        CallCnvntn: [DEFAULT]
        ReturnType: Void
        No arguments.
        CustomAttribute #1 (0c000001)
        ------------------------------------------------------------
            CustomAttribute Type: 0a000003
            CustomAttributeName: System.STAThreadAttribute ::
              instance void .ctor()
            Length: 4
            Value : 01 00 00 00
                                    >              <
            ctor args: ()
```

Listing 2-1 Output from Ildasm.exe that shows metadata for HelloDotNet.exe

```
    CustomAttribute #1 (0c000002)
    -------------------------------------------------------------
        CustomAttribute Type: 0a000002
          CustomAttributeName:
          Microsoft.VisualBasic.CompilerServices.StandardModuleAttribute
            :: instance void .ctor()
        Length: 4
        Value : 01 00 00 00
                                        >              <
        ctor args: ()
TypeRef #1 (01000001)
-------------------------------------------------------------
Token:              0x01000001
ResolutionScope:    0x23000001
TypeRefName:        System.Object


TypeRef #2 (01000002)
-------------------------------------------------------------
Token:              0x01000002
ResolutionScope:    0x23000001
TypeRefName:        System.Console
    MemberRef #1
    -------------------------------------------------------------
        Member: (0a000001) WriteLine:
        CallCnvntn: [DEFAULT]
        ReturnType: Void
        1 Arguments
            Argument #1:  String


TypeRef #3 (01000003)
-------------------------------------------------------------
Token:              0x01000003
ResolutionScope:    0x23000002
TypeRefName:
  Microsoft.VisualBasic.CompilerServices.StandardModuleAttribute
    MemberRef #1
    -------------------------------------------------------------
        Member: (0a000002) .ctor:
        CallCnvntn: [DEFAULT]
        hasThis
        ReturnType: Void
        No arguments.


TypeRef #4 (01000004)
-------------------------------------------------------------
Token:              0x01000004
ResolutionScope:    0x23000001
TypeRefName:        System.STAThreadAttribute
    MemberRef #1
```

(continued)

Listing 2-1 *continued*

```
        ------------------------------------------------------
         Member: (0a000003) .ctor:
         CallCnvntn: [DEFAULT]
         hasThis
         ReturnType: Void
         No arguments.

Assembly
------------------------------------------------------
     Token: 0x20000001
     Name : HelloDotNet
     Public Key   :
     Hash Algorithm : 0x00008004
     Major Version: 0x00000000
     Minor Version: 0x00000000
     Build Number: 0x00000000
     Revision Number: 0x00000000
     Locale: <null>
     Flags : [SideBySideCompatible]  (00000000)

AssemblyRef #1
------------------------------------------------------
     Token: 0x23000001
     Public Key or Token: b7 7a 5c 56 19 34 e0 89
     Name: mscorlib
     Major Version: 0x00000001
     Minor Version: 0x00000000
     Build Number: 0x00000c1e
     Revision Number: 0x00000000
     Locale: <null>
     HashValue Blob:
     Flags: [none] (00000000)

AssemblyRef #2
------------------------------------------------------
     Token: 0x23000002
     Public Key or Token: b0 3f 5f 7f 11 d5 0a 3a
     Name: Microsoft.VisualBasic
     Major Version: 0x00000007
     Minor Version: 0x00000000
     Build Number: 0x00000000
     Revision Number: 0x00000000
     Locale: <null>
     HashValue Blob:
     Flags: [none] (00000000)

User Strings
------------------------------------------------------
70000001 : (17) L"Hello .NET World!"
```

The first thing you'll notice is that the metadata contains lots of information. The metadata is organized into tables, which essentially describe what your code defines and references. For example, *TypeDef #1* is a definition table that includes information about the *Main* procedure that is defined in the code. In the *TypeDef #1* table, you can see that the *Main* procedure doesn't return a value (*ReturnType: Void*) and doesn't take any arguments (*No arguments*). *TypeRef #2* is a reference table that includes information about the .NET Framework *System.Console* class that is referenced in the code. The *TypeDef #2* table references the *WriteLine* method, which doesn't return a value and takes one argument of type *String*. The metadata can also include name and version information, referenced files and assemblies, security permissions, and other information.

You might be asking yourself, Why is all this metadata needed? One reason is that it provides a language-independent description of the code. Another reason is that it makes your assembly self-describing and enables other environments to discover functionality about your assembly. An assembly is one or more files that can be logically grouped and deployed. HelloDotNet.exe is actually a single file assembly. I'll talk more about assemblies in Chapter 6.

When designing Web services, the metadata can be used to create a WSDL (Web services Description Language) file, which can be used to discover information exposed by the service. You'll learn more about Web services in Chapter 10, but briefly a Web service is a software component or service that is exposed over the Web. To give you a sneak preview, Figure 2-3 shows a Web page automatically generated by pointing to an ASP.NET page designed as a Web service.

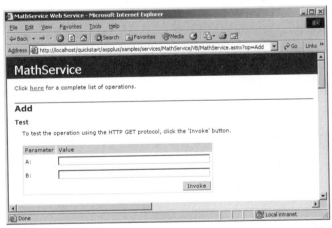

Figure 2-3 A Web page automatically generated from a Web service

As you can see, the Web service being run has an *Add* method that, not surprisingly, expects two parameters. Type *2* in each of the Value boxes, and click Invoke. The result is returned as an XML result set, as shown in Figure 2-4. I'll cover XML and data access in general in Chapter 8.

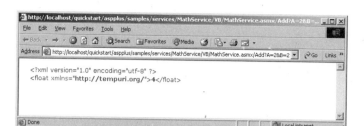

Figure 2-4 The result screen that appears when you invoke the *Add* method in Figure 2-3

The information gathered from examining the metadata lets potential users discover the required parameters and test the Web service without constructing any test frames. This capability will become increasingly important as Web services become the default method for exposing functionality over the Web.

> **Note**   In general, the ability to discover the details of code created based on the .NET Framework is beneficial. However, developers who are distributing binary code to run on client workstations rather than creating Web pages and Web services might not consider this capability an asset. As of this writing, there's no supported way to suppress this information, although in theory there's nothing to prevent the obfuscation of the information. For example, you could rename a method named *GetSecretCode* with a nonsense name such as *DDFeewsayppfgeEk* to change its visibility without compromising the runtime's ability to look at the code as required for security checks. This sort of obfuscation is used to conceal client-side JScript code as well as C language code that needs to be distributed in source code form. Fortunately, developers creating ASP.NET applications don't usually need to be concerned with this issue.

Getting the JITters—Just in Time!

In theory, as with Java, MSIL can be compiled and run in any environment that supports the runtime. As of this writing, this environment includes only the Intel architecture running Microsoft Windows, but it's safe to assume that the runtime will become available in other environments as well. What makes the potential for multiple platforms possible is the just-in-time (JIT) compiler. Figure 2-5 shows the compilation and execution process.

Compilation

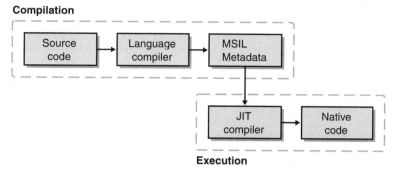

Execution

Figure 2-5 The compilation and execution of managed code

When you think about it, compiling an application from assembly code such as MSIL should impose some burden on the performance of the application. In practice, the overhead seems to be a difference small enough that in most cases no one will notice. Part of the reason for this low cost is certainly cleverness on the part of the developers of the JIT compiler, but just as much of the credit goes to the way programs are commonly used. Generally, not every single line of code within a program is used each time the program is run. For example, code re-lated to error conditions might virtually never be executed. To take advantage of this fact, rather than compile the entire MSIL code into a native executable file at the start, the JIT compiler compiles code only as it is needed, and it then caches the compiled native code for reuse. The mechanics of the JIT compila-tion are fairly straightforward. As a class is loaded, the loader attaches a stub to each method of the class. The first time the method is called, the stub code passes control to the JIT compiler, which compiles the MSIL into native code. The stub is then modified to point to the native code just created, so subsequent calls go directly to the native code.

Managed Code and Data

So what is managed code, then? *Managed code* is code that provides enough information to allow the common language runtime to perform the following tasks:

- Given an address inside the code, locate the metadata describing the method
- Walk the stack
- Handle exceptions
- Store and retrieve security information

For the runtime to carry out these tasks, the code must pass a *verification process*—unless a network administrator has established a policy that allows code to run without verification. During the verification process, the JIT compiler examines the MSIL code and the metadata to determine whether the code can be classified as type-safe. *Type-safe* code is code that can be determined to access only memory locations that it owns. This restriction ensures that the code works and plays well with other programs and that the code is safe from causing accidental or malicious corruption. Without type safety, there's no way to reliably enforce security restrictions.

Related to managed code is managed data. *Managed data* is data that is allocated and freed automatically through the runtime using a process called *garbage collection*. With garbage collection, whenever an allocated item goes out of scope, the runtime cleans it up.

One consequence of using garbage collection is that the time and potentially even the order of destruction of objects can't be determined. For instance, consider the following C# code snippet. (I'll introduce C# in Chapter 3; but even without knowing anything about C#, you should be able to understand this simple example.)

```
class MainApp {
    public static void Main()
    {
        System.String Hello = "Hello";
        System.String World = "World!";
        System.Console.WriteLine(Hello);
        System.Console.WriteLine(World);
    }
}
```

Here two *String* objects are created, one containing the literal "Hello" and the other containing the literal "World!". Although the literals are declared in that order, there's no assurance that they will be destroyed in any particular order. Furthermore, there's no assurance that they will be destroyed as the strings go out of scope. The order, or timing, in the preceding example is meaningless, but it might make a difference in other examples.

The nondeterministic freeing of objects isn't a problem unless the object holds some persistent resources that the runtime doesn't manage—for instance, a database connection or a window handle. When an object holds such resources, the solution is to provide a *Dispose* method and implement the *IDisposable* interface, which can be explicitly called to free resources. You'll see examples of this technique in subsequent chapters.

About Unsafe Code

There are cases in which you can't use managed code. For instance, many native Win32 functions require pointers. One of the problems C/C++ programmers often had with Visual Basic was the lack of pointers. Visual Basic .NET still doesn't support pointers, but it does support a similar mechanism called a *reference type*. Still, in some cases, pointers can come in handy. You might also need to access unmanaged legacy code. In the best of all worlds, all our programs would magically be converted to managed code because of the advantages it offers, but sometimes this isn't possible. So what about the times when you really need a pointer or need to access legacy code? For these situations, C# provides a special keyword: *unsafe*. A method or a section of code can be declared as *unsafe*, and when compiled using the */unsafe* compiler switch, will generate unsafe (unmanaged) code that isn't verifiable by the runtime.

In addition to *unsafe*, C# provides the *fixed* keyword. During the process of garbage collection, variables are often moved to make more efficient use of memory. If several smaller blocks of free memory are required for a single, larger allocation, the garbage collector can move the blocks to make the single larger block available. Such rearranging would obviously be disastrous for any program that had stored, within unsafe code, a pointer to one of the variables the garbage collector moved. The *fixed* keyword was added for just this situation. Within a *fixed* block, the variables referenced will be pinned and won't be movable. After exiting the *fixed* block, the variables are once again available for the garbage collector to move as required.

Conclusion

ASP programmers seldom needed to understand the underlying Win32 API that supported ASP within IIS. Indeed, VBScript and JScript offered extremely limited options for doing anything more than the language itself allowed.

ASP.NET programmers, on the other hand, have full access to all that the .NET Framework has to offer. Using C# or Visual Basic .NET, along with the .NET Framework, enable the ASP.NET programmer to do virtually anything the Win32 programmer can do.

3

The .NET Framework Objects and Languages

When developing real-world systems today, you'll encounter two significant problems: one is the problem of making software work on multiple platforms, and the other is the problem of enabling the various pieces of an application written in different languages to communicate. As you'll see in this chapter, the .NET Framework offers elegant solutions to both these problems. But first, let's review a little history.

One attempt to solve the problem of creating software that will work on multiple platforms has been to use Sun Microsystems' Java programming language. To run Java, a computer must have a Java Virtual Machine (JVM), which will interpret the Java byte code at runtime. Because JVMs are available in browsers for multiple platforms, it would appear that Java has solved part of the problem. In reality, however, there can be incompatibility in the execution of the same Java byte code even on the same platform. For example, in a recent Java project, I needed to use radio buttons but without any text associated with them. I accomplished this by setting the radio button text to an empty string. This approach worked, but in Microsoft Internet Explorer, when the radio button with no text was selected, a small dotted-line box appeared next to the radio button where the text would have been. The solution seemed simple: instead of not setting the text of the radio button or setting the text of the radio button to an empty string, I explicitly set the text of the radio button to null. This remedy worked for a time. Unfortunately, when a new version of Netscape Navigator came out, setting the text of the radio button to null not only didn't work, but also actually caused the browser to end hard, displaying an error message referencing some C++ source code. So much for Java's cross-platform compatibility.

In the beginning of the PC revolution, cross-platform compatibility was a much bigger requirement. With so many slightly different variants of PCs, as well as other platforms, having a single development environment was very important. Several circumstances have minimized this issue. First, Intel x86 assembly code has become close to a universal assembly language. Virtually any application of any significance these days is available for an Intel-based machine. Even other hardware platforms, notably the Apple Macintosh, provide emulation environments that allow Intel-based applications to run.

The second important change that has affected the issue of cross-platform compatibility has been the explosion of the Internet. The Internet provides a single platform that allows applications from a variety of platforms to work on virtually any other platform, including even the newer ones, such as wireless devices. For many applications, HTML, along with client-side JavaScript, provides a rich enough environment. Of course, in some places, the Internet boom has increased the requirement for cross-platform execution—notably in creating richer user interfaces on the client side—and here's where Java has found a place.

As I mentioned at the beginning of the chapter, another difficulty for software developers today is enabling the various pieces of an application written in different languages to communicate. Currently, a number of languages and technologies are used on the dominant platform (Microsoft Windows running on an Intel processor). Common languages include Microsoft Visual Basic, C/C++, and Borland Delphi. Less common, but still used, are languages such as COBOL, Fortran, and PERL.

From the first days of Windows development, it has been possible to call into dynamic-link libraries (DLLs) from virtually any significant program development environment, but that doesn't mean it's always been easy. For example, something as simple as passing a string as a parameter that will accept some information can cause great problems. In most programming languages, you must ensure that before the string is passed in, it has sufficient allocated space. This task isn't something that many programmers in some programming environments are used to doing. For instance, in Visual Basic, strings are managed, and if you pass a string into another function by reference, the string can have information added to it without worrying about who allocated the space. User-defined data types are much worse, and on at least one occasion not so long ago, the way that Visual Basic padded members of user-defined types wreaked havoc on many a program that had relied on structures being packaged just so.

In recent years, COM has been the glue that holds components from the various languages together. COM provides a least common denominator approach

37

to things like data types and does nothing to address issues involved with using the Win32 API. Using the Win32 API from Visual Basic requires some very un-Visual-Basic-like data structures, and the Win32 API can often be difficult to use from other languages as well. The string type supported by COM is *BSTR*, a not entirely friendly type for C/C++ programmers.

The .NET Framework offers solutions to all these problems. First it provides a system of data types that can be marshaled between multiple .NET languages without any loss of fidelity. Developers using the .NET Framework will no longer have to worry about what language might be consuming the class or component they're writing. They can spend more time solving the problem at hand and less time worrying about how the C++ client for the server program is going to interpret a string or a currency type.

Next the .NET Framework provides a virtual execution environment that addresses the need for portability without forsaking performance. Applications built on the .NET platform run as native applications on whatever platform they're running on. I'll explain the technological magic that allows this to occur in the following sections.

The .NET Solution to Type Compatibility

One of the traits that distinguishes any great programming environment is a well thought out object model. It's difficult to work with a patchwork of poorly designed objects and continue to create world-class software. Given a good object model, you can easily extend it with your own code. The underlying support for the object model of the .NET Framework is the type system the framework offers.

Let me clarify a few terms here. When I talk about the *type* of a variable, I'm talking about what the variable is designed to hold. For example, if a variable is an integer type, you wouldn't expect that setting it equal to "dog" or "Fred" would work. Likewise, if the type were a date type, 7/24/1956 would be a reasonable value, but 7 wouldn't be.

Classic Active Server Pages (ASP) programmers are used to a development language that doesn't use variables with types. More accurately, *every* variable is a single type: *Variant*. Thus, a variable can hold 7 in one line and "Fred" in the next. Many beginning programmers find having a single data type convenient, but more experienced programmers realize the mess that this limitation can cause. Although forcing you to explicitly change variables from one type to another can be more work, it does ensure that you're converting a variable in a way you intended.

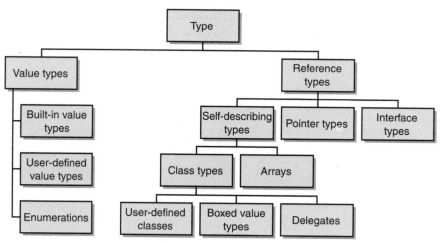

Figure 3-1 The .NET Framework type system

Figure 3-1 shows the relationship between the various types the .NET Framework supports. Some of the types are probably familiar to you, and some refer to concepts that might be new to you, such as *boxing* and *value types* vs. *reference types*. I'll explain the new concepts associated with .NET Framework types as they come up in this chapter.

Value Types

Value types refer to generally small types that are represented as a series of bits. For example, native C/C++ and Visual Basic 6.0 both have *int* and *long* types used to represent numbers. These types are commonly used for much of the processing within any program.

> **Note**   One of the problems with the type system in the Visual Studio 6.0 programming languages is the lack of consistency. Here's an example: Imagine my surprise when one day I discovered that an ASP page that had worked for some time suddenly broke very badly. The error message indicated some kind of numeric overflow. Upon inspection, the error was obvious. The user ID field within the system had exceeded the upper bound for an integer within Visual Basic, and my call to *CInt* broke. The confusion was understandable for an old C/C++ programmer. In the Win32 C/C++ world, an *int* type is 4 bytes wide, whereas in Visual Basic 6.0, it is only 2 bytes wide. Using the .NET Framework, with its common set of types across all languages, should reduce this sort of confusion.

Table 3-1 lists some of the built-in value types in the .NET Framework and indicates whether they are common language specification (CLS) compliant.

Table 3-1 Various Value Types in the .NET Framework

Class Name	CLS Compliant	Description
System.Byte	Yes	Unsigned 8-bit integer
System.SByte	No	Signed 8-bit integer
System.Int16	Yes	Signed 16-bit integer
System.Int32	Yes	Signed 32-bit integer
System.Int64	Yes	Signed 64-bit integer
System.UInt16	No	Unsigned 16-bit integer
System.UInt32	No	Unsigned 32-bit integer
System.UInt64	No	Unsigned 64-bit integer
System.Single	Yes	32-bit floating point number
System.Double	Yes	64-bit floating point number
System.Boolean	Yes	True or false value
System.Char	Yes	Unicode 16-bit character
System.Decimal	Yes	96-bit decimal number
System.IntPtr	Yes	Signed integer that is platform dependent
System.UIntPtr	No	Unsigned integer that is platform dependent
System.Object	Yes	Root object
System.String	Yes	Fixed-length string of Unicode characters

Note Visual Basic .NET doesn't allow the use of signed bytes (*System.SByte*) or unsigned integer values of any kind (*System.UInt16*, *System.UInt32*, or *System.UInt64*). Any reference to these types will generate an error. There are no such restrictions in C# code, but to achieve the highest cross-language audience, you should avoid signed byte or unsigned integer values unless they are absolutely required. Using unsigned types should be less of an issue in Visual Basic .NET because of the large range of the *System.Int64* type.

All the types ending in *16* would be referred to as *WORD* size values in Win32. Those ending in *32* would be referred to as *DWORD* size values in Win32, and those ending in *64* would be referred to as *QWORD* size values in Win32. In reality, when using any of the languages that support .NET, you won't generally use the full *System* value types. For example, in C#, the *int* type is internally a *System.Int32*. You could use *System.Int32* rather than *int*, of course, but that's not a good idea because it will make your code more difficult to read. In some situations, using the full *System* value type name makes sense. If you're creating components for commercial release, it might be better to be explicit about the type used because .NET language implementers might not implement types exactly as you would expect.

Reference Types

Reference types are types that are represented as a location for a sequence of bits. In fact, these types store only a reference to the real data. In many respects, these types are like pointers in that they point to the actual data stored on the common language runtime heap and can be accessed only through the reference. Remember that direct access to the underlying data isn't allowed so that the garbage collector can track outstanding references and then release the data when all references are released.

One potential problem with consistent object models, such as the one included with the .NET Framework, is the overhead they can bring. For example, all the objects available in the .NET Framework are derived from the *System.Object* base type. Table 3-2 shows the methods that *System.Object* provides.

Although *System.Object* is still a relatively lightweight object, carrying around a full-fledged object for each integer could hinder performance. Imagine that rather than just an integer here or there you have a large array of integers, each carried in its own object. This situation would not be workable.

The three general reference type declarations are listed here:

- **Self-describing types** The type of any self-describing type can be determined from its value. Self-describing types are further broken down into class types and arrays. Much like classes in other languages and frameworks, a class in the .NET Framework serves as a container for the properties and methods of an object. Classes are further divided into user-defined classes, boxed value types, and delegates.

- **Interface** This type provides a way to package a description of a set of functionality.

Table 3-2 **Methods of *System.Object***

Method	Description
Equals(Obj)	Returns *true* if the *Obj* is the same instance as the instance that *Equals* is called on by default; can be overridden to test for equality for value types.
Equals(ObjA, ObjB)	Returns *true* if *ObjA* is the same as *ObjB*.
Finalize	Protected method called to allow the object to clean up resources when it is garbage collected; default implementation does nothing. In C#, you would use the destructor rather than *Finalize*.
GetHashCode	Serves as a hash function for a particular type; suitable for hashing algorithms and data structures.
GetType	Returns a *Type* object that exposes the metadata associated with the object the method is called on.
MemberwiseClone	A protected method that provides a shallow copy of the object. A *shallow copy* copies only the contents of the current object, not any referenced objects.
New	A Visual Basic .NET method for object construction.
Object	A C# method for object construction.
ReferenceEquals(ObjA, ObjB)	Returns *true* if *ObjA* and *ObjB* are the same instance or both are null.
ToString	Returns a string representing the object. For example, for an integer type, would return the value.

- ■ **Pointer**   This type refers to a value that is used to point to another object. The value of a pointer type is not an object, so you can't determine the exact type from such a value. (You don't need a deep understanding of pointers to follow most of the code presented in this book.)

These types are not tightly bound to any particular .NET language. Both Visual Basic .NET and C# provide syntax to support each of these reference types.

Built-In Reference Types

One of the built-in reference types that Visual Basic .NET and C# provide is the *Object* class (in C#, *object* with a lowercase *o*). Both types are based on the *System.Object* type described earlier.

Value types have many purposes and allow for the more efficient use of resources. What happens when you want to use a value type as an object? For example, one of the methods of *System.Object* is *ToString*, often used for debugging purposes. The process is called *boxing* variables.

For example, suppose you have an *int* variable named *i* and you want to do something with a string representation of that variable. Consider this code fragment:

```
using System;

class test
{
    static void Main()
    {
        int i=5;
        object box=i;
        System.Console.WriteLine(box.ToString());
        System.Console.WriteLine(i.ToString());
        System.Console.WriteLine(box.GetType());
        System.Console.WriteLine(i.GetType());
    }
}
```

First we assign the integer *i* the value 5. Next we declare an object named *box* and assign it the value *i*. This line internally boxes the simple value type into an object and makes *box* refer to that reference type variable—hence the term *boxing*. On the following line, we print to the console (using *System.Console.WriteLine)box.ToString()*. *ToString* is a method of *object*, and the result is what you would expect: a 5 is displayed on the console.

A bit more surprisingly, the next line, which prints *i.ToString()*, also displays 5 on the console. This case is a bit different because there's not an object in sight and yet calling *ToString*, a method of *object,* still does exactly what you would hope. This occurs through the magic of the .NET Framework, which boxes the value type (in this case, the integer *i*) in an object. Thus, the method is called on the boxed version of the integer variable.

The next two lines use the same principles to display the type of object, using the *GetType* method of *object*. Notice that both the explicit boxed version of *i* held in the *box* object and the version boxed on the fly implicitly are of type *System.Int32*. Neither of these methods will likely be used except for debugging, but the ability to have an object contain a reference to any number of different types is useful.

Boxing of a value type implies making a copy of the value being boxed. For example, suppose we added the following lines to the preceding code:

```
i=12;
System.Console.WriteLine(box.ToString());
System.Console.WriteLine(i.ToString());
```

The first line (which refers to a copy of *i* as it existed at the first assignment) will still display *5* on the console, but the second line, which refers to a copy of *i* boxed just for this statement, will refer to the new value of *i* and will thus display *12* on the console. This happens because the type being boxed is a value type.

If, on the other hand, we were boxing a reference type, the object would not reference a copy but rather the object, as in the following code:

```
using System;

class intHolder
{
    public int i;
}

class test{
    static void Main()
    {
        object box;
        intHolder ih = new intHolder();
        ih.i=22;

        box=ih;

        ih.i=99;
        System.Console.WriteLine(((intHolder)box).i.ToString());
        System.Console.WriteLine(ih.i.ToString ());
    }
}
```

Both calls to *System.Console.WriteLine* would display *99* because *box* now refers to the reference type *intHolder*, not to a copy of it. If the type *intHolder* were declared as a *struct* rather than a *class*, the first line would display *22* because that would be the value of the copy of *ih* used when *ih* was boxed in the *box* object.

Note   These examples have been using C#, but the general principles apply to all languages designed to support the .NET runtime.

The *String* class, available in both Visual Basic .NET and C#, provides virtually all the string handling you could ever need. Just as important, the methods offered are identical in both languages, and future supported .NET languages should also provide the same functionality. The following code snippet only hints at the capabilities available within the *String* class:

```
Public Module test

Sub Main()
    Dim s as String
    Dim i as integer
    s="This is a test       "
    System.Console.WriteLine(s & "|")

    s=s.Trim()
    System.Console.WriteLine(s & "|")

    s="46"
    i=4
    System.Console.WriteLine(i + System.Convert.ToInt32(s))
End Sub

End module
```

When run, this short program produces the following output:

```
This is a test       |
This is a test|
50
```

First a string is created, with lots of trailing spaces. This string is sent to the console, and the result is exactly as you might expect. Next the *Trim* method is called, and the string is now printed without any spaces between the word "test" and the vertical bar. Next we set *s* equal to the literal "46". In doing so, notice that the old string ("This is a test") isn't modified by setting *s* equal to "46" but rather a new copy is created. Strings are immutable—once created, they are not directly modified. There is a *StringBuilder* class that can be used if it's convenient to directly modify an existing string rather than create a new copy. Situations in which you might make many modifications to a large string might be appropriate places to use the *StringBuilder* class rather than creating a new string for each modification because the overhead of allocating and freeing a large block repeatedly might cause a performance problem. Finally, we convert the string to an *Int32*, add it to another integer value, and display the result.

Most Visual Basic programmers are used to working with strings as you've seen here (making assignments directly to variables, with system support for tasks such as trimming strings). However, this isn't something that all C/C++ programmers are used to (although many C++ programmers are using the Standard Template Library's string classes and would thus be accustomed to this kind of convenience).

Essentially, the same code could be written in C#, and just as important, when strings are sent from code in one .NET language to another, there's not the sort of confusion that was possible with traditional Win32 languages. In the course of working with lots of different Win32 programming languages, I've encountered at least three varieties of strings:

- The zero-terminated string, native to Win32 programming and C/C++

- The Basic string, or *BSTR*, native to Visual Basic and COM

- The length-prefixed string, with a length byte followed by the actual string, native to Pascal

In addition, there are variants of the zero-terminated string that use 2-byte-wide characters (Unicode). The .NET Framework provides a cross-language standard for storing strings.

Other Objects in the .NET Framework

The .NET Framework provides literally hundreds of other classes that enable you to do things that would have previously required dropping to the Win32 API. Table 3-3 lists some of these classes, along with a brief description of what they do.

Table 3-3 Overview of Some Classes Within the .NET Framework

Object	Description
Microsoft.Win32.Registry	Manipulates the registry.
System.Array	Provides support for arrays, including searching and sorting.
System.Collections	Provides support for collections and includes classes such as *ArrayList, BitArray,* and *Stack* that make using data simpler.
System.Data	Provides support for all sorts of data access, including support for ADO.NET. (ADO.NET is covered in Chapter 8.)
System.DateTime	Provides support for working with dates and times.

(continued)

Table 3-3 *continued*

Object	Description
System.Diagnostics	Provides convenient support for writing to the event log and for other debugging tasks, as well as for accessing process information.
System.Net	Provides support for the Domain Name System (DNS), cookies, Web requests, and Web responses.
System.Net.Sockets	Provides support for using TCP/IP sockets, much like WinSock in Win32, but somewhat cleaner.
System.Reflection	Provides a managed view of loaded types and methods, as well as the ability to create and invoke types.
System.Threading	Provides support for creating and managing multiple threads of execution.
System.Web.UI	Enables you to create controls and pages that will appear in Web applications.
System.Xml	Provides support for XML, including Document Object Model (DOM) level 2 core and Simple Object Access Protocol (SOAP) 1.1.

Operations That Still Require Dropping to the Win32 API

Although the set of objects present in the .NET Framework is rich, there are still occasions in which you'll have to drop to the Win32 API. For example, Memory Mapped Files (MMF) is one feature that as of this writing won't be directly supported within the .NET Framework. MMF allows multiple applications to share data in a convenient way. I've used MMF to allow a Win32 program written in C++ to communicate with another Win32 program written using Borland Delphi. In both languages, the result was a pointer that could be written to and read just like a traditional in-memory pointer.

Both Visual Basic .NET and C# have the ability to call down to the Win32 API as well as to any standard Win32 DLL that you need to call.

Table 3-3 just touches on the capabilities of the .NET Framework classes. Until now, some of the services offered haven't been available even as a standard part of the Win32 environment (for instance, XML support). Other things, such as threading, are supported in a way that makes possible what wasn't possible previously. These threading objects allow Visual Basic programmers to safely use multiple threads of execution. Because these objects execute within a managed context, all the advantages of managed code are there (security and reliability), and you're still able to do most of what you really need to do to build powerful applications.

Overview of Visual Basic .NET

Seldom has a company the size of Microsoft taken such a chance with one of its flagship products as Microsoft has done with Visual Basic .NET. Visual Basic .NET maintains much of the ease of use that has made Visual Basic famous, but it does so while breaking virtually all existing programs. Furthermore, ASP programmers accustomed to Visual Basic Scripting Edition (VBScript) face a learning curve to be able to take full advantage of what Visual Basic .NET has to offer.

That said, the changes to Visual Basic should also silence the critics who often berate Visual Basic as a toy language. Among the major complaints of programmers who are not fans of Visual Basic is the error handling—sometimes called "On Error Goto Hell" error handling. In fact, the Visual Basic error handling *can* be made to work correctly, but in practice, it's difficult to get right, and it's often handled badly. VBScript's error handling was even more limited, making the error handling available in Visual Basic look good, which was bad news for ASP programmers. The changes to Visual Basic's error handling are just one of several areas in Visual Basic that have improved dramatically in Visual Basic .NET, albeit at the cost of compatibility with all existing code.

Out with the Old!

In many respects, Visual Basic is a victim of its own success. There's a joke about the universe being created in seven days: God was able to do it because there was no installed base. I expect the Visual Basic team can appreciate this punch line all too well. Making changes in the primary development platform for many Windows developers is a tricky business. Each new version has brought along new features but for the most part has allowed older code to continue to function. Visual Basic .NET marks a break with that tradition.

Such drastic changes are required for a lot of reasons. The most significant is that the underlying platform Visual Basic .NET is written for is no longer Win32 but rather the .NET Framework. This in and of itself requires many changes. For example, although it's possible to use the exception handling offered by the .NET Framework while continuing with the earlier "On Error Goto" model, doing so would have been at the price of fully exploiting the new framework. Before we get into all the new features offered, it's worthwhile to take a moment to look at the two biggest compatibility issues between Visual Basic 6.0 and Visual Basic .NET, which involve the *Set* statement and the default calling convention.

The *Set* Statement Goes Away

One of the many areas in which Visual Basic could be confusing to newcomers was in its use of the *Set* keyword. For example, if you wanted to create an instance of an ActiveX control with the ProgID *Foo.Bar*, you would use code such as the following:

```
Dim foo As Foo.Bar
Set foo = New Foo.Bar
```

Creating an object requires using the *Set* keyword. Unfortunately, many developers don't have a good understanding of what exactly is and is not an "object" from the Visual Basic point of view; I've seen more than a few programmers who play with using or not using the *Set* keyword in a vain attempt to get their programs going. Sometimes the result is a working program, because the presence or absence of the *Set* keyword was the problem, but as often as not the real problem remains hidden until you look at the code more closely.

Why was the *Set* keyword ever used? In Visual Basic 6.0 and earlier, objects had default properties that didn't require a parameter. So if an object *foo* had a parameterless default property called *bar*, without using *Set* there was the chance for ambiguity, as in the following example:

```
Dim f as foo
Dim o as Object
foo=o
```

In this case, it's unclear whether *foo.bar* should be set to *o* or whether *foo* should be set to *o*. Visual Basic .NET eliminates the need for using *Set* by eliminating parameterless default properties. More than eliminating the need for *Set*, in Visual Basic .NET, the *Set* keyword is no longer allowed.

Default Parameter Calling Conventions

The second area that will require significant source code changes in the move to Visual Basic .NET involves changes to the way parameters are passed to functions and subroutines. In earlier versions of Visual Basic, by default, all parameters were passed in by reference. A parameter passed in by reference means that instead of getting a copy of the parameter, the parameter is really a pointer to the parameter being passed. Consider the following code that could be used in Visual Basic 6.0:

```
Private Sub Command1_Click()
    Dim l As Long
    Dim OldL As Long
    Dim t As Long
    l = CLng(Timer())
    OldL = l
    t = CallingByReference(l)
    MsgBox "l was " & CStr(OldL) & " but is now " & l
End Sub

Function CallingByReference(Ref As Long) As Integer
    Ref = Ref Mod 60
    CallingByReference = Ref
End Function
```

Running this code any time (after 12:01 a.m.) will result in two different values, as shown in Figure 3-2.

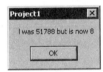

Figure 3-2 Message box displayed after calling *CallingByReference*

The ability to modify parameters is often useful, but it can sometimes confuse beginners. For example, a beginning programmer glancing at this code won't see the relationship between the variable *l* and the variable *Ref* in *CallingByReference*.

Of course, in Visual Basic 6.0 and earlier, you could always declare the parameter explicitly to be passed by value. Here's a Visual Basic 6.0 function that uses call by value:

```
Function CallingByValue(ByVal Ref As Long) As Integer
    Ref = Ref Mod 60
    CallingByValue = Ref
End Function
```

By using the *CallingByValue* function rather than *CallingByReference*, the *l* value isn't modified. Figure 3-3 shows a sample message box after using *CallingByValue* instead.

Figure 3-3 Message box displayed after calling *CallingByValue*

It's good form to explicitly declare the calling convention to avoid any confusion, and that will be the standard for the Visual Basic .NET programs that follow.

> **Note**   If a parameter is very large, passing it by reference can be more efficient than passing it by value, even if it's not the intention of the function to modify the parameter.

In with the New!

Although for some, the break with compatibility will be the big news about Visual Basic .NET, the far more important news is about the improvements to the language. The pain of the compatibility breaks will be temporary, but the gain from the new features will be long lasting. For developers familiar with working under the constraints of VBScript in ASP, the improvements are nothing short of earth shattering.

Inheritance and Polymorphism

In recent versions, Visual Basic has tried to become a more object-oriented language, with some success. To be considered object oriented, a language must meet three primary requirements. The language must be *polymorphic*, meaning that you can call a method of an object and, depending on the exact type of the object, different underlying methods are called. A second requirement for a language to be considered object oriented is *encapsulation*. Encapsulation means that there is a separation between what the object exposes and the internal workings of the object. For example, if an object exposes a collection of strings, it shouldn't expose details of implementation, such as whether the collection of strings is stored in an array, a linked list, or a stack. Perhaps the most important requirement is *inheritance*. Inheritance is the ability to derive one type from another. For example, given a simple class

```
Public Class Base
    Public Function foo
        System.Console.Writeline("Base Foo")
    End Function
End Class
```

we could create another class:

```
Public Class Derived
    Inherits Base
    Public Function bar
        System.Console.Writeline("Derived Bar")
    End Function
End Class
```

If we created an instance of class *Derived* and called *foo*, "Base Foo" would be displayed on the console.

Inheritance is a convenient way to reuse code, well beyond the cutting and pasting that has often been the standard technique for code reuse in the past. For example, imagine a set of classes representing shapes. All shapes have some characteristics in common—for instance, they might have a position as well as a length and a width. You might also have some common actions that the shapes would take—for example, *Draw* or *Move*. Using inheritance, a hierarchy of shapes could be created, all originally descended from the class *Shape*, which might look like this (in abbreviated form):

```
MustInherit Class Shape
    Private myX as Integer
    Private myY as Integer
    Public Sub New()
        myX = 0
        myY = 0
    End Sub
    Public Property X
        Get
            X = myX
        End Get
        Set
            myX = Value
            Draw()
        End Set
    End Property
    Public Property Y
        Get
            Y = myY
        End Get
        Set
            myY = Value
            Draw()
        End Set
    End Property
    MustOverride Function Draw()
End Class
```

(continued)

```
Class Square
    Inherits Shape
    Overrides Function Draw()
        ' A Square-Specific Implementation
    End Function
End Class
```

In this simple example, if you create an instance of class *Square* named *s*, setting the property *s.X* will call the *Set* property as defined in *Shape* and call the *Draw* method that is part of the *Square* class. Furthermore, if the *Square* object *s* is passed to a method that takes a *Shape* object, when *Draw* is called on the object in that method, the *Draw* associated with the *Square* object is called.

Classes can have behaviors with the same name. The ability of the language to determine, based on the type of object, what behavior is used when requested is called *polymorphism*.

A Word About Multiple Inheritance

Visual Basic .NET doesn't support multiple inheritance—there can be only one *Inherits* keyword per class. In some object models (notably C++), multiple inheritance is used as a way to allow, for example, a *Dog* object to derive from both *Animal* and *Pet*. Single inheritance isn't a terrible limitation, and it eliminates the possibility of method ambiguity. For example, if *Dog* is derived from both *Animal* and *Pet*, and if both hierarchies have a method *MakeNoise*, there could be ambiguity over exactly which method should be called.

You can get around this single inheritance restriction in many ways. In this case, *Animal* could be used as the base class, *Pet* could be derived from *Animal,* and *Dog* could be derived from *Pet*. This is *not* multiple inheritance because there is only a single *Inherits* at each level. (This solution would eliminate the *PetRock* class because a Pet Rock might be considered a pet, but it isn't an animal.)

An alternative solution is to create *Animal*, from that derive a *Dog* class, and then also have the *Dog* class implement the *Pet* interface. An *interface* is like a class except that it contains only methods, and the methods aren't implemented at the interface level. A class can implement an interface simply by declaring that it does implement the interface by using the *Implements* keyword and by providing methods that match each of the methods in the interface. Methods can implement any number of interfaces.

Structured Exception Handling

There are two general models for handling errors. The first model makes reporting errors the responsibility of any given function, with any code that calls the function responsible for taking action based on the report of an error. This approach is typified by code such as the following:

```
Ret = SomeFunc(SomeParam)
If Ret = 0 then
    ' An error occurred, so do something about it.
End If
' Continue processing.
```

This kind of error handling has several problems. Using it often requires error processing to be mixed up with returned results. For example, in C, the *fopen* function returns a file pointer that can be used for other functions that require a file pointer, such as *fgets* and the like. If the file can't be opened, however, *fopen* returns not a file pointer but *NULL*, indicating that an error occurred opening the file. Thus, the return value from the function is either a file handle *or* something entirely different, a signal that an error occurred.

Many developers can live with the lack of purity of the returned value, but most developers don't always remember to check the return result for the exceptional value indicating an error. In practice, most C programmers *do* check for the return code from calls to *fopen* because it has a fairly large chance of failure. However, many C programmers do *not* check for errors in functions like *fputs* because that function, using a valid file pointer, fails relatively rarely. Thus, many file writes will fail because the disk is full or, for other reasons, go unnoticed.

The second model for error handling is exception handling. In this sort of system, an error throws an exception and that exception bubbles up the stack until an appropriate handler is found. Although Visual Basic offers a sort of exception handling using the *On Error* statement, the form in which it was exposed wasn't the most convenient. For VBScript programmers in ASP, the options were even more limited because the system didn't allow all the control over exception handling Visual Basic or Visual Basic for Applications (VBA) allowed.

The preferred sort of exception handling is *structured exception handling*. Although structured exception handling is more a feature of the .NET Framework than of Visual Basic .NET per se, it is a critical change that will allow developers to create far more robust and reliable applications. The general form of structured exception handling is shown here:

```
Try
    ' Some code that might throw an exception
Catch e As Exception
    ' Handle the error.
Finally
    ' Used to do things that should always be done,
    ' whether or not an exception occurs
End Try
```

Any code that might throw an exception should be placed within a *Try* block. It's possible that some or all exceptions might not be appropriately handled at this level. If that's the case, the exception can be rethrown (using the *Throw* keyword) and the *Finally* block will still be executed. For example, if within the *Try* block you're opening a database connection, the *Finally* block should be where the database connection will be closed because that block of code will always be executed. Within the *Finally* block, you might need to ensure that the database connection is in fact open because the exception could've been thrown before the database connection was successfully opened. You can have multiple *Catch* blocks so that you can catch specific exceptions. The *Finally* block allows all cleanup for the code in the *Try* block to appear in only a single place, rather than existing once for when the code executed normally and once in each of the *Catch* blocks.

Function Overloading

Function overloading allows the existence of multiple functions with the same name, differing only in the parameters. For example, if you were creating a method to send a string to a browser, you might declare several functions, each named *Write*. One version would accept a string as a parameter; another, an integer; and yet another, a *DateTime* object.

If you're a VBScript programmer, you might wonder what the big deal is. In the old ASP object model under VBScript, you could, for example, call the *Response.Write* method with a string—or an integer, or a date—and it would seem to work as you would expect. There's a subtle difference, however. In VBScript, all variables are the *Variant* type, a sort of chameleon variable that becomes whatever is poured into it. The *Response.Write* method simply takes whatever is passed and writes the resulting string to the HTML stream. Function overloading is different in that the specific *Write* methods provided will be called based on the type of argument. If the *Write* method is called with an argument that can't be converted implicitly to one of the types that one of the overloaded *Write* functions expects, a compile time error is generated.

Overloading can also be used to cleanly extend existing systems without breaking existing code. For example, if a *Write* method exists that accepts a string, and if there were an option to write with a color, a *Write* method that accepts a string and a color could be created. The code inside the existing *Write* method that takes a string could then be replaced cleanly with a call to the new *Write* method that accepts a string and a color, with the color being passed in the default color. Existing consumers of the *Write* method would be none the wiser, and the natural extension to the *Write* method could be used in new code.

Stronger Typing of Variables

One of the big changes for ASP programmers moving from VBScript to Visual Basic .NET is the introduction of stronger typing of variables. Although it was possible to require declaration of variables in VBScript, it wasn't possible to declare specific types. Statements such as the following were possible:

```
Dim X

X="Hello There"
X=7

Response.Write(X)
```

In this example, the variable *X* is set to a string, and in the next line, it's set to an integer. The result of the *Response.Write* method is a string containing the number 7. This is possible because all variables in VBScript are the *Variant* type. To help catch potential data conversion errors, Visual Basic .NET has a new statement named *Option Strict* that is stricter than *Option Explicit*. Using *Option Strict* will cause Visual Basic .NET to generate an error if a data type conversion results in data loss, if a variable is undeclared, or if a variable is late bound.. This isn't news to most non–Visual Basic programmers, but for Visual Basic .NET programmers trying to create professional, reliable applications, it's a huge step forward.

Short-Circuit Evaluation

Another problem that C/C++ programmers coming to Visual Basic face is the way in which logical expressions are evaluated. For example, imagine that you have the following code in an ASP page:

```
While rs.EOF=False And rs("Grouping")=thisGroup
    ' Do something for all members of "thisGroup".
Wend
```

Programmers used to C and C++ will presume that if *rs.EOF* is *True*, the evaluation of the expression will end. In VBScript and Visual Basic 6.0, this isn't the case. In this example, even if *rs.EOF* is *True*, *rs("Grouping")* will be evaluated, causing an error to be raised. Of course, once *rs.EOF* is *True*, we really don't care about the other part of the expression because by definition it has no meaning.

Visual Basic .NET includes two new logical operators (*AndAlso* and *OrElse*) that are used for *short-circuit evaluation* of expressions. In the preceding example, you could replace the *And* operator with *AndAlso*:

```
While rs.EOF=False AndAlso rs("Grouping")=thisGroup
    ' Do something for all members of "thisGroup".
Wend
```

Once *rs.EOF* evaluates to *True*, the program can just stop the expression evaluation because it's guaranteed that the expression in total can never evaluate to *True*. We can use this evaluation order to our advantage by ordering the parts of a logical expression from least expensive to evaluate to most expensive. However, you need to remember that short-circuit evaluation means that parts of an expression might not always run, which can cause side effects. *And* and *Or* continue to operate as they did in Visual Basic 6.0 and earlier, forcing evaluation of all parts of a predicate.

Miscellaneous Changes

Here's a list of some of the other changes in Visual Basic .NET.

- All arrays use zero-based indexing. There are ways around this, using classes from the .NET Framework, but within the language itself, all arrays are zero-based. One interesting change designed to help port existing code is what happens when you declare an array. Consider the following declaration:

  ```
  Dim a(5) as Integer
  ```

  The result will be a *six* element array, from *a(0)* through *a(5)*. This allows developers to continue using arrays as they have in the past. Developers who are creating cross-language components need to be aware of this behavior and explicitly document how the component will base the array.

- The *Option Base* statement isn't supported.

- Arrays don't have a fixed size. Arrays can be declared with a size; declared without a size and sized by calling *New*; or declared, initialized, and sized in a single statement, like this:

  ```
  Dim Month() As Integer = {1, 2, 3, 4, 5, 6, 7, 8, 9, 10, 11, 12}
  ```

  In Visual Basic .NET, you can resize arrays with the *ReDim* statement. In Visual Basic 6.0, you couldn't resize arrays with a specified size.

- String lengths can't be explicitly declared.

- *ReDim* can't be used as a declaration. The variable must be declared using *Dim* first.

- The Currency data type is no longer supported. The Decimal data type can be substituted.

- The *Type* statement is no longer supported. Use the *Structure...End Structure* construction instead. Each *Structure* member must have an access modifier: *Public, Protected, Friend, Protected Friend*, or *Private*. *Dim* can be used—in which case, the access to the member is *Public*.

- Multiple variable declarations on a single line without the type repeated result in all variables on the line being declared as the same type, as in the following example:

```
Dim I, J as Integer
```

   In Visual Basic 6.0, this line will result in *I* being a Variant and *J* being an integer, but in Visual Basic .NET, both *I* and *J* are integers.

- Variables declared within a block of code have block-level scope rather than procedure-level scope. Thus, if a variable *I* is declared within a *While* block, it's visible only within the block. Note that the lifetime of the variable is the same as that of the procedure, so if a block that declares a variable will be entered more than once, the variable should be initialized on each entry to the block.

- Parentheses are always required when you're calling procedures with nonempty parameter lists.

- Rather than *While* and *Wend*, Visual Basic .NET uses *While* and *End While*. *Wend* isn't supported.

- *IsNull* is replaced by *IsDBNull*, and *IsObject* is replaced by *IsReference*.

C# (C Sharp) Overview

For many C and C++ programmers, the most anxiously anticipated feature of ASP.NET is the ability to use C#. C# is a new language, crafted specifically to work well within the .NET Framework. In particular, it is designed to work well within a managed code environment. One of the elements of C and C++ that makes these languages unsuitable for such an environment is the use of pointers. Although C and C++ can be used without using pointers, it's extremely difficult to do so. As discussed in Chapter 2, pointers make for unsafe code and thus can't be allowed in ASP.NET, except under extraordinary circumstances.

C# provides a syntax much like that of C++, while at the same time making use of all the features of the .NET Framework, including the class library and garbage collection. Curly braces mark blocks, and many of the keywords (*while, for, if,* and so on) work exactly as they would in C++. These similarities make C# a comfortable starting place for C++ programmers looking to begin ASP.NET development.

Differences Between C++ and C#

If C# were exactly the same as C++, there'd be no reason for its existence. Clearly, there was a need for a programming language somewhat lighter and considerably safer than C++. For many people, Java has been that language, but Java too has some weaknesses that have been addressed in C#. Because C++ programmers moving to the ASP.NET environment will be a primary target for C#, let's begin with a look at the differences between C++ and C#.

Safer Memory Management

One of the places in which virtually all C++ programmers create trouble for themselves is in the use of memory management and pointers. For example, although most modern C++ compilers issue warnings about using uninitialized pointers, the warnings can be ignored. Just as important, when a pointer is initialized and the object or block of memory it points to is freed, nothing prevents the program from using the pointer again, since it's likely not pointing to *NULL*, but instead to the memory that has just been freed. This situation can make for some errors that are terribly difficult to debug. In some cases, the errors will appear only in certain circumstances, and even completely disappear when debugging code is in place—a C++ programmer's worst nightmare. C# has the answer.

In C#, rather than having to explicitly free objects that have been created, the garbage collector keeps track of the references to managed objects. When there are no longer any references to an object, the object can be deleted. This approach is much cleaner than, for instance, the methods used for COM objects, which required programmer intervention to track the count of references.

C# doesn't support pointers in safe or managed code. C# does support a reference mechanism when passing parameters to functions, which has the same effect as pointers, but eliminating pointers in safe code decreases the likelihood of incorrectly accessing memory.

No Templates

One of the disappointments for C++ programmers moving to C# is the lack of *templates*. Templates provide the ability to create parameterized types. For example, if you create an integer array class, you might someday need a floating-point array class. Templates provided a clean way to accomplish this, without requiring you to cut and paste code from the integer array class to the floating-point array class. Templates generally were implemented in such a way that behind the scenes the compiler was in fact doing almost exactly that, but it wasn't something the programmer needed to get involved with.

It's extremely unlikely that templates will ever be added to C#. Currently, the developers of C# are looking at other alternatives for providing generic implementations that won't involve templates as such. The .NET Framework provides features such as array classes, so scenarios such as the preceding example won't likely present a problem. In other scenarios, however, some form of generics would be extremely useful.

No Multiple Inheritance

Like Visual Basic .NET, C# doesn't provide multiple inheritance. And as with Visual Basic .NET, this isn't a major problem. In C# (and Visual Basic .NET) you can create a class that implements multiple interfaces, which is often sufficient. Many C++ programmers have survived without the use of multiple inheritance, and I'm sure C# programmers won't be significantly harmed by this C++ feature not being present in C#.

No Global Functions

Unlike C++, which was designed from the ground up as a language that would allow programmers to move naturally toward using classes and other object-oriented features, C# is designed to force the use of many object-oriented practices. When C++ was designed, virtually all C programs could be converted to C++ simply by changing the extension from .c to .cpp and recompiling. Of course, these "C++" programs weren't really in C++, and the major benefit of compiling them as C++ programs was to take advantage of enhanced warnings for things like functions used but not declared.

Moving to C# is a totally different experience. For example, every C and C++ programming book or class for the last 20 years has contained a Hello World program that looked something like this:

```
main()
{
    printf("hello, world\n");
}
```

This program, which will compile and run with most C or C++ compilers, is *not* a valid C# program. All functions in a normal C# program are methods of a class. For example, here's a C# version of Hello World:

```
public class Hello1
{
    public static void Main()
    {
        System.Console.WriteLine("Hello, World!");
    }
}
```

All standard C# console applications use the method of some class named *Main* as the entry point. In practice, this isn't an issue for most ASP.NET programs, but it *is* important to remember that there are no global functions—everything is a method of a class.

No Preprocessor Macros

In C and C++, it was common to use macros that the preprocessor interpreted. The preprocessor works before the code is compiled, and in the case of macros, one string is replaced by another before compiling takes place. The preprocessor was extremely convenient, but it also was used in ways that eventually caused problems.

C# doesn't have a separate preprocessor, but it processes preprocessor directives as if there was one. The preprocessor directives are mostly the same as for the C and C++ preprocessor, such as *#if*, *#else*, and *#endif* as well as preprocessor directives used by Visual Studio .NET, such as *#region* and *#endregion*. However, the *#ifdef* directive is not present.

Things You Can Do in C# but Not in Visual Basic .NET

One of the most common questions on the Usenet newsgroups about C# and Visual Basic .NET is, "What can I do in C# that I can't do in Visual Basic .NET?" As of this writing, C# has only one significant feature that isn't present in Visual Basic .NET and has several features that are mandatory in C# but optional in Visual Basic .NET.

Operator Overloading

In our examination of Visual Basic .NET, we looked at function overloading—that is, the ability to have multiple functions with the same name but different argument lists. C# offers this sort of overloading, as well as *operator overloading*, which Visual Basic .NET doesn't support. Operator overloading allows you to create a method that will be called when an operator, such as +, -, ++ (increment), or -- (decrement) is used. Operator overloading in C# is similar to operator overloading in C++, but there are some notable differences. Table 3-4 lists the operators and indicates whether they can be overloaded in C#.

Table 3-4 C# Operators and Their Overloadability

Operators	Operator Type	Overloadability
+, -, !, ~, ++, --, true, false	Unary	Can be overloaded.
+, -, *, /, %, &, |, ^, <<, >>	Binary	Can be overloaded.
==, !=, <, >, <=, >=	Comparison	Can be overloaded, but only in pairs. For example, if == (equality comparison operator) is overloaded, != (inequality operator) must also be overloaded.
&&, ||	Conditional logical	Can't be overloaded, but are evaluated using the & and | operators, which can be overloaded.
[]	Array indexing	Can't be overloaded, but the same effect can be obtained using indexers. This operator can be used, for example, to create a virtual array.
()	Cast	Can't be overloaded, but the same effect can be obtained using conversion operators (implicit and explicit).
+=, -=, *=, /=, %=, &=, |=, ^=, <<=, >>=	Assignment	Can't be overloaded, although they are evaluated so that, for example, += uses the + operator.
=, comma (,), ?:, ->, new, is, sizeof, typeof	Other	Can't be overloaded.

There's a television commercial in my part of the country that shows a group of people anxiously awaiting one of those big building implosions. The building is surrounded by lots of other buildings, and so when it seems to implode correctly, everyone looks relieved, but then suddenly the contractor gives a signal and several other buildings nearby implode as well. A reporter asks, "What are you doing?" and the contractor replies, "We had some extra dynamite, and so we figured, what the heck." Overloading operators is a lot like that. It certainly has a place, and it is often quite useful. But just because you *can*, doesn't mean you *should*. A brief example might help you understand how you can use operator overloading:

```
public class MyColor
{
    public int red=0;
    public int green=0;
    public int blue=0;
    public MyColor(int red,int green,int blue)
    {
        this.red=red;
        this.green=green;
        this.blue=blue;
    }
    public static MyColor operator + (MyColor c1, MyColor c2)
    {
        return new MyColor(c1.red+c2.red,
            c1.green+c2.green,
            c1.blue+c2.blue);
    }

    public static void Main()
    {
        MyColor red = new MyColor(255,0,0);
        MyColor green = new MyColor(0,255,0);

        MyColor yellow = red + green;
        System.Console.WriteLine("RGB of yellow={0},{1},{2}",
            yellow.red,
            yellow.green,
            yellow.blue);
    }
}
```

This isn't a terribly useful example of operator overloading; it simply illustrates how overloading is done. In this example, the plus sign (+) operator is overloaded for the *MyColor* class. Here, the *MyColor* instance *c1* is the instance to the left of the plus sign, and the instance *c2* is the instance to the right of the plus sign.

The following rules of thumb apply to operator overloading[*]:

■ *Do* supply standard math operators (+, −, * and /) for all classes that represent numbers. The classic example is a complex number class.

---

[*] From Douglas J. Reilly, *Computer Language* (October 1992), page 57.

- *Do* supply overloaded operators to do things folks will expect. For example, providing an equality operator for strings is a no-brainer.

- *Do* remember the audience's expectations that some operators (such as + and −, * and /) are opposites. Overloaded operators should have opposite effects.

- *Don't* violate people's expectations of what an operator will do. Making an overloaded plus sign (+) operator subtract is an easy example of a bad idea, but confusion can be subtler as well. For example, what should the increment operator do to the string "Hi there"? Should it be "i there"? How about "Ij!uidsd"? (Each character has its ASCII value increased by 1.) If it's not obvious what an operator should do, don't create one.

- *Don't* overload an operator to modify data where the operator for native types doesn't do so. For example, don't overload a comparison operator such as the equality operator (==) so that it modifies either side of the equality test.

- *Do* create a method that will allow users of .NET languages that don't work with operator overloading to get the same functionality.

Forced Early Binding

One of the things that C++ programmers expect is that variables will always be declared and will always have a specific type associated with them. Visual Basic programmers have historically not been required to do this, although the better Visual Basic programmers will *always* use *Option Explicit* to force variables to be declared. Prior to Visual Basic .NET, not only was declaring a variable at all not required, but it was also not possible to force the type of variables to be declared.

Visual Basic .NET provides a new directive, *Option Strict*, that prevents implicit conversions as well as *late binding*. Late binding occurs when an object is created and only at runtime is the type of the object determined. This approach can be useful, but in the case of COM objects, for example, it can force almost a doubling of communications overhead between the client program and the COM object. Deciding early (at compile time) the sort of object that will be used can enable the compiler to create faster code.

> **Note**   One problem with the *Option Explicit* and *Option Strict* directives in Visual Basic is that you have to remember to use them. Fortunately, there's a way within ASP.NET to force the use of these options on an application-by-application basis. You'll learn much more about these options in Chapter 4.

C# doesn't require such directives as *Option Explicit* and *Option Strict*. More to the point, you *can't* use variables without declaring them, and you *can't* use variables without declaring the type of the variable. I've actually read reviews of Internet dynamic content development systems, including ASP, in which extra points were awarded to ASP simply because it allowed users to use variables without declarations. ASP.NET still gives you that option using Visual Studio .NET; however, I encourage you to use the *Option Strict* directive in Visual Basic .NET code.

C# doesn't allow late binding, and this may be the only area in which you can be assured that C# programs will outperform Visual Basic .NET programs. In general, all .NET languages perform about the same. In the case of Visual Basic .NET and C#, similar programs will generate similar MSIL code, and thus the .NET Framework will execute both programs with about the same speed. In complicated programs, it's possible to use late binding in Visual Basic .NET inadvertently, resulting in a program that will perform somewhat more slowly than a C# program with equivalent functionality.

Conclusion

In this chapter, you've learned most of what you need to know to be comfortable with ASP.NET. I hope this brief introduction to types, objects, and the standard languages the .NET Framework supports has been helpful. In the next chapter, we'll dive into ASP.NET programming. If you're comfortable with HTML, you should be ready to go. If not, you might want to skip ahead to Appendix B, which covers everything you need to know about HTML to enjoy the balance of this book.

Enough introduction! Let's get into Chapter 4, where we'll start creating ASP.NET applications.

4

ASP.NET Development 101

Once you've decided that you need to create dynamic Web content (and you certainly will), your next decision is to choose the tools you'll use to develop it. In Chapter 1, you learned about some of the traditional options, such as the Common Gateway Interface (CGI), the Internet Server Application Programmers Interface (ISAPI), and Active Server Pages (ASP). ASP.NET is the newest tool for developing dynamic Web applications, and in this chapter, you'll find out what you need to know to start using it. ASP.NET development has much in common with traditional ASP development, but it also has many differences. Throughout the chapter, you'll see special notes that I've added to highlight the differences between ASP and ASP.NET for you ASP programming veterans.

Hello ASP.NET World!

As with all discussions of programming languages, it's almost mandatory that the first example presented be of the "Hello World" variety. The brief introduction to ASP in Chapter 1 showed the typical "Hello World" example. This example is reproduced in Listing 4-1.

```
<% Option Explicit %>
<HTML>
<HEAD>
<TITLE>Hello ASP World</TITLE>
</HEAD>
<BODY>
<CENTER>
<%
Dim x
```

Listing 4-1   SayHelloASP.asp sample application listing   *(continued)*

Listing 4-1 *continued*

```
For x=1 to 5
    Response.Write("<FONT size=" & x)
    Response.Write(">Hello ASP World</FONT><BR>" & vbCrLf)
Next
%>
</CENTER>
</BODY>
</HTML>
```

A C# Example

The source code to produce basically the same result, written for ASP.NET, is shown in Listing 4-2.

```
<%@ Page Language="C#" %>

<HTML>
<HEAD>
<TITLE>
My First ASPX Page
</TITLE>
</HEAD>
<BODY>
<CENTER>
<%

int loop;
String s="";
for ( loop=1 ; loop<=5 ; loop++ )
{
    s=s +
        String.Format(
        "<FONT SIZE={0}>Hello ASP.NET World</FONT><BR>",
        loop);
}
Message.InnerHtml=s;
%>
<SPAN id="Message" runat=server/>

</CENTER>
</BODY>
</HTML>
```

Listing 4-2 SayHelloASPDOTNET.aspx sample application listing

> **ASP.NET Differences** ASP file names have the extension .asp. ASP.NET file names generally have the extension .aspx. (Other extensions are associated with ASP.NET, but the rough equivalent of .asp for ASP.NET applications is .aspx.) ASP and ASP.NET files can coexist side by side on a Web site; however, they won't share common application settings or session information. It's generally better to have ASP and ASP.NET applications in separate directories, interacting only via standard arguments on URLs or through a common database.

As you go through Listing 4-2, you'll notice lots of differences between the ASP.NET version and the ASP version in Listing 4-1. The first difference is the language used. Rather than Visual Basic Scripting Edition (VBScript), or even any version of Visual Basic, the page uses C#. In the first line, rather than the *Option Explicit* directive in the ASP example, SayHelloASPDOTNET.aspx uses a *Page* directive that also specifies the language to be used—in this case, C#. Because the page uses C#, *Option Explicit* isn't required to force declaration of variables, and in any event, it isn't supported.

The *Page* directive has several attributes that are important to know about. A partial list is shown in Table 4-1.

Table 4-1 Attributes of the *Page* Directive

Attribute	Description
Buffer	Indicates whether HTTP response buffering is enabled. If *true* (the default), page buffering is enabled; if *false*, buffering is not enabled. Generally, buffering a page until all content is written can improve performance of the page, although it can make the page appear to be slower because nothing is visible on the browser until all content is written. Complex pages often exist within HTML tables. If an entire page is contained within a table, it won't be rendered until the table is closed out, so explicit buffering when content is within a table has no downside.
ContentType	Defines the HTTP content type of the response as a standard Multipurpose Internet Mail Extensions (MIME) type. For instance, if this attribute is set to *Application/MSWord*, the application associated with the .doc file type will be called to open the document, instead of the standard HTML browser.
EnableSessionState	If *true*, enables session state; if *ReadOnly*, allows reading but not writing of session state; and if *false*, disables session state.

(continued)

Table 4-1 *continued*

EnableViewState	Indicates (*true* or *false*) whether view state is maintained across page requests.
ErrorPage	Sets a target URL for redirection if an unhandled error occurs.
Explicit	If set to *true*, the *Option Explicit* mode in Visual Basic .NET is enabled, requiring variables be declared.
Inherits	Defines a code-behind class for the page to inherit. This attribute can be any class derived from the *Page* class.
Language	Specifies the language used in all inline code blocks (enclosed in <% %>). This attribute can be any .NET supported language, including Visual Basic, C#, or JScript .NET.
Strict	If set to *true*, the *Option Strict* mode in Visual Basic .NET is enabled, forcing the type of variable to be declared and disallowing narrowing type conversions.
Trace	Indicates (*true* or *false*) whether tracing is enabled. The default setting is *False*. This attribute is used for debugging.
Transaction	Indicates whether transactions are supported on the page. This attribute can be set to *NotSupported*, *Supported*, *Required*, or *RequiresNew*.
WarningLevel	Indicates the warning level at which the compiler should abort compilation of a page. This attribute can be set to *0* through *4*.

There can be only one page directive per .aspx page. After the *Page* directive, the next few lines of SayHelloASPDOTNET.aspx are fairly standard HTML. Inside the code block (between the opening <% and the closing %>), you can see that the language used is C#. C/C++ programmers should be comfortable with the code that follows within the script block.

Two variables are declared, an integer named *loop* and a string named *s*. The *for* loop steps through the font sizes between 1 and 5. I use the variable *s* to hold all the HTML code to be written out. After the loop, rather than using *Response.Write* to write the output (a *very* ASP way of doing things), I set the *InnerHtml* property of the *Message* object. *Message* is an HTML <SPAN> tag declared farther down in the actual HTML, as follows:

```
<SPAN id="Message" runat=server/>
```

ASP.NET Differences   If you tried to use *Response.Write* to write the text in this example, it wouldn't compile. Strictly speaking, this isn't a limitation of ASP.NET, but rather a difference between Visual Basic and C#. Visual Basic isn't case-sensitive; C# is.

Notice that the *id* attribute of the *SPAN* element is what is used to reference the HTML object. One other important feature of the *SPAN* element is that it has a *runat* attribute, indicating that it should be run at the server. Running controls on the server is common in ASP.NET applications. Also notice that there's no closing *</SPAN>* tag. This seeming omission isn't a problem because the trailing */>* in the tag indicates that it's a start tag and an end tag.

> **Note**   Even if you explicitly place text within the *<SPAN id="Message" runat=server>* tag and a *</SPAN>* end tag, the text won't be rendered in the browser because the line *Message.InnerHtml=s;* resets the text to the string in the variable *s*. If instead you changed that line to read *Message.InnerHtml= Message.InnerHtml + s;*, the text in the actual HTML between the *<SPAN></ SPAN>* tags would be displayed, followed by the text created in the loop.

A Visual Basic .NET Example

The same page created using Visual Basic .NET is shown in Listing 4-3. This listing isn't much different from the C# example presented in Listing 4-2.

```
<%@ Page Language="VB" %>

<HTML>
<HEAD>
<TITLE>
My First ASPX Page
</TITLE>
</HEAD>
<BODY>
<CENTER>
<%

Dim tLoop as Integer
Dim s as String
s=""
For tLoop=1 to 5
    s= s + String.Format( _
        "<FONT SIZE={0}>Hello ASP.NET World</FONT><BR>", _
        tLoop)
```

Listing 4-3 SayHelloASPDOTNETVB.aspx sample application listing   *(continued)*

Listing 4-3 *continued*

```
Next
Message.InnerHtml=s
%>
<SPAN id="Message" runat=server />

</CENTER>
</BODY>
</HTML>
```

Figure 4-1 shows the output from the Visual Basic .NET version of the page; however, both the Visual Basic .NET and the C# versions produce nearly identical output.

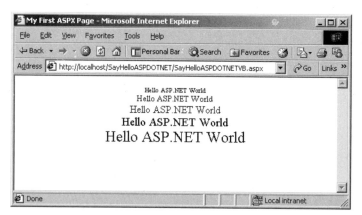

Figure 4-1 Output of the Visual Basic .NET version of the ASP.NET example shown in Listing 4-3

I've made some obvious syntax changes in this example, such as removing semicolons at the ends of statements, changing curly braces ({ and }) and the *for* loop syntax, as well as changing variable declarations. In addition, although I commonly use a variable named *loop* in C/C++ and now in C#, *loop* is a reserved word in Visual Basic .NET—therefore, I changed the variable name.

The ASP.NET Development Model

Developing applications using ASP.NET is similar to developing applications using earlier versions of ASP, as far as the overall development model is concerned. Figure 4-2 shows the general workflow from the ASP developer's perspective. The process consists of editing the page, testing the page, possibly returning to edit the page again, and so on.

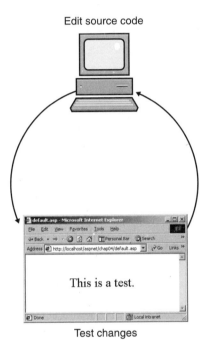

Edit source code

Test changes

Figure 4-2 The ASP development cycle

For the ASP.NET developer, the process is exactly the same, but the underlying activity is slightly different. Figure 4-3 shows the real process, which is edit-compile-test. The compile portion of the process is transparent to the developer. Every time an application is run, if the page being run hasn't been compiled, it's compiled automatically.

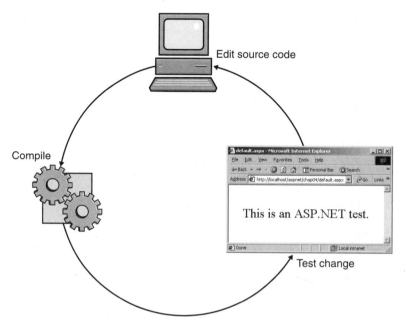

Figure 4-3 The ASP.NET development cycle

What's interesting about the ASP.NET development cycle is that while the developer's impression is that nothing has changed in moving from ASP to ASP.NET, the change under the covers has a tremendous impact. The primary benefits, aside from the new languages and the .NET Framework, are that ASP.NET applications offer better performance than ASP and greater reliability, since compiling the application ensures that blatant syntax errors are caught on the first compilation, instead of being discovered only when the actual code is run.

Creating an ASP.NET Web Application with Visual Studio .NET

Although the ASP.NET Web Application is just one of the types of applications that are possible with ASP.NET, it's the type of application you'll create most often. You don't have to use Visual Studio .NET to create an ASP.NET Web application, but your life as a developer will sure be easier if you do.

When you start Visual Studio .NET, the Start Page is the first screen that appears. The Start Page is designed to introduce you to the Visual Studio .NET environment as well as to allow you to perform many common tasks easily. One of the nicer features of the Start Page is the My Profile option. When this option is selected, you'll see a page similar to the screen shown in Figure 4-4.

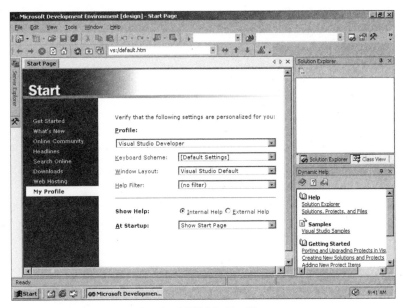

Figure 4-4 The Visual Studio .NET My Profile screen

Many developers moving to Visual Studio .NET will be coming from one of three integrated development environments (IDEs): Visual InterDev, Visual Basic, or Visual C++. Historically, these IDEs have been quite different, and developers who work in one IDE often have strong feelings about the other IDEs. To allow each developer to feel more comfortable with the new, common IDE, Visual Studio .NET allows you to configure different screen layouts and keyboard schemes to resemble what you're used to. Of course, not everyone will be happy with all the decisions the designers of the new IDE made, but having a common IDE is a necessary step toward supporting multilanguage development.

> **Note**   Although the IDE supports creating applications in Visual Basic .NET, C#, or C++, it doesn't currently allow you to create a single ASP.NET application with both Visual Basic .NET and C# pages in any clean way. I would hope that future versions of the IDE will allow greater integration of different languages within the same solution. The term *solution*, by the way, is the Visual Studio .NET term used to describe a container that can group multiple related projects.

Changing the screen layouts to emulate the various Visual Studio 6.0 IDEs is an interesting exercise and can give you a feeling of déjà vu. Although I've been quite fond of the Visual C++ 6.0 layout, for the examples in the book, I've used the Visual Studio Default layout. After months of use in one form or another, I find the default layout to be quite good.

Once Visual Studio .NET is open, you can create a new project in a variety of ways. The most general way is to click the File menu, point to New, and then click Project. Doing this displays the dialog box shown in Figure 4-5.

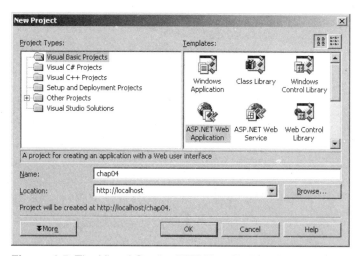

Figure 4-5 The Visual Studio .NET New Project dialog box

The folder view on the left enables you to select the language you want to use for the project or one of several types of special projects. Most often, you'll create a project in one of the language folders. In the Other Projects folder, if you're using the Enterprise edition of Visual Studio .NET, you'll see enterprise template projects that can be useful when you're creating larger distributed applications.

Depending on the type of project you select, the Location text box in the New Project dialog box might change to a folder location or a URL of the local Web server. In Figure 4-5, the location is a virtual directory on the root of the current Web directory because the project type selected is ASP.NET Web Application.

Visual Studio .NET Interactions with Internet Information Services (IIS)

For this example, I'll select the Visual Basic ASP.NET Web Application and name the project chap04. When I click OK, several things happen. As with Visual C++ 6.0, the name of the project becomes the name of the directory where the application is stored. In addition, Visual Studio .NET contacts the Web server (in this example, the local Web server) and creates an application directory by the same name. After the project is created, when I look at the Internet Information Services console, I see the application directory created, as shown in Figure 4-6.

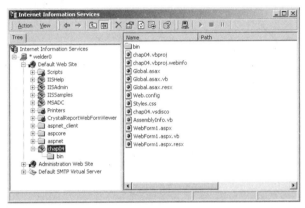

Figure 4-6 The Web application directory created by Visual Studio .NET when a new ASP.NET application is created

The right pane lists all the files created by Visual Studio .NET. The most significant files for you as the developer are the Web Form file (cleverly named WebForm1.aspx) and the code-behind file (named WebForm1.aspx.vb). If this were a C# project, the code-behind file would be named WebForm1.aspx.cs. You can use the Web.config file to customize the application settings, as I'll discuss shortly. Visual Studio .NET also creates a bin folder, in which all the compiled code for the application is stored.

Looking at the properties of the application directory (right-click on the chap04 application package icon and select Properties), you see nothing that unusual. From the Properties page, you can click the Configuration button to display the Application Configuration dialog box shown in Figure 4-7.

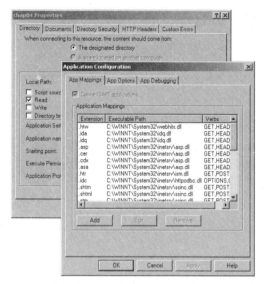

Figure 4-7 Application Configuration dialog box for newly created chap04 application directory

The App Mappings tab displays the executable or DLL that will process a given extension. In this case, the entire executable path is too large to be seen in the dialog box, but you can take my word for it that all ASP.NET extensions are mapped in IIS to C:\WINNT\Microsoft.NET\Framework\v1.0.2941\aspnet_isapi.dll. As I write this, I'm using version 1.0.2941 of the .NET Framework, so you can see that the version is part of the path to the DLL that handles ASP.NET applications. The significance of the long path that includes the version number is that it should be possible to have different ASP.NET applications using different versions of ASP.NET.

Your First Visual Studio .NET Web Page

Once Visual Studio .NET has created the project files and the application directory in IIS, Visual Studio will look something like Figure 4-8. A couple of things are significant about Visual Studio. First, notice the faint grid on the WebForm1.aspx tab. These lines are shown when *Grid Layout* is enabled. Grid Layout allows you to place components precisely, as you would on a traditional Visual Basic form.

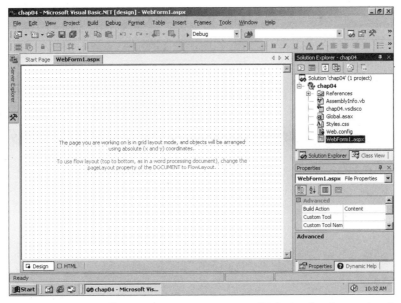

Figure 4-8 Visual Studio as soon as the new Web Application project has been created in Grid Layout

Note   The way this magic of providing precise component layout works is worth a brief note. Traditionally, HTML hasn't been able to give you such fine control of the exact placement of components within a Web page. When you place a component using Grid Layout, the component is positioned using DHTML and Cascading Style Sheets (CSS) to it to tell the browser exactly where to render it. This idea is very cool but presents two possible problems. The first is what to do about downscale browsers that don't support DHTML and CSS. To allow the illusion of precise placement to continue, a complex set of tables is sent to the browser, doing an acceptable job of placing components in most cases. A second problem is that trying to use such precise control of a page might cause some developers to create layouts that are fragile. For example, if the fonts installed don't *exactly* match the fonts the developer used, the layout will likely be different. The decision is left to the developer: the Page Layout can be changed from Grid Layout to Flow Layout if you don't want that level of control. This setting is in the property dialog box of the page. If you're developing applications for the Internet rather than an intranet, on which you have control over the clients, it might not be reasonable to take advantage of the admittedly convenient Grid Layout. In general, examples in this book won't use Grid Layout but will instead use tables to align components. The next example is an exception because I'm trying to show the IDE, and Grid Layout does show that off quite well.

Display the Toolbox by clicking the Toolbox tab on the left of the screen (just below the Server Explorer) or by clicking the Toolbox button on the toolbar. In this example, I'll add two labels and place them on the design grid, one on the top and one below it, both just about centered. I'll make the lower label a bit wider than the top label. Your screen should look something like the screen shown in Figure 4-9.

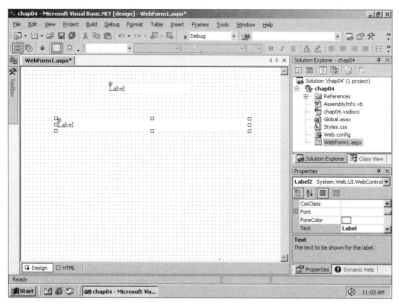

Figure 4-9 The chap04 main form with two labels added to the form

There are two major ways to modify objects on an ASP.NET page at design time. One way is to use the Properties window. This window is by default in the lower right corner of Visual Studio. To change the top label, just click that label (it should be Label1 on the form) and modify the properties. Then change the *Text* property to read, "Your First ASP.NET Page". You may need to resize the label to keep all the text on a single line. Next, go to the *Font* property. This property has a + next to it, meaning that you can expand it to get to subproperties. Change the *Bold* subproperty to *True*. As you make the preceding changes, the changes will show up in the designer immediately.

The second way to modify objects at design time is to change the code. Let's use code to change the other label, *Label2*. You have a couple coding options for changing the text of a label. First, notice the two tabs at the bottom of the design surface: the active tab, Design, and another tab, HTML. Click the HTML tab, and you'll see the HTML code, looking very much like HTML displayed in Visual InterDev 6.0. Figure 4-10 shows what that screen will look like.

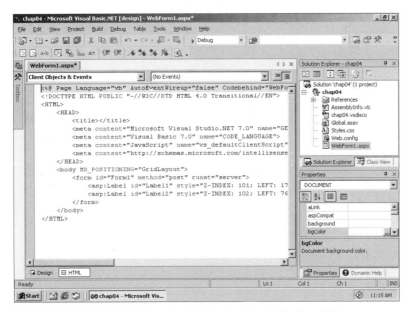

Figure 4-10 HTML code as it appears in Visual Studio .NET

Although it's not visible in the figure, at the very end of the line with the Label1 tag, the text I entered in the Properties window is between the opening and closing *asp:Label* tags. The *Font-Bold* attribute is also set to *True*, based on the change I made in the Properties window. The designer is a two-way designer; that is, changes made in HTML view also appear on the Design view. For example, if you click the *<body>* opening tag, the Properties window changes to reflect the properties of the body tag. Scroll down in the Properties window to the *bgcolor* property, click on the field, and you can either enter a valid HTML color directly or click the ellipsis button and use the Color Picker dialog box to pick the color. I selected a pale yellow, also known as *#ffffcc*. The appropriate attribute/value pair is added to the body tag. Now, if you click back to Design view, the background will be the selected color.

Changing text in Design view or HTML view is fine, but you often need to change properties at runtime. To see the Visual Basic code for this page, select Code from the View or simply press the F7 key. The active pane will change to Webform1.aspx.vb, and the Visual Basic .NET code will appear. There is very little code, and some of that is hidden from view, by default. Ignore the hidden code for now. The method that matters is *Page_Load*, which should look like the following (reformatted a bit here for clarity):

```
Private Sub Page_Load(ByVal sender As System.Object, _
   ByVal e As System.EventArgs) Handles MyBase.Load
     'Put user code to initialize the page here
End Sub
```

Rather than putting just static text into Label2, I will put some static text and the current date and time, something that is certain to change each time I refresh. I add the following code just under the wizard comment about placing user code to initialize the page here:

```
Label2.Text = "The current date and time is " + Now()
```

This code is very Visual Basic–like, and it should be clear exactly what I'm doing. Notice that I'm using the plus sign (+) rather than the ampersand (&) for concatenating strings. Use of the plus sign was discouraged in previous versions of Visual Basic but works correctly in both Visual Basic .NET and C#, and so I'll always use the plus sign to concatenate strings throughout this book.

Once I've made all the changes I want to, I can go to the Debug menu and select Start, which will start the application with the debugger. If anything has been changed since the last time the application was run, the affected items will be compiled, so the first time you run the application, it will take longer than normal. If all has gone well, a screen similar to the one shown in Figure 4-11 will appear.

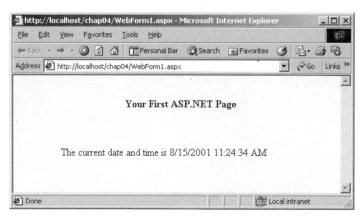

Figure 4-11 The chap04 example page when run after the modifications described in the text

This is a very simple application, but I hope it gives you a feel for some of what is possible in the Visual Studio .NET IDE. Although some of the design features have been available in tools such as Visual InterDev 6.0, the implementation in Visual Studio .NET is much better. I virtually never used the designer in Visual InterDev 6.0 because it had a nasty habit of completely reformatting my nicely formatted HTML. Visual Studio .NET is more intelligent about how it formats your text moving from the designer to the editor, and there are configuration options to control most of the reformatting Visual Studio .NET does.

The server components, such as the Label control, haven't been available before. The label components are barely the tip of the iceberg as far as server controls go. In subsequent chapters, we'll return to developing ASP.NET Web Forms as well as using server controls—even creating your own server controls.

Other Types of ASP.NET Applications

Except for the preceding ASP.NET example, the examples we've looked at so far are very similar to existing ASP applications. A page is requested, and after server-side processing, the HTML code is sent to the browser. If all ASP.NET had to offer was greater efficiency doing what ASP has always allowed, it would still be a great improvement over ASP. But as the late-night infomercial hucksters often say, "But wait, there's more!"

In addition to the ASP-like applications you're already familiar with, you can use ASP.NET to help develop two other types of scalable applications: XML Web services and applications using the HTTP runtime, HTTP handlers, and HTTP modules.

XML Web Services

How often have you had a neat bit of processing that you needed to share with another application, either on an enterprise-wide intranet or over the Internet? For example, suppose you have a bit of code that does some specialized validation, such as a credit card validation function. Given a credit card number, the function returns feedback on whether the card is valid. The function might directly interact with a database, or perhaps it might even interact with some service that has a less than convenient programmer's interface. If you have multiple applications that need to access that functionality, you've had a few ways to make the functionality available.

One way would have been to create a service application that would communicate with the various users of the function via TCP/IP, using a custom protocol. This option isn't terrible, but it does lead to a Tower of Babel of interfaces and protocols. Does the system expect the credit card confirmation result in uppercase ("YES" or "NO") or lowercase ("yes" or "no")? Does the system use commas to delimit the confirmation result from the authorization code, or tildes (~)? What port is it on? Will it work through firewalls? Will anyone remember this a year from now?

The second option has been to create a Web page that, given arguments appended on the URL, will produce a result and return it as a page that can be read by the requesting application rather than displayed in the browser. This option does resolve the problem of making the function available through firewalls, but it does nothing to address the problem of a custom interface that can be easily forgotten.

The solution is XML Web services. Briefly, XML Web services are software components that provide services to applications over the Web and use Extensible Markup Language (XML) for sending and receiving messages (I'll cover XML Web services in greater detail in Chapter 10.) XML Web services are not dependent on the .NET Framework. As a matter of fact, XML Web services don't even require a Windows operating system on the server, and they can be created using any tool that can create a Simple Object Access Protocol (SOAP) compliant application. (MSDN contains an article, "Develop a Web Service: Up and Running with the SOAP Toolkit for Visual Studio" that describes creating an XML Web service using the SOAP Toolkit in conjunction with Visual Studio 6.0; see *http://msdn.microsoft.com/library/periodic/period00/webservice.htm*.)

So why are XML Web services in ASP.NET such a big deal? The reason is the simplicity ASP.NET brings to creating them.

> **Note** XML Web services will revolutionize the way services are available on the Web. For example, at the time of this writing, Microsoft and eBay had announced an agreement to use XML Web services to integrate Microsoft services, such as Carpoint, bCentral, and WebTV, with eBay's marketplace. The kind of cooperation planned would be difficult without using XML Web services.

How simple is it to use the .NET Framework to create XML Web services? Listing 4-4 shows the XML Web service code required in Visual Basic .NET, including the code generated by Visual Studio .NET. The generated code appears between the *#Region* and *#End Region* tags.

```
Imports System.Web.Services

Public Class Service1
    Inherits System.Web.Services.WebService

#Region " Web Services Designer Generated Code "

    Public Sub New()
        MyBase.New()

        'This call is required by the Web Services Designer.
        InitializeComponent()

        'Add your own initialization code after the
        'InitializeComponent() call

    End Sub

    ' Required by the Web Services Designer
    Private components As System.ComponentModel.Container

    'NOTE: The following procedure is required by the Web Services Designer
    'It can be modified using the Web Services Designer.
    'Do not modify it using the code editor.
    <System.Diagnostics.DebuggerStepThrough()> _
      Private Sub InitializeComponent()
        components = New System.ComponentModel.Container()
    End Sub

    Protected Overloads Overrides Sub Dispose(ByVal disposing As Boolean)
        'CODEGEN: This procedure is required by the Web Services Designer
        'Do not modify it using the code editor.
    End Sub

#End Region

    ' WEB SERVICE EXAMPLE
    ' The HelloWorld() example service returns the string Hello World.
    ' To build, uncomment the following lines then save and build the project.
    ' To test this web service, ensure that the .asmx file is the start page
    ' and press F5.
    '
    <WebMethod()> Public Function HelloWorld() As String
        HelloWorld = "Hello World"
    End Function

End Class
```

Listing 4-4 Simple HelloWorld XML Web service code

Figure 4-12 shows the results of calling the XML Web service—the XML message that is the string returned by the *HelloWorld* method of the class *Service1*. Of course, the more interesting case is when parameters are passed into the service and the service does something interesting with them to generate results.

Figure 4-12 The results returned by calling the HelloWorld XML Web service shown in Listing 4-4

XML Web services open up a new world for application developers and let even the smallest development firm expose services over the Web that will create entirely new market opportunities.

HTTP Handlers and HTTP Modules

Additional types of ASP.NET applications are HTTP handlers and HTTP modules. These applications are roughly equivalent to ISAPI extensions and ISAPI filters, respectively. In the ASP world, you would resort to ISAPI extensions or filters under the following two circumstances:

- You hit a performance or scalability wall.

- You need the flexibility offered only by ISAPI extensions or filters.

The first condition isn't likely to be an issue with the current ASP.NET applications that you can develop. Given that ASP.NET applications are compiled using the same runtime as HTTP handlers and HTTP modules, performance and scalability aren't likely to be an issue.

The second condition is much more likely to persist—thus the need for HTTP handlers and HTTP modules. HTTP handlers are helpful if, for example, you need to port an existing CGI application to ASP.NET or if you need to do somewhat unusual things, like return binary data. HTTP modules can act like the binary equivalent of the Global.asax file, catching various events, and giving the application developer the greatest flexibility.

Configuring an Application

One element seems to be missing from the Visual Basic .NET code shown in Listing 4-3. Although I've often extolled the virtue of using *Option Explicit*, I didn't use it in this example, which can be done by setting *Explicit="true"* in *@ Page*. I can assure you that the page does require variables to be declared—I missed one of the references to *loop* when converting the application from C# to Visual Basic .NET and an error page did in fact appear, as shown in Figure 4-13.

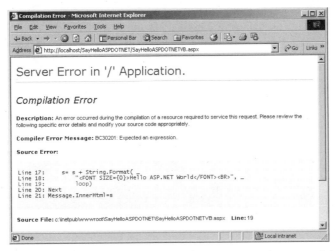

Figure 4-13 The error message that appears when a variable is not declared in the source from Listing 4-3

This error message contains quite a bit more information than ASP error messages had, and it includes the section of code that produced the error, with the line in which the error occurred displayed in red. By default, this detailed error message will appear only on the machine on which the application is running. This is good default behavior because it's possible that the source code displayed could include information about database user names and passwords, or worse.

So if I didn't set *Explicit* to true, why did I get the error message about the undeclared variable (badly reported in this example as "Expected an expression")? The answer is the Web.config file. In addition to specifying *Explicit* and *Strict* on each page, Web.config provides an application-global way to configure these and other application settings. Listing 4-5 shows a simple Web.config file.

```
<?xml version="1.0" encoding="utf-8" ?>
<configuration>
    <system.web>
        <compilation
            debug="true"
            defaultLanguage="C#"
            explicit="true"
            batch="true"
            batchTimeout="30"
            strict="true" >
        </compilation>
    </system.web>
</configuration>
```

Listing 4-5 Simple Web.config file, with *explicit* and *strict* set to *"true"*, eliminating the need for setting these on each Visual Basic .NET page

If you're familiar with XML, you'll recognize Listing 4-5 as a simple, well-formed XML document. In Chapter 8, we'll discuss XML, but in the meantime, you'll need to be aware of the following aspects of XML:

■ XML always uses matched start and end tags, unlike HTML, which allows omission of many end tags. For some tags, the start and end tags can be represented as a single tag. For example, the following tag is valid:

```
<compilation debug="true" />
```

■ XML is case-sensitive. Thus, the following tag is *not* valid, because *</Compilation>* is not seen as a closing tag for *<compilation>*:

```
<compilation debug="true"> </Compilation>
```

Although early betas of the .NET Framework were forgiving about the case of attributes values (for example, *true* and *True* were considered the same), from Beta 2 onward, the configuration files are, correctly, completely case-sensitive.

■ XML values are enclosed in quotation marks. Thus, the following tag is not valid:

```
<compilation debug=true />
```

XML is the preferred data language of the .NET Framework. As of this writing, however, no automated administrative tool is available for editing the Web.config file. This isn't a terrible problem because XML is an easy format to follow, but it does mean that you'll need to manually tweak these files using a normal editor program such as Notepad (known affectionately as Notepad.NET to some of the early ASP.NET adopters). I won't cover all the many possible configuration options because they're described in the .NET Framework Software Development Kit (SDK) documentation; however, I will go through the important configuration options and their implications and explain each of the sections of the Web.config file.

Where Does the Web.config File Go?

One of the frustrations for ASP programmers is the odd patchwork of files that grows up around any complex Web site. With ASP, the only configuration file was Global.asa, and in fact, this file is similar to the ASP.NET Global.asax file. ASP beginners often ask, "Where do I put the Global.asa file?" It turns out that in practice you had to put a Global.asa file in almost every directory.

In ASP.NET, the Web.config file provides a mechanism that should allow many sites to have far fewer redundant configuration settings within each virtual site. There is a root configuration file, in the same format as the Web.config files, named Machine.config. This file is included with the .NET Framework and contains many default settings. It is located under the Windows root, in the %windir%\Microsoft.NET\Framework\<version>\CONFIG folder. All other directories on the site inherit settings from this root file and from all Web.config files that exist higher in the logical hierarchy.

For example, one possible elementsection in the Web.config file is *appSettings*. This section is normally used to make certain variables available to all pages within an application, to multiple applications (if the variable exists in a virtual directory with other applications located logically under it), or even to all applications on the machine (if the *appSettings* section is located in the Machine.config file). Individual *appSettings* values can be overridden based on the location of the Web.config file in the hierarchy. Suppose, for example, that Machine.config contains the following section (within the *<configuration></configuration>* tags):

```
<appSettings>
    <add key="dsn" value="myDSN" />
</appSettings>
```

Suppose further that there is a virtual directory named Test that has the following section within the *<configuration></configuration>* tags:

```
<appSettings>
    <add key="dsn" value="myLocalDSN" />
</appSettings>
```

If these are the only *appSettings* sections on the machine, any page that retrieves the "dsn" key from *appSettings* will receive the value "myDSN", *except* any page within the Test application. Pages within the Test application or directories logically located below Test will receive the value "myLocalDSN".

> **Caution**   If hacking in the registry isn't enough fun for you and you're looking for a new way to hose your machine, do try improperly nesting sections of the Web.config or Machine.config files. Although this will mess up only your ASP.NET applications, it will *thoroughly* mess them up. It's possible that future versions of ASP.NET will be more forgiving of such errors, but the current version is not. Starting with Beta 2 of ASP.NET, all Web.config files are also case-sensitive. This requirement is reasonable from the standpoint that a well-formed XML file is case-sensitive, and the Web.config files are designed to be well-formed XML files. That said, the need for case-sensitivity can still be a pain.

Don't Try This at Home!

Imagine, if you will, a resource that's physically located at c:\Subdir1\Subdir2\Resource.aspx. VirtualDirectory1 is mapped to c:\SubDir1, and VirtualDirectory2 is mapped to c:\Subdir1\Subdir2. If you access Resource.aspx via http://localhost/VirtualDirectory1/Subdir2/Resource.aspx, you could access the file with completely different settings than if you used http://localhost/VirtualDirectory2/Resource.aspx. You can do this because the inheritance of configuration information from Web.config isn't based on the physical directory hierarchy but rather on the logical hierarchy defined by the virtual directory structure.

Obviously, avoiding this kind of setup is important to ensure that all access to a resource uses the same set of configuration settings.

The configuration files contain many sections. What follows in this section is an alphabetic listing and description of the significant sections, along with an example here and there to clarify things as needed.

The *authentication* Section

ASP.NET allows you to authenticate users in a number of ways. An example of the *authentication* section of the Web.config file, set up for forms-based authentication, is shown here:

```
<authentication mode="Forms">
    <forms name=".ASPXUSERDEMO" loginUrl="login.aspx"
        protection="All" timeout="60" />
</authentication>
```

The options for the *mode* attribute of the *<authentication>* tag are listed in Table 4-2.

Table 4-2 Options of the *mode* Attribute

Option	Description
Forms	Uses a user-provided form to gather identifying information
Windows	Uses Windows authentication to obtain the identity of the user
Passport	Uses Microsoft Passport authentication
None	Uses no authentication

Windows authentication in ASP.NET is similar to Windows authentication in earlier versions of ASP. Windows authentication generally piggybacks on IIS support for authentication using the Windows user database. One addition is the use of Windows authentication in addition to specific user and role authorization, as discussed in the next section.

Passport authentication uses an external user database. Computers using Passport authentication must have the Passport SDK installed. ASP.NET provides a wrapper around the Passport SDK.

Forms-based authentication is commonly used for Internet applications, where it's likely that not all users will be members of a Windows domain. Although this type of authentication can be implemented using traditional ASP, ASP.NET makes forms-based authentication much easier by creating a formalized framework to support it.

ASP.NET Differences   In ASP, the standard method for conducting forms-based authentication is to use the *Session_OnStart* event handler, placed in Global.asa to redirect new sessions to a login page. This method doesn't scale well because the session state in ASP can't be maintained across a Web server farm. The forms-based authentication method provides a cleaner way to ensure that users are logged in.

Note   When most of the attributes within all the configuration files are specified, they are specified using *camel casing*, meaning that the initial letter of the attribute name is lowercase but the initial letter of embedded words are capitalized, for example *loginUrl*. This convention is different from some earlier public betas, in which the same attribute might have been specified using *Pascal casing*, resulting in *LoginUrl*.

When forms-based authentication is specified, the *<forms>* subtag can be used. The *<forms>* tag has the attributes listed in Table 4-3.

Table 4-3 Attributes of the *<forms>* Tag

Attribute	Description
loginUrl	The URL to which unauthenticated users are redirected. This URL can be on the same machine or on a different machine, but if it's on a different machine, the *decryptionKey* attribute must be the same for both machines. *decryptionKey* is an attribute of the *<machineKey>* tag in Machine.config.
name	The name of the cookie to use for authentication purposes. If more than a single application on the machine uses forms-based authentication, the cookie name should be different for each application. ASP.NET uses / as the path of the cookie.
timeout	The number of minutes for expiration of the cookie. The cookie will be refreshed if half the *timeout* number of minutes has elapsed—an effort to reduce the number of warnings users will get about receiving cookies, if they have cookie warnings turned on. Because cookies can be refreshed, the timeout value might lose precision. Thus, you can't absolutely depend on a cookie timing out in exactly the number of seconds specified by the timeout attribute. The default value is *30*.
path	The path for cookies. Defaults to /. This attribute can be changed by specifying a value in the *<forms>* tag or can be changed programmatically.
protection	The type of cookie protection. Allowed values are *Validation*, *Encryption*, *None*, and *All*. *Validation* validates the cookie data but doesn't encrypt it. *Encryption* encrypts the cookie data but doesn't validate it. *None* does neither. *All* (the default) both encrypts the cookie data and validates it, detecting any alteration in transit. For all but the least important data, the default is a reasonable choice, at the cost of some performance.

Note   Why validate the cookie? Because the cookie can be used to tie into information that shouldn't be shared, validating the cookie data and rejecting it if it has been tampered with can ensure that no one can, say, "hijack" another shopper's shopping cart.

A simple example of forms-based authentication is shown in Listings 4-6, 4-7, and 4-8. This simple-minded example uses a hard-coded user name and password within Login.aspx, as shown in Listing 4-6. These listings also introduce a new class of user interface objects. In Listing 4-6, the button used on the screen isn't a standard HTML submit button or even a standard HTML button but rather an *asp:button*. We'll examine these objects in much greater detail in Chapter 5. For now, just assume that they behave as you might expect. And just take it on faith that the *OnClick* event causes the code in *Login_Click* at the top of the page to be fired. Some of the details within *Login_Click* in Listing 4-6 aren't important, but the call to *FormsAuthentication.RedirectFromLoginPage* is. The first parameter passed to this method is the name of the user, obtained from *UserEmail.Value*, using magic not yet described (See Chapter 5 for more information on getting values from server controls.) The second parameter, hard-coded to *false* here, indicates that a persistent cookie shouldn't be used.

```
<%@ Import Namespace="System.Web.Security " %>

<html>

    <script language="C#" runat=server>
    void Login_Click(Object sender, EventArgs E)
    {
        // Authenticate user: This sample accepts only one user with
        // a name of doug@programmingasp.net and a password of
        // 'password'
        if ((UserEmail.Value == "doug@programmingasp.net") &&
          (UserPass.Value == "password"))
        {
            FormsAuthentication.RedirectFromLoginPage(
                UserEmail.Value, false);
        }
        else
        {
            Msg.Text = "Invalid Credentials: Please try again";
        }
    }
    </script>
    <body>
    <form runat=server>
        <center>
        <h3>
        <font face="Verdana" color=blue>Login Page</font>
        </h3>
        <table>
            <tr>
                <td>
                    Email:
                </td>
```

Listing 4-6 A login page for authentication sample (Login.aspx)   *(continued)*

Listing 4-6 *continued*

```
            <td>
                <input id="UserEmail"
                type="text"
                runat=server
                size=30 />
            </td>
            <td>
                <ASP:RequiredFieldValidator
                ControlToValidate="UserEmail"
                Display="Static" ErrorMessage="*"
                runat=server />
            </td>
        </tr>
        <tr>
            <td>
                Password:
            </td>
            <td>
                <input id="UserPass"
                type=password
                runat=server size=30 />
            </td>
            <td>
                <ASP:RequiredFieldValidator
                ControlToValidate="UserPass"
                Display="Static" ErrorMessage="*"
                runat=server />
            </td>
        </tr>
        <tr>
            <td colspan=3 align="center">
                <asp:button text="Login"
                OnClick="Login_Click"
                runat=server>
                </asp:button>
                <p>
                <asp:Label id="Msg" ForeColor="red"
                Font-Name="Verdana"
                Font-Size="10" runat=server />
            </td>
        </tr>
    </table>
    </center>
    </form>
    </body>
</html>
```

Listing 4-7 also shows a pedestrian example (well, pedestrian once you understand how all the ASP.NET form magic works—and you'll learn all about that in Chapter 5). The form simply identifies the user and allows the user to log out.

```
<%@ Import Namespace="System.Web.Security " %>

<html>

    <script language="C#" runat=server>
    void Page_Load(Object Src, EventArgs E ) {
        Welcome.Text = "Hello, " + User.Identity.Name;
    }

    void Signout_Click(Object sender, EventArgs E) {
        FormsAuthentication.SignOut();
        Response.Redirect("login.aspx");
    }
    </script>

    <body>
        <h3>
        <font face="Verdana">Using Cookie Authentication</font>
        </h3>
        <form runat=server>
            <h3>
                <asp:label id="Welcome" runat=server />
            </h3>
            <asp:button text="Signout" OnClick="Signout_Click" runat=server /
>
        </form>
    </body>
</html>
```

Listing 4-7 A restricted page for authentication sample that allows you to logout (Default.aspx)

Listing 4-8 is the configuration file for this application, named Web.config. This too is a plain vanilla file. The *authentication* section is the part we're interested in, and it's essentially the same as the *authentication* tag shown earlier. Also of interest is the *authorization* tag, which is related to *authentication* as well, as described in the next section.

> **Note**   This Web.config file must be at the root of the Web application directory in IIS. Also, the directory must be configured as an application directory, not a virtual directory.

```
<configuration>
  <system.web>
    <authentication mode="Forms">
      <forms name=".ASPXUSERDEMO" loginUrl="login.aspx" protection="All"
        timeout="60" />
    </authentication>
    <authorization>
      <deny users="?" />
    </authorization>
    <globalization requestEncoding="UTF-8" responseEncoding="UTF-8" />
  </system.web>
</configuration>
```

Listing 4-8 Configuration file for authentication sample

There's one more possible twist to forms-based authentication. Within the *<authentication>* tags, a *credentials* section is allowed, where user and password information is allowed. For example, these lines could be added to the *authentication* section of the Web.config file shown in Listing 4-8.

```
<credentials passwordFormat="Clear" >
    <user name="Mary" password="littlelamb"/>
    <user name="Jill" password="uphill"/>
</credentials>
```

The *<credentials>* tag has one attribute, named *passwordFormat*. The possible values for the *passwordFormat* attribute are shown in Table 4-4.

Table 4-4 Options of the *passwordFormat* Attribute

Option	Description
Clear	Stores passwords in clear text. This value is not at all secure, but it is convenient for testing.
SHA1	SHA stands for Secure Hash Algorithm. *SHA1* stores passwords as SHA1 digests. SHA1 uses a 160-bit hash size. SHA1 was designed to correct a problem in the original SHA algorithm.
MD5	Stores passwords as MD5 digests. *MD5* produces a 128-bit "fingerprint." This value is much more reliable than a traditional checksum.

To validate a user name and password from the form, the form needs to call the *Authenticate* method of the *System.Web.Security.FormsAuthentication* class.

The *authorization* Section

After the system has identified a user, you might want to control whether the user is allowed to use the application. The *authorization* section enables you to do exactly that by using *<allow>* and *<deny>* tags, which can specify individual users, or groups of users, called *roles*. Using Windows authentication, as described in the previous section, will cause Windows NT groups to be mapped to roles.

The *<allow>* and *<deny>* tags are searched until the first match is found for the user being authorized. If the first match is in the *<allow>* tag, the user is allowed; if the first match is in the *<deny>* tag, the user is denied. Access is denied if no matching rule is found. In general, for sites where authorization is important, a *<deny users="*" />* tag should be present to make the denial explicit.

The *customErrors* Section

For developers, one of the problems with ASP is a lack of clarity in error messages. ASP.NET has addressed this issue by creating far better error messages, often including not only the single line of code that triggered the error but also a couple lines before and after. This additional information is important because often an error on one line is in fact caused by an error on the previous line. Figure 4-14 shows an example ASP.NET error message.

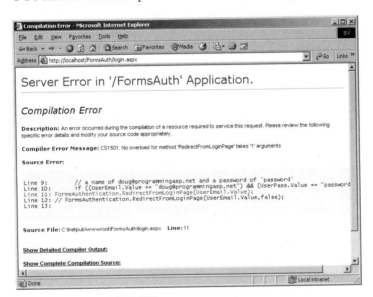

Figure 4-14 An ASP.NET error message

This error page provides a couple links at the bottom that are useful to the developer. The first is Show Detailed Compiler Output. Clicking this link shows the output that would be seen if the command-line compiler were called directly. This output can be useful if there are warnings that occur before the error that might give clues to exactly what's happening. The second link is Show Complete Compilation Source. Clicking this link shows a detailed listing of exactly what the compiler is using to generate the page. The simple Login.aspx page shown in Listing 4-6 is expanded to over 400 lines of detailed listing as ASP.NET takes the source provided (both the code and the HTML source) and produces the code required to create the page. Understanding this code isn't essential, but it can be useful in some debugging situations.

One thing you should notice about the error page is that in showing the context, it actually shows the user name and password that the login page is expecting! Of course, this example is contrived. No one would use such a "security" system in a real application. However, people might have other code that they'd prefer users not see, such as database user names and passwords embedded in connection strings. Embedding connection strings into the application is a bad idea for lots of reasons, but in any event, preventing exposure of source code to users is always a good idea.

The *customErrors* section of Web.config can be used to ensure that this sort of error message appears only to developers during development and testing, and not to users. The *<customErrors>* tag supports the attributes listed in Table 4-5.

Table 4-5 Attributes of the *<customErrors>* Tag

Attribute	Option	Description
defaultRedirect		Specifies a URL to redirect the user to
mode		Specifies whether custom errors are enabled, disabled, or shown only on remote clients
	On	Specifies that custom errors are enabled
	Off	Specifies that custom errors are disabled
	RemoteOnly	Specifies that custom errors are shown only on remote clients

The default behavior for *mode* is *RemoteOnly*, meaning that the type of error page shown in Figure 4-14 will *not* be shown to remote users; instead, a custom error page will appear. The default page shown to remote users is really designed for developers. It explains how to view the details of the error by making changes to the *customErrors* section of Web.config. By setting the *defaultRedirect* attribute, the user can be redirected to a page that can, for example, notify the administrator of the site where an error occurred.

There is also an *<error>* subtag for the *<customErrors>* tag. The *<error>* subtag can occur multiple times. The two attributes in Table 4-6 are supported for the *<error>* subtag.

Table 4-6 Attributes of the *<error>* Subtag

Attribute	Description
statusCode	Specifies an error code that redirects a browser to a nondefault error page
redirect	Specifies the page to redirect to when the error specified in *statusCode* occurs

The *httpHandlers* Section

The *httpHandlers* section maps incoming requests to the appropriate *IHttpHandler* or *IHttpHandlerFactory* class, according to the URL and the HTTP verb requested.

> **Note**   When I talk about *HTTP verbs,* I mean the keywords used to specify what action the Web server should take. If you're an HTML developer, the most common HTTP verbs will be *POST* and *GET*. When you create an HTML form, you have these two options for the *METHOD* attribute of the *<FORM>* tag. When *GET* is specified, any form values are appended to the URL specified in the *ACTION* attribute. When *POST* is specified, form element data is sent as part of the message body. The practical difference is that when *GET* is used, all form elements are sent on the URL, possibly displaying information in the address box that you'd rather not display. (Imagine using *GET* for a login form—the form data, user name, and password will be appended to the URL.) *POST* is preferred, but in practice ASP.NET developers generally allow the framework to handle this type of detail. As you'll see in Chapter 5, most ASP.NET form tags simply use the *runat=server* attribute/value pair.

The *httpHandlers* section in Web.config specifies the HTTP handlers that the applications will use as well as the order in which they will be used. The *httpHandlers* section supports three subtags: *<add>, <remove>*, and *<clear>*. The HTTP handler that will be used by an incoming request is determined by looking at all directories that are at a higher level (logically, *not* physically) and processing all the *<add>* and *<remove>* tags. An HTTP module included at a higher level with an *<add>* tag can be removed at a lower level with a *<remove>* tag.

The *<add>* subtag adds an HTTP handler, and it supports the three attributes listed in Table 4-7.

Table 4-7 Attributes of the *<add>* Subtag in *httpHandlers*

Attribute	Description
verb	A comma-separated list of HTTP verbs, such as *GET, PUT, POST,* or the wildcard character (*).
path	A single URL path or a simple wildcard, such as *.aspx.*
type	An assembly and class combination. Assemblies are groups of functionality grouped together for convenience. The .NET Framework first searches in the application's private bin directory and then in the system assembly cache.

The *<remove>* subtag removes an HTTP handler specified previously in an *<add>* subtag. The *verb/path* in a *<remove>* subtag must *exactly* match the *verb/path* specified in a previous *≤add>* subtag. Although it might seem silly to add and remove HTTP handlers, remember that the configuration files are read from the root through to the current directory (logically speaking, *not* physically), so it's not unreasonable to expect that there will be times when a handler needed at a higher level isn't needed in every application located logically below. The *<remove>* subtag supports two attributes, *verb* and *path*. These are exactly the same as their *<add>* subtag counterparts.

The final subtag supported by the *httpHandlers* section is the *<clear>* subtag. When this subtag is present, all HTTP handler mappings inherited or configured are cleared. Here is a simple example of an *httpHandlers* section:

```
<httpHandlers>
    <add verb="*" path="MyApp.New" type="MyApp.New, MyApp" />
    <add verb="*" path="MyApp.Baz" type=" MyApp.Baz, MyApp" />
</httpHandlers>
```

In this example, all HTTP verbs that are used on *MyApp.New* will be mapped to *MyApp.New* class in the *MyApp* assembly. All HTTP verbs used on *MyApp.Baz* will be referred to *MyApp.Baz class*, in the *MyApp* assembly.

The *httpModules* Section

The *httpModules* section of Web.config contains information similar to the *httpHandlers* section described in the preceding section. The *httpModules* section supports three subtags, *<add>*, *<remove>*, and *<clear>*, just as in the *httpHandlers* section. The *<add>* subtag supports two attributes, *type* and *name*, as described in Table 4-8.

Table 4-8 Attributes of the *<add>* Subtag in *httpModules*

Attribute	Description
type	Specifies a comma-separated class/assembly combination. ASP.NET searches the application's private bin directory and then the system assembly cache.
name	Specifies the name that the application uses to refer to the module identified in *type*.

The *<remove>* subtag works exactly the same as the *<remove>* subtag in the *httpHandlers* section. The *type* and *name* attributes are used to match previously added HTTP modules. The *<clear>* subtag removes all HTTP module mappings from an application.

The *identity* Section

The *identity* section of Web.config controls the application identity of the Web application. This section allows you to set up *impersonation*. Impersonation is when the identity of the user on the client machine is used to determine what files on the server can be accessed. For example, suppose you have two virtual directories on an intranet-accessible Web server, one named Employees and the other named Managers. If all users are using Windows and have Windows 2000 domain user accounts and the Web server has both directories on an NTFS volume, instead of using application logic to prevent nonmanagers from accessing the Managers virtual directory, you could apply NTFS permissions to the files in the Managers directory that allowed only managers to access the files in that directory.

The *<identity>* tag supports three attributes, as described in Table 4-9.

Table 4-9 Attributes of the *<identity>* Tag

Attribute	Option	Description
impersonate		Specifies whether client impersonation is used on each request
	true	Specifies that client impersonation is used
	false	Specifies that client impersonation is not used, which is the default
userName		Specifies the user name to use if *impersonate* is set to *false*
password		Specifies the password to use if *impersonate* is set to *false*

The *pages* Section

The *pages* section of the Web.config file contains page-specific information that can be configured on the machine, site, application, or virtual directory level. The *<pages>* tag supports six attributes, as listed in Table 4-10.

Table 4-10 Attributes of the *<pages>* Tag

Attribute	Option	Description
buffer		Specifies whether the URL resource uses response buffering
	true	Specifies that response buffering is enabled
	false	Specifies that response buffering is disabled
enableSessionState		Specifies whether session state is enabled
	true	Specifies that session state is enabled
	false	Specifies that session state is disabled
	ReadOnly	Specifies that session state data can be read but not written
enableViewState		Specifies whether view state (the state of controls) is enabled
	true	Specifies that view state is enabled
	False	Specifies that view state is disabled
pageBaseType		Specifies a code-behind class that .aspx pages inherit
userControlBaseType		Specifies a user control that user controls inherit
autoEventWireup		Indicates whether page events are automatically enabled
	true	Indicates that page events are automatically enabled
	false	Indicates that page events are not automatically enabled

> **Note**   The *autoEventWireup* attribute seemed like a good idea at the time. Events are wired up based on the names of methods and components. Given a control named *button1*, *button1_Click* would handle the click event. In general, the attribute is more trouble than it's worth and has been the cause of no end of confusion on the ASP.NET newsgroups. All the examples in this book will use manual event *wireup*.

ASP.NET Differences   ASP developers are used to the fact that if you move beyond a single server, session state can't be saved using the standard ASP session state mechanisms. The problem is that in ASP, session state is stored directly on the Web server. In a clustered Web server farm environment, there's no assurance that each request from a particular client will go to a particular server in the cluster. Workarounds in ASP include saving small bits of session state in encrypted cookies and then using that little bit of session state to go to a database to get other information. Another workaround is to use a session identifier that gets passed from page to page and use that to get to a database. ASP.NET eliminates the need for these workarounds. Session state can be saved in a state server or SQL Server database. You'll find more information on session state in the section "The *sessionState* Section" later in this chapter.

The *processModel* Section

The *processModel* section of Web.config controls the ASP.NET process model settings on an IIS Web server. This section is different from the other sections we've looked at in that it's read by the aspnet_isapi unmanaged DLL rather than the managed code configuration system. The *processModel* section sets many performance-tuning details.

Caution   Many features can be configured using the *processModel* section, including attributes that specify how ASP.NET runs on multiprocessor machines. You can do things such as set the CPU mask, meaning that you can control which processors ASP.NET will use to execute its code. If this sounds like a good idea, think again. Microsoft has spent perhaps millions of dollars and untold hours creating the Windows 2000 process scheduling system, which efficiently handles doling out works to the multiple processors in a multiple CPU system. Only under unique circumstances are you likely to do better manually mucking with setting processor affinity.

The *<processModel>* tag supports many attributes. The most common ones are described in Table 4-11.

ASP.NET runs one process per eligible CPU. On a four-processor system, if all CPUs are eligible to run ASP.NET (based on the settings for the *cpuMask* and *webGarden* attributes), four ASP.NET processes will be started. Given a *cpuMask* of 7 (as described earlier), only three ASP.NET processes will be created.

Table 4-11 Attributes of the _<processModel>_ Tag

Attribute	Option	Description
enable		Specifies whether the process model is enabled.
	true	Indicates that the process model is enabled.
	false	Indicates that the process model is not enabled.
timeout		Specifies the number of minutes until ASP.NET launches a new worker process to take the place of the current one. The default is _infinite_.
idleTimeout		Specifies the number of minutes of inactivity until ASP.NET automatically shuts down the worker process. The default is _infinite_.
shutdownTimeout		Specifies the number of minutes allowed for a worker process to shut itself down. If the timeout expires and the worker process hasn't shut itself down, ASP.NET shuts down the process. The format is hr:min:sec. The default is 5 seconds, or 0:00:05.
requestLimit		Specifies the number of requests allowed before ASP.NET automatically launches a new worker process to take the place of the current one. The default is infinite.
requestQueueLimit		Specifies the number of requests allowed in the queue before ASP.NET launches a new worker process and reassigns the requests. The default is _5000_.
memoryLimit		Specifies the maximum memory size, as a percentage of total system memory, that the worker process can consume before ASP.NET launches a new process and reassigns existing requests. The default is _40_. A percent sign (%) is _not_ specified; only the number.
cpuMask		Specifies a bitmask value that indicates which processors in a multiple-processor system are eligible to run ASP.NET processes. On a computer with four CPUs, a value of 0111 binary (7 decimal) would mean that CPUs 0 through 2 would run an ASP.NET process and CPU 3 would not. This attribute interacts with the _webGarden_ attribute.

Table 4-11   *continued*

Attribute	Option	Description
webGarden		Controls CPU affinity when used in conjunction with the *cpuMask* attribute. A multiple-processor system is called a Web garden, presumably in contrast to a multiple-PC cluster, often called a Web server farm.
	true	Specifies that the system should use the Windows CPU scheduling system. This is the default.
	false	Specifies that *cpuMask* is used to specify which CPUs are eligible to run ASP.NET processes.
userName		Specifies an account that worker processes should use. By default, processes run using the IIS account.
password		Specifies the password for the account specified in the *username* attribute.
logLevel		Specifies event types logged to the event log.
	All	Specifies all process events are logged.
	None	Specifies no process events are logged.
	Errors	Specifies only errors are logged. These include unexpected shutdowns, memory limit shutdowns, and deadlock shutdowns. *Errors* is the default.
clientConnectedCheck		Specifies the time a request is left in the queue before a check is made to see if client is still connected.
comAuthenticationLevel		Specifies the level of authentication for DCOM security. The options for this attribute are: *Default, None, Connect, Call, Pkt, PktIntegrity*, and *PktPrivacy*. The default is *Connect*.
comImpersonationLevel		Specifies the authentication level for COM security. The options for this attribute are: *Default, Anonymous, Identify, Impersonate*, and *Delegate*. (*Anonymous* is currently not supported.)
maxWorkerThreads	5 to *100*	Specifies the maximum number of worker threads to be used for the process on a per CPU basis. The default is 25.
maxIoThreads	5 to *100*	Specifies the maximum number of I/O threads to used for the process on a per CPU basis. The default is 25.

The *sessionState* Section

Session state support in ASP.NET is much more extensive and flexible than it was in ASP. For developers of small Internet or intranet Web sites, the session support offered by ASP was adequate. The problem was that ASP session state didn't scale out to multiple Web servers. ASP session state was stored on the Web server, and so using a system like Microsoft's Network Load Balancing provided no assurance that the same server in a Web server farm would service each request from a particular client. Another limitation of ASP session state is that it requires cookies to work. This constraint has become less of a problem because now virtually all browsers support cookies, and the sheer number of Internet sites that require cookies enabled have forced all but the most paranoid users to accept at least nonpersistent cookies.

The *sessionState* section of Web.config controls how session state is managed. The *<sessionState>* tag supports five attributes, as described in Table 4-12.

Table 4-12 Attributes of the *<sessionState>* Tag

Attribute	Option	Description
mode		Specifies where session state is stored.
	Off	Specifies that no session state is saved.
	Inproc	Specifies that session state is saved locally, similar to ASP session state.
	StateServer	Specifies that session state is saved on a remote state server.
	SqlServer	Specifies that session state is saved in a SQL Server.
cookieless		Specifies whether session state should be saved without using client cookies.
	true	Specifies that sessions without cookies are being used.
	false	Specifies that sessions do use cookies. This is the default.
timeout		Specifies the number of minutes a session can be idle before it is abandoned. The default is 20 minutes, the same as in ASP.

Table 4-12   *continued*

Attribute	Option	Description
stateConnectionString		Specifies the server name and port where session state is stored remotely (for example, *192.168.1.100:8484*). This attribute is required when mode is set to *StateServer*.
sqlConnectionString		Specifies the connection string for the SQL Server where the state is to be saved (for example, *data source=192.168.1.100;user id=sa;password=*). This attribute is required when mode is set to *SqlServer*.

The same rules about trying to minimize the amount of data stored in session state that applied in ASP still apply in ASP.NET.

The *trace* Section

One of the problems developers experienced with ASP was difficulty obtaining detailed debugging information. Exactly what was the page doing when an error occurred? What portions of the code had been run? ASP.NET has much improved debugging information, and the *trace* section of the Web.config file allows you to specify settings for the trace service. Figure 4-15 shows a page that has been run with tracing enabled and *pageOutput* set to *true*.

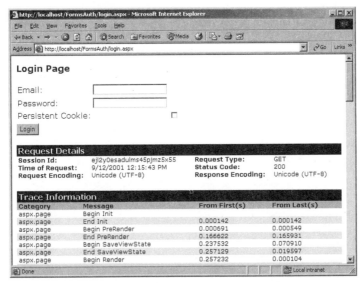

Figure 4-15 The output of the Login.aspx page shown in Listing 4-6 when tracing is enabled and *pageOutput* is set to true

The *<trace>* tag supports five attributes, as described in Table 4-13.

Table 4-13 Attributes of the *<trace>* Tag

Attribute	Option	Description
enabled		Specifies whether tracing is enabled.
	true	Specifies that tracing is enabled.
	false	Specifies that tracing is disabled. This is the default.
requestLimit		Specifies the number of trace requests to save on the server. The default is *10*.
pageOutput		Specifies whether trace information should be displayed at the end of each page.
	true	Specifies that trace output is appended to each page.
	false	Specifies that trace output is not appended to each page. This is the default.
traceMode		Sets the order of trace output.
	SortByTime	Specifies that output is sorted by time (thus, displayed in the order the events being traced occurred). This is the default.
	SortByCategory	Specifies that output is displayed alphabetically by category. See the text in this section for information about user-defined categories.
localOnly		Specifies whether the trace viewer is available only on the host Web server.
	true	Specifies that trace output is available only on the server console. This is the default.
	false	Specifies that trace output is available on any client, not just the Web server.

In Figure 4-15, all trace output has a category of *aspx.page*, and it is generated automatically by the .NET Framework, with no explicit trace code in the page source. However, this is only half the power of ASP.NET tracing. Suppose, for example, that the login page from Listing 4-6 wasn't responding the way you expected. Perhaps the following code seemed not to be working correctly:

```
if ((UserEmail.Value == "doug@programmingasp.net") &&
  (UserPass.Value == "password"))
{
    FormsAuthentication.RedirectFromLoginPage(
      UserEmail.Value, false);
```

```
}
else
{
    Msg.Text = "Invalid Credentials: Please try again";
}
```

You can use the *Trace* class to add user-defined trace statements in the trace output, like this:

```
if ((UserEmail.Value == "doug@programmingasp.net") &&
  (UserPass.Value == "password"))
{
    Trace.Write("MyCategory", "Authenticated");
    FormsAuthentication.RedirectFromLoginPage(
      UserEmail.Value,false);
}
else
{
    Msg.Text = "Invalid Credentials: Please try again";
    Trace.Write("MyCategory", "Invalid Credentials");
}
```

If you ran the page shown in Listing 4-6 with the modifications shown above and entered an invalid user name or password, the trace would have one "MyCategory" trace line inserted into the output, as shown in Figure 4-16.

In addition to the Web.config sections described in this chapter, there are a couple other sections that are not generally modified (such as the *globalization* section).

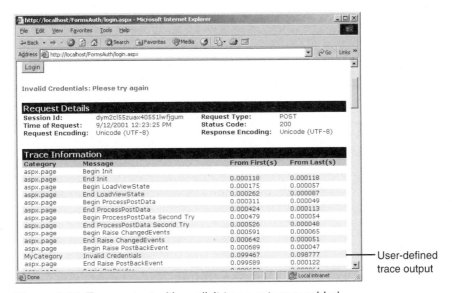

Figure 4-16 Trace output with explicit trace category added

Conclusion

One important thing to keep in mind about these configuration settings is that in many cases, the default values are completely acceptable. In the real world, most of the sections described in this chapter won't exist in your Web.config files because the default values will suffice. In addition, tools such as Visual Studio .NET will interact with some of these settings on their own; thus, the default behavior you see if you're using Visual Studio .NET might be slightly different from what has been described as the ASP.NET default. Users of Visual Studio .NET will notice other significant differences compared to the experience of someone using an editor that isn't at all .NET aware. In general, most of the examples in the following chapters use Visual Studio .NET, but with special attention paid to the "magic" that Visual Studio .NET performs on your behalf. Generally, Visual Studio .NET is doing things that are helpful, but understanding what is going on "behind the curtain" will help on those occasions when the special Visual Studio .NET behavior isn't what you're looking for.

With this background, you should know enough to move on to Chapter 5, which covers the most important type of ASP.NET application—the Web Form. Web Forms provide ASP.NET developers with the kind of rapid application development (RAD) for the server that ASP programmers could only dream of. The dream has arrived, and in Chapter 5 you'll see how to make it work for you!

5

Web Forms

The most common requirement for a dynamic Web application is getting the user's input, processing it, and providing feedback in the event of data-entry errors. HTML provides basic support for many widgets, including text boxes, drop-down lists, list boxes, check boxes, and radio buttons as well as traditional buttons and submit buttons. This basic HTML support for forms was the building block for Active Server Pages (ASP) developers, who were able to add additional processing and validation to user input in HTML forms. Validation especially is different in HTML forms than in traditional Microsoft Windows application forms. For instance, 5/35/2001 isn't correct input when a date is required. Unlike a Microsoft Visual Basic 6.0 application or a Windows Forms application, your ASP.NET application can't conveniently create forms with masked inputs that will make invalid entries impossible. There is no ASP.NET equivalent for the *DateTimePicker* control in the Windows Common Controls, which automatically ensures that each part of the date—month, day, and year—is correct and consistent.

> **Note** It's certainly possible to use JavaScript to micromanage the input on a Web Form, disallowing invalid entries such as 5/35/2001 as a date as they're entered, but generally that isn't the way Web applications work. ASP developers commonly code defensively, writing basic validation code using JavaScript that will be executed on the Web client, as well as writing additional validation code that will be executed on the server, in case the client-side validation isn't effective because the browser doesn't have the required features or the required settings.

Using the Classic ASP Program Architecture

ASP provided little direct support for form validation, and thus you were free to do pretty much as you pleased. Even within the same development group, you can generally find one or more models for accepting and validating input. I'm sorry to report that even within a single developer's code, you might find more than one structure for handling form validation (at least if I'm the developer in question…).

Every HTML form has an *action* attribute in the *<FORM>* tag that points to a URL. The URL can be *absolute*, beginning with *http://*, or *relative*, perhaps beginning with a slash (/) to refer to the root of the current site, or just a file name that must exist in the same folder as the page the form is in. When the form is submitted, the contents of the form are sent to the URL referred to by the *action* attribute of the *<FORM>* tag.

The two common ASP structures are shown in Figures 5-1 and 5-2.

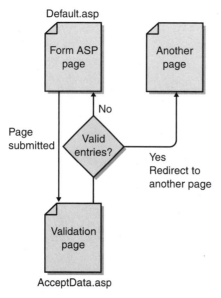

Figure 5-1 One possible ASP structure for form validation

The ASP structure in Figure 5-1 has a form in Default.asp with the *action* attribute of the *<FORM>* tag pointing to AcceptData.asp. The job of AcceptData.asp is to validate the information in the form from Default.asp and then return the user to Default.asp to correct some information, process the information and then display a status message, or redirect the user to another page.

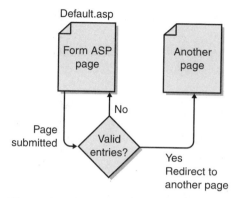

Figure 5-2 Another possible ASP structure for form validation

The ASP structure in Figure 5-2 has a form in Default.asp with the *action* attribute of the *<FORM>* tag pointing to Default.asp. This page is self-referencing, meaning that the information entered in the form will be posted back to the same page the form is on, and the page should allow different behaviors based on whether this is the first time the form is displayed or this is a *postback*. A postback occurs when a form is filled in and the submit button is clicked. There are several ways to detect whether a postback is in progress, but my preferred method is to have a hidden field in the form, named *postback*.

The structures shown in Figures 5-1 and 5-2 both have advantages, but I generally prefer the structure shown in Figure 5-2, for the following reasons:

- All logic for a given form is located in a single place. If you need to add or delete a control in the form, all logic to handle it should be in one page.

- No redirect is required to allow the user to correct an error. This is also an advantage in cases where the user interface needs to be refreshed based on information entered by the user in a first pass. For instance, in a recent hospital registration system I worked on, the user admitting a patient would first select the patient service, and then based on whether the service was for an inpatient or an outpatient, when the user submitted the form, the form would be refreshed with an additional control where the room and bed could be specified.

- When an error occurs, all the information passed doesn't need to be reconstructed for the redirection back to the original page.

Commonly, when the postback succeeds and the information entered is valid, the information is processed and the user is redirected to another page.

Redirecting to another page for validation has some advantages. First, if multiple pages need to perform similar validations, it's possible to do them all on one page, which might be important when certain validations involve lots of complex code. An alternative to centralizing all such complex validations on a single page is to use include files, but this solution comes with its own problems.

The ASP.NET form validation architecture is much more structured than what ASP had to offer. The goal of ASP.NET was to bring RAD to the server. To a great extent, ASP.NET has succeeded in doing this.

ASP.NET Differences   ASP.NET provides a richer framework for form validation than ASP, but ASP.NET really works best if you use the preferred structure mentioned earlier (in Figure 5-2), in which pages postback to themselves. You can force some other structure on ASP.NET, but it won't be fun, and you'll be working against, rather than with, ASP.NET. "Use the Force, Luke!"

ASP.NET Forms vs. Visual Basic 6.0 Forms

Most of this chapter compares classic ASP to ASP.NET. The differences are striking. If you're moving from Visual Basic 6.0 to ASP.NET, whether you decide to use Visual Basic .NET or C#, the changes in the overall architecture of forms are even more striking.

Certain things that are reasonable and easy to do in a traditional Visual Basic application are less reasonable, and certainly harder to do, in the ASP.NET forms model. For example, it's not uncommon to create a traditional application in which exiting from one control changes the contents of the next control. I've worked on an application in which users select a facility type in a drop-down list. After they tab out of the facility type drop-down list, the facility name drop-down list changes its contents to reflect only facilities of the selected type. Modifying controls on the fly might not be the best structure for an ASP.NET form because repopulating the next control commonly requires a round-trip to the server.

At a deeper level, the biggest shock for Visual Basic developers who begin developing ASP.NET forms will be the lifetime of a page and the variables defined within it. An ASP.NET page is like a forgetful child. Tell it something (set a variable in the underlying page class), and the next time you see the page and ask it about that variable, the page will have forgotten everything you ever told it about the variable. This lack of retention isn't unreasonable, given that HTTP is a stateless protocol. If you connect to a large commercial Web site—for instance, MSDN—there's no guarantee that each time you request the same page from the site, the page will come from the same Web server.

One solution for maintaining state information is to use the *ViewState* property. The *ViewState* property persists values between round-trips to the server using a hidden variable in the page, named *__VIEWSTATE*. This variable is opaque (its meaning is not obvious, or even easily discernible), and you shouldn't alter it directly.

Imagine you have an integer value within a page class, named *tries*, used to count the number of times a particular user has refreshed a page. To persist this integer, you could do something like the following:

```
ViewState ("tries")=tries
```

An alternative would be to encapsulate the value into a property of the class. In Visual Basic .NET, you could do something like this:

```
Public Property tries() As Integer
    Get
        Return CInt(ViewState ("tries"))
    End Get
    Set(ByVal Value As Integer)
        ViewState("tries") = Value
    End Set
End Property
```

Using a property enables your Visual Basic .NET code to cleanly use *MyClass1.tries* when it needs to access the value of *tries*, but under the covers, the value will be retrieved and set on the *ViewState* property.

Adding to the confusion, some things *are* saved automatically between round-trips to the server. By default, ASP.NET automatically saves the contents entered into controls between round-trips to the server as well as the properties of controls declared on the page.

An Example of ASP.NET Form Validation

In the discussion of forms authentication in Chapter 4, Listing 4-6 showed a simple login page that allowed entry of a user's e-mail address and password, to be compared with a hard-coded set of acceptable values. Listing 5-1 shows this same form.

```
<%@ Import Namespace="System.Web.Security " %>

<html>

    <script language="C#" runat=server>
    void Login_Click(Object sender, EventArgs E)
    {
        // Authenticate user: This sample accepts only one user with
        // a name of doug@programmingasp.net and a password of
        // 'password'
        if ((UserEmail.Value == "doug@programmingasp.net") &&
          (UserPass.Value == "password"))
        {
            FormsAuthentication.RedirectFromLoginPage(
               UserEmail.Value,false);
        }
        else
        {
            Msg.Text = "Invalid Credentials: Please try again";
        }
    }
    </script>

    <body>
    <form runat=server>
        <center>
        <h3>
        <font face="Verdana" color=blue>Login Page</font>
        </h3>
        <table>
            <tr>
                <td>
                    Email:
                </td>
                <td>
                    <input id="UserEmail"
                    type="text"
                    runat=server
                    size=30 />
                </td>
```

Listing 5-1 Login.aspx, a login page

```
                    <td>
                        <ASP:RequiredFieldValidator
                            ControlToValidate="UserEmail"
                            Display="Static" ErrorMessage="*"
                            runat=server />
                    </td>
                </tr>
                <tr>
                    <td>
                        Password:
                    </td>
                    <td>
                        <input id="UserPass"
                        type=password
                        runat=server size=30 />
                    </td>
                    <td>
                        <ASP:RequiredFieldValidator
                            ControlToValidate="UserPass"
                            Display="Static" ErrorMessage="*"
                            runat=server />
                    </td>
                </tr>
                <tr>
                    <td colspan=3 align="center">
                        <asp:button text="Login"
                            OnClick="Login_Click"
                            runat=server>
                        </asp:button>
                        <p>
                        <asp:Label id="Msg" ForeColor="red"
                        Font-Name="Verdana"
                        Font-Size="10" runat=server />
                    </td>
                </tr>
            </table>
            </center>
        </form>
        </body>
</html>
```

Login.aspx has a great deal in common with both a traditional ASP page and a traditional HTML page. At the very top of the page is an import declaration, used to import the *System.Web.Security* namespace. As you might recall, Login.aspx is the page that users will be redirected to when they first visit the site, specified by a configuration setting in the Web.config file. The *System.Web.Security* namespace is used to enable the page to properly redirect the user to the page initially requested.

ASP.NET Differences   In traditional ASP programming, one way to import functionality into a page was to use *include* statements. ASP.NET supports the *import* statement that allows you to import namespaces. However, the .NET implementation does not allow wildcards in the import as Java does—that is, you can't import *System.Web.** and then use the *System.Web.Security* namespace.

After the *<HTML>* start tag comes a script block, delimited by *<SCRIPT></SCRIPT>* tags. The script block contains a single C# function, *Login_Click*. This function does little more than compare some values from the form to some hard-coded values and either uses a method from *System.Web.Security. FormsAuthentication* to redirect the user back to the originally requested page or sets the text property of a label on the form to instruct the user to try again.

ASP.NET Differences   In ASP, functions can be enclosed in *<SCRIPT></SCRIPT>* tags, as in the example shown in Listing 5-1, or in *<%* and *%>* tags, which are used to enclose code. ASP.NET only supports functions inside script blocks. Currently, the error message that appears if you inadvertently use *<%* and *%>* tags to enclose function declarations might not clearly describe the problem. You can, however, still use *<%* and *%>* tags inline to display results. In any event, as you'll see shortly, there's a better way to code ASP.NET applications.

Also note that within the *<SCRIPT></SCRIPT>* tags the *Login_Click* function is never directly called. In a moment, I'll explain exactly how this function gets called.

Within the body of the page (just inside the *<BODY></BODY>* tags), a form is started, using a *<FORM>* start tag. Unlike a traditional ASP or HTML form tag, the only attribute specified here is the *runat* attribute, set to *server*. There's no mention of using *post* or *get*, and no *action* attribute to specify the page to be called when the form is submitted. An ASP.NET form that uses a *runat=server* attribute/value pair always posts back to itself. Although using the *runat* attribute here isn't something you'd do in classic ASP, using the *runat* attribute for script blocks should be familiar to ASP programmers. ASP.NET supports the *runat* attribute for many HTML tags, and using *runat* always implies the same thing— that there will be some activity on the server to support this component.

The form contains a great deal of standard-looking HTML code, including tables and text box input elements. The text box input elements do have one unfamiliar feature, the same *runat=server* attribute/value pair that the *<FORM>* tag uses.

ASP.NET Server Controls vs. HTML Server Controls

You'll notice some unfamiliar tags contained within Listing 5-1. These tags begin with *<ASP:*. In some cases, the string after *ASP:* does look familiar (as in *ASP:Button* and *ASP:Label*), and in others, it is unfamiliar (for example, *ASP:RequiredFieldValidator*). These tags are ASP.NET server controls. These controls run on the server, and in some respects, they behave like the HTML controls we've seen with the *runat=server* attribute/value pair. When controls have the *runat=server* attribute/value pair, they can trigger server-side functions. In this example, the *Login_Click* method is called when the ASP.NET button server control is clicked. But if these controls are similar, why do both sets exist?

There are several reasons for having two sets of controls. First, some of the controls don't have pure HTML equivalents. Although creating an HTML server control for an input box or a button by using a standard HTML tag and adding *runat=server* seems like a natural extension, a control like *RequiredFieldValidator* requires something different, as it has no pure HTML equivalent. But before we delve into exactly what a *RequiredFieldValidator* control would do, it's useful to understand the basic differences between the two types of server controls, HTML server controls and ASP.NET server controls.

HTML server controls provide the following features:

- An object model that allows controls to be manipulated programmatically.

- An event model that allows you to handle events for the controls in a way similar to client-side event handling, except here event handling happens on the server.

- The ability to handle events on the client side, the server side, or both. It might seem odd to handle events on both the client and the server, but there are good reasons why this might be appropriate and reasonable. I'll supply more information on this feature in Chapter 7.

- Automatic maintenance of values between trips to the server. Enter a value in an HTML text box server control, and after a submit operation, the control can maintain the text that was entered.

- Interaction with validation controls. We'll look at this feature in more detail in the next section, "Using Validator Controls."

- Data binding to one or more properties of the control.

- Support for HTML 4.0 style sheets, if the browser supports it.

- Pass-through custom attributes. You can add attributes to the HTML server control, and the .NET Framework will read attributes and render them without any change in functionality.

ASP.NET server controls provide everything that HTML server controls provide and more. However, ASP.NET server controls don't have a one-to-one mapping to standard HTML elements. (For example, the *RequiredFieldValidator* control has no standard HTML equivalent.) ASP.NET server controls provide the following features:

- A rich object model that allows for type-safe programming.

- Automatic browser detection. The controls detect the browser's capabilities and provide client-side code appropriate to the client.

- For some controls, the ability to modify the look and feel using templates. (C++ programmers, these are not at all what you think of as templates!)

- For some controls, the ability to specify whether an event for a control should be cached for later form submission or posted immediately to the server.

- The ability to pass events to a parent control from a nested control. For example, a button in a table can have an event passed to the containing table.

Login.aspx in Listing 5-1 uses both HTML server controls and ASP.NET server controls. Most of the examples in this book use ASP.NET server controls. For programmers used to working in type-safe languages, such as C and C++, using ASP.NET server controls will be more comfortable, as they provide a type-safe object model.

Using Validator Controls

Because the *RequiredFieldValidator* control is the first of the validator controls we'll look at in this section, it's useful to review the class hierarchy for the *RequiredFieldValidator* class (shown in Figure 5-3). We know that everything in the .NET Framework descends from *Object*, so it's no surprise that the most remote descendant of the *RequiredFieldValidator* class is *Object*.

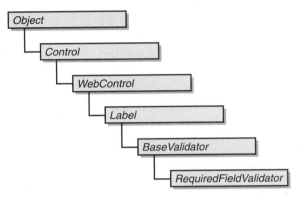

Figure 5-3 Object class hierarchy for *RequiredFieldValidator* in the .NET Framework

The *RequiredFieldValidator* Control

To understand this hierarchy, it's useful to see the *RequiredFieldValidator* control at work. Login.aspx, shown in Listing 5-1, uses the *RequiredFieldValidator* control. Figure 5-4 shows Login.aspx and what happens when we submit the form with neither field filled in.

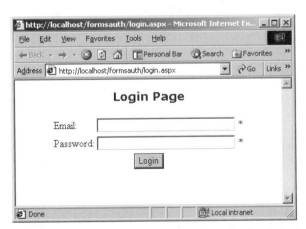

Figure 5-4 The Login.aspx page when the Login button is clicked and the fields are not filled in

The form validator controls all have an *ErrorMessage* attribute that in this example has been set to "*", and thus an asterisk is displayed next to any field that doesn't validate properly. The *RequiredFieldValidator* control is perhaps the simplest validator control—it checks to see whether a field has a value. How does a validator control work? That depends on several factors. As with many aspects of ASP.NET, it's useful to look at the HTML code that the browser sees, to determine how your request for a validator control is translated into something that a browser can work with. Listing 5-2 shows the HTML sent to the browser before the validator controls are fired (with the listing reformatted to make it easier to read).

```html
<html>
    <body>
    <form name="_ctl0" method="post"
    action="login.aspx"
    language="javascript"
    onsubmit="ValidatorOnSubmit();"
    id="_ctl0">
    <input type="hidden" name="__VIEWSTATE"
    value="dDwxMDgxMzYzOTAxOzs+" />

    <script language="javascript"
    src="/aspnet_client/system_web/1_0_3217_0/WebUIValidation.js">
    </script>
        <center>
        <h3>
        <font face="Verdana" color=blue>Login Page</font>
        </h3>
        <table>
            <tr>
                <td>
                    Email:
                </td>
                <td>
                    <input name="UserEmail"
                    id="UserEmail"
                    type="text"
                    size="30" />
                </td>
                <td>
                    <span id="_ctl1"
                    controltovalidate="UserEmail"
                    errormessage="*"
                    evaluationfunction=
                        "RequiredFieldValidatorEvaluateIsValid"
                    initialvalue=""
                    style="color:Red;visibility:hidden;">*</span>
                </td>
            </tr>
```

Listing 5-2 The HTML source that the browser sees when Login.aspx is requested and before the validator controls are fired

```
            <tr>
                <td>
                    Password:
                </td>
                <td>
                    <input name="UserPass" id="UserPass"
                    type="password" size="30" />
                </td>
                <td>
                    <span id="_ctl2" controltovalidate="UserPass"
                    errormessage="*"
                    evaluationfunction=
                      "RequiredFieldValidatorEvaluateIsValid"
                    initialvalue=""
                    style="color:Red;visibility:hidden;">*</span>
                </td>
            </tr>
            <tr>
                <td colspan=3 align="center">
                    <input type="submit"
                    name="_ctl3" value="Login"
                    onclick="if (typeof(Page_ClientValidate) == 'function')
                      Page_ClientValidate(); "
                    language="javascript" />
                    <p>
                    <span id="Msg"
                    style="color:Red;font-family:Verdana;font-size:10pt;">
                    </span>
                </td>
            </tr>
        </table>
    </center>

<script language="javascript">
<!--
    var Page_Validators =
      new Array(document.all["_ctl1"],
      document.all["_ctl2"]);
        // -->
</script>


<script language="javascript">
<!--
var Page_ValidationActive = false;
if (typeof(clientInformation) != "undefined" &&
  clientInformation.appName.indexOf("Explorer") != -1)
```

(continued)

Listing 5-2 *continued*

```
{
    if (typeof(Page_ValidationVer) == "undefined")
        alert("Unable to find script library " +
            "'/aspnet_client/system_web/1_0_3217_0" +
            "/WebUIValidation.js'. " +
            "Try placing this file manually, " +
            "or reinstall by running 'aspnet_regiis -c'.");
    else if (Page_ValidationVer != "125")
        alert("This page uses an incorrect " +
            "version of WebUIValidation.js. The page expects " +
            "version 125. The script library is " +
            Page_ValidationVer + ".");
    else
        ValidatorOnLoad();
}

function ValidatorOnSubmit() {
    if (Page_ValidationActive) {
        ValidatorCommonOnSubmit();
    }
}
}
// -->
</script>

        </form>
    </body>
</html>
```

> **Note** Listing 5-2 contains one unusual field: a hidden field named
> __*VIEWSTATE*. This field is used to maintain the state of controls from
> submission to submission. You should leave this field alone. It's designed so
> that it can't be modified, to prevent you from, for example, hijacking another
> user's state information. For more information about this topic, see the sidebar
> "ASP.NET Forms vs. Visual Basic 6.0 Forms," earlier in this chapter.

Wow. That's a lot of code! Not surprisingly, the C# script block at the top
of Listing 5-1 isn't present in Listing 5-2, since it is identified as a *runat=server*
script block. However, there is a new *<SCRIPT>* block, as follows:

```
<script language="javascript"
    src="/aspnet_client/system_web/1_0_3217_0/WebUIValidation.js">
</script>
```

This code, of course, doesn't look even a little familiar! Looking at the Internet Information Services console, we can see that, sure enough, a directory is logically located where the *src* attribute on the *<SCRIPT>* tag points to, as shown in Figure 5-5.

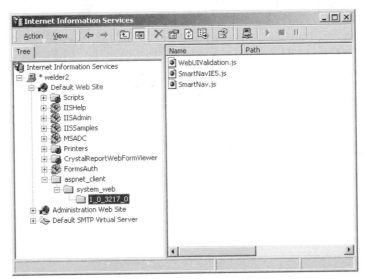

Figure 5-5 The Internet Information Services console, showing the ASP.NET client code directory

I won't show the entire WebUIValidation.js file because the version you'll be using will probably differ slightly from the version I'm using. The significant point here is that a script library designed for the client side is used in your pages when you're doing client-side validation.

> **Note**   You can also set the location of the client-side scripts in the *webControls* tag in the Machine.config file. Generally, it's best to leave this location setting alone, but the ability to have the location of these client-side JavaScript files might be useful.

The next major change in the resulting HTML is the *<SPAN>* tag that seems to replace the first *RequiredFieldValidator* element, as follows:

```
<span id="_ctl1"
controltovalidate="UserEmail"
errormessage="*"
evaluationfunction=
```

(continued)

```
"RequiredFieldValidatorEvaluateIsValid"
initialvalue=""
style="color:Red;visibility:hidden;">*</span>
```

An HTML *<SPAN>* tag is used to provide a container for a section of text that might require special rendering. In this case, the special rendering is that the text shouldn't be visible. This is accomplished using a standard *style* attribute. The validator control associated with the Password text box is similarly changed to a *<SPAN>* tag. The *<ASP:Button>* element from Listing 5-1 is transformed into a traditional HTML submit button, as shown here:

```
<input type="submit"
name="_ctl3" value="Login"
onclick="if (typeof(Page_ClientValidate) == 'function')
  Page_ClientValidate(); "
language="javascript" />
```

As you can see, the page validation we requested is now handled by client-side JavaScript. But how exactly? A script tag below the form actually sets a variable named *Page_Validators* that contains an element for each of the validator controls. The *onclick* event of the submit button calls *Page_ClientValidate*. The version of *Page_ClientValidate* present in my version of WebUIValidation.js looks like this:

```
function Page_ClientValidate() {
    var i;
    for (i = 0; i < Page_Validators.length; i++) {
        ValidatorValidate(Page_Validators[i]);
    }
    ValidatorUpdateIsValid();
    ValidationSummaryOnSubmit();
    Page_BlockSubmit = !Page_IsValid;
    return Page_IsValid;
}
```

Each element of the *Page_Validators* array is individually validated by calling *ValidatorValidate,* another function in WebUIValidation.js. This function calls the function specified in the *evaluationFunction* attribute of the *<SPAN>* tag for each of the validator controls. The details of how this all works aren't critical, but you should be aware of where the processing is taking place.

The *CompareValidator* Control

Referring back to Login.aspx, in Listing 5-1, you'll see that logic is used to compare the e-mail address and password entered to hard-coded values. If the e-mail and password don't match what's expected, another label on the form will be set to a message requesting the user to try again. We haven't seen that message yet, because when we clicked the Login button, the client-side validators fired and displayed those red asterisks before the form was submitted. Because the client-side validators didn't indicate that the page was valid, a round-trip to the server wasn't necessary.

ASP.NET includes a *CompareValidator* control to compare two values. Using a *CompareValidator* control could be useful for creating, for example, a password change page, on which the new password must be entered correctly twice to ensure that the password is set to the value the user intended. Suppose that we wanted to use the *CompareValidator* control rather than the *Login_Click* server-side logic. For the password, we could change the *RequiredFieldValidator* control to a *CompareValidator* control, as follows:

```
<asp:CompareValidator id="comp1"
    ControlToValidate="UserPass"
    ValueToCompare = "password"
    Type="String" runat="server"/>
```

The *ValueToCompare* attribute is one way to specify what is to be compared in a *CompareValidator* control, but another possible way is to use the *CompareToControl* attribute. Set this attribute to the ID of another control on the form, and the *CompareValidator* control will instead compare the value of the *ControlToValidate* attribute to the value of the control pointed to by *CompareToControl*. If you use the *ValueToCompare* attribute, an unfortunate side effect can occur. For example, if you use the previous *CompareValidator* code, the following code would replace the *CompareValidator* code and be returned to the client:

```
<span id="comp1"
    controltovalidate="UserPass"
    evaluationfunction="CompareValidatorEvaluateIsValid"
    valuetocompare="password"
    style="color:Red;visibility:hidden;"></span>
```

This is almost certainly *not* what you would want to do. In the generated HTML returned to the client browser, the *<SPAN>* tag contains, in clear text, the *ValueToCompare* attribute. This example is obviously contrived, but in the real world, you'll certainly encounter situations in which you'd prefer not to expose so much to the client.

One solution is to change the *clienttarget* attribute of the *Page* directive. Listing 5-1 didn't have a *Page* directive, but you could add the following line:

```
<%@ Page Language="c#" clienttarget=downlevel %>
```

When this directive is added to the Login.aspx code shown in Listing 5-1, rather than the HTML code shown in Listing 5-2, the browser sees the code shown in Listing 5-3.

```
<html>

    <body>
        <form name="_ctl0" method="post"
        action="login.aspx" id="_ctl0">
        <input type="hidden"
        name="__VIEWSTATE"
        value="dDwxMDgxMzYzOTAxOzs+" />


        <center>
        <h3>
        <font face="Verdana" color=blue>Login Page</font>
        </h3>
        <table>
            <tr>
                <td>
                    Email:
                </td>
                <td>
                    <input name="UserEmail"
                    id="UserEmail"
                    type="text" size="30" />
                </td>
                <td>
                     
                </td>
            </tr>
            <tr>
                <td>
                    Password:
                </td>
                <td>
                    <input name="UserPass"
                    id="UserPass"
                    type="password"
                    size="30" />
                </td>
                <td>
                     
                </td>
            </tr>
```

Listing 5-3 The HTML sent to the browser when Login.aspx in Listing 5-1 has the *clienttarget=downlevel* attribute added to the *Page* directive

```
        <tr>
          <td colspan=3 align="center">
            <input type="submit"
            name="_ctl3"
            value="Login"
            onclick="if (typeof(Page_ClientValidate) == 'function')
              Page_ClientValidate(); "
            language="javascript" />
            <p>
            <span id="Msg">
            <font face="Verdana"
            color="Red"
            size="2">
            </font>
            </span>
          </td>
        </tr>
      </table>
      </center>
      </form>
  </body>
</html>
```

Note   With the current build of ASP.NET, using the *clienttarget=downlevel* attribute/value pair in the *Page* directive also causes the emitted HTML code to drop to HTML 3.2 compatible level, with potentially undesired results. Hopefully, future versions of ASP.NET will offer a finer grain of control over the level of HTML sent to the client.

Using *clienttarget=downlevel* certainly results in much cleaner HTML code! If I were using an older browser, or possibly any browser other than Microsoft Internet Explorer 4.0 or later, the code sent to the browser would look more like that in Listing 5-3, even if *clienttarget=downlevel* wasn't set. One of the most noticeable differences in the code is that the table cell that previously held the <SPAN> tags for the validators now holds just a nonbreaking space ( ).

One other consequence of changing the client target to a downlevel browser is what happens when you actually submit the form. For instance, clicking the Login button with both fields not filled in results in the page shown in Figure 5-6.

Figure 5-6 The page that appears after clicking Login with both fields blank, and the page targeted at downlevel browsers

Figure 5-6 looks a little different from the page that appeared when we clicked Login without targeting downlevel browsers (shown in Figure 5-4). This page contains a message that reads "Invalid Credentials: Please try again". What's significant is that this message comes from the server-side *Login_Click* function. Because this code has fired, we know that this page was generated after a round-trip to the server. Using a downlevel browser, or targeting your page for a downlevel browser, will result in more round-trips to the server, but in some cases it's worth the cost.

Several additional attributes are available for the *CompareValidator* control. MSDN has the complete documentation, but the *Type* and *Operator* attributes can be quite useful so we'll look at these in more detail here.

The *Type* attribute allows you to specify the data type when performing the comparison. The following values are allowed for the *Type* attribute:

- **String**   Specifies a string comparison
- **Integer**   Specifies a whole number numeric comparison
- **Double**   Specifies a floating-point number comparison
- **Date**   Specifies a date comparison
- **Currency**   Specifies a comparison of currency values

The *Operator* attribute can be used to control the type of comparison that takes place. The examples in this chapter use the default value for *Operator*, *Equal*. In this case, we're checking for equality between the control being validated and either some other control specified by *ControlToCompare* or a constant value specified as *ValueToCompare*. The other relational operators are listed here and perform the expected comparison:

- *GreaterThan*
- *GreaterThanEqual*
- *LessThan*
- *LessThanEqual*
- *NotEqual*

There's another allowed value for *Operator*: *DataTypeCheck*. By using *DataTypeCheck*, the control indicates whether the input is the same or can be converted to the type specified by the *Type* attribute.

Using *DataTypeCheck* might not seem useful until you think about the checking you must do to ensure that users enter, for example, a valid date where a date value is expected. The following code shows an example of how to ensure that a valid date is entered in a text box:

```
<asp: TextBox id=txtDate runat="server"/>
<asp:CompareValidator ControlToValidate="txtDate"
Operator="DataTypeCheck" Type="Date" runat="server">
Must input a date
</asp:CompareValidator>
```

This data type checking is much simpler than what you might need to do on a classic ASP page, and the validator properly handles generation of client-side code, where appropriate (unless you explicitly set *clienttarget* to *downlevel*).

Other Validators

Listed here are the three other types of validator controls available in addition to *RequiredFieldValidator* and *CompareValidator*:

- ***RangeValidator***   Verifies that a user's entry is between specified upper and lower boundaries. The upper and lower boundaries can be numbers, strings, or dates. These boundaries can be specified directly or calculated from the values of other controls.

- ***RegularExpressionValidator***   Verifies that a user's entry matches a pattern defined by a regular expression. Using a *RegularExpressionValidator* control, you could ensure that an entry was, for example, a valid social security number, including numeric entries and dashes where appropriate.

■ ***CustomValidator*** Allows you to create custom validation logic. Using this validator control, you could, for example, validate an entry against a database table or use some other complex criteria, such as an XML Web service that would validate a credit card number.

Listing 5-4 shows a validation page with each of these three types of validators.

```
<%@ Import Namespace="System.Web.Security " %>

<html>

    <script language="C#" runat=server>
    void Validate_Click(Object sender, EventArgs E)
    {
        if ( Page.IsValid )
        {
            Msg.Text="Page Valid";
        }
    }


    void CustomServerVal (object source, ServerValidateEventArgs args)
    {
        try
        {
            if ( args.Value.Equals("Hello") )
            {
                Msg.Text="ServerValidation called and TRUE returned.";
                args.IsValid=true;
            }
            else
            {
                Msg.Text="ServerValidation called and FALSE returned.";
                args.IsValid=false;
            }
        }
        catch
        {
            Msg.Text="ServerValidation called and FALSE returned.";
            args.IsValid=false;
        }
    }
    </script>
```

Listing 5-4 ValidatorTest.aspx, which uses the *RangeValidator*, *RegularExpressionValidator*, and *CustomValidator* controls

```
<body>
    <form runat=server>
        <center>
        <h3>
        <font face="Verdana" color=blue>Validator Test Page</font>
        </h3>
        <table>
            <tr>
                <td>
                Range Validation (1-12):
                </td>
                <td>
                    <input id="Range"
                    type="text"
                    runat=server size=10 />
                </td>
                <td>
                    <ASP:RangeValidator ID="ValRange"
                        ControlToValidate="Range"
                        Display="Static"
                        Type="Integer"
                        MinimumValue="1"
                        MaximumValue="12"
                        ErrorMessage="Out of Range"
                        runat=server />
                </td>
            </tr>
            <tr>
                <td>
                    Regular Expression Validation (nnn-nn-nnnn):
                </td>
                <td>
                    <input id="RegEx"
                    type="text"
                    runat=server size=11 />
                </td>
                <td>
                    <ASP:RegularExpressionValidator ID="ValRegEx"
                        ControlToValidate="RegEx"
                        runat="SERVER"
                        ErrorMessage=
                          "Enter a valid U.S. SSN (nnn-nn-nnnn)."
                        ValidationExpression=
                          "[0-9]{3}-[0-9]{2}-[0-9]{4}" />
                </td>
            </tr>
```

(continued)

Listing 5-4 *continued*

```
                    <tr>
                        <td>
                            Custom Validation
                            (It wants you to enter
                            "Hello" WITHOUT THE QUOTES):
                        </td>
                        <td>
                            <input type="text"
                            id="txtCustom"
                            runat=server size=11 />
                        </td>
                        <td>
                            <ASP:CustomValidator ID="ValCustom"
                                runat="server"
                                ControlToValidate="txtCustom"
                                OnServerValidate="CustomServerVal"
                                Display="Static"
                                >
                                Enter "Hello".  Case-Sensitive.
                            </ASP:CustomValidator>
                        </td>
                    </tr>
                    <tr>
                        <td colspan=3 align="center">
                            <asp:button
                                text="Validate"
                                OnClick="Validate_Click"
                                runat=server>
                            </asp:button>
                            <p>
                            <asp:Label id="Msg"
                                ForeColor="red"
                                Font-Name="Verdana"
                                Font-Size="10" runat=server />
                        </td>
                    </tr>
                </table>
                </center>
            </form>
        </body>
</html>
```

Figure 5-7 shows ValidatorTest.aspx when displayed in a browser.

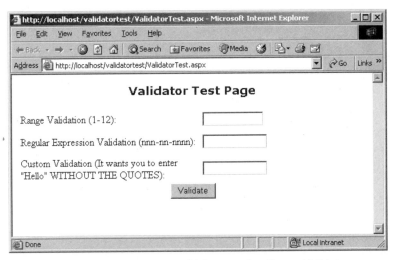

Figure 5-7 ValidatorTest.aspx, which uses the *RangeValidator*, *RegularExpressionValidator*, and *CustomValidator* controls

The *RangeValidator* control has several attributes that are unique to this type of validator. In Listing 5-4, the code that declares *RangeValidator* is as follows:

```
<ASP:RangeValidator ID="ValRange"
    ControlToValidate="Range"
    Display="Static"
    Type="Integer"
    MinimumValue="1"
    MaximumValue="12"
    ErrorMessage="Out of Range"
    runat=server />
```

Three of the attributes used here are already familiar (*ControlToValidate*, *Type*, and *RunAt*), one has been shown previously but not explained (*Display*, to be described in the next section), and a couple are new (*MinimumValue* and *MaximumValue*). *Type* is the type of comparison that should be done. For example, consider whether *1234* is greater than *13*. If these are string values, *1234* is alphabetically smaller, but if these are numeric values, *1234* is numerically greater. The values allowed for *Type* in *RangeValidator* are the same as are allowed for a *CompareValidator* control's *Type* attribute.

MinimumValue and *MaximumValue* are compared to the value of *ControlToValidate*, using the type conversion specified by the *Type* attribute. In this example, we're looking for an integer from 1 through 12.

RegularExpressionValidator is useful because of its flexibility. The code used to specify *RegularExpressionValidator* in Listing 5-4 is shown here:

```
<ASP:RegularExpressionValidator ID="ValRegEx"
    ControlToValidate="RegEx"
    runat="SERVER"
    ErrorMessage="Enter a valid U.S. SSN (nnn-nn-nnnn)."
    ValidationExpression="[0-9]{3}-[0-9]{2}-[0-9]{4}" />
```

The unique attribute in the code to create this validator is *ValidationExpression*. The value of this attribute is a regular expression pattern to match against the value of the control specified in *ControlToValidate*.

If you're unfamiliar with regular expressions in general, refer to the following "Regular Expressions" sidebar.

Regular Expressions

Regular expressions are strings used to match patterns of text. Why is matching patterns of text so much more useful than just comparing against a string or against another control (as the *CompareValidator* control does)? Think about the kind of things you validate. Often you're validating input such as telephone numbers, ZIP Codes, and social security numbers. The *CompareValidator* control is of no value in these situations.

The simplest kind of regular expression that virtually all computer users were familiar with when the command line was king was a file name with a wildcard. Want to see all the .doc files in a folder? From the command prompt, you would type the following:

```
Dir *.doc
```

This command would result in a list of all files with the .doc extension. Or you might want to look for a file named either TEST0501.DOC or TEST0601.DOC. To do so, you would type the following:

```
Dir TEST0?01.DOC
```

SQL programmers are also used to a form of regular expressions that can be used with the LIKE keyword, as shown here:

```
SELECT * FROM Users WHERE LastName LIKE 'R__lly'
```

This statement would show a list of users with the last name Reilly, or even Rielly, a common misspelling. It would *not* show a name like Rilly because in this case, the underscore (_) is used as a single-character place-holder, and so two underscores could take the place of exactly two characters.

Regular expressions in .NET are much more powerful, and a complete description is beyond the scope of this book, so here we'll look only at the regular expression I'm using in the *RegularExpressionValidator* example in ValidatorTest.aspx, shown in Listing 5-4.

The regular expression *"[0-9]{3}-[0-9]{2}-[0-9]{4}"* is one of many ways you can validate for a plausible U.S. social security number, which must be in the form *nnn-nn-nnnn*, where the *n*s each represent a single digit. Characters within square brackets ([and]) can be either a list of characters or a range of characters. In each of the instances of square brackets in this example, the characters allowed are represented by a range of characters from 0 through 9. Following each of the sets of characters in square brackets is a number in curly braces ({ and }). The value within the curly braces specifies the number of characters matching the previous expression that must be present. The hyphens (-) outside the brackets and braces represent literal characters that must be present.

This example could have been satisfied just as easily in several different ways, as in the following examples:

```
[0123456789]{3}-[0123456789]{2}-[0123456789]{4}
\d{3}-\d{2}=\d{4}
```

In the first alternative, I've simply listed the digits individually within the square brackets. In the second alternative, I've used a shortcut to specify digits, *\d*, and followed it with the count in curly braces. There are lots of other shortcuts. In addition to specifying the characters allowed, you can precede the character set within the square brackets with a caret (^) to indicate characters *not* allowed. Thus, the following string would match seven non-numeric characters.

```
[^0-9]{7}
```

This brief introduction is by no means complete. You can refer to the MSDN documentation for more information.

With the *RequiredFieldValidator*, *CompareValidator*, *RangeValidator*, and *RegularExpressionValidator* controls, most of your validation needs are met. These validators can handle many different types of fields. But suppose you needed something a little different? That's where *CustomValidator* comes in.

The *CustomValidator* control can be used whenever the other stock validators don't do the job. For example, if instead of just comparing a value against a fixed value or a regular expression you want to validate the value entered against a database, *CustomValidator* is one way to go. The code used to specify *CustomValidator* in ValidatorTest.aspx in Listing 5-4 is shown here:

```
<ASP:CustomValidator ID="ValCustom"
    runat="server"
    ControlToValidate="txtCustom"
    OnServerValidate="CustomServerVal"
    Display="Static"
    >
    Enter "Hello".  Case-Sensitive.
</ASP:CustomValidator>
```

One thing that stands out in this example in comparison with previous example validators is that rather than using a single tag to open and close the validator and specifying the error message as an attribute (the *ErrorMessage* attribute), here I enter the error message I want associated with the validator between the start and end tags. There's no practical difference between the two methods of specifying the error message.

A new attribute is included with *CustomValidator* in this example, *OnServerValidate*. This attribute points to a server-side function that takes two parameters—in this example, the function *CustomServerVal*, shown here:

```
void CustomServerVal (object source, ServerValidateEventArgs args)
{
    try
    {
        if ( args.Value.Equals("Hello") )
        {
            Msg.Text="ServerValidation called and TRUE returned.";
            args.IsValid=true;
        }
        else
        {
            Msg.Text="ServerValidation called and FALSE returned.";
            args.IsValid=false;
        }
    }
```

```
catch
{
    Msg.Text="ServerValidation called and FALSE returned.";
    args.IsValid=false;
}
}
```

ServerValidateEventArgs has two properties that are important for this example: *Value* and *IsValid*. *Value* is used to get the value of the control, useful for performing the custom validation that's the goal of *CustomServerVal*. *Value* is a read-only property.

The *CustomServerVal* function does nothing more than perform a simple comparison between the value and the literal string "Hello". If *Value* equals "Hello" and no exception is thrown during the check, the function sets the *IsValid* property of the *ServerValidateEventArgs* instance to *true*. If *IsValid* is set to *false*, the *CustomValidator* control will fire, displaying the error message specified either in the *ErrorMessage* attribute or between the start and end tags of the *CustomValidator* control.

As with the other validators, *CustomValidator* can also perform some of its checking on the client side. The *ClientValidationFunction* attribute allows you to specify which function on the client side should be used to validate the control pointed to by the *ControlToValidate* attribute. This example contains no client-side validation, but a reasonable implementation would be as follows:

```
<script language="javascript">
    function ClientValidate(source, value)
    {
        if (value == "Hello")
            return true;
        else
            return false;
    }
</script>
```

The important thing to recognize about the client-side validation is that you'll almost certainly be using a different language than you use to code the server-side validator function. This can lead to interesting problems. For instance, in this simple example, is the comparison of the string "Hello" case sensitive on both the client side and the server side? Ensuring the same case sensitivity would require knowledge of each of the languages involved.

Multiple Validators on a Single Field

Loading the ValidatorTest.aspx page from Listing 5-4 and clicking Validate displays the page shown in Figure 5-8.

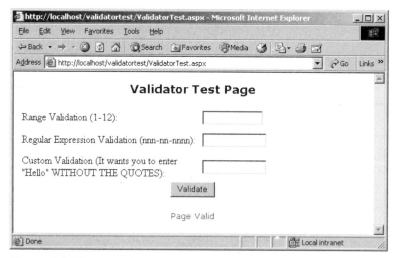

Figure 5-8 The page that results from clicking the Validate button with no values filled in

Notice that it displays the message "Page Valid". This is almost certainly not what you wanted! You specified that the first field should be a number between 1 and 12, that the second field should be some string that looks like a social security number, and that the last field should be "Hello". But it turns out that, by design, all validators except *RequiredFieldValidator* don't validate against an empty control. There must be a solution.

One solution is to use the *RequiredFieldValidator* control. Listing 5-5 shows a modified version of ValidatorTest.aspx, named ValidatorTestRequired.aspx. The difference between ValidatorTest.aspx (which is shown in Listing 5-4) and ValidatorTestRequired.aspx is the addition of a *RequiredFieldValidator* control for each of the fields covered by another validator.

```
<html>
    <script language="C#" runat=server>
    void Validate_Click(Object sender, EventArgs E)
    {
        if ( Page.IsValid )
        {
            Msg.Text="Page Valid";
        }
    }
```

Listing 5-5 ValidatorTestRequired.aspx, a page that requires all fields to be filled, with valid data

```
void CustomServerVal (object source, ServerValidateEventArgs args)
{
    try
    {
        if ( args.Value.Equals("Hello") )
        {
            Msg.Text="ServerValidation called and TRUE returned.";
            args.IsValid=true;
        }
        else
        {
            Msg.Text="ServerValidation called and FALSE returned.";
            args.IsValid=false;
        }
    }
    catch
    {
        Msg.Text="ServerValidation called and FALSE returned.";
        args.IsValid=false;
    }
}
</script>

<body>
    <form runat=server>
        <center>
        <h3>
        <font face="Verdana"
        color=blue>
        Validator Test Page - Required Entry
        </font>
        </h3>
        <table>
            <tr>
                <td>
                    Range Validation (1-12):
                </td>
                <td>
                    <input id="Range"
                    type="text"
                    runat=server size=10 />
                </td>
                <td>
                    <ASP:RangeValidator ID="ValRange"
                        ControlToValidate="Range"
                        Display="Dynamic"
                        Type="Integer"
```

(continued)

Listing 5-5 *continued*

```
                        MinimumValue="1"
                        MaximumValue="12"
                        ErrorMessage="Out of Range"
                        runat=server />
                    <ASP:RequiredFieldValidator
                        ControlToValidate="Range"
                        Display="Dynamic"
                        ErrorMessage="Must enter a value."
                        runat=server />
                </td>
            </tr>
            <tr>
                <td>
                    Regular Expression Validation (nnn-nn-nnnn):
                </td>
                <td>
                    <input id="RegEx"
                    type="text"
                    runat=server size=11 />
                </td>
                <td>
                    <ASP:RegularExpressionValidator ID="ValRegEx"
                        ControlToValidate="RegEx"
                        runat="SERVER"
                        Display="Dynamic"
                        ErrorMessage=
                          "Enter a valid U.S. SSN (nnn-nn-nnnn)."
                        ValidationExpression=
                          "[0-9]{3}-[0-9]{2}-[0-9]{4}" />
                    <ASP:RequiredFieldValidator
                        ControlToValidate="RegEx"
                        Display="Dynamic"
                        ErrorMessage="Must enter a value."
                        runat=server />
                </td>
            </tr>
            <tr>
                <td>
                    Custom Validation
                    (It wants you to enter
                    "Hello" WITHOUT THE QUOTES):
                </td>
                <td>
                    <input type="text"
                    id="txtCustom"
                    runat=server
                    size=11 />
                </td>
```

```
                    <td>
                        <ASP:CustomValidator ID="ValCustom"
                            runat="server"
                            ControlToValidate="txtCustom"
                            OnServerValidate="CustomServerVal"
                            Display="Dynamic"
                            >
                            Enter "Hello".  Case-Sensitive.
                        </ASP:CustomValidator>
                        <ASP:RequiredFieldValidator
                            ControlToValidate="txtCustom"
                            Display="Dynamic"
                            ErrorMessage="Must enter a value."
                            runat=server />
                    </td>
                </tr>
                <tr>
                    <td colspan=3 align="center">
                        <asp:button
                        text="Validate"
                        OnClick="Validate_Click"
                        runat=server>
                        </asp:button>
                        <p>
                        <asp:Label id="Msg"
                        ForeColor="red"
                        Font-Name="Verdana"
                        Font-Size="10"
                        runat=server />
                    </td>
                </tr>
            </table>
            </center>
        </form>
    </body>
</html>
```

One attribute of all validators we haven't yet looked at is the *Display* attribute. The *Display* attribute expects one of three values: *None*, *Static*, or *Dynamic*. When the *Display* attribute is set to *None*, the validation error message isn't displayed. When the *Display* attribute is set to *Static*, the layout of the page won't change when the validator control displays an error message. In this case, the validator contents are physically part of the page, and space will be allocated for them in the layout. When *Display* is set to *Dynamic*, the validator output is not part of the page until it's displayed. In Listing 5-5, I set each validator's *Display* attribute to *Dynamic*. Using *Dynamic* has the unfortunate effect of possibly causing the layout of the page to change when validators are fired, but the result is generally better than setting *Display* to *Static*. For example, when I changed *RangeValidator* to *Static* and then submitted the form with no value in the Range field, the page shown in Figure 5-9 was displayed.

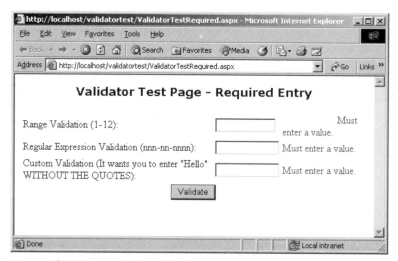

Figure 5-9 The result when the first validator on a given field is set to *Static* display

The *ErrorMessage* associated with the first validator (which hasn't been fired) is "Out of Range". Looking at Figure 5-9, you can see that the space between the text box and the beginning of the first "Must enter a value" string is about what might be required to fit "Out of Range". Because we have the actual source that generated this page, we can see what the browser uses to render the page. The following HTML code is the table row returned to the browser in which the range validator is located. (The code has been reformatted for readability.)

```
<tr>
    <td>
        Range Validation (1-12):
    </td>
    <td>
        <input name="Range"
        id="Range" type="text"
        size="10" />
    </td>
    <td>
        <span id="ValRange"
            controltovalidate="Range"
            errormessage="Out of Range"
            type="Integer"
            evaluationfunction="RangeValidatorEvaluateIsValid"
            maximumvalue="12" minimumvalue="1"
```

```
        style="color:Red;visibility:hidden;">
        Out of Range
    </span>
    <span id="_ctl1"
        controltovalidate="Range"
        errormessage="Must enter a value."
        display="Dynamic"
        evaluationfunction="RequiredFieldValidatorEvaluateIsValid"
        initialvalue=""
        style="color:Red;display:none;">
        Must enter a value.
    </span>
    </td>
</tr>
```

From this HTML output, you can verify that the space for the "Out of Range" text is present in the rendered HTML. Thus, in general, when two validators are present, you'll want to set *Display* to *Dynamic*.

The *ValidationSummary* Control

Sometimes, you might want to simply summarize the errors on a page, perhaps because the errors might involve multiple fields, and so signaling an error on a single field might be misleading. For example, if we were to use a *CompareValidator* control to compare two new password entries, placing an error message next to one or the other of the fields could be misleading. On the other hand, it could just be a part of the user interface standards at your organization that you display a single error message, either at the top or the bottom of the page. How do you do that with ASP.NET?

ASP.NET offers another kind of validation control, *ValidationSummary*. This control handles all the error messages from all validators and displays them in a single place. Listing 5-6 demonstrates how this control is used in ValidatorTestSummary.aspx.

```
<html>

    <script language="C#" runat=server>
    void Validate_Click(Object sender, EventArgs E)
    {
        if ( Page.IsValid )
        {
            Msg.Text="Page Valid";
        }
    }
```

Listing 5-6 ValidatorTestSummary.aspx, showing how the *ValidationSummary* control is used

(continued)

Listing 5-6   *continued*

```
void CustomServerVal (object source, ServerValidateEventArgs args)
{
    try
    {
        if ( args.Value.Equals("Hello") )
        {
            Msg.Text="ServerValidation called and TRUE returned.";
            args.IsValid=true;
        }
        else
        {
            Msg.Text="ServerValidation called and FALSE returned.";
            args.IsValid=false;
        }
    }
    catch
    {
        Msg.Text="ServerValidation called and FALSE returned.";
        args.IsValid=false;
    }
}
</script>

<body>
    <form runat=server>
        <center>
        <h3>
        <font face="Verdana" color=blue>
        Validator Test Page - Summary
        </font>
        </h3>
        <table>
            <tr>
                <td>
                    Range Validation (1-12):
                </td>
                <td>
                    <input id="Range"
                    type="text"
                    runat=server
                    size=10 />
                </td>
                <td>
                    <ASP:RangeValidator ID="ValRange"
                        ControlToValidate="Range"
                        Display="None"
                        Type="Integer"
                        MinimumValue="1"
```

```
                    MaximumValue="12"
                    ErrorMessage="Range"
                    runat=server />
                <ASP:RequiredFieldValidator
                    ControlToValidate="Range"
                    Display="None"
                    ErrorMessage="Range"
                    runat=server />
            </td>
        </tr>
        <tr>
            <td>
                Regular Expression Validation (nnn-nn-nnnn):
            </td>
            <td>
                <input id="RegEx"
                type="text"
                runat=server
                size=11 />
            </td>
            <td>
                <ASP:RegularExpressionValidator ID="ValRegEx"
                    ControlToValidate="RegEx"
                    runat="SERVER"
                    Display="None"
                    ErrorMessage="Regular Expression"
                    ValidationExpression=
                        "[0-9]{3}-[0-9]{2}-[0-9]{4}" />
                <ASP:RequiredFieldValidator
                    ControlToValidate="RegEx"
                    Display="None"
                    ErrorMessage="Regular Expression"
                    runat=server />
            </td>
        </tr>
        <tr>
            <td>
                Custom Validation
                (It wants you to enter "Hello"
                WITHOUT THE QUOTES):
            </td>
            <td>
                <input type="text"
                id="txtCustom"
                runat=server
                size=11 />
            </td>
```

(continued)

Listing 5-6 *continued*

```
                    <td>
                        <ASP:CustomValidator ID="ValCustom"
                            runat="server"
                            ControlToValidate="txtCustom"
                            OnServerValidate="CustomServerVal"
                            Display="None"
                            >
                            Custom
                        </ASP:CustomValidator>
                        <ASP:RequiredFieldValidator
                            ControlToValidate="txtCustom"
                            Display="None"
                            ErrorMessage="Custom"
                            runat=server />
                    </td>
                </tr>
                <tr>
                    <td colspan=3 align="center">
                        <asp:button
                            text="Validate"
                            OnClick="Validate_Click"
                            runat=server>
                        </asp:button>
                        <p>
                        <asp:Label id="Msg"
                            ForeColor="red"
                            Font-Name="Verdana"
                            Font-Size="10"
                            runat=server />
                        <asp:ValidationSummary
                            id="valSum"
                            DisplayMode="BulletList"
                            ShowSummary="true"
                            runat="server"
                            HeaderText=
                            "You must enter a value in the following fields:"
                            Font-Name="Verdana"
                            Font-Size="12"/>
                    </td>
                </tr>
            </table>
            </center>
        </form>
    </body>
</html>
```

Figure 5-10 shows the page that is returned when all fields are left empty and the Validate button is clicked.

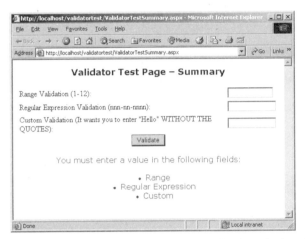

Figure 5-10 The validation summary displayed when ValidatorTestSummary.aspx is submitted with no values entered

The most important change in Listing 5-6 is the addition of a *ValidationSummary* control at the bottom of the page, below the button and label, as follows:

```
<asp:ValidationSummary
    id="valSum"
    DisplayMode="BulletList"
    ShowSummary="true"
    runat="server"
    HeaderText="You must enter a value in the following fields:"
    Font-Name="Verdana"
    Font-Size="12"/>
```

Let's quickly review the attributes of the *ValidationSummary* control that aren't obvious by their names. *DisplayMode* is the attribute that tells ASP.NET how to display errors. The values allowed are part of the *ValidationSummaryDisplayMode* enumeration in the *System.Web.UI.WebControls* namespace. The allowed values are shown here:

■ **BulletList** Displays a bulleted list of the error messages

■ **List** Displays a list of the error messages

■ **SingleParagraph** Displays all error messages in a single paragraph

The *ShowSummary* attribute accepts a *true* or *false* value and indicates whether the validation summary is shown in line within the HTML. Not shown in this example is the *ShowMessageBox* attribute, which controls whether the validation summary is displayed in a message box on the client. *ShowMessageBox* also expects a *true* or *false* value. The *HeaderText* attribute sets the text used as the header of the validation summary.

Other changes made to ValidatorTestSummary.aspx (shown in Listing 5-6) from ValidatorTestRequired.aspx (shown in Listing 5-5) are the settings for the *Display* attribute (all set to *None*) and the error text, set to a user-friendly version of the control being validated so that the message makes sense in combination with *HeaderText*.

Maintaining the State of Controls in ASP.NET

In classic ASP form handling code, a large amount of code is typically required for validation of entered data. The next largest bit of code often is maintaining the state of controls between times the form is submitted. HTTP is a stateless protocol—it doesn't provide a static, long-term connection. Each trip to the server is treated as a new request, and even if there's the *appearance* of a session, it is just that, an appearance that the .NET Framework provides. No connection exists and, by default, the server remembers nothing about the client between page submissions.

When using classic ASP to create standard forms, I typically use the following steps to maintain state information while allowing the user to view and edit information from a database:

1. Determine whether this is a postback. If it isn't, skip to read from database, step 4.

2. If this is a postback, validate the input. If the input is all valid, save the information and redirect the user to another page. If the input is not valid, continue to step 3.

3. Save the entered values into local variables.

4. If this is *not* a postback, read the values from database into local variables.

5. Display the form. On all appropriate controls, set the *value* attribute to the appropriate local variable from step 3 or 4.

There's a lot of processing going on here, and while it's not rocket science, it definitely leaves a lot of room for error. The cost in terms of confusion to the user and grief to the developer trying to track down inconsistencies in such code is not trivial. For instance, in a recent project, I inadvertently used two different naming conventions for controls, one using a prefix describing the type of control (for example, *txtFirstName*) and another that used just a descriptive name for the control (for example, *FirstName*). Tracking down the inconsistencies in exactly how I had named the various controls was no fun. I had to check the postback logic, the validation logic, and the values used as the default values for the HTML widgets. As we'll see, ASP.NET makes it easier to maintain state information.

When an ASP.NET form is submitted, maintaining the state of controls on the form is handled by the .NET Framework. This isn't something you need to specially code or ask for. When a form is submitted and redisplayed, the previous entries are automatically the default entries on the form. For example, Listing 5-7 shows a simple form named StateTest.aspx.

```
<%@ Import Namespace="System.Web.Security " %>
<%@ Page ClientTarget="Downlevel" %>
<html>
    <script language="VB" runat=server>
    Sub ValidateBtn_OnClick(sender As Object, e As EventArgs)
        If (Page.IsValid) Then
            Msg.Text = "Page is Valid!"
        Else
            Msg.Text = "Page is InValid!"
        End If
    End Sub
    </script>

<body>
    <form runat=server>
        <center>
        <h3>
        <font face="Verdana"
        color=blue>Control Test Page - State
        </font>
        </h3>
        <table>
            <tr>
                <td>
                    Name:
                </td>
                <td>
                    <input id="Name"
                    type="text"
                    runat=server
                    size=30 />
                </td>
```

Listing 5-7 StateTest.aspx page used to show how form entries are maintained from submission to submission

(continued)

Listing 5-7 *continued*

```
            <td>
                <ASP:RequiredFieldValidator
                    ControlToValidate="Name"
                    Display="Static"
                    ErrorMessage="Please enter name."
                    runat=server />
            </td>
        </tr>
        <tr>
            <td>
                SSN:
            </td>
            <td>
                <input id="SSN"
                type="text"
                runat=server size=11 />
            </td>
            <td>
                <ASP:RequiredFieldValidator
                    ControlToValidate="SSN"
                    Display="Dynamic"
                    ErrorMessage=
                    "Enter a valid U.S. SSN (nnn-nn-nnnn)."
                    runat=server />
                <ASP:RegularExpressionValidator ID="ValRegEx"
                    ControlToValidate="SSN"
                    runat="SERVER"
                    Display="Dynamic"
                    ErrorMessage=
                      "Enter a valid U.S. SSN (nnn-nn-nnnn)."
                    ValidationExpression=
                      "[0-9]{3}-[0-9]{2}-[0-9]{4}" />
            </td>
        </tr>
        <tr>
            <td colspan=3 align="center">
                <asp:button text="Validate"
                    OnClick="ValidateBtn_OnClick"
                    runat=server>
                </asp:button>
                <p>
                <asp:Label id="Msg"
                    ForeColor="red"
                    Font-Name="Verdana"
                    Font-Size="10"
                    runat=server />
            </td>
```

```
            </tr>
        </table>
        </center>
      </form>
   </body>
</html>
```

> **Note**   Listing 5-7 uses Visual Basic .NET rather than C#. The general
> structure is the same, and although the function called when the Validate
> button is clicked is named *ValidateBtn_OnClick*, there's no reason other than
> convention for my using this naming format. Visual Studio .NET will com-
> monly generate event handlers in this format, but the format is *not* required
> by the .NET Framework.

This form has validators on both the Name field and the SSN field. Entering a name (the form isn't fussy about names) and an invalid social security
number (in this case, 111-111-111 rather than 111-11-1111) displays the page
shown in Figure 5-11, with the entries appearing as the default entries when the
page is redisplayed.

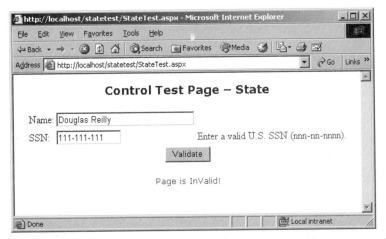

Figure 5-11 The result of submitting StateTest.aspx with a name and an invalid social
security number

> **Note**   The StateTest.aspx sample doesn't use client-side validation be-
> cause I specifically used the *Page* directive's *ClientTarget=Downlevel* attri-
> bute/value pair to ensure that the page was in fact submitted to the server.
> The fact that the message at the bottom of the page displays "Page is InValid!"
> proves it, because this message is generated from a server-side method.

Manipulating Server Controls Programmatically

In addition to the controls you've already seen, all the other standard HTML
widgets have both HTML server controls and ASP server controls, including the
following:

- *HyperLink (<A> tag)*

- *Label*

- *DropDownList*

- *ListBox*

- *Checkbox*

- *RadioButton*

Using the HTML server controls is simply a matter of using the same syntax as you've used with standard HTML controls, with a couple qualifications:

- The *ID* attribute must be set if you want to manipulate the controls
  and their values programmatically.

- The *RunAt* attribute must be set to *Server*.

In general, you'll define the ASP server controls in exactly the same way
you defined HTML controls, but again with a couple exceptions. First, all ASP
server controls use a tag name of *<ASP:controltypename>*. In addition, some of
the properties of the ASP controls are more similar to traditional Visual Basic
controls than HTML controls. One striking example of how the ASP controls are
very similar to the Visual Basic controls is the *ASP:TextBox* control. The first thing
you'll notice is that it is named *TextBox*. In the HTML world, it would be an *INPUT*
of type *Text*. When you begin to investigate properties, the parallel to Visual Basic
becomes even clearer. What would be *Value* in HTML is named *Text* in the ASP
server controls.

> **Note**   You could argue, and many have, that the properties of ASP server controls and HTML server controls should, where they exist in both models, use the same name. Microsoft apparently quite consciously made a decision to keep the HTML server controls true to their heritage, and at the same time create an ASP control hierarchy that would be comfortable for Visual Basic programmers moving to ASP.NET. I think it's a reasonable compromise.

Beyond the list of server controls that mirror the HTML controls, there are a number of ASP server controls that don't have exact analogs in HTML. We've seen one family of these controls, the validator controls. Another large family of controls is designed to make developing database-driven applications easier. We'll postpone looking at these data controls until Chapter 9.

Several other controls enable ASP.NET developers to provide a richer user interface. A simple example is the *LinkButton* control, a hyperlink-style button control.

A much more complicated control is the *Calendar* control. Until now, one of the benefits that developers have had to leave behind when moving to Web applications is the *DateTimePicker* common control provided in Windows. Although it's certainly possible to use client-side ActiveX controls to get a similar effect, using a client-side ActiveX control isn't practical for most developers of Internet applications.

The *Calendar* ASP.NET server control is a pure HTML solution to the problem of date selection in a Web page. The *Calendar* control has attributes that are too numerous to list here; again, they're well documented in the MSDN documentation. To insert a *Calendar* ASP.NET server control in your page, you need to add a set of tags something like the following:

```
<asp:Calendar id="Calendar1"
    runat="server"
    Width="277px"
    Height="188px"
    OnSelectionChanged="Selection_Change">
    <TodayDayStyle
        ForeColor="#0000C0"
        BorderStyle="Solid"
        BorderColor="Red">
    </TodayDayStyle>
</asp:Calendar>
```

Most attributes of the *Calendar* control are self-explanatory, such as *Width*, *Height*, and *ID*. This example also uses a subtag inside the *<ASP:Calendar>* start and end tags. The *TodayDayStyle* subtag is used to set the appearance of the current date in the *Calendar* control. *TodayDayStyle* alone has over 10 individual elements that can be set, including attributes such as *BorderStyle* and *BorderColor* and details about the font. Setting multiple elements using attributes can be tedious. Fortunately, when you're using the Visual Studio .NET development environment, you can set these attributes in the Properties window, similar to the Properties window that Visual Basic programmers have come to expect. You can also set the individual attributes programmatically.

Using Code-Behind Files

All the examples I've shown so far have been created primarily using Notepad—a tool that knows nothing of the .NET Framework. The next example, named WebForm1.aspx, as well as most future examples, will be created using Visual Studio .NET. One of the important differences between classic ASP and ASP.NET is the location of code. With ASP, all code had to be located in the ASP file, or included in the ASP file. ASP.NET encourages a different model. In WebForm1.aspx, all the code is located in a separate file, by convention named WebForm1.aspx.vb (because the code is Visual Basic .NET code). The code-behind file, as it is called, would be named WebForm1.aspx.cs if the example used C# rather than Visual Basic .NET. The ability to conveniently separate content from the code is critical for development groups that place page designers and page developers in two different groups.

The rest of this section describes an example named ControlShowAndTell. The example uses four ASP.NET server controls (*Label*, *Calendar*, *LinkButton*, and *TextBox*), which will be manipulated programmatically. Listing 5-8 shows WebForm1.aspx, which contains the content for the page. Later we'll see the code behind this page, which is in a separate file.

```
<%@ Page Language="vb"
AutoEventWireup="false"
Codebehind="WebForm1.aspx.vb"
Inherits="ControlShowAndTell.WebForm1"%>
<!DOCTYPE HTML PUBLIC "-//W3C//DTD HTML 4.0 Transitional//EN">
<HTML>
    <HEAD>
        <title></title>
        <meta content="Microsoft Visual Studio.NET 7.0" name="GENERATOR">
```

Listing 5-8 WebForm1.aspx, a Visual Studio .NET–generated content file

```
        <meta content="Visual Basic 7.0" name="CODE_LANGUAGE">
        <meta content="JavaScript" name="vs_defaultClientScript">
        <meta content="Internet Explorer 5.0" name="vs_targetSchema">
    </HEAD>
    <body>
        <CENTER>
            <form id="Form1" onsubmit="FormSubmit"
            method="post" runat="server">
                <p>
                <asp:label
                    id="Label2"
                    runat="server"
                    Width="175px"
                    Height="35px"
                    BackColor="#FFC0C0"
                    BorderStyle="Dotted"
                    Font-Size="18pt"
                    Font-Bold="True">
                    Other Controls
                </asp:label>
                </p>
                <p>
                <asp:calendar id="Calendar1"
                    runat="server"
                    Width="277px"
                    Height="188px"
                    OnSelectionChanged="Selection_Change">
                    <TodayDayStyle ForeColor="#0000C0"
                        BorderStyle="Solid"
                        BorderColor="Red">
                    </TodayDayStyle>
                </asp:calendar>
                </p>
                <p>
                <asp:linkbutton id="LinkButton1"
                    runat="server"
                    Width="81px"
                    Height="19px">
                    LinkButton
                </asp:linkbutton>
                </p>
                <asp:textbox id="TextBox1"
                    runat="server">
                </asp:textbox>
            </form>
        </CENTER>
    </body>
</HTML>
```

Listing 5-9 shows WebForm1.aspx.vb, which is the Visual Basic .NET code behind the content page WebForm1.aspx.

```vb
Public Class WebForm1
    Inherits System.Web.UI.Page
    Protected WithEvents Calendar1 As System.Web.UI.WebControls.Calendar
    Protected WithEvents LinkButton1 As System.Web.UI.WebControls.LinkButton
    Protected WithEvents Label2 As System.Web.UI.WebControls.Label
    Protected WithEvents Form1 As System.Web.UI.HtmlControls.HtmlForm
    Protected WithEvents TextBox1 As System.Web.UI.WebControls.TextBox

#Region " Web Form Designer Generated Code "

    'This call is required by the Web Form Designer.
    <System.Diagnostics.DebuggerStepThrough()> _
    Private Sub InitializeComponent()

    End Sub

    Private Sub Page_Init(ByVal sender As System.Object, _
      ByVal e As System.EventArgs) _
      Handles MyBase.Init
        'CODEGEN: This method call is required by the Web Form Designer
        'Do not modify it using the code editor.
        InitializeComponent()
    End Sub

#End Region

    Private Sub Page_Load(ByVal sender As System.Object, _
      ByVal e As System.EventArgs) _
      Handles MyBase.Load
        'Put user code to initialize the page here
        If Page.IsPostBack() = False Then
            Calendar1.BackColor = System.Drawing.Color.BlanchedAlmond
            Calendar1.ForeColor = System.Drawing.Color.Red
            Calendar1.TodaysDate = "7/24/2001"
            LinkButton1.Enabled = False
            TextBox1.Text = "Hello"
        End If
    End Sub
End Sub
```

Listing 5-9 WebForm1.aspx.vb, a Visual Basic .NET–generated code-behind file for WebForm1.aspx, showing how to manipulate a calendar control programmatically

```
Sub Selection_Change(ByVal sender As Object, _
  ByVal e As EventArgs)
    Dim s As String
    s = Calendar1.SelectedDate.ToString()
    TextBox1.Text = s.Substring(0, s.IndexOf(" "))
End Sub 'Selection_Change

End Class
```

The first difference from previous examples you'll notice in Listing 5-8 is the *Page* directive, shown here:

```
<%@ Page Language="vb"
AutoEventWireup="false"
Codebehind="WebForm1.aspx.vb"
Inherits="ControlShowAndTell.WebForm1"%>
```

AutoEventWireup and *Codebehind* are attributes specific to Visual Studio .NET. *AutoEventWireup* is almost always set to *false*. Setting this attribute to *true* or omitting it causes an event handler named *Page_Init* to automatically be wired up to the *Init* event of the page. Using *AutoEventWireup* seemed like a good idea at the time but can cause some confusion in practice. There were many reports during early ASP.NET betas of developers accidentally using *AutoEventWireup* and manually wiring up the events as well, resulting in two calls to the event rather than the desired single call. Visual Studio .NET uses *Codebehind* at design time, and the .NET Framework ignores it. Projects that don't use Visual Studio .NET commonly use the *Src* attribute of the *Page* directive to point to the code to run for the page.

WebForm1.aspx next has a number of *Meta* tags placed by Visual Studio .NET. *Meta* HTML elements convey hidden information about the document to both the server and the client. Search engines commonly read *Meta* tags to index pages. The remainder of Listing 5-8 is similar to previous examples, defining ASP.NET server controls for the page. Some bells and whistles are used for the title label (a dotted border and a background color), but the rest of the controls are declared with the minimum number of attributes.

WebForm1.aspx.vb, in Listing 5-9, begins with the opening of a class declaration, as follows:

```
Public Class WebForm1
    Inherits System.Web.UI.Page
    Protected WithEvents Calendar1 As System.Web.UI.WebControls.Calendar
    Protected WithEvents LinkButton1 As System.Web.UI.WebControls.LinkButton
    Protected WithEvents Label2 As System.Web.UI.WebControls.Label
    Protected WithEvents Form1 As System.Web.UI.HtmlControls.HtmlForm
    Protected WithEvents TextBox1 As System.Web.UI.WebControls.TextBox
```

The public class *WebForm1* is declared and described as inheriting from *System.Web.UI.Page*. Complete documentation on this class is available in MSDN. Next, four controls are declared, one each for *Label2*, *Calendar1*, *LinkButton1*, and *TextBox1*. Each of these controls is declared as an ASP server control in WebForm1.aspx (Listing 5-8), and they are declared here so that they can be manipulated programmatically. These controls are declared using the *WithEvents* Visual Basic .NET keyword to specify that these objects will respond to events raised by the instance assigned to the variable. All the ASP server controls are located in the *System.Web.UI.WebControls* namespace.

Immediately after the instance variables are declared in WebForm1.aspx.vb in Listing 5-9, you'll see the following curious line:

```
#Region " Web Form Designer Generated Code "
```

The code between this line and the *#End Region* line below it in Listing 5-9 is hidden, by default, when the code is edited within Visual Studio .NET. Visual C++ MFC and ATL programmers might be familiar with this generated code, but Visual Basic programmers might not be.

> **Note** In Microsoft Visual C++, programmers have long been familiar with sections of code that were maintained by the development environment. In time, some even learned to manipulate these lines of code manually, although doing so is certainly not recommended. Visual Basic programmers are not used to having this same sort of code exposed to the programmer but really designed for the development environment's use. In Visual Basic, some "secret sauce" ingredients were magically added but were not represented by code that the developer could see. The .NET model moves all the Visual Studio .NET–supported languages away from any secret ingredients. If the code is doing something, even if that something isn't intended for end user modification, it's in there! For now, just overlook the regions declared as "Web Form Designer Generated Code". In Listing 5-9, this generated code is quite straightforward, but other examples will be more complex.

Because Visual Studio .NET has taken over the *Page_Init* event for its own purposes, we need to find another place where we can place code to be executed at the start of processing. There is such a place, of course: the *Page_Load* event. The *IsPostBack* property of the *Page* class will help us handle the two situations that we'll encounter on the *Page_Load* event.

ASP.NET Web Form Stages

The life cycle of an ASP.NET Web Form has five basic stages:

- **_Page_Init_**   The ASP.NET page framework uses this event to restore control properties and postback data (data entered in controls by the user before the form was submitted).

- **_Page_Load_**   The developer uses this event either to perform some initial processing (if this is the first visit to the page) or to restore control values (if this is a postback).

- **Validation**   The _Validate_ method of ASP.NET server controls is called to perform validation for the controls.

- **Other event handling**   Various controls expose many events. For example, the _Calendar_ control exposes a _SelectionChanged_ event, as we'll see later in this section. There's no assurance that events will be raised in any particular order, except that cached control events (as specified in the control's _AutoPostBack_ property) are always processed before the posting event. If the page contains validation controls, you should check the _IsValid_ property of the page and individual validation controls to determine whether validation has been passed.

- **_Page_Unload_**   This event is called as the page has finished rendering. This would be the place to clean up any resources allocated, especially expensive resources like file handles and database connections. Simply allowing these resources to pass out of scope might not be enough, especially on a busy site, where waiting for garbage collection to occur might hinder performance.

When a page is loaded, two scenarios are possible: this could be the first time this page is loaded, or this could be a postback. In the _Page_Load_ event handler, the following code handles the two possible page-loading scenarios:

```
Private Sub Page_Load(ByVal sender As System.Object, _
  ByVal e As System.EventArgs) _
  Handles MyBase.Load
    'Put user code to initialize the page here
    If Page.IsPostBack = False Then
       Calendar1.BackColor = System.Drawing.Color.BlanchedAlmond
       Calendar1.ForeColor = System.Drawing.Color.Red
       Calendar1.TodaysDate = "7/24/2001"
       LinkButton1.Enabled = False
       TextBox1.Text = "Hello"
    End If
End Sub
```

In this example, processing is done only when *Page.IsPostBack* is *false*—that is, the first time the page is processed, not when a form is filled in. When *Page.IsPostBack* is *false*, the page programmatically sets several properties of the *Calendar* control as well as the *Enabled* property of the link button and the *Text* property of the text box. For the *Calendar* control, the *BackColor* and *ForeColor* properties are set, along with the *TodaysDate* property. The *TodaysDate* property is used to set the control's view of what today's date is, which can be different from the system date on the server or the client. These simple examples of setting properties are just the tip of the iceberg as far as the level of programmatic control you can have over components.

Figure 5-12 shows the ControlShowAndTell example when WebForm1.aspx is requested.

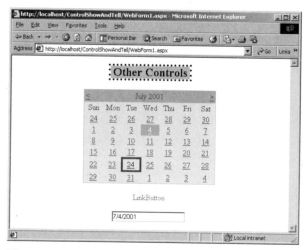

Figure 5-12 WebForm1.aspx, showing *TodaysDate* as set in code, with July 4 as the selected date

In WebForm1.aspx.vb (Listing 5-9), the link button control was disabled in code, and indeed it is disabled in Figure 5-12. However, the *Text* property of the text box just below that was set to "Hello" in the *Page_Load* method. In Figure 5-12, the text box is set to "7/4/2001", which happens to be the selected date as well. How did that happen?

The answer is the code in the *Selection_Change* method in Listing 5-9:

```
Sub Selection_Change(ByVal sender As Object, _
    ByVal e As EventArgs)
    Dim s As String
    s = Calendar1.SelectedDate.ToString()
    TextBox1.Text = s.Substring(0, s.IndexOf(" "))
End Sub 'Selection_Change
```

The *OnSelectionChanged* attribute of the *Calendar* control is set to *Selection_Change*. Whenever the selection is changed, this method is called on the server. This simple method changes the *Text* property of the text box to the date that the *Calendar* control is set to.

Strings, Dates, and a Rich Framework

The ControlShowAndTell example demonstrates the richness of the object model in the .NET environment. Notice that I actually set an intermediate string *s* to the result of the *ToString* method on the *SelectedDate* property. When I first did this, there was a problem. Rather than displaying "7/4/2001" when I selected July 4, 2001, the text box showed "7/4/2001 12:00:00 AM". To get just the date, I used the *Substring* method. To display the date, I could have also used another approach. Rather than having the *Selection_Change* method hard-coded to work on *Calendar1*, I really could have used the *Sender* parameter passed into the event handler. Here's another approach that would also work:

```
Sub Selection_Change(ByVal sender As Object, ByVal e As EventArgs)
    Dim c As Calendar
    Try
        c = CType(sender, Calendar)
        c.SelectedDate.ToShortDateString()
        TextBox1.Text = c.SelectedDate.ToShortDateString()
    Catch
    End Try
End Sub 'Selection_Change
```

First, I converted the *sender* parameter to a *Calendar* object. I placed the code in a *Try/Catch* block, because it could fail if I used the same event handler for some other, non-calendar-related event. Once I had the *Calendar* object, I simply used the *ToShortDateString* method on the date so that I got the date only, without the time. The *Catch* block does nothing, because this event handler is designed only for *Calendar* objects, and so if this is not a *Calendar* object or a class that can be converted to a *Calendar* object, I do nothing.

When you create an ASP.NET Web Application project in Visual Studio .NET, multiple supporting files are created. Figure 5-13 shows the files created for the ControlShowAndTell example.

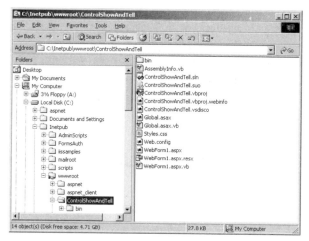

Figure 5-13 The files created by Visual Studio .NET for the ControlShowAndTell example

Listing 5-10 shows the Global.asax.vb file for the ControlShowAndTell example, a file that contains the code elements somewhat analogous to the event handlers in Global.asa in classic ASP.

```
Imports System.Web
Imports System.Web.SessionState

Public Class Global
    Inherits System.Web.HttpApplication

#Region " Component Designer Generated Code "

    Public Sub New()
        MyBase.New()

        'This call is required by the Component Designer.
        InitializeComponent()

        'Add any initialization after the InitializeComponent() call

    End Sub


    'Required by the Component Designer
    Private components As System.ComponentModel.Container
```

Listing 5-10 Global.asax.vb, generated by Visual Studio .NET

```
'NOTE: The following procedure is required by the Component Designer
'It can be modified using the Component Designer.
'Do not modify it using the code editor.
<System.Diagnostics.DebuggerStepThrough()> _
  Private Sub InitializeComponent()
    components = New System.ComponentModel.Container()
End Sub

#End Region

  Sub Application_BeginRequest(ByVal sender As Object, _
    ByVal e As EventArgs)
      ' Fires at the beginning of each request
  End Sub

  Sub Application_AuthenticateRequest(ByVal sender As Object, _
    ByVal e As EventArgs)
      ' Fires upon attempting to authenticate the use
  End Sub

  Sub Application_Error(ByVal sender As Object, _
    ByVal e As EventArgs)
      ' Fires when an error occurs
  End Sub

End Class
```

Global.asax.vb also has a region of code that is generated by the development environment, and this code is hidden by default when viewed in Visual Studio .NET.

When you compile or run a Visual Studio .NET project, a bin folder is created. The bin folder contains the DLL (named ControlShowAndTell.dll) with the compiled functionality from WebPage1.aspx.vb as well as a file used for debugging.

> **Note**   If you use the Depends.exe tool included with Visual Studio 6.0, you'll see that the only DLL that the ControlShowAndTell.dll file relies on is Mscoree.dll. This DLL contains the majority of the .NET Framework functionality.

Conclusion

We've now looked at the basic building blocks of Web Forms, and how they can be used to move RAD to the server. Although the examples presented in this chapter were relatively simple, the power of the ASP.NET Framework should be clear. You can develop applications and factor out all the detail work that used to be required for each page you designed. Instead, you can concentrate on what makes each of your pages unique to your organization.

Just as important, you can concentrate on the part of the job you're responsible for, if the development task in your organization is divided between content and code. An interface designer has a wonderful set of tools that can be used to create a user interface the designer never dreamed of before. And the person designing the guts of the application can independently proceed in developing the core functionality required by the application.

What if the controls discussed in this chapter aren't enough to meet all your needs? We'll be looking at the database-related controls in Chapter 9, but what if some twist on a component requires a slightly different behavior? Developing your own components is the subject of Chapter 6. While much of the code so far has made use of just the .NET Framework, some of the code to develop components will use special features of each of the major .NET languages, Visual Basic .NET and C#.

6

Creating ASP.NET Components

One of the features that drove the unprecedented (and somewhat unexpected) success of Microsoft Visual Basic when it was introduced was that it could be extended with components. Even though the benefits possible with object-oriented development wouldn't be fully realized until the arrival of Visual Basic .NET, Visual Basic succeeded initially in no small part because it allowed Microsoft as well as third parties to develop and use components within it.

In the first section of this chapter, I'll talk about the mixed blessing components have been until now. In the rest of the chapter, I'll explain how ASP.NET has come to the rescue, solving many of the problems that developers have had to endure when using COM components in Active Server Pages (ASP). I'll go over the control classes in ASP.NET and then walk you through the life cycle of an ASP.NET control. In the final two sections of the chapter, you'll learn the ins and outs of creating and using both user controls and custom controls within ASP.NET.

The Trouble with Components

According to object-oriented purists, an object should support polymorphism, inheritance, and encapsulation. Software components or controls aren't always a perfect match for what objects should be, although they're often "good enough." Certainly the initial VBX controls, and even the more current COM controls, weren't designed to enable easy inheritance. In addition, problems with version compatibility persist. The idea of an immutable interface that will endure and be compatible with all future versions of a component that implements it is a good one, but in the real world, it's often difficult to create a new component that perfectly mimics the behavior of the previous version.

For example, I once used a third-party text control to create encrypted rich text format (RTF) files. The initial two versions of the text control interacted perfectly with my encryption routine, which was a simple routine designed (because of the memory limitations inherent in 16-bit Microsoft Windows programming) to operate on chunks of text no larger than 2048 characters. This limitation wasn't a problem because the text control always gave me the text with real newline characters at every line break (denoted by a *{para}* RTF tag). All went well until I moved to the third version of the text control, and then suddenly, everything broke!

The reason for the problem, in retrospect, was simple. The interface contract between the developer of the control and the end user of the control did specify exactly how to get the text in and out of the control, how to calculate the length of the text in the control, how to select certain characters, and many other details. However, the interface contract for the control said *nothing* about how physical line breaks would be handled. Nonetheless, I relied on the behavior of the first version. There was no need for physical line breaks in the RTF text, and in fact, the third version of the text control *never* inserted a line break. That meant that, including control characters and the like, I could receive between 4000 and 8000 characters without any physical line break. Such large text chunks broke the encryption routine, which was designed specifically to work with small blocks of text.

The new text control properly implemented the same interface that had previously existed, but nonetheless it broke my code. Reverting to a previous version of the control until I could address the encryption routine's buffer limit was a nightmare.

Deploying COM components is also a bit more difficult than it should be and can include the following problems:

- Version dependencies can cause a newer version of a COM component to break an older application.

- COM components must have the proper entries in the registry.

- There's no easy way to deploy a new COM component while the existing component is running.

- Developing and debugging COM components is difficult.

The .NET Framework addresses the first problem of version dependency by allowing different versions of components to live side by side on the same machine. Therefore, applications can request a particular version, so older applications can use an older version of a component and won't break if another application residing on the same computer requires the newer version.

The second problem made deployment and configuration of COM components more difficult. The components created for the .NET Framework are self-describing and don't rely on the registry. Removing this dependency on the registry makes it easier to deploy components because the components can just be copied to the proper location.

The third problem wasn't much of an issue initially, when COM components were used primarily for desktop applications. Frankly, shutting down and restarting a desktop application, or even rebooting the machine, wasn't a catastrophe. There was still the hassle of having someone walk from machine to machine to perform the upgrade, but at least that was possible. As more and more COM components were used for server-based applications, and especially Web servers, however, the need to shut down an application to install a new version of the component became a serious liability. Many Web sites must be up and running 24 hours a day, 7 days a week. There's no convenient time for a shutdown. Fortunately, some alternatives are available, though they're not without problems of their own.

For example, I work on a four-machine Web server cluster. If I need to update a COM component, I have to understand the difference in behavior between the old and the new versions and then make my plans accordingly. If the new component is designed to be compatible with the existing COM component and the change is merely a bug fix, all I need to do is drop the servers out of the cluster, stop required services (often the World Wide Web Publishing service and Component Services), and install the new component. I can then bring the machine with the updated component on line and move to the next server.

What happens if the upgrade isn't just a bug fix but is instead adding new functionality? This scenario gets a bit tricky. If the Active Server Pages (ASP) code that calls the component will be changed to use the new functionality, I need to move through all the servers to change the component and then move through the servers again to add the changed ASP code on each server. Even this plan presents potential problems. If one request to the Web server goes to a machine that knows about the added functionality of the control and the next request based on new information goes to a different server that doesn't yet have the ASP code to understand the new functionality, a problem could arise. This window of opportunity for bad things to happen isn't terribly large on a four-server cluster, but if you're working with a larger cluster, you might have real trouble.

ASP.NET, in conjunction with some other services available as part of the .NET Framework, allows this transition to take place much more cleanly. (See MSDN for information about the Microsoft Application Center, one service that can help with this kind of upgrading.) As for the components themselves, new ASP.NET components are designed to be copied on top of the older versions, and users connected to an old version are allowed to cleanly spin down, while new requests will receive the new component. Of course, potential problems still lurk, but the ability to copy in a new component without shutting down services like IIS and Component Services is a huge advance.

Finally, the fourth problem is developing and debugging COM components, which is a difficult process. Developing COM components using Visual Basic is definitely easier than using C++, but it's still more difficult than it should be. Debugging COM components that are called from an ASP page isn't impossible, but it involves a very different process than standard ASP script debugging.

ASP.NET components address all these issues and more, as you'll see in this chapter. But first, let's take a look at exactly what makes up a component in ASP.NET.

ASP.NET Control Classes

Everything in the .NET Framework is an object. OK, that's an oversimplification, since value types, like integers and structures, aren't actually objects by default. But it shouldn't surprise you that the components you build will, ultimately, derive from the *Object* class. Figure 6-1 shows the hierarchy of classes that will be the basis for any component you build.

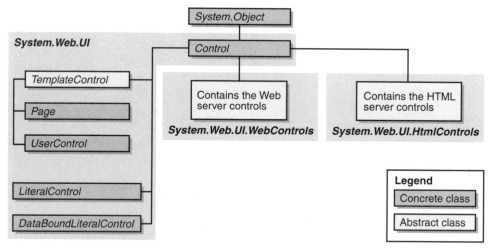

Figure 6-1 The class hierarchy for server control classes

The *System.Web.UI* namespace contains the *System.Web.UI.Control* class, from which all server controls derive. The two most important namespaces under

System.Web.UI are *System.Web.UI.WebControls* and *System.Web.UI.HtmlControls*. The *HtmlControls* namespace contains the controls that directly map to standard HTML server controls (created by using the standard HTML syntax, with the addition of a *RunAt=Server* attribute/value pair). The *WebControls* namespace contains all the ASP.NET server controls whose tags in the .aspx files are preceded by *ASP:*, such as *ASP:TextBox*.

> **Note**   If you're thinking that the world would be a perfect place if the Windows Forms control classes were also in the same control hierarchy, this note is a reminder that, alas, the developer's world is still far from perfect. In fact, if you look at the *System.Windows.Forms.Control* class, you'll quickly be reminded of just how different the two control environments—the Web and Windows—really are. For example, Web controls have no concept of things like z-order or window handles, while Windows controls have no concept of rendering or view state. The classes do have similarities, and certainly Visual Basic programmers will be comfortable with many of the properties now exposed on the Web controls, such as *Text*. But these similarities shouldn't lead you to overlook the very great differences in both implementation and purpose of Web controls and Windows controls.

Although the *WebControls* and *HtmlControls* namespaces contain most of the controls you'll normally be deriving from, they're not the only namespaces that have classes you might derive from. As you can see in Figure 6-1, the two most important classes in this hierarchy are *Page* and *UserControl*. *Page* is the base class used for all ASP.NET Web pages. Keep in mind that although the *Page* class is used in a very different way than the other control classes, at its heart, it's similar to any other control. (Learning about controls is important, even if, as a Visual Basic programmer, you shied away from creating controls and concentrated on consuming them.) Related to the *Page* class is the *UserControl* class. The *UserControl* class can be derived and used much like the *Page* class, except that rather than defining an entire page, it defines a fragment of a page. Multiple *UserControl*-derived objects can be used on a single page, and they can also be nested.

> **Note**   In early beta releases of ASP.NET, user controls were called *pagelets*. I prefer the earlier names to *UserControl*, but *UserControl* is the final name.

The Life Cycle of a Control

One key to understanding all controls is to understand the execution life cycle of a control. For example, when is the view state restored? What happens first, the *Load* event or the postback event notifications?

Table 6-1, which is based on the table included in the MSDN documentation, shows the life cycle of an ASP.NET control. One critical point to remember as you look at this table is that HTTP is a stateless protocol. The control life cycle is designed to create the illusion of state maintenance. Because you can modify the life cycle via exposed events, you can effect the illusion of state, for good or for ill.

Table 6-1 Execution Life Cycle of an ASP.NET Control

Phase	Control Duties	Method or Event to Override
Initialize	Initializes settings needed during the lifetime of the incoming Web request.	*Init* event (*OnInit* method)
Load view state	Customizes how view state is restored by overriding the *LoadViewState* method.	*LoadViewState* method
Process postback data	Processes incoming form data and updates properties. (Only controls that process postback data participate in this phase. The control must implement the *IPostBackDataHandler* interface to handle this event.)	*LoadPostData* method
Load	Performs tasks common to all requests, such as opening database connections. When the *Load* event takes place, server controls are created and initialized, state has been restored, and form controls reflect client-side changes.	*Load* event (*OnLoad* method)
Send postback change notifications	Raises change events in response to state changes between the current and previous postbacks. As with the "process postback data" phase, this phase occurs only for controls that implement the *IPostBackDataHandler* event.	*RaisePostDataChangedEvent* method

Phase	Control Duties	Method or Event to Override
Handle postback events	Handles the client-side event that caused the postback and raises appropriate events on the server. As with the "process postback data" phase, this phase occurs only for controls that implement the *IPostBackDataHandler* event.	*RaisePostBackEvent* method
Prerender	Performs any changes required before the control is rendered. *Rendering* a control means writing out the HTML that will create the control on the client's browser. Changes to state made here will be saved, whereas changes made in the rendering phase are not.	*PreRender* event (*OnPreRender* method)
Save state	Saves the current state of the control. The *ViewState* property of a control is automatically persisted to a string object after this phase. The string object is sent to the client as a hidden field in the HTML that goes to the client's browser. A control can override the *SaveViewState* method to change the contents of the *ViewState* property, possibly to create a more efficient view state.	*SaveViewState* method
Render	Generates the output to be rendered to the client.	*Render* method
Dispose	Performs any final cleanup. Although garbage collection will eventually recover any unreferenced objects, objects that require deterministic freeing of expensive resources, such as database connections, can be freed here.	*Dispose* method
Unload	Performs any final cleanup before the control is torn down. Control authors generally perform cleanup in *Dispose* and don't handle this event.	*Unload* event (*OnUnload* method)

When you're creating components, you might find yourself referring to Table 6-1 often. If you discover that an action doesn't have the desired effect, look carefully at where in the life cycle of the component you're taking an action that doesn't seem to work. In most cases, moving the action to a more appropriate event will eliminate the problem.

Creating User Controls

Creating Web Forms should be fresh in your mind (recall that we created several forms in Chapter 5), so it seems worthwhile to start a discussion of creating controls with a very similar process of creating a *UserControl*-derived object and including it on a test page. A user control can be created in two ways. The first, and perhaps the simplest, technique is to create a page with the attributes and controls you want on the user control and then convert the page to a user control. The second technique is to create the user control programmatically and then test it on another page. In general, I prefer to create the user control as a regular Web page and then modify it for use as a user control. In any event, the result will be a file with an .ascx extension that contains the code on the page or that contains an *Src* attribute pointing to a code-behind file containing a class derived from *UserControl*. The .ascx file will contain an @ *Control* directive rather than an @ *Page* directive.

Preparing a Web Page to Be Converted to a User Control

Converting a Web page to a user control is often the easiest way to test the user control, especially if the user control will have some nontrivial functionality. For instance, the logic to allow a login might need to be repeated on multiple pages. A task like this is a perfect candidate for a user control. For this example, we'll start with the simple login page from Chapter 5, modified somewhat in Listing 6-1.

```
<%@ Import Namespace="System.Web.Security " %>

<html>

    <script language="C#" runat=server>
    void Login_Click(Object sender, EventArgs E)
    {
        // Authenticate user: This sample accepts only one user with
        // a name of doug@programmingasp.net and a password of
        // 'password'.
        if ((UserEmail.Value == "doug@programmingasp.net") &&
          (UserPass.Value == "password"))
```

Listing 6-1 Login.aspx form from Listing 5-1, modified to be converted to a user control

```
        {
            // FormsAuthentication.RedirectFromLoginPage(
            // UserEmail.Value, false);
            FormsAuthentication.GetRedirectUrl(UserEmail.Value, false);
        }
        else
        {
            Msg.Text = "Invalid Credentials: Please try again";
        }
    }
</script>

<body>
<table width=120 bgColor="0000ff">
<tr>
    <td>
    <form runat=server>
    <center>
    <h3>
    <font face="Verdana" color=Yellow>Login<font>
    </h3>
    <table width=100%>
        <tr>
            <td>
            <font color=yellow>Email:</font>
            </td>
        </tr>
        <tr>
            <td>
                <input id="UserEmail"
                type="text"
                runat=server
                size=20 maxlen=30 />
            </td>
            <td>
                <ASP:RequiredFieldValidator
                    ControlToValidate="UserEmail"
                    Display="Static"
                    ErrorMessage="*"
                    runat=server />
            </td>
        </tr>
        <tr>
            <td>
                <font color=yellow>Password:</font>
            </td>
        </tr>
```

(continued)

Listing 6-1   *continued*

```
        <tr>
            <td>
                <input id="UserPass" type=password
                runat=server
                size=20
                maxlen=30 />
            </td>
            <td>
                <ASP:RequiredFieldValidator
                    ControlToValidate="UserPass"
                    Display="Static" ErrorMessage="*"
                    runat=server />
            </td>
        </tr>
        <tr>
            <td colspan=3 align="center">
            <asp:button text="Login"
                OnClick="Login_Click"
                runat=server>
            </asp:button>
            <p>
            <asp:Label id="Msg" ForeColor="red"
                Font-Name="Verdana"
                Font-Size="10" runat=server />
            </td>
        </tr>
    </table>
    </center>
    </form>
    </td>
    </tr>
    </table>
    </body>
</html>
```

The changes between this listing and Listing 5-1 are primarily cosmetic. I've added tables to constrain the width and set a background color that will be appropriate for the page I'm adding the user control to. I've also made minor changes to the text boxes on the form. I used the *size* attribute to set the width of the text boxes, and I used the *maxlen* attribute to set the maximum number of characters that can be entered into the text boxes.

The one substantive change is in the *Login_Click* function, as shown here:

```
if ((UserEmail.Value == "doug@programmingasp.net") &&
  (UserPass.Value == "password"))
{
    // FormsAuthentication.RedirectFromLoginPage(
    // UserEmail.Value,false);
    FormsAuthentication.GetRedirectUrl(UserEmail.Value,false);
}
```

Here I'm using a different method of the *FormsAuthentication* class so that rather than being redirected to the originally requested page, I'm getting the redirection URL and ignoring it. I've done this because calling *RedirectFromLoginPage* is designed to redirect the user from the login page specified in the Web.config file back to the originally requested page, or if there is no originally requested page, back to default.aspx in the same application. This user control is designed to just sit on a page as a component and to allow the user to log in and likely remain on the same page, rather than be a complete page that the user will be redirected to when calling a page that requires authentication. *GetRedirectUrl* accepts the user name and a *Boolean* parameter specifying whether a persistent cookie should be issued with the authentication ticket.

> **Note**   There has long been a great deal of fuss over cookies and the possible invasion of privacy they can cause. As you know, a cookie is a bit of information that's held on the client's machine. There are two types of cookies: *session cookies,* which are held in memory and survive only as long as the browser is open on the client machine, and *persistent cookies*, which are written to the hard disk of the client machine. In general, it's good practice to ask the user's permission before trying to write persistent cookies to a user's machine.

When run, the .aspx page in Listing 6-1 produces the page shown in Figure 6-2.

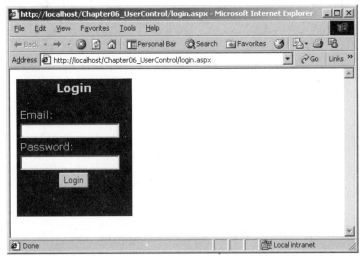

Figure 6-2 An .aspx page reformatted to be ready for conversion to a user control

Converting a Web Page to a User Control

Our goal for the user control we're creating is to use it in part of a side navigation panel. The page shown in Figure 6-2 is in the format we want—a relatively narrow, compact table that's 120 pixels wide. Once the Web page has the appearance you want, follow these steps to convert it to a user control:

1. Remove all *<HTML>*, *<BODY>*, and *<FORM>* tags from the page.

2. If the page includes an *@ Page* directive, change it to an *@ Control* directive. (There is no *@ Page* directive in Listing 6-1.)

3. Add a *className* attribute to the *@ Control* directive. (If necessary, add an *@ Control* directive.) The *className* attribute allows you to specify a class name for the user control. Specifying a class name allows strong typing of the control when it's added to a page or other server controls programmatically.

4. Change the extension of the file from .aspx to .ascx, to reflect its intended use.

Listing 6-2 shows the completed Login.ascx page.

```
<%@ Control className="login" %>
<%@ Import Namespace="System.Web.Security " %>

    <script language="C#" runat=server>
    void Login_Click(Object sender, EventArgs E)
    {
        // Authenticate user: This sample accepts only one user with
        // a name of doug@programmingasp.net and a password of
        // 'password'.
        if ((UserEmail.Value == "doug@programmingasp.net") &&
          (UserPass.Value == "password"))
        {
            // FormsAuthentication.RedirectFromLoginPage(
            // UserEmail.Value, false);
            FormsAuthentication.GetRedirectUrl(UserEmail.Value, false);
            Msg.Text = "Logged In!";
        }
        else
        {
            Msg.Text = "Invalid Credentials: Please try again";
        }
    }
    </script>
```

Listing 6-2 Login.ascx, a user control that was converted from Login.aspx

```
<table width=120 bgColor="0000ff">
<tr>
    <td>
    <center>
    <h3>
    <font face="Verdana" color=Yellow>Login<font>
    </h3>
    <table width=100%>
        <tr>
            <td>
            <font color=yellow>Email:</font>
            </td>
        </tr>
        <tr>
            <td>
                <input id="UserEmail"
                    type="text"
                    runat=server
                    size=20
                    maxlen=30 />
            </td>
            <td>
                <ASP:RequiredFieldValidator
                    ControlToValidate="UserEmail"
                    Display="Static"
                    ErrorMessage="*"
                    runat=server />
            </td>
        </tr>
        <tr>
            <td>
                <font color=yellow>Password:</font>
            </td>
        </tr>
        <tr>
            <td>
                <input id="UserPass"
                    type=password
                    runat=server
                    size=20
                    maxlen=30 />
            </td>
            <td>
                <ASP:RequiredFieldValidator
                    ControlToValidate="UserPass"
                    Display="Static"
                    ErrorMessage="*"
                    runat=server />
            </td>
        </tr>
```

(continued)

Listing 6-2   *continued*

```
            <tr>
                <td colspan=3 align="center">
                    <asp:button text="Login"
                        OnClick="Login_Click"
                        runat=server>
                    </asp:button>
                    <p>
                    <asp:Label id="Msg" ForeColor="Yellow"
                        Font-Name="Verdana"
                        Font-Size="10"
                        runat=server />
                </td>
            </tr>
        </table>
        </center>
        </td>
    </tr>
    </table>
```

As with the original Login.aspx, the script code is located within this file rather than in a code-behind file. Some minor complications arise when you don't use a separate code-behind file. First, if others will be using your user control, you'll have to distribute the .ascx file, source and all. If the script code were in a code-behind file, you could instead distribute just the source for the .ascx file (which would contain only user interface elements) along with the compiled dynamic-link library (DLL) created from the code-behind file. Second, there are differences in how you register the component on the page using the user control.

To test the Login.ascx user control, I've created a page named UseLogin.aspx, shown in Listing 6-3.

```
<%@ Page %>
<%@ Register TagPrefix="Chapter06" TagName="login" Src="Login.ascx" %>
<html>
<head>
<title>Use Login User Control</title>
</head>
<body leftmargin="0" topmargin="0">

<form runat=server>
<table width=600 height=600 border=0
cellpadding=0 cellspacing=0>
```

Listing 6-3 UseLogin.aspx, a page that uses the Login.ascx user control

```
    <tr>
        <td width=120 bgcolor="blue" valign=top>
            <font face="verdana"
            color="yellow" size=2><b>
            Just before the user control is included...
            </b></font>
            <Chapter06:login
                ID="LoginControl"
                RunAt=Server />
            <font face="verdana"
            color="yellow" size=2><b>
            Just after the user control was included...
            </b></font>
        </td>
        <td valign=top>
            <center>
            <br>
            <b><font face="verdana" size=4>
            This is the rest of the page!
            </font></b>
            </center>
        </td>
    </tr>
</table>
</form>
</body>
</html>
```

The first step in using any custom control in ASP.NET is the *@ Register* directive, as shown here:

```
<%@ Register TagPrefix="Chapter06"
    TagName="login"
    Src="Login.ascx" %>
```

In this example, the *TagPrefix* attribute specifies the prefix to be used within the tag that will place the control on the page. The *TagName* attribute specifies the name of the control. Taken together, these attributes mean that to create an instance of the control in the .aspx file, we need to use the tag *<Chapter06:login />*.

Note   Although you might presume that ASP.NET would know that *<Chapter06:login>* is a user control and thus a server control that should be run on the server, you'd be incorrect. If you don't include a *RunAt=Server* attribute/value pair inside the *<Chapter06:login>* tag, the tag will be sent back to the client browser unaltered.

The *Src* attribute points to the location of the .ascx file. This location is relative to the current directory, so in this example, we don't precede the name with any path qualifier.

> **Note**   One magical character can be used when declaring source paths in ASP.NET. The tilde (~) character starts the path at the root of the application, similar to the way the slash (/) character starts the path at the root of the site. This shortcut seems less useful than it really is, and you might think you don't need it, but wait until you work with Web applications that have many directories.

An alternative form of the *@ Register* directive allows you to register a component when all you have is the DLL created from the source. This alternative is commonly used for controls created entirely in code. The format of the directive is shown here:

```
<%@ Register tagprefix="tagprefix"
    Namespace="namespace"
    Assembly="assembly" %>
```

The *tagprefix* attribute is the same as the other variant of the *@ Register* directive. The *Namespace* attribute is used to specify the namespace within the code in which the control exists. Finally, the *Assembly* attribute specifies the name of the compiled .NET DLL that contains the namespace specified by the *Namespace* attribute. The assembly name is specified *without* the extension. The .NET Framework will search for the assembly first in the application's private bin directory and then in the system assembly cache.

What Is an Assembly?

I referred to assemblies in Chapter 2, and I just mentioned them in reference to the @ Register directive This seems like a good place to offer a more complete explanation of exactly what an assembly is.

In the world of COM, immutable interfaces were supposed to be the solution to the problem of DLL conflicts. Unfortunately, this solution didn't completely resolve this problem. As mentioned, creating new versions of a COM component that didn't break existing applications, even if the actual interface exposed remained the same, was more difficult than anticipated.

What Is an Assembly?   *continued*

The .NET solution is the *assembly*. An assembly is one or more files that can be logically grouped and deployed. An assembly is most often a single file, but it can also represent resources in several files. Assemblies can contain executable code, images, resource files, and so on. Assemblies are the basic unit of deployment, versioning, security, and reuse.

An assembly contains an *assembly manifest*, which is similar to a type library in COM. Listing 2-1 contained the Microsoft intermediate language (MSIL) code from a simple HelloDotNet application. One of the sections of that code is repeated here:

```
Assembly
-----------------------------------------------------------
    Token: 0x20000001
    Name : HelloDotNet
    Public Key   :
    Hash Algorithm : 0x00008004
    Major Version: 0x00000000
    Minor Version: 0x00000000
    Build Number: 0x00000000
    Revision Number: 0x00000000
    Locale: <null>
    Flags : [SideBySideCompatible]  (00000000)
```

This portion of the MSIL code describes the single assembly that makes up the HelloDotNet application.

So how does this approach differ from COM components? First, COM components envisioned a world in which each machine could hold only a single version of a component that implemented a particular interface. The .NET Framework embraces the idea of *side-by-side execution*. Multiple versions of an assembly can coexist, and both the developer and the system administrator have some control over which assembly is used when multiple assemblies exist. The system administrator can make the final decision as to which assembly is used.

In most cases, the examples in this book will use the local assembly directory. The registry isn't used, and nothing more is required than copying files when you use assemblies in the local assembly directory. Assemblies can also be placed in the global assembly cache. When you use the global assembly cache, you're required to install the assembly, using a tool such as the global assembly cache utility (Gacutil.exe). See the MSDN documentation for details on using Gacutil.exe.

When you load UseLogin.aspx (Listing 6-3), you'll see the page shown in Figure 6-3.

Chapter06:login user control

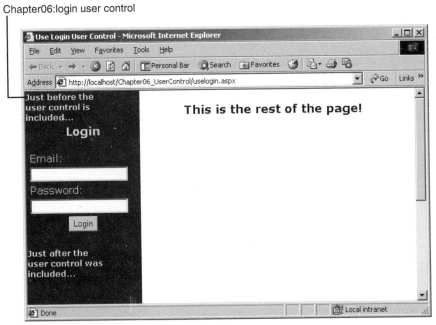

Figure 6-3 The page created by running UseLogin.aspx as shown in Listing 6-3

The user control appears to integrate seamlessly within the page. The login section can be included in many pages. Although this was possible using server-side include files in ASP, user controls offer the advantage of compiled code. Listing 6-4 shows the HTML sent to the browser when UserLogin.aspx is requested.

```
<html>
<head>
<title>Use Login User Control</title>
</head>
<body leftmargin="0" topmargin="0">

<form name="_ctl0"
    method="post"
    action="uselogin.aspx"
    language="javascript"
    onsubmit="ValidatorOnSubmit();"
    id="_ctl0">
<input type="hidden" name="__VIEWSTATE"
    value="dDwtMzg3OTgxNDYyOzs+" />
```

Listing 6-4 The HTML sent to the browser when UseLogin.aspx as shown in Listing 6-3 is requested

```
<script language="javascript"
    src="/aspnet_client/system_web/1_0_3125_0/WebUIValidation.js">
</script>

<table width=600 border=0 height=600
cellpadding=0 cellspacing=0>
    <tr>
        <td width=120 bgcolor="blue" valign=top>
            <font face="verdana"
            color="yellow" size=2><b>
            Just before the user control is included...
            </b></font>

    <table width=120 bgColor="0000ff">
    <tr>
        <td>
        <center>
        <h3>
        <font face="Verdana" color=Yellow>Login<font>
        </h3>
        <table width=100%>
            <tr>
                <td>
                <font color=yellow>Email:</font>
                </td>
            </tr>
            <tr>
                <td>
                    <input name="LoginControl:UserEmail"
                    id="LoginControl_UserEmail"
                    type="text"
                    size="20"
                    maxlen="30" />
                </td>
                <td>
                    <span id="LoginControl__ctl0"
                    controltovalidate="LoginControl_UserEmail"
                    errormessage="*"
                    evaluationfunction=
                      "RequiredFieldValidatorEvaluateIsValid"
                    initialvalue=""
                        style="color:Red;visibility:hidden;">*</span>
                </td>
            </tr>
            <tr>
                <td>
                    <font color=yellow>Password:</font>
                </td>
            </tr>
```

(continued)

Listing 6-4 *continued*

```
            <tr>
                <td>
                    <input name="LoginControl:UserPass"
                    id="LoginControl_UserPass"
                    type="password"
                    size="20"
                    maxlen="30" />
                </td>
                <td>
                    <span id="LoginControl__ctl1"
                    controltovalidate=
                      "LoginControl_UserPass"
                    errormessage="*"
                    evaluationfunction=
                      "RequiredFieldValidatorEvaluateIsValid"
                    initialvalue=""
                        style="color:Red;visibility:hidden;">*</span>
                </td>
            </tr>
            <tr>
                <td colspan=3 align="center">
                    <input type="submit"
                    name="LoginControl:_ctl2" value="Login"
                    onclick="if (typeof(Page_ClientValidate) ==
                      'function')
                    Page_ClientValidate(); "
                    language="javascript" />
                    <p>
                    <span id="LoginControl_Msg"
                    style="color:Yellow;font-family:Verdana;
                    font-size:10pt;">
                    </span>
                </td>
            </tr>
        </table>
        </center>
        </td>
    </tr>
</table>

        <font face="verdana"
        color="yellow" size=2><b>
        Just after the user control was included...
        </b></font>
    </td>
    <td valign=top>
        <center>
        <br>
```

```
        <b><font face="verdana" size=4>
        This is the rest of the page!
        </font></b>
        </center>
      </td>
    </tr>
</table>

<script language="javascript">
<!--
    var Page_Validators =
      new Array(document.all["LoginControl__ctl0"],
      document.all["LoginControl__ctl1"]);
        // -->
</script>

<script language="javascript">
<!--
var Page_ValidationActive = false;
if (typeof(clientInformation) != "undefined" &&
clientInformation.appName.indexOf("Explorer") != -1) {
    if (typeof(Page_ValidationVer) == "undefined")
        alert("Unable to find script library " +
        "'/aspnet_client/system_web/1_0_3125_0/WebUIValidation.js'." +
        " Try placing this file manually, "+
        "or reinstall by running 'aspnet_regiis -c'.");
    else if (Page_ValidationVer != "124")
        alert("This page uses an incorrect version of " +
        "WebUIValidation.js. The page expects version 124. " +
        "The script library is " + Page_ValidationVer + ".");
    else
        ValidatorOnLoad();
}

function ValidatorOnSubmit() {
    if (Page_ValidationActive) {
        ValidatorCommonOnSubmit();
    }
}
// -->
</script>
        </form>
</body>
</html>
```

The important thing to notice in Listing 6-4 is that code that was contained in Login.ascx in Listing 6-2 replaces the *Chapter06:login* tag in UseLogin.aspx in Listing 6-3.

User controls are easy to create and relatively easy to use. They support nested controls as well as multiple controls on a single user control, as in UserLogin.aspx. User controls can exist in a separate namespace, and they can even be created in a different language than the page that consumes them. One concern early on about ASP.NET was the fact that, unlike ASP, you could use only a single server-side language on an ASP.NET page. User controls make this limitation much less onerous.

What are the problems with user controls? The major problem is illustrated in Figure 6-4. In the Visual Studio .NET designer, instead of a representation of what the user control looks like, you see just a gray box with the name of the user control.

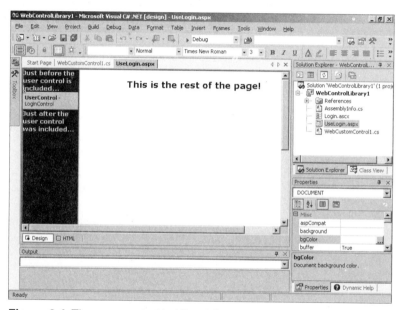

Figure 6-4 The user control in Visual Studio .NET

The lack of designer support is not a total showstopper, and for many elements, especially elements that expose a great deal of user interface, user controls are a good choice. One example of when user controls are a good choice is a situation in which a team is split between user interface designers and back-end developers. In this case, using code-behind files, the user interface designer can work on the .ascx file, and the back-end developer can work somewhat independently on the code-behind file. Another situation in which user controls come in handy is when the content is syndicated and must present a completely different user interface appearance in multiple application directories.

Creating Custom Controls

For most ASP developers, user controls might be enough to boost their productivity. However, Visual Basic programmers moving to ASP.NET might be a little disappointed by the lack of designer support. More important, user controls aren't the ideal type of control for third-party developers to distribute. Third-party developers have been essential to the growth of Visual Basic throughout its history, and it's safe to assume that they will be essential to the next phase of Visual Basic .NET and C# development within ASP.NET.

The solution to the limitations of user controls is custom controls. Custom controls are server controls that derive from a base control class and are compiled into a DLL. Custom controls have great design-time support within Visual Studio .NET. The trade-off is that they're harder to build, and if a control needs to have a different appearance in different circumstances (for example, in multiple syndications that each have a different look), the change in appearance must be made by changing the values of parameters.

A Simple Custom Control

Let's start with a simple custom control. This control will display a line of text like a label but will center the text and make it boldface. I named this custom control *CenteredLabel*.

You must make a couple of design decisions when you decide to create a custom control. The first, and probably most important, is the decision of what class to use as your base class. Your new custom control will inherit the base behaviors and attributes of whatever base class you use. In this example, the choice is simple: *System.Web.UI.WebControls.Label*.

> **Note**   MSDN documentation lists multiple pages of properties, methods, and events for *System.Web.UI.WebControls.Label*. All but one of these properties, methods, and events are inherited from the *WebControl* or *Control* classes. The single exception is the *Text* property. Inheriting from *Label* means that all of its properties, methods, and events are available in our new class.

The next decision is what additional properties, methods, and events need to be exposed. In this example, there's no need to add any properties, methods, or events. The only property we'll use is the *Text* property inherited from *Label*. The *CenteredLabel* source (written in Visual Basic .NET) is shown in Listing 6-5.

```
Imports System.ComponentModel
Imports System.Web.UI

Public Class CenteredLabel
    Inherits System.Web.UI.WebControls.Label

    Protected Overrides Sub Render( _
    ByVal output As System.Web.UI.HtmlTextWriter)
        output.Write("<CENTER><B>" + Me.Text + "</B></CENTER><br>")
    End Sub

End Class
```

Listing 6-5 The *CenteredLabel* custom control

This code is mostly self-explanatory (although not exactly as you'd write it for production purposes). After a couple of imports, I declare the class, named *CenteredLabel*. Visual Studio .NET automatically adds a namespace with the same name as the project name for Visual Basic .NET projects. C# projects have the namespace explicitly declared. Explicitly declaring a namespace in a Visual Basic .NET custom control will result in a nested namespace.

The heart of the *CenteredLabel* custom control is the *Render* method override, shown here:

```
Protected Overrides Sub Render( _
ByVal output As System.Web.UI.HtmlTextWriter)
    output.Write("<CENTER><B>" + Me.Text + "</B></CENTER><br>")
End Sub
```

Recall from Table 6-1 that the render phase of the execution life cycle of a control is where the content is actually written. The *output* parameter of the *Render* method is an instance of the *System.Web.UI.HtmlTextWriter* class. This is a utility class with a large number of methods for outputting HTML content. In this case, the content is straightforward, consisting of the *Text* property with a literal string prepended and appended.

Although using the *Write* method of the *HtmlTextWriter* class seems convenient, it's not the preferred way to render HTML to the browser. *HtmlTextWriter* provides a number of utility methods for generating HTML. These utility methods are the preferred way to output HTML in the *Render* method for the following reasons:

■   They make the code more readable and reusable, and they don't require great HTML proficiency.

■   They provide automatic conversions between different versions of HTML for uplevel and downlevel rendering.

■   Multiple calls to these utility methods are more efficient than concatenating multiple strings and then calling *Write* with the resulting string.

Using these utility methods, the *Render* method override in Listing 6-5 becomes the following:

```
Protected Overrides Sub Render( _
ByVal output As System.Web.UI.HtmlTextWriter)
    output.RenderBeginTag(HtmlTextWriterTag.Center)
    output.RenderBeginTag(HtmlTextWriterTag.B)
    output.Write(Me.Text)
    output.RenderEndTag()
    output.RenderEndTag()
    output.RenderBeginTag(HtmlTextWriterTag.Br)
    output.RenderEndTag()
End Sub
```

Although the result is a bit more verbose, for more complex examples, this code will not only be more efficient but the result will also be properly rendered for both uplevel and downlevel browsers.

The *RenderBeginTag* method has two versions. The first takes a string representing the tag. Thus, the first call to *RenderBeginTag* would be as follows:

```
output.RenderBeginTag("Center")
```

The second version uses the *HtmlTextWriterTag* enumeration (part of the *System.Web.UI* namespace), for example:

```
output.RenderBeginTag(HtmlTextWriterTag.Center)
```

I use the enumeration because I expect that doing so will result in consistent casing for HTML tags. Strictly speaking, consistent casing isn't required for most browsers, but it's certainly a good idea.

The *RenderEndTag* method requires no parameters, and it will write the appropriate end tag, properly nesting the end tags. Most modern browsers are tremendously forgiving of improperly nested—and even missing—end tags. Still, it's a good idea to supply properly nested end tags, for those cases in which the browser might not handle errors. Counting *RenderBeginTag* and *RenderEndTag* calls is a reasonable way to ensure correctly terminated tags.

> **Note**　The *
* tag normally doesn't include an end tag, but there's no harm in including it. I do so here for completeness, as well as to make it possible to count calls to *RenderBeginTag* and *RenderEndTag*.

To compile this custom control, you need to use the following command line (all entered on the same line):

```
Vbc.exe CenteredLabel.vb /reference:System.dll
    /reference:System.Web.dll
    /target:library
```

Once compiled, you can place the resulting DLL (CenteredLabel.dll) in the bin folder of an ASP.NET Web application, add a reference to the control, and generate a page, which will look like the one shown in Figure 6-5.

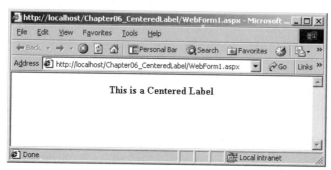

Figure 6-5 The *CenteredLabel* control on a test form

We'll look at adding custom controls to Web application projects more completely in the next section.

Creating Custom Controls in Visual Studio .NET

Most developers creating custom controls and other .NET projects won't use Windows Notepad to create their projects. It's certainly possible to do so , but given the size of the common language runtime, features like IntelliSense and statement completion make using the Visual Studio .NET development environment very handy.

The only downside of using Visual Studio .NET is that it contains some generated code that the developers of the project skeletons thought was important that might not be important to you. For example, if you create a new Web Control Library project in Visual Studio .NET, the generated code will look like the following (reformatted for clarity):

```
Imports System.ComponentModel
Imports System.Web.UI

<DefaultProperty("Text"),
ToolboxData("<{0}:WebCustomControl1 runat=server>
</{0}:WebCustomControl1>")>
Public Class WebCustomControl1
    Inherits System.Web.UI.WebControls.WebControl

    Dim _text As String

    <Bindable(True), Category("Appearance"), DefaultValue("")>
      Property [Text]() As String
        Get
            Return _text
        End Get

        Set(ByVal Value As String)
            _text = Value
        End Set
    End Property

    Protected Overrides Sub Render( _
      ByVal output As System.Web.UI.HtmlTextWriter)
        output.Write([Text])
    End Sub

End Class
```

In addition to some default names that obviously should be changed (such as the default class name, *WebCustomControl1*), you'll likely need to make other changes as well. First, Visual Studio generates a class that inherits from *System.Web.UI.WebControls.WebControl*. In many cases, this will be what you want to do, but in others, you'll want to inherit from a different class, as we did earlier with the *CenteredLabel* control. Next, there's the *Text* property and the *_text* data element within the class. In many cases, you might want to retain this property and the supporting data element, but just as often you won't. One thing to note here is the relationship between the name of the property and the name of the data element. The property is Pascal cased, and in the case of Visual Basic .NET (a case-insensitive language), the actual class data element is preceded by an underscore. In a C# Web Control Library project, the property name would remain the same, but the class data member would simply be *text*, because C# is case-sensitive.

There are attributes for both classes and namespaces. The first, in this case *not* created by default when you create a custom control using Visual Studio .NET, is the *TagPrefix* attribute. If you don't specify a *TagPrefix* attribute, Visual Studio .NET will generate a tag prefix for you, so your custom controls, when dragged onto the form, will begin with *cc1*, continuing with *cc2* for the next control, and so on. Using a *TagPrefix* attribute allows Visual Studio .NET to use a more convenient name for the tag prefix. For example, the following code specifies that the tag prefix for the *RequiredTextBox* class is *MyControls*:

```
[ assembly:TagPrefix("MyControls","RequiredTextBox") ]
```

This is the C# syntax. The Visual Basic .NET syntax is similar, but with angle brackets (<>) enclosing the attribute.

At the class level, there's another important attribute: *ToolboxData*, which is provided by Visual Studio .NET. An example of this attribute using the Visual Basic .NET syntax is shown here:

```
<ToolboxData("<{0}:WebCustomControl1 runat=server>
</{0}:WebCustomControl1>")>
```

Visual Studio .NET will provide a default tag when a control is dropped on a form; however, the *ToolboxData* attribute allows you to specify additional attributes that will be set whenever you drag a control on a form. In this example, the *runat=server* attribute/value pair appears by default whenever the control defined by the class is dropped on the form. After you've experienced the failure of your custom control, only to discover that you forgot to add the *runat=server* attribute/value pair, you'll really appreciate having all custom server controls dropped on the form complete with *runat=server*.

The attributes used for properties by the Visual Studio .NET design-time environment are shown in Table 6-2.

Table 6-2 Attributes Available for Controlling the Design-Time Environment for a Custom Control Property

Attribute	Description
Bindable	Specifies whether a property should be displayed in the DataBindings dialog box
Category	If the property grid is sorted by category, specifies the category the property should be in
DefaultValue	Specifies the default value in the designer
PersistenceMode	Specifies how (or whether) changes made to the property should be persisted
Browsable	Specifies whether a property is displayed in the designer
TypeConverter	Specifies the type converter to use for converting the property type to another type
Editor	Hooks up the extended user interface for setting the property

A More Complicated Custom Control

Our simple *CenteredLabel* custom control example was a good starting place for learning about custom controls. However, it doesn't even begin to touch on what you can achieve using custom controls. In the next example, we'll create a more complicated custom control to handle a more common scenario.

Whenever you're laying out a Web Form, you'll almost certainly want to lay out text boxes with labels that describe the required entry. A great number of variables are inherent within this situation. Should the text box be to the right of the label or below the label on the next line? Does the text box have default text? What about the style of the label and the text box?

Just as with the *CenteredLabel* custom control, the first and most important decision here is to determine what class to inherit from. Because C# and Visual Basic .NET offer only single inheritance, you'll have to select a single class. In this example, we have two possible alternatives: the label or the text box. Presented with such a choice, we should look at exactly what it is we're trying to create. Is it a label with a text box, or a text box with a label? Pretty clearly, what we want is a text box with a label. Looking at it another way, this control *is* a text box, and it *has* a label. This example is greatly oversimplified, but you'll still have to decide which single class to inherit from, no matter how complicated your control.

> **Note**   You do have another alternative for creating a custom control such as this label/text box example: composite controls. We'll discuss composite controls in the next section.

This more complicated custom control is named *LabelTextBox*. Listing 6-6 shows LabelTextBox.vb, which declares and implements the *LabelTextBox* class.

```
Imports System.ComponentModel
Imports System.Web.UI

Public Enum LabelLocation As Long
    LabelLeft
    LabelAbove
End Enum

Public Class LabelTextBox
    Inherits System.Web.UI.WebControls.TextBox

    Dim _labelText As String
    Dim _labelStyle As String
    Dim _labelLocation As LabelLocation

    Property [LabelText]() As String
        Get
            Return _labelText
        End Get

        Set(ByVal Value As String)
            _labelText = Value
        End Set
    End Property

    Property [LabelStyle]() As String
        Get
            Return _labelStyle
        End Get

        Set(ByVal Value As String)
            _labelStyle = Value
        End Set
    End Property
```

Listing 6-6 *LabelTextBox* custom control in Visual Basic .NET used to create a label and a text box

```
    Property [LabelLocation]() As LabelLocation
        Get
            Return _labelLocation
        End Get

        Set(ByVal Value As LabelLocation)
            _labelLocation = Value
        End Set
    End Property

    Protected Overrides Sub Render(ByVal output As _
    System.Web.UI.HtmlTextWriter)
        If _labelStyle Is DBNull.Value Then
            output.Write("<Span Style="""")
            output.Write(_labelStyle)
            output.Write("""">")
            output.Write([_labelText])
            output.Write("</Span>")
        Else
            output.Write([_labelText])
        End If
        If _labelLocation = LabelLocation.LabelAbove Then
            output.RenderBeginTag(HtmlTextWriterTag.Br)
            output.RenderEndTag()
        End If
        MyBase.Render(output)
    End Sub

End Class
```

As you can see in Listing 6-6, after the *Imports* are listed, an enumeration
is declared. This enumeration is used to allow the user of the class or component it creates to describe the label position. The enumeration is declared so that
the default will be *LabelLeft*, meaning that the label will be on the same line as
the text box, to its left.

After the class declaration, the class declares that it inherits from
System.Web.UIWebControls.TextBox. The three data elements that act as the storage data items for the three properties of the class are declared next. Following
this, the *LabelText* property is declared, as follows:

```
Property [LabelText]() As String
    Get
        Return _labelText
    End Get

    Set(ByVal Value As String)
        _labelText = Value
    End Set
End Property
```

The pattern for each property is the same, no matter what the type. In each case, the property is declared. The *Get* section returns the underlying data element. The property doesn't have a direct data element that it cleanly maps to. In such situations, the property is *synthesized,* or created from some other information stored in the class. For example, if your class contains a *StartDate* property and an *EndDate* property and you need a *Duration* property, you probably wouldn't want to declare an additional internal data element named *_duration* but would instead calculate the duration whenever the *Duration* property was requested.

The *Set* section allows the property to be set. By tradition, the parameter passed in is named *Value,* and the type is that of the property itself. In this example, the *Set* section just assigns the value to the underlying data element, but the *Set* section can also do something more complex.

The meat of the *LabelTextBox* class is in the *Render* method:

```
Protected Overrides Sub Render(ByVal output As _
    System.Web.UI.HtmlTextWriter)
    If _labelStyle Is DBNull.Value Then
        output.Write("<Span Style=""")
        output.Write(_labelStyle)
        output.Write(""">")
        output.Write([_labelText])
        output.Write("</Span>")
    Else
        output.Write([_labelText])
    End If
    If _labelLocation = LabelLocation.LabelAbove Then
        output.RenderBeginTag(HtmlTextWriterTag.Br)
        output.RenderEndTag()
    End If
    MyBase.Render(output)
End Sub
```

The *Render* method first checks to see whether *_labelStyle* has been set. If *_labelStyle* has been set, a span tag with a *Style* attribute is written, followed by the *_labelText* string, followed by the end tag for the span. If the style hasn't been set, *_labelText* is written directly.

The *_labelLocation* value is next compared to one of the members of the *LabelLocation* enumeration, *LabelLocation.LabelAbove.* If the label location is set so that the label should be above the text box, a *
* tag is written. Finally, the text box itself is rendered, by calling the *Render* method of *MyBase,* a keyword that allows you to access members of the immediate base class. I use *MyBase* to make it clear that I'm calling the base implementation of *Render.*

Listing 6-7 shows the same class from Listing 6-6 written using C#.

```csharp
using System;
using System.Web.UI;
using System.Web.UI.WebControls;
using System.ComponentModel;

namespace LabelTextBoxCS
{
    /// <summary>
    /// Summary description for WebCustomControl1.
    /// </summary>
    public enum LabelLocationCS
    {
        LabelLeft,
        LabelAbove
    }
    public class LabelTextBox : System.Web.UI.WebControls.TextBox
    {
        private string labelText;
        private string labelStyle;
        private LabelLocationCS labelLocation;

        public string LabelText
        {
            get
            {
                return labelText;
            }
            set
            {
                labelText = value;
            }
        }

        public string LabelStyle
        {
            get
            {
                return labelStyle;
            }
            set
            {
                labelStyle = value;
            }
        }

        public LabelLocationCS LabelLocation
```

Listing 6-7 C# version of *LabelTextBox*, named *LabelTextBoxCS*   *(continued)*

Listing 6-7 *continued*

```
    {
        get
        {
            return labelLocation;
        }
        set
        {
            labelLocation = value;
        }
    }

    /// <summary>
    /// Render control to output parameter specified.
    /// </summary>
    /// <param name="output"> The HTML writer
    /// to write out to </param>
    protected override void Render(HtmlTextWriter output)
    {
        if ( labelStyle != null )
        {
            output.Write("<Span Style=\"");
            output.Write(labelStyle);
            output.Write("\">");
            output.Write(labelText);
            output.Write("</Span>");
        }
        else
        {
            output.Write(labelText);
        }
        if ( labelLocation == LabelLocationCS.LabelAbove )
        {
            output.RenderBeginTag(HtmlTextWriterTag.Br);
            output.RenderEndTag();
        }
        base.Render(output);
    }
  }
}
```

You'll notice some minor differences between the two classes. The first difference is the three-slash (///) comment marker used for XML documentation. Using the XML documentation provided by Visual Studio as a starting point, you can add documentation on classes and class members that can be parsed out to create an XML file.

The C# property syntax is also a little different from the Visual Basic .NET syntax, but it's similar enough that you shouldn't have any difficulty following the intent of the code. One characteristic of properties in both Visual Basic .NET and C# is that the access modifier (in Listings 6-6 and 6-7, *Public*) applies to both the *Get* and *Set* methods. This is an unfortunate limitation, but you can overcome it by providing a property with a *Get* method with one level of protection and then a separate nonproperty setter method with another level of protection, although this solution isn't ideal. For example, this fragment of a class allows all classes to read *ReadOnlyText*, but it provides a nonproperty setter method to allow the class to update the internal buffer that is returned as the *ReadOnlyText* property:

```
private string _readOnlyText;
public string ReadOnlyText
{
    get
    {
        return _readOnlyText;
    }
}
private setReadOnlyText(string Value)
{
    _readOnlyText=Value;
}
```

A more realistic example would be one in which the property isn't simply getting and setting an underlying field but is synthesizing the value in a more complex way.

> **Note**   One difference between Visual Basic .NET properties and C# properties is that in Visual Basic .NET properties, the type of the property is present twice in the declaration of the property: once as the property is declared and once as the type of the *Value* parameters to the *Set* method. The C# syntax mentions the type only once, which is somewhat more convenient if during development you're changing the type of the parameter.

The *Render* method in Listing 6-7 is similar to the Visual Basic .NET version in Listing 6-6, discounting obvious syntax differences between the two languages. One more significant difference between the two *Render* methods is the use of a different keyword to access the base implementation of the class. C# uses *base*, whereas Visual Basic .NET uses *MyBase*.

A Composite Custom Control

A composite custom control shares many of the benefits of user controls, and at the same time offers the benefits of normal custom controls. If you're a developer for an internal Internet or intranet site, the functional difference between a user control and a composite custom control isn't that great. However, if you need to distribute a component to other groups within your organization or if you're a third-party vendor planning to sell a component, the composite custom control offers tremendous advantages. First, it's completely compiled, with no .ascx file that must be exposed to the end user. Second, as a custom control, your component offers certain advantages within a design-time environment such as Visual Studio .NET.

> **Caution**   One problem you might discover when you use a tool like Visual Studio .NET instead of something like Notepad is that the tool can sometimes add its own tool-specific restrictions or bugs. For example, in preparing this composite control example, I foolishly used the same name for the namespace and the class. In initial testing of a page generated using just Notepad, the control worked as expected. However, one of the points of this example is to show the support for custom controls within Visual Studio .NET. I followed all instructions and was able to get the control installed, yet try as I might, I kept getting this strange error: "CS0103: The name '__ctrl' does not exist in the class or namespace 'ASP.WebForm1_aspx'". I had no control named __ctrl, so I was puzzled. In the end, I discovered that the error was in the code Visual Studio .NET generated to create the control. Renaming the namespace solved the problem, but not before it cost me several hours I would rather have spent doing something else.

One of the good things about ASP.NET is that it allows you to automate some of the more common and boring tasks, such as providing validation for text boxes. The problem is that even with automation it's still more work than most Visual Basic developers are used to. Rather than associating a "Required" Boolean with the text box control, you need to drop two controls on the form—a text box and a validator—and wire them up. An alternative technique is to create a composite custom control, combining both a required field validator and a text box in a single control, and then wire them up automatically.

Listing 6-8 shows the code for a composite custom control named *RequiredTextBox* written in C#. This control requires that the user enter text into a text box. The control uses a text box control and a required field validator.

```
using System;
using System.IO;
using System.Web.UI;
using System.Web.UI.WebControls;
using System.ComponentModel;
using System.Collections;
using System.Collections.Specialized;
using System.Web.UI.Design;

[ assembly:TagPrefix("MyControls","RequiredTextBox") ]

namespace MyControls
{
    /// <summary>
    /// Summary description for WebCustomControl1.
    /// </summary>
    ///

    [DefaultProperty("Text"),
        ToolboxData(
        "<{0}:RequiredTextBox runat=server></{0}:RequiredTextBox>"),
        Designer("MyControls.RequiredTextBoxDesigner, RequiredTextBox")  ]
    public class RequiredTextBox : System.Web.UI.Control,
      INamingContainer
    {

        [Bindable(true),
        Category("Appearance"),
        DefaultValue("Text")]
        public string Text
        {
            get {return (string)ViewState["text"]; }
            set {ViewState["text"] = value; }
        }
        [Bindable(false),
        Category("Validator")]
        public string ErrorMessage
        {
            get {return (string)ViewState["errorMessage"]; }
            set {ViewState["errorMessage"]= value; }
        }
        [Bindable(false),
        Category("Validator"),
        DefaultValue("")]
        public string ValidatorText
        {
            get {return (string)ViewState["validatorText"]; }
            set {ViewState["validatorText"]= value; }
        }
```

Listing 6-8 RequiredTextBoxCs.cs, an example composite custom control   *(continued)*

Listing 6-8   *continued*

```
        [Bindable(false),
        Category("Validator")]
        public System.Drawing.Color ValidatorColor
        {
            get {
                // This will throw an exception the first time.
                // An alternative would be to initialize this in
                // a constructor.
                try
                {
                    return (System.Drawing.Color)
                        ViewState["validatorColor"];
                }
                catch (Exception e)
                {
                    return System.Drawing.Color.Red;
                }
            }
            set {ViewState["validatorColor"]= value; }
        }
        protected override void CreateChildControls()
        {
            System.Web.UI.WebControls.TextBox textBox;
            System.Web.UI.WebControls.RequiredFieldValidator
                requiredValidator;

            textBox=new TextBox();
            textBox.ID=UniqueID;
            textBox.Text=this.Text;

            requiredValidator=new RequiredFieldValidator();
            requiredValidator.ErrorMessage=this.ErrorMessage;
            requiredValidator.ForeColor=this.ValidatorColor;
            requiredValidator.Text=this.ValidatorText;
            requiredValidator.ID=UniqueID + "Validator";
            requiredValidator.ControlToValidate=textBox.ID;

            Controls.Add(textBox);
            Controls.Add(new LiteralControl(" "));
            Controls.Add(requiredValidator);


        }
    }
```

```
public class RequiredTextBoxDesigner : ControlDesigner
{
    public RequiredTextBoxDesigner()
    {
    }
    public override string GetDesignTimeHtml()
    {
        RequiredTextBox rtb = (RequiredTextBox) Component;

        StringWriter sw = new StringWriter();
        HtmlTextWriter tw = new HtmlTextWriter(sw);

        HyperLink placeholderLink = new HyperLink();

        placeholderLink.Text="RequiredTextBox Designer";
        placeholderLink.RenderControl(tw);

        return sw.ToString();
    }
}
}
```

The first thing to notice in Listing 6-8 is the inclusion of several namespaces I haven't previously used. *System.IO* and *System.Web.UI.Design* are both used to add designer support to the component. *System.Web.UI.Design* requires adding a reference to *System.Design.dll* to the project. This and all other system-supplied DLLs are located in the *<windir>/Microsoft.NET/Framework/<version>* directory.

The attributes for the *RequiredTextBox* class are the defaults provided by Visual Studio .NET, with the addition of the *Designer* attribute, which will be described when we look at the designer in the section "Enhancing Design-Time Support" later in this chapter. The class implements *INamingContainer*, a marker interface that has no methods that need to be implemented. Implementing *INamingContainer* tells the framework that a new namespace should be created to ensure unique names within the application.

Several properties are declared, and all are persisted in the *ViewState* rather than in class members. In the following *get* and *set* methods, notice that when the value is retrieved, it must be cast to the type expected:

```
public string Text
{
    get {return (string)ViewState["text"]; }
    set {ViewState["text"] = value; }
}
```

Several of the properties are related to the required field validator, and so I use the *Category* attribute to create a new category named *Validator* that will allow all the validator-related properties to be displayed together when properties are displayed in categories.

The bulk of the work in the class is done within the *CreateChildControls* method. This method is called by the .NET Framework in preparation for posting back or rendering. This method actually creates the instances of the text box and required field validator controls. An additional method not used here can be handy when creating composite controls: *EnsureChildControls*. This method will check to see whether the child controls have been created, and if they haven't, it creates them.

Within *CreateChildControls*, I first create the *TextBox* control, assign it a unique ID, and then set the *Text* property to the *Text* property of the composite control. To get the ID, I use the *UniqueID* property of *Control*, which gives me an ID I can use. The ID is required because I need to assign the *ControlToValidate* property of the *RequiredFieldValidator* control I create next. Once the *RequiredFieldValidator* instance is created, I assign appropriate properties from the main control. To set the *RequiredFieldValidator ID*, I use the *UniqueID* property with the literal "Validator" appended. C/C++ programmers will notice that a function call such as *strcat* isn't required. I simply use the + operator to combine the strings.

After I've created both major controls, I add them to the composite control, using the *Add* method of *Controls*. I also add a literal control between the text box and the validator, simply to provide some white space between the text box and the validator. *LiteralControl* is a class that represents HTML elements and text that doesn't need to be processed on the server. Once these controls are added, I can reference them using the *Controls* array, which is 1-based. In this example, the text box would be *Controls[1]*, the literal control would be *Controls[2]*, and the validator control would be *Controls[3]*. To use the *Controls* array, you generally need to cast the element of the array to the correct type. For example, to get a usable reference to the text box control, you would use *((TextBox)Controls[1])*.

Composition vs. Rendering

When presented with the need to create a composite control, you have two options: composition or rendering. Composition allows you to create the individual objects, manipulate properties, and insert each of the objects into the final control. Rendering allows you just to emit arbitrary HTML code, formatted in whatever way is convenient. This example uses composition, a method that creates multiple server side controls that the ASP.NET framework will render for you. This is done in the *CreateChildControls* method.

Another alternative is to use the *Render* method. Recall that I used the *Render* method earlier in this chapter with the *CenteredLabel* custom control. This same *Render* event can also be used for composite controls, though it becomes awkward with large numbers of controls, and there are additional tasks you must perform.

When using the rendering option, rather than creating server controls where you can set properties, you need to create the code to render the HTML controls. This is similar to the way you created the noncomposite *CenteredLabel* control earlier in this chapter, but likely somewhat more complex because you might need to also have code to set up the relationship between the two controls. Next, there are two additional interfaces that you may need to implement, *IPostBackEventHandler* and *IPostBackDataHandler*. Finally, you need to override the *Render* method.

The *RequiredTextBox* example isn't a good candidate for rendering because you'd end up writing server-side code that would be quite a bit more complex than the code I'm using for composition. You'd have to manually handle the validation part of the control since all you could render would be HTML.

Installing a Control in Visual Studio .NET

To install a control for use within a project in Visual Studio .NET, you have two options. First, you can manually copy the control to the bin folder for the project and manually add the *@ Register* tag to the form. This method isn't terribly onerous; however, if you're committed to using Visual Studio .NET, there's an easier way.

To begin, open the project in which you'll be using the control. While in design mode on one of the Web Forms in the project, select the Toolbox tab where you want to add the control. Right-click the Toolbox, and choose Customize Toolbox on the shortcut menu. Select the .NET Framework Components tab in the Customize Toolbox dialog box, and click the Browse button. Navigate to the folder containing the assembly with the control you want to add, often in the bin folder under the project, or in the bin\Release folder for a C# project. Select the assembly, which is a file with a .dll extension. The control should show up in the list of controls on the .NET Framework Components tab. Make sure there's a check mark next to the control, as shown in Figure 6-6, and click OK in the Customize Toolbox dialog box.

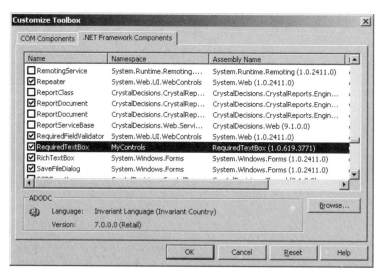

Figure 6-6 Adding the *RequiredTextBox* control to the Toolbox

When you add the control to the Web Form for the first time, the following results will occur:

■   The control's *TagPrefix* and *Namespace* attributes are added to the @ Register directive for the page.

■   A tag for the control is added to the page.

■   A reference to the control is added to the project. This has the effect of copying the assembly to the bin folder of the application.

■   If applicable, the control's designer is loaded.

■   The control is displayed in the designer.

Of course, none of these tasks are particularly difficult, but anything that can be properly automated by the development environment is one less thing for the developer to worry about. In general, in the rest of this book, the components used in the examples will be added to the Toolbox.

Figure 6-7 shows a simple form with a *RequiredTextBox* control dropped on it.

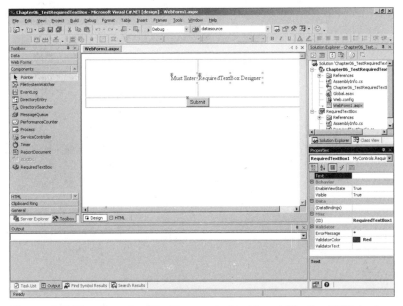

Figure 6-7 The *RequiredTextBox* control in Visual Studio .NET designer

Listing 6-9 shows the code for WebForm1.aspx, which uses the *RequiredTextBox* control.

```
<%@ Register TagPrefix="requiredtextbox"
    Namespace="MyControls"
    Assembly="RequiredTextBox" %>
<%@ Page language="c#"
    Codebehind="WebForm1.aspx.cs"
    AutoEventWireup="false"
    Inherits="Chapter06_TestRequiredTextBox.WebForm1" %>
<!DOCTYPE HTML PUBLIC "-//W3C//DTD HTML 4.0 Transitional//EN" >
```

Listing 6-9 WebForm1.aspx, used to test the *RequiredTextBox* control   *(continued)*

Listing 6-9 *continued*

```html
<HTML>
    <HEAD>
        <meta name="GENERATOR" Content="Microsoft Visual Studio 7.0">
        <meta name="CODE_LANGUAGE" Content="C#">
        <meta name="vs_defaultClientScript"
          content="JavaScript (ECMAScript)">
        <meta name="vs_targetSchema"
          content="http://schemas.microsoft.com/intellisense/ie5">
    </HEAD>
    <body>
        <form id="Form1" method="post" runat="server">
            <TABLE
            cellSpacing="1"
            cellPadding="1"
            width="600"
            border="0">
                <TR height="100">
                    <TD width="50%" align="right">
                        <asp:Label id="Label1"
                            runat="server">
                            Must Enter:
                        </asp:Label>
                    </TD>
                    <TD>
                        <RequiredTextBox:RequiredTextBox
                            id="RequiredTextBox1"
                            runat="server"
                            ErrorMessage="*">
                        </RequiredTextBox:RequiredTextBox>
                    </TD>
                </TR>
                <TR>
                    <TD colspan="2" align="middle">
                        <asp:Button
                            Runat="server"
                            Text="Submit"
                            id="Button1">
                        </asp:Button>
                    </TD>
                </TR>
            </TABLE>
        </form>
    </body>
</HTML>
```

Listing 6-10 shows the code-behind file located in WebForm1.aspx.cs.

```csharp
using System;
using System.Collections;
using System.ComponentModel;
using System.Data;
using System.Drawing;
using System.Web;
using System.Web.SessionState;
using System.Web.UI;
using System.Web.UI.WebControls;
using System.Web.UI.HtmlControls;

namespace Chapter06_TestRequiredTextBox
{
    /// <summary>
    /// Summary description for WebForm1.
    /// </summary>
    public class WebForm1 : System.Web.UI.Page
    {
        protected MyControls.RequiredTextBox RequiredTextBox1;
        protected System.Web.UI.WebControls.Button Button1;
        protected System.Web.UI.WebControls.Label Label1;

        public WebForm1()
        {
            Page.Init += new System.EventHandler(Page_Init);
        }

        private void Page_Load(object sender, System.EventArgs e)
        {
            // Put user code to initialize the page here.
        }

        private void Page_Init(object sender, EventArgs e)
        {
            //
            // CODEGEN: This call is required by
            // the ASP.NET Web Form Designer.
            //
            InitializeComponent();
        }

        #region Web Form Designer generated code
        /// <summary>
        /// Required method for Designer support - do not modify
        /// the contents of this method with the code editor.
        /// </summary>
        private void InitializeComponent()
```

Listing 6-10 WebForm1.aspx.cs C# code-behind file for the page to test the *RequiredTextBox* composite control

(continued)

Listing 6-10   *continued*

```
        {
            this.Load +=
                new System.EventHandler(this.Page_Load);

        }
        #endregion
    }
}
```

Figure 6-8 shows the test page for the *RequiredTextBox* control before any text has been entered.

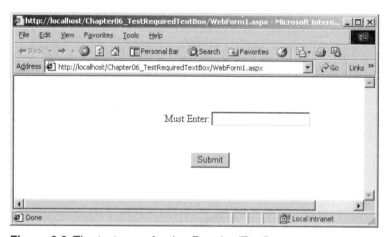

Figure 6-8 The test page for the *RequiredTextBox* custom control

Figure 6-9 shows the test page after it has been submitted, with the validator fired, displaying an asterisk (*).

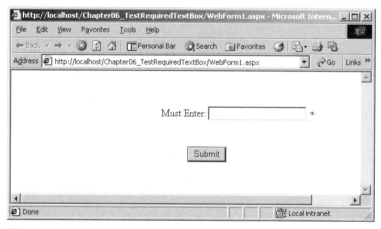

Figure 6-9 The test page for *RequiredTextBox* after the page is submitted with a blank field

The validation that has taken place in Figure 6-9 is on the client. Add a *ClientTarget=Downlevel* attribute/value pair to the @ *Page* directive and each click of the submit button will require a round-trip to the server.

> **Note**   There are a couple of other ways to disable client-side validation (without dumbing down the rendering of the entire page). First, you can set the *Click* event of a submit button to *Page_ValidationActive=false;*. This technique is useful if, for example, you provide a cancel button on a form and want to allow the form to be cancelled without firing the client-side validation. Another, perhaps better, alternative is to set the *CausesValidation* attribute of an *<asp:Button>* to *false*. This will disable both client-side and server-side validation, something that you'd likely want to do on a cancel button.

Enhancing Design-Time Support

Referring back to Figure 6-7, notice the selected control, which reads "RequiredTextBox Designer". By default, a control in design mode will show just what would be displayed by a call to *RenderControl*. If this call would result in nothing being displayed, Visual Studio .NET will instead display the type and ID of the control, something like "RequiredTextBox:RequiredTextBox1". If you want to create your own display in the designer, you do have a few alternatives.

The usual way to display the text is to use the *Designer* attribute for the class. In Listing 6-8, the *Designer* attribute is specified as follows:

```
Designer("MyControls.RequiredTextBoxDesigner, RequiredTextBox")
```

The *Designer* attribute tells the design-time environment that *MyControls. RequiredTextBoxDesigner* is the class that will serve as the designer and that it's in the *RequiredTextBox* assembly. In some examples, I've seen the .dll extension explicitly specified to identify the assembly, but this extension isn't required, and for consistency with other parts of ASP.NET such as the @ *Register* directive, I've omitted it here.

The designer class is often in a subsidiary namespace—for example, something like *MyControls.Design*. The designer class can be in any namespace and in any assembly. Placing the designer in the same assembly as the component is more convenient and imposes additional size in the assembly, even if the control will never be used in design mode. No runtime performance penalty is incurred, however, for having the designer in the same assembly.

The *RequiredTextBoxDesigner* class, at the bottom of Listing 6-8, derives from the *ControlDesigner* class. A designer must derive from one of the following three classes:

- **System. Web. UI. Design. ControlDesigner**   A general-purpose designer that derives from *Control* and *WebControl*.

- **System. Web. UI. Design. WebControls. TemplatedControlDesigner**
  Adds support for template editing. I'll provide more information about templated controls in Chapter 9.

- **System. Web. UI. Design. WebControls. ReadWriteControlDesigner**
  Adds support for in-place editing, as in the *Panel* control. This support allows you to place other controls on top of a control in design time.

The *RequiredTextBoxDesigner* parameterless constructor is provided so that the class can be created without requiring any parameters.

The bulk of the work of the designer is done in the *GetDesignTimeHtml* method. The method first gets an instance of the control. This instance can be used for retrieving or setting parameters. In this case, it's just there to show how you would obtain the current instance of the class. A *StringWriter* and an *HtmlTextWriter* are created (from the *System.IO* namespace). A new *HyperLink* object is created, and the placeholder link is rendered. The text of the hyperlink object is set to "RequiredTextBox Designer", but it could be any arbitrary HTML code.

Another option, which will result in the design-time appearance of a gray raised box similar to a button, is to use the *CreatePlaceHolderDesignTimeHtml* method, passing in a string parameter that will then be rendered on the gray box.

Looking back again at Figure 6-7, two things about the Properties window are worth noting. First, the items in the Properties window are displayed in categories, and so the parameters I declared through the use of attributes as part of the *Validator* category are displayed together. Just as important, the *ValidatorColor* property is not just a text box in which you would enter names or numbers for colors but is instead a complete color picker, as shown in Figure 6-10.

The same behavior will occur with any type that has a complex property picker. Declare a property of the correct type, and the enhanced property picker becomes available with no additional programming required.

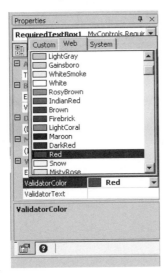

Figure 6-10 The color picker, made available to our *RequiredTextBox* custom control

Conclusion

User controls and custom controls will be critical in the acceptance of ASP.NET by the bulk of Visual Basic programmers. These programmers have long relied on the wide range of components available to allow them to focus on the business-specific code. Between user controls, most often produced within the enterprise, and custom controls, often created by centralized component librarians or third parties, components will be present on the vast majority of ASP.NET pages.

I hope this introduction to controls will open your mind to what can be done with controls. Although VBX controls were popular in Visual Basic, ActiveX controls, especially after it was possible to build them using Visual Basic, continue to be huge. ASP.NET, in a version 1.0 product, provides what I think you'll agree is an easy control-creation tool.

In future chapters, I'll cover several other aspects of user controls and custom controls. In Chapter 7, you'll find out how to decide when to use the client for processing and when the server is best, as well as the many times when using both is appropriate. In Chapters 8 and 9, we'll examine database and XML access. There are many built-in controls that use data, and many custom controls that can be built to use data more efficiently.

7

Balancing Server and Client Functionality

Monitor the ASP.NET newsgroups for any time at all, and you'll likely see a frustrated message from a programmer new to ASP.NET in particular and probably new to Web development in general. The message will be something like this:

If C# [or Visual Basic .NET—your pick] is so powerful, how come I can't get my ASP.NET application to put up a simple message box?!

Experienced classic ASP developers will perhaps chuckle a bit at this question, but it's a real issue for many developers new to Web development. Why can't you display a simple message box like you're used to doing in Visual Basic? Much like in the *Wizard of Oz,* when Dorothy discovered that she wasn't in Kansas anymore, the answer here is that you're not a client-side programmer anymore.

ASP.NET is a server-based technology. Using ASP.NET gives you access to the newest and greatest in many areas of server programming, but if you want to use ASP.NET to display a message box, you're out of luck. However, there is a way to present message boxes and other similar close user interactions. The answer is *client-side scripting.*

> **Note** By the way, the JavaScript command to present the user with a message box is the *alert* function. This chapter introduces client-side scripting, but it is not a tutorial or a reference on JavaScript. Many good books on JavaScript are available, including *JavaScript: The Definitive Guide* by David Flanagan (O'Reilly, 1996).

Client-Side Scripting

One important thing to remember about Web applications is that there is at best a very tenuous connection between the client browser and the server while the user is interacting within a single page. The lack of a constant connection is actually a feature of the HTTP protocol. Because the client and server are not coupled during most of the time a Web application is in use, a single server can support hundreds of users at a time. A model of a Web application is shown in Figure 7-1.

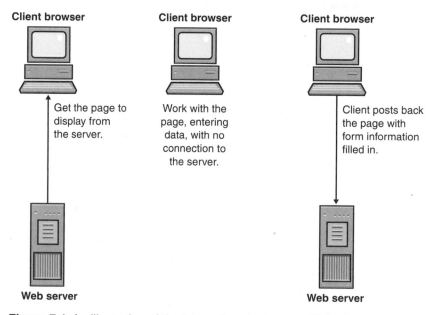

Figure 7-1 An illustration of the interactions between a Web client browser and a Web server

After the browser gets all the information it needs to display and format the page, the user can interact with the page, filling in fields, selecting items from list boxes, and so on. All this work is done without any interaction between the client and the server. When the user clicks the submit button, the form data is submitted to the server.

One result of this lack of connection is the frustrated new ASP.NET user wanting to pop up a message box on the client machine. Fortunately, virtually all browsers these days do support client-side scripting.

> **Note**   Although it's possible in some circumstances to use Visual Basic Scripting Edition (VBScript) on the client side, none of the ASP.NET components do so, and I won't do so in any of the examples in this chapter. Instead, I'll use JScript, Microsoft's implementation of JavaScript.

> **Tip**   JavaScript and JScript have been rechristened, at least in the ASP.NET documentation, as ECMAScript. This name doesn't have quite the same ring as JavaScript or JScript, but it does reflect the variant that is designed to be cross-browser compatible. You'll find more details on the ECMAScript scripting language at *http://www.ecma.ch/ecma1/STAND/ ECMA262.HTM*. Browsers continue to use *JavaScript* or *JScript* as the value for the *Language* attribute in *<SCRIPT>* tags.

Only a couple of standard HTML controls will initiate a return trip to the server—the submit button and a hyperlink are two such controls that come to mind. It's not an accident that only a limited number of controls initiate interactions with the server.

As you'll see in this chapter, it's possible to create a control other than a submit button or a hyperlink that will initiate a round-trip to the server. To create such a control, you need to use client-side JavaScript. For example, using client-side JavaScript, you could initiate a round-trip to the server when the user exits a drop-down list. Generally this isn't a good idea, because it will be a greater burden on the server. However, sometimes causing a postback is appropriate; knowing when to cause one is something you can learn with experience. On lightly used intranet applications, the increased server burden might be worth the richer user interface that the greater server interactions can provide. On a busy Internet site, the burden is most often not worth it, because the round-trip to the server would make the application less responsive for the user.

One of the problems with using client-side JavaScript is that rather than executing in the warm cocoon of the server, the code executes out in the cold cruel world of the client's browser. One of the reasons server-based computing has become so popular is that it's easier to ensure that a server environment is set up correctly than it is to ensure that the client has the proper environment.

Warning!   Because you have no control over client-side scripting, you should use it only as a way to reduce round-trips to the server. It is *not* a replacement for server-side validation. Your server-side code should always presume that the data coming in from a form, even a form with client-side validation, is invalid until proven otherwise. Additionally, if the browser in use is considered a *downlevel* browser, the client-side scripting won't occur for the standard controls that use client-side scripting, such as the validator controls.

How ASP.NET Uses Client-Side Scripting

One common control used on many forms is a drop-down list with several options. Based on the user's selection in the drop-down list, options in the form are customized to reflect the current selection. Selecting an item in a drop-down list doesn't cause a round-trip to the server, but client-side scripting can be used to cause a round-trip to the server.

Listing 7-1 shows PostTest.aspx, an .aspx file created in Visual Studio .NET.

```
<%@ Page Language="vb" AutoEventWireup="false"
Codebehind="PostTest.aspx.vb"
Inherits="Chapter07_DropDownPost.PostTest"%>
<!DOCTYPE HTML PUBLIC "-//W3C//DTD HTML 4.0 Transitional//EN">
<HTML>
    <HEAD>
        <title></title>
        <meta name="GENERATOR" content="Microsoft Visual Studio.NET 7.0">
        <meta name="CODE_LANGUAGE" content="Visual Basic 7.0">
        <meta name="vs_defaultClientScript" content="JavaScript">
        <meta name="vs_targetSchema"
            content="http://schemas.microsoft.com/intellisense/ie5">
    </HEAD>
    <body>
        <form id="Form1" method="post" runat="server">
        <table width="600" border="0">
```

Listing 7-1 PostTest.aspx, a page that generates a postback when the drop-down list selection is changed

```
        <tr>
            <td align="middle">
            <asp:dropdownlist
                id="DropDownList1"
                runat="server"
                AutoPostBack="True">


                <asp:ListItem Value="Black">
                --Select Color--</asp:ListItem>
                <asp:ListItem Value="Red">Red</asp:ListItem>
                <asp:ListItem Value="Green">Green</asp:ListItem>
                <asp:ListItem Value="Blue">Blue</asp:ListItem>
            </asp:dropdownlist>
            <br>
            <br>
            <asp:Label id="Label1"
                runat="server"></asp:Label>
            <br>
            <br>
            <br>
            </td>
        </tr>
    </table>
    </form>
    </body>
</HTML>
```

The code (reformatted slightly for presentation here) creates a simple form, with a drop-down list and a label. The label is initially blank. The drop-down list has an initial value, "--Select Color--", as well as list items for Red, Green, and Blue. In addition to the normal attributes in the *asp:dropdownlist* tag, *AutoPostBack* is set to *True*. The *AutoPostBack* attribute is available for various controls, including drop-down lists, list boxes, check boxes, and text boxes. When *AutoPostBack* is set to *True* in one of these controls and when the control is changed (by selecting an item in a list, changing the value of a check box, and changing the text in a text box), a round-trip is made to the server so that the server can react to changes in the control.

Listing 7-2 shows the code-behind file for PostTest.aspx, named PostText.aspx.vb.

```
Public Class WebForm1
    Inherits System.Web.UI.Page
    Protected WithEvents DropDownList1 _
      As System.Web.UI.WebControls.DropDownList
    Protected WithEvents Label1 As _
      System.Web.UI.WebControls.Label

#Region " Web Form Designer Generated Code "

    'This call is required by the Web Form Designer.
    <System.Diagnostics.DebuggerStepThrough()> _
    Private Sub InitializeComponent()

    End Sub

    Private Sub Page_Init(ByVal sender As System.Object, _
      ByVal e As System.EventArgs) _
      Handles MyBase.Init
        'CODEGEN: This method call is required by the Web Form Designer
        'Do not modify it using the code editor.
        InitializeComponent()
    End Sub

#End Region

    Private Sub Page_Load(ByVal sender As System.Object, _
      ByVal e As System.EventArgs) _
      Handles MyBase.Load
        'Put user code to initialize the page here.
        If IsPostBack Then
            If DropDownList1.SelectedIndex <> 0 Then
                Label1.Text = "You selected " + _
                    DropDownList1.SelectedItem.Text
                Label1.ForeColor = Label1.ForeColor.FromName( _
                    DropDownList1.SelectedItem.Value)
            Else
                Label1.Text = "Please select a color"
                Label1.ForeColor = Label1.ForeColor.FromName("Black")
            End If
        End If
    End Sub

End Class
```

Listing 7-2 PostText.aspx.vb, the code-behind file for PostTest.aspx from Listing 7-1

The most significant aspect of the code in Listing 7-2 is the use of the *Page_Load* method to test for a postback. If this is a postback, meaning that the user has selected an item from the drop-down list, the label displays the name of the color selected, and the label becomes that color.

Setting the label color is a little different from setting the label text, as you can see here:

```
Label1.ForeColor = Label1.ForeColor.FromName( _
    DropDownList1.SelectedItem.Value)
```

Unlike in earlier versions of Visual Basic, here the *ForeColor* property isn't a simple number made up of the red, green, and blue values. Instead, *ForeColor* is a specific type, *System.Drawing.Color*. You can't, for example, set *ForeColor* to *255* to get red. A couple of helper functions are available that allow you to set a color using a color name (as in this example) or from a system color, such as *ActiveBorder*. You can also use one of the predefined colors in the *System.Drawing.Color* class, which includes everything from *SaddleBrown* to *BlanchedAlmond*. Because we've set the *Value* attribute of each of the *asp:ListItem* tags to a color name, we can pass the *Value* attribute from the selected item to the *FromName* method and set the *ForeColor* property to the returned *System.Drawing.Color*.

Figure 7-2 shows the page that appears after you select Green from the drop-down list. (Notice that there is no submit button on this page.)

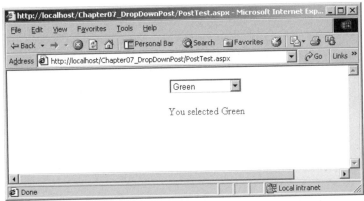

Figure 7-2 PostTest.aspx after Green has been selected from the drop-down list

As you can see, the page recognizes that you've selected Green. (You'll have to take my word for it that the text is also displayed in green.)

So, given that there's no submit button on this page and pure HTML drop-down lists don't cause a postback, how does the *AutoPostBack* attribute cause a postback to occur? The answer is shown in Listing 7-3, the HTML actually received by the browser.

```
<!DOCTYPE HTML PUBLIC "-//W3C//DTD HTML 4.0 Transitional//EN">
<HTML>
    <HEAD>
        <title></title>
        <meta name="GENERATOR" content="Microsoft Visual Studio.NET 7.0">
        <meta name="CODE_LANGUAGE" content="Visual Basic 7.0">
        <meta name="vs_defaultClientScript" content="JavaScript">
        <meta name="vs_targetSchema"
          content="http://schemas.microsoft.com/intellisense/ie5">
    </HEAD>
    <body>
        <form name="Form1" method="post" action="PostTest.aspx" id="Form1">
        <input type="hidden" name="__VIEWSTATE"
          value="dDw4MzQ2Mzg4MzY7dDw7bDxpPDE+Oz47bDx0PDtsPGk8Mz47Pjts
          PHQ8cDxwPGw8VGV4dDtGb3J1Q29sb3I7XyFTQjs+02w8WW91IHN1bGVjdGGV
          kIEdyZWVuOzI8R3J1ZW4+02k8NT47Pj47Pjs7Pjs+Pjs+Pjs+" />

        <table width="600" border="0">
            <tr>
                <td align="middle">
                <select name="DropDownList1" id="DropDownList1"
                  onchange="__doPostBack('DropDownList1','')"
                  language="javascript">
                    <option value="Black">--Select Color--</option>
                    <option value="Red">Red</option>
                    <option selected="selected"
                      value="Green">Green</option>
                    <option value="Blue">Blue</option>
                </select>
                <br>
                <br>
                <span id="Label1"
                  style="color:Green;">You selected Green
                </span>
                <br>
                <br>
                <br>
                </td>
            </tr>
        </table>

<input type="hidden" name="__EVENTTARGET" value="" />
<input type="hidden" name="__EVENTARGUMENT" value="" />
```

Listing 7-3 The HTML output from the page shown in Listings 7-1 and 7-2

```
<script language="javascript">
<!--
    function __doPostBack(eventTarget, eventArgument) {
        var theform = document.Form1;
        theform.__EVENTTARGET.value = eventTarget;
        theform.__EVENTARGUMENT.value = eventArgument;
        theform.submit();
    }
// -->
</script>
</form>
    </body>
</HTML>
```

The significant additions in the HTML output shown in Listing 7-3 are the __doPostBack JavaScript function within the <SCRIPT> tags and the onchange attribute in DropDownList1. There was no onchange event specified in the code in Listing 7-1, and neither Listing 7-1 nor 7-2 had any JavaScript. But here it is in the output to the browser.

The addition of this JavaScript by ASP.NET is what allows the drop-down list to force a postback when an item in the drop-down list is selected. The JavaScript function in Listing 7-3 works in conjunction with two hidden fields in the form, __EVENTTARGET and __EVENTARGUMENT. These two hidden fields are sent out empty and are filled in by the __doPostBack JavaScript function just before the theform.submit is called. When a postback occurs, the page can use these hidden fields to determine which control was modified to cause the postback.

Firing Postbacks from a Custom Control

Some controls support the AutoPostBack attribute and so can cause a postback to occur after a change in the data. Unfortunately, the custom controls you design might not descend from a control that supports AutoPostBack. Fortunately, there is a solution.

The Page class exposes a method named GetPostBackEventReference that emits client-side script that allows a control to cause a postback. The resulting JavaScript is nearly identical to the JavaScript in Listing 7-3. Listing 7-4 shows a Visual Basic .NET hyperlink control that reacts to a click by causing a postback rather than directly calling another page, as a traditional hyperlink would do.

```
Imports System.ComponentModel
Imports System.Web.UI
<Assembly: TagPrefix("PostLink", "PostLinkStuff")>

<DefaultProperty("Text"), ToolboxData( _
"<{0}:PostLinkControl runat=server></{0}:PostLinkControl>")> _
Public Class PostLinkControl
    Inherits System.Web.UI.WebControls.WebControl

    Dim _text As String

    <Bindable(True), Category("Appearance"), DefaultValue("")> _
      Property [Text]() As String
        Get
            Return _text
        End Get

        Set(ByVal Value As String)
            _text = Value
        End Set
    End Property

    Protected Overrides Sub Render( _
      ByVal output As System.Web.UI.HtmlTextWriter)
        output.Write("<a id=""" + Me.UniqueID + _
          """ href=""javascript:" + _
          Page.GetPostBackClientEvent(Me, _text) + """>")
        output.Write(_text + "</a>")
    End Sub

End Class
```

Listing 7-4 PostLink.vb, a postback link control

> **Note** ASP.NET includes a *LinkButton* control that does much of what this example control does. In general, the technique shown here would be used on more complex controls, but adding this functionality to a hyperlink control makes the process easier to understand.

PostLink.vb, shown in Listing 7-4, began as a Visual Basic Web Control Library project created in Visual Studio .NET. I added the following line:

```
<Assembly: TagPrefix("PostLink", "PostLinkStuff")>
```

This code tells Visual Studio .NET to use the tag prefix *PostLinkStuff* for any control in the *PostLink* namespace that is dragged onto the design surface. Recall from Chapter 6 that if you don't specify a *TagPrefix*, Visual Studio .NET will use *cc1*, *cc2*, and so on.

The other section of code modified from the Web Control Library project is the *Render* method, shown here:

```
Protected Overrides Sub Render( _
  ByVal output As System.Web.UI.HtmlTextWriter)
    output.Write("<a id=""" + Me.UniqueID + _
    """ href=""javascript:" + _
    Page.GetPostBackClientEvent(Me, _text) + """>")
    output.Write(_text + "</a>")
End Sub
```

One confusing part of this *Render* code is the use of multiple quotation marks in the *output.Write* call. To include quotation marks within a string, each quotation mark must be preceded by a quotation mark so that the quotation mark isn't interpreted as the end of the string.

In C#, the same method would be written as follows:

```
protected override void Render(HtmlTextWriter output)
{
    output.Write("<a id=\"" + this.UniqueID +
    "\" href=\"javascript:" +
    Page.GetPostBackClientEvent(this, text) + "\">")
    output.Write(text + "</a>")
}
```

C# follows the C/C++ convention of using the backslash character to prefix a quotation mark within a quoted literal string. In addition, C# uses the *this* keyword to identify the current instance, whereas Visual Basic .NET uses *Me*.

The *Render* method creates an anchor tag that includes JavaScript code in the *href* attribute. The JavaScript includes a call to *Page.GetPostBackClientEvent*, which is passed a reference to the current instance (using *Me* in Visual Basic .NET, or *this* in C#) and the value of *_text*. Both of these values are available on the server in the *__EVENTTARGET* and *__EVENTARGUMENT* variables, as shown in the *Page_Load* method of the code-behind file TestPostLink.aspx.vb in Listing 7-5.

```
Public Class WebForm1
    Inherits System.Web.UI.Page
    Protected WithEvents PostLinkControl1 _
      As PostLink.PostLinkControl
    Protected WithEvents Label1 _
      As System.Web.UI.WebControls.Label

#Region " Web Form Designer Generated Code "

    'This call is required by the Web Form Designer.
    <System.Diagnostics.DebuggerStepThrough()> _
    Private Sub InitializeComponent()

    End Sub

    Private Sub Page_Init(ByVal sender As System.Object, _
      ByVal e As System.EventArgs) _
      Handles MyBase.Init
        'CODEGEN: This method call is required by
        'the Web Form Designer
        'Do not modify it using the code editor.
        InitializeComponent()
    End Sub

#End Region

    Private Sub Page_Load(ByVal sender As System.Object, _
      ByVal e As System.EventArgs) _
      Handles MyBase.Load
        If Me.IsPostBack = True Then
            Label1.Text = "Postback from " + _
            Request("__EVENTTARGET") + " - " + _
            Request("__EVENTARGUMENT")
        End If
    End Sub

End Class
```

Listing 7-5 TestPostLink.aspx.vb, the code-behind file to test the *PostLink* control

Listing 7-6 shows the TestPostLink.aspx file, which is used to test the *PostLink* control.

```
<%@ Register TagPrefix="PostLink"
    Namespace="PostLink"
    Assembly="PostLink" %>
<%@ Page Language="vb"
    AutoEventWireup="false"
    Codebehind="WebForm1.aspx.vb"
    Inherits="Chapter07_PostControl.WebForm1"%>
<!DOCTYPE HTML PUBLIC "-//W3C//DTD HTML 4.0 Transitional//EN">
<HTML>
    <HEAD>
        <title></title>
        <meta name="GENERATOR"
          content="Microsoft Visual Studio.NET 7.0">
        <meta name="CODE_LANGUAGE" content="Visual Basic 7.0">
        <meta name="vs_defaultClientScript"
          content="JavaScript">
        <meta name="vs_targetSchema"
          content="http://schemas.microsoft.com/intellisense/ie5">
    </HEAD>
    <body>
        <form id="Form1" method="post" runat="server">
            <PostLink:PostLinkControl
                id="PostLinkControl1"
                runat="server"
                Text="This is a test">
            </PostLink:PostLinkControl>
            <p>
            </p>
            <asp:Label id="Label1"
            runat="server"></asp:Label>
        </form>
    </body>
</HTML>
```

Listing 7-6 TestPostLink.aspx, the file used to test the *PostLink* control

As you can see in Listing 7-5, when the page is loaded, the *Page_Load* event handler is called. If *IsPostback* returns *True*, the label text is changed to report the value of *__EVENTTARGET* and *_EVENTARGUMENT*. When the *PostLink* control is clicked, the page shown in Figure 7-3 is returned to the browser.

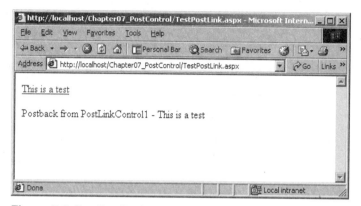

Figure 7-3 TestPostBack.aspx after the link has been clicked and the label modified by the server code

The *PostLink* control is rendered in the browser as follows:

```
<a id="PostLinkControl1"
    href="javascript:__doPostBack('PostLinkControl1',
    'This is a test')">
    This is a test
</a>
```

Using *Page.GetPostBackClientEvent* ensures that the *__doPostBack* JavaScript function is written to the browser and that only a single copy of the script is written to the resulting HTML file.

Several other methods of the *Page* class are involved with using client-side code. The next section describes the most significant of these methods, named *RegisterClientScriptBlock*.

Creating an Extensive Client-Side Web Control

In the previous examples in this chapter, the client-side script wasn't central to the operation of the control. In this section, we'll look at a control that uses client-side script not as a minor part of its existence but as its primary reason for being.

One common problem that developers encounter is the need to duplicate the behavior of an existing system. For example, I recently needed to create a downtime patient registration system to be used while the main system was disabled for scheduled maintenance or due to a system failure. The users of this system were willing to be a little flexible, but certain things were non-negotiable. The main patient registration system allowed users to enter dates in *mmddyy* or *mmddyyyy* format. As they left the date field, the date would be changed to *mm/dd/yyyy* format, or a message would appear saying that the date was invalid.

It's certainly possible to format the date on the server side, with every change in the text box for the date causing a round-trip to the server, but processing all of this information on the server side could require a great deal of interaction between the client and the server. JavaScript on the client side is capable of handling this kind of problem.

With ASP, using client-side code requires a great deal of coordination between the designer of the page and the JavaScript developer. A better solution in the ASP.NET world is a component that encapsulates all of the required logic in a convenient package that can be dragged from the Toolbox onto the Web Form design surface.

Figure 7-4 shows an ASP.NET control named *ReformatDate* that properly formats a date when the control is exited.

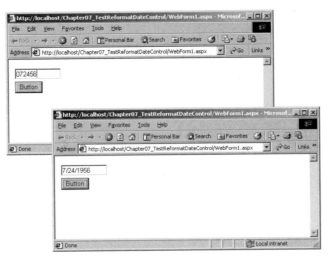

Figure 7-4 The *ReformatDate* control, before and after tabbing out of it

Listing 7-7 shows the code for the completed *ReformatDate* control.

```
using System;
using System.Web.UI;
using System.Web.UI.WebControls;
using System.ComponentModel;
using System.Collections.Specialized;

[assembly: TagPrefix("Chapter07_ReformatDate","Chapter07")]
```

Listing 7-7 WebCustomControl1.cs, the source for the *ReformatDate* control *(continued)*

Listing 7-7 *continued*

```
namespace FormatDateControl
{
    /// <summary>
    /// Summary description for WebCustomControl1.
    /// </summary>
    [DefaultProperty("Text"),
    ToolboxData("<{0}:ReformatDate runat=server></{0}:ReformatDate>")]
    public class ReformatDate : System.Web.UI.WebControls.BaseValidator,
        IPostBackDataHandler,IPostBackEventHandler
    {

        private bool bIsValid;

        protected override bool EvaluateIsValid()
        {
            this.ServerFormatDate();
            return bIsValid;
        }

        public ReformatDate()
        {
            bIsValid=true;
            this.ErrorMessage="*";
        }

        [Bindable(true),
        Category("Appearance"),
        DefaultValue("")]
        override public String Text
        {
            get
            {
                return (String) ViewState["Text"];
            }
            set
            {
                ViewState["Text"] = value;
            }
        }

        protected override void OnLoad(EventArgs e)
        {
            base.OnLoad(e);
            if ( Page.IsPostBack )
            {
                ServerFormatDate();
                IsValid=bIsValid;
            }
```

```
        if ( Page.ClientTarget.ToLower()!="downlevel" )
        {
            Page.RegisterClientScriptBlock("FormatDateClientScript",
                "<" + "SCRIPT Language=JavaScript " +
                "SRC=\"FormatDate.js\"></" + "SCRIPT>");
        }
    }


    protected override void OnInit(EventArgs e)
    {

    }


    /// <summary>
    /// Render this control to the output parameter specified.
    /// </summary>
    /// <param name="output"> The HTML writer to write out to </param>
    protected override void Render(HtmlTextWriter output)
    {
        if ( Page.ClientTarget.ToLower()!="downlevel" )
        {
            output.Write("<INPUT TYPE=\"TEXT\" ID=" +
                this.UniqueID + " Name= " +
                this.UniqueID + " Value=\"" +
                Text + "\" OnChange=\"FormatDate('" +
                this.UniqueID + "');\" Size=10 maxlen=10>");
        }
        else
        {
            output.Write("<INPUT TYPE=\"TEXT\" ID=" +
                this.UniqueID + " Name= " +
                this.UniqueID + " Value=\"" +
                Text + "\" Size=10 maxlen=10>");
        }

//          this.ControlToValidate=this.UniqueID;
        output.Write("<span id=val" + this.UniqueID + ">");
        if ( IsValid==false )
        {
            output.Write("<font color=" + this.ForeColor + ">" +
                this.ErrorMessage + "</font>");
        }
        output.Write("</span>");
    }
```

(continued)

Listing 7-7 *continued*

```
protected void ServerFormatDate()
{
    string tstr;
    System.DateTime dt;
    bIsValid=false;
    tstr=Text;
    try
    {
        dt=System.DateTime.Parse(tstr);
        Text=dt.ToShortDateString();
        bIsValid=true;
    }
    catch(FormatException fe)
    {
        if ( tstr.Length==6 || tstr.Length==8 )
        {
            int mo,da,yr;
            string dtPart;
            try
            {
                dtPart=tstr.Substring(0,2);
                mo=System.Int32.Parse(dtPart);

                dtPart=tstr.Substring(2,2);
                da=System.Int32.Parse(dtPart);

                dtPart=tstr.Substring(4,tstr.Length-4);
                yr=System.Int32.Parse(dtPart);
                if ( yr<30 )
                {
                    yr+=2000;
                }
                else
                {
                    if ( yr<100 )
                    {
                        yr+=1900;
                    }
                }
                Text=mo.ToString() +
                    "/" + da.ToString() +
                    "/" + yr.ToString();
                bIsValid=true;
            }
            catch (Exception e)
```

```
                            {
                                bIsValid=false;
                            }
                    }
            }
        }


        // IPostBackDataHandler related items follow.
        public event EventHandler TextChanged;

        public virtual bool LoadPostData(string postDataKey,
            NameValueCollection values)
        {
            String presentValue = Text;
            String postedValue = values[postDataKey];
            try
            {
                if (!presentValue.Equals(postedValue))
                {
                    Text = postedValue;
                    return true;
                }
            }
            catch ( Exception e )
            {
                Text=postedValue;
            }
            return false;
        }

        public virtual void RaisePostDataChangedEvent()
        {
            ServerFormatDate();
            IsValid=bIsValid;
            OnTextChanged(EventArgs.Empty);
        }

        public void RaisePostBackEvent(string EventArgument)
        {
            return;
        }

        protected virtual void OnTextChanged(EventArgs e)
        {
            if (TextChanged != null)
                TextChanged(this,e);
        }
    }
}
```

Designing Microsoft ASP.NET Applications

For this example, I won't need to add designer support for Visual Studio .NET because the default rendering of the control is reasonable, showing a text box that displays the *Text* property in the designer. (Chapter 6 explained how to add designer support to display a custom control in design mode.)

The vast majority of the server-side work in the *ReformatDate* control is done in the *Render* method. Within *Render*, I simply output the HTML required to render an HTML text input control. I set the *ID* on the text control using *this.UniqueID*. (In Visual Basic .NET, this would be *Me.UniqueID*.) I also set the *Size*, *Maxlen*, and *Value* attributes in the HTML input control. In addition, I set the *OnChange* event to the *FormatDate* JavaScript function, passing in the *ID* of the control as the single parameter to the function. The *OnChange* event handler is called whenever the control is exited and the value is different from the value when the control was entered.

> **Caution**   One thing that caused me no end of confusion while creating the *ReformatDate* control was how it should be rendered. I've become used to setting the *ID* of the ASP.NET server controls and really forgot about the *Name* attribute. For the data to post back properly, a rendered control *must* have both the *ID* and *Name* attributes specified. In this example (and in virtually any case I can think of), I use the same value for *ID* and *Name*: the *UniqueID* of the control.

> **Tip**   A point of confusion is the difference between server-side and client-side events. In the *ReformatDate* control, it's clear that the *OnChange* event is a client-fired event, but in some cases, this distinction can be confusing. If you're in doubt as to whether you're properly setting the client-side events from a server-side control, you can always view the control in a Web browser and view the source. This technique is a powerful tool in resolving problems with how the control is rendered.

In the *OnLoad* server-side method of *ReformatDate*, I first call the ancestor *OnLoad* method, by calling *base.OnLoad*. Remember that in Visual Basic .NET, this would be *MyBase.OnLoad*. Since this class is derived from *BaseValidator*, the ancestor class *OnLoad* must be called because it allows the component to emit the required JavaScript that any validator needs.

> **Caution**   Using *BaseValidator* as the class that *ReformatDate* derives
> from is not an obvious choice. You might want to create a composite con-
> trol that contains two server-side controls: a *TextBox* control and a
> *CustomValidator* control. This option would be reasonable, but in the end,
> not as good a solution as deriving from *BaseValidator* (especially in light of
> what the *ReformatDate* control example is trying to show—client-side code
> integrated into a control). The *BaseValidator* class allows the *ReformatDate*
> control to participate in deciding whether or not the page is valid.

Next, I call *Page.RegisterClientScriptBlock* to send the client script to the
browser. Why use this method rather than just sending out the script directly? The
reason is to ensure that if there is more than one *ReformatDate* control on a page,
only a single copy of the script is written per page. *Page.RegisterClientScriptBlock*
expects two parameters: a key, used to uniquely identify the script block, and
the actual script. Notice that I use the *Src* attribute of the *<SCRIPT>* tag to include a file, rather than trying to embed the entire script in a string. This technique allows you to centralize scripts and also to correct the client-side script
without requiring a recompile of the control using it.

Listing 7-8 shows the JavaScript file FormatDate.js.

```
// JScript source code

function isLeapYear(year)
{
    var bIsLeapYear;

    bIsLeapYear=false;
    if ( year%4 )
    {
        bIsLeapYear=true;
        if ( (year%100) && !(year%400) )
        {
            bIsLeapYear=false;
        }

    }
    return(bIsLeapYear);
}
```

Listing 7-8 FormatDate.js, the JavaScript used by the *ReformatDate* control *(continued)*

Listing 7-8 *continued*

```
function FormatDate(ControlName)
{
    var ctrl;
    var text;
    var dt;
    var slash1;
    var slash2;
    var loop;
    var mo;
    var da;
    var yr;
    var bIsDate;
    var arrMonthLen=new Array(-1,31,28,31,30,31,30,31,31,30,31,30,31);

    bIsDate=false;

    slash1=-1;
    slash2=-1;
    ctrl=window.event.srcElement;
    text=ctrl.value;
    dt=Date(text);
    slash1=text.indexOf('/');
    if ( slash1>=0 )
    {
        slash2=text.indexOf('/',slash1+1);
    }
    if ( slash2<0 )
    {
        if ( text.length==6 || text.length==8 )
        {
            tstr=text.substring(0,2);
            mo=parseInt(tstr,10);

            tstr=text.substring(2,4);
            da=parseInt(tstr,10);

            tstr=text.substring(4,text.length);
            yr=parseInt(tstr,10);
            if ( yr<30 )
            {
                yr+=2000;
            }
            else
            {
                yr+=1900;
            }
```

```
        if ( isNaN(yr) || isNaN(mo) || isNaN(da) ||
            mo<1 || mo>12 || da<1 || da>31 )
        {
            // not a date...
        }
        else
        {
            if ( mo==2 && isLeapYear(yr) )
            {
                arrMonthLen[2]=29;
            }
            if ( da<=arrMonthLen[mo] )
            {
                text=mo.toString() + "/" +
                  da.toString() + "/" + yr.toString();
                window.event.srcElement.value=text;
                bIsDate=true;
            }
        }
    }
    else
    {
        bIsDate=true;
    }

    if ( bIsDate==false )
    {
        alert('Invalid Date');
    }
    return (bIsDate);
}
```

The purpose of the JavaScript function *FormatDate* shown in Listing 7-8 is to perform a cursory test for a valid date, regardless of whether the date has been entered using slashes. To gain access to the contents of the control, I use *window.event.srcElement*, which will be available because this function is called as an event handler.

If two slashes aren't found in the entered value, I try to interpret the entry as a date without slashes. If the string is six or eight characters, I split it into month, day, and year. To get a numeric value (for easier formatting later), I use the JavaScript function *parseInt*. One interesting feature of this function is that it interprets strings with leading zeros as octal by default. Thus, *parseInt('09')* would not be considered a number because there's no *9* in the octal number system. Thankfully, there's a second parameter, which accepts the base of the number. Calling *parseInt('09', 10)* returns a correct value. If I've determined that the string entered without slashes is likely to be a date, I reformat it with slashes and update the *value* property of *window.event.srcElement*. If the date isn't valid, I use the *alert* function to display a message box on the client. All of this activity occurs without any intervention on the part of the client.

> **Note**   How important is it to be able to change JavaScript files? In Beta 2 of ASP.NET, there was a bug in the JavaScript files. Fortunately, because the code wasn't baked into the controls, Microsoft was able to provide instructions that allowed developers to fix the problem themselves. In this example, the behavior of the date formatting could be changed independently of the control, allowing, for example, a date entered in *ddmmyy* format.

Let's look back at Listing 7-7. Because *ReformatDate* is derived from *BaseValidator*, the *ReformatDate* control needs to implement a single function, *EvaluateIsValid*. My implementation is brief:

```
protected override bool EvaluateIsValid()
{
    this.ServerFormatDate();
    return bIsValid;
}
```

EvaluateIsValid is a method that returns *true* if the form is valid or *false* if the form is not valid. *ServerFormatDate*, a method of *ReformatDate*, does much the same kind of checking that the *FormatDate* JavaScript function does. In general, if the browser is capable of using JavaScript, no invalid dates will get to the server, and so this function is used as a second line of defense.

> **Caution**   In addition to acting as a validator of last resort, if the client browser doesn't support JavaScript, *ServerFormatDate* can also prevent users *trying* to enter or send invalid data. Remember, you have no control over *exactly* how the data gets to your server. All data posted from a client should be treated as suspect, unless proven otherwise!

The *ReformatDate* control also implements two interfaces; *IPostBackDataHandler* and *IPostBackEventHandler*. If you need to have a control notified when data is posted back by the client, you must implement *IPostBackEventHandler*. Two methods must be implemented on this interface:

LoadPostData and *RaisePostDataChangedEvent*. The implementation of these methods is shown here:

```
public virtual bool LoadPostData(string postDataKey,
    NameValueCollection values)
{
    String presentValue = Text;
    String postedValue = values[postDataKey];
    try
    {
        if (!presentValue.Equals(postedValue))
        {
            Text = postedValue;
            return true;
        }
    }
    catch ( Exception e )
    {
        Text=postedValue;
    }
    return false;
}

public virtual void RaisePostDataChangedEvent()
{
    ServerFormatDate();
    IsValid=bIsValid;
    OnTextChanged(EventArgs.Empty);
}
```

LoadPostData is passed in a *postDataKey* parameter as a string. *postDataKey* is used as a key into the second parameter, named values in this example—a *NameValueCollection* object. Using *postDataKey*, you can find the value for the current control and access it. In this example, I'm setting the Text property to the string retrieved from the *NameValueCollection*, if the value differs from the present value. The *RaisePostDataChanged* event is used in this example to call *ServerFormatDate*. *ServerFormatDate* sets the class variable *bIsValid*; doing so allows the control to signal that it isn't valid if the field returned can't be interpreted as a date.

The *IPostBackEventHandler* has a single method that must be implemented, *RaisePostBackEvent*. This event can be used to trigger an event whenever a postback occurs.

The *OnTextChanged* method calls the event handler *TextChanged*, if *TextChanged* is not set to *null*. *TextChanged* is an event handler that I've declared in this class. A client program could use this event to perform some action in the event that the text is changed. In many instances, declaring event handlers and calling them will allow consumers of your control to customize the control's behavior.

Conclusion

Decisions about how an application is to be partitioned are never easy, and the Web doesn't change that. On the server side, ASP.NET makes language choice irrelevant. You can use Visual Basic .NET, C#, or any of the third-party languages that are becoming available for the .NET Framework. Of course, even here you do have to be aware of certain language differences, but for the most part, you can just work with the language you prefer.

The client side is quite a bit more constrained. On the client, your only cross-browser-compatible language choice is JavaScript. There's nothing wrong with JavaScript, but this remains the one area in which you don't have a real choice. Add to this the lack of control you have over the state of the client's JavaScript execution environment, and you can see that moving too much data processing to the client isn't a good idea.

Still, there's a place for client-side scripting. Especially on a busy Internet site, performing initial validation and some minor processing on the client side can make the user's experience with the application more immediate, while reducing the load on the server. This can't be a bad thing.

Most compelling Internet and intranet applications have, at their heart, access to dynamic content derived from various databases. In Chapter 8, we'll begin to gather the information you'll need to build such applications. ADO.NET is used to get the data within an ASP.NET application. Don't let the name confuse you: ADO.NET is really more like a distant cousin to ActiveX Data Objects (ADO) than a chip off the old block. Knowing how to take advantage of the changes in ADO.NET can mean the difference between designing a good application and designing a good application that performs and scales well.

8

Time to Get the Data!

One of the most important tasks of any Web application is getting and displaying data. The ability to create data-driven, dynamic content is at the heart of what made Active Server Pages (ASP) such a hit. ASP.NET continues the tradition of easy data access. More than just providing for simple access to data, however, ASP.NET adds integrated, pervasive support for XML. XML is the data language of the Internet, and so it's not surprising that ASP.NET, through the .NET Framework, offers tremendous support for it.

What is a bit surprising about database access in the .NET Framework is that it's *so* different from the database access that ASP and Microsoft Visual Basic 6.0 programmers are used to. The .NET technology for database access is ADO.NET. ASP programmers accustomed to ActiveX Data Objects (ADO) shouldn't assume that ADO.NET is a minor update to the classic ADO they know and love. ADO.NET isn't just a version upgrade to ADO but rather a completely new way to access data.

In this chapter, I'll introduce XML and explain how you might be able to use it in your solutions. I'll also discuss some of the differences between ADO and ADO.NET and show how you can use ADO.NET in your ASP.NET applications.

XML as the Universal Data Language

In Chapter 4, I introduced XML in the context of the ASP.NET configuration files, Web.config and Machine.config. Briefly, XML is a plain-text data description language, in many ways paralleling HTML, a plain-text data presentation description language.

There's a lot to recommend XML as a universal data language. Think about what you need to do when you're partitioning an application. If you need to send data from application tier to application tier, the decision about how to transport the data is dependent on whether the tiers are on the same machine or different machines. If the tiers are on different machines with different operating systems, your choices are even more limited.

Using XML to transport data solves most of these problems. Imagine that you need to send customer information across machine boundaries. To send information from machine to machine, you need some sort of wire format that both machines can readily understand. Two possible solutions are shown here—the first uses fixed-length buffers and the second uses delimited buffers:

```
REILLY        DOUGLAS        1422345819560724DOUG@PROGRAMMINGASP.NET
REILLY,DOUGLAS,14223458,19560724,DOUG@PROGRAMMINGASP.NET
```

A casual observer could figure out some of the data from the fixed-length representation. In this example, it's easy to see that "Douglas Reilly" is the name and that the last part of the record is likely an e-mail address. In the delimited example, the name and e-mail address are still clear, and now that the fields are split, you might notice that one of the two string fields appears to be a date. Of course, you don't know what this date represents, but given that this is a customer record and the date is 45 years ago, perhaps it's a birth date.

Let's consider another delimited example, in which the problem of identifying the data becomes even harder:

```
LEE,FRANK,22321234,19920403,YELLOWFISH@PROGRAMMINGASP.NET
```

Is the person named in this example Frank Lee or Lee Frank? Both are plausible. And is the date (19920403) a birth date for a very young customer or the first purchase date for an older long-time customer? It's impossible to tell.

Current Solutions to Formatting Data vs. the XML Approach

Dozens of notable attempts have been made by individual companies and industry consortiums to create a standard data transport language. One that I'm familiar with is Health Level 7 (HL7). HL7 is used as a format for data about patient transactions, most often as the wire format in a point-to-point TCP/IP transmission. A simple example of HL7 is shown in this transaction, which admits a patient:

```
MSH|^~\&|ADT1|MMC|DTS|MMC|20010828131127||ADT^A01|P|2.3|<cr>
EVN|A01|20010828131127||<cr>
PID|||0000984249||JONES^BEVERLY^L^||19560214|M||W|
    100 PROSPECT ST^^LAKEWOOD^NJ^08701|OCEA||||M||0400233919||||9
    <cr>
NK1|1|JONES^AMY^|B||||||<cr>
PV1|1|I|B5^551^A||||001218^TEST^DOCTOR^^^MD|||MED||NOF||||<cr>
```

There's no need to understand the full details of this transaction. Briefly, the first line is a message header (*MSH*). The first line also declares the delimiters that will be used for the various levels within the message. The next line is an event submessage (*EVN*). In both the *MSH* and *EVN* lines, the message is declared to be an inpatient admittance (signified by the *A01* code in both lines). The third line is the patient identifying information (*PID*). (Here the *PID* is shown on several lines for clarity, but it's really a single line of text ending with a carriage return.) This line includes the text ⌊*JONES^BEVERLY^L^* ⌋. The vertical bars (⌊) are the outermost delimiters, and the carat (^) is used for delimiting the next level within individual segments. Because we know that this is a patient information line within the admittance message, we can probably assume that this is the name of the patient. The fourth line declares Amy as her next of kin (*NK1*). The final line has patient visit information specific to this visit (*PV1*). Every single segment within the hundreds of lines is comprehensively documented, and hospitals all over the country use this HL7 standard to convey information from system to system.

Compare this HL7 example with an example of a possible XML solution to just the patient visit information:

```
123456789 123456789 123456789 123456789 12345
<patientVisit>
<admissionType>I</admissionType>
<patientLocation>
<unit>B5</unit>
<room>551</room>
<bed>A</bed>
</patientLocation>
<doctor>
<doctorID>001218</doctorID>
<lastName>TEST</lastName>
<firstName>DOCTOR</firstName>
<mi></mi>
</doctor>
<service>MED</service>
<ambulatoryStatus>NOF</ambulatoryStatus>
</patientVisit>
```

The HL7 example makes it fairly clear what the purpose of the data is, but the XML representation of the same information makes it crystal clear what the data means. XML is said to be self-describing, and although you might have to do a little work to parse out the data programmatically, looking at a file with this information, even 20 years from now, you'll be able to determine exactly what data is where.

Is XML Perfect?

Of course, there's no such thing as a free lunch. The cost of the convenience offered by XML is a larger payload. The example patient-visit information rendered using HL7 takes up about 64 bytes (assuming 1 byte per character). The XML alternative uses about 308 bytes. In real-world applications, the size difference is generally not that great, and while it's not insignificant, it probably doesn't matter all that much, for a couple of reasons. The first is the increased bandwidth available to many users these days. The difference between sending 64 bytes and 308 bytes, in terms of time perceived by the user, is inconsequential. Second, the XML data is highly compressible. Given current technologies, compressing the XML for transport over a limited bandwidth line, or for storage, is a reasonable option.

As you'll see in Chapter 10, XML is also at the heart of XML Web services. By using XML as a way to communicate information, XML-enabled applications written in any language on any platform can work with other XML-enabled applications written in any language and on any platform. Given that XML is so critical to .NET data handling in general and to XML Web services in particular, you'd expect to find generous support for XML within the .NET Framework, and you'd be correct.

Using the *IEnumerator* Interface

As we examine the support within the .NET Framework for various types of data handling, it's important to understand some of the details of implementation. As you'll see, using the .NET Framework, you'll be able to use a great variety of objects to access data. All of this access, whether the underlying data is in an array, in a SQL Server database, or in an XML document, will have one thing in common: it will take place through the *IEnumerator* interface.

Recall that interfaces are the definition of a set of behaviors that a class can agree to support. Although .NET doesn't allow multiple inheritance, it *does* allow a class to implement multiple interfaces. The *IEnumerator* interface is a simple interface, containing one property and two methods, as listed in Table 8-1.

Table 8-1 Members of the *IEnumerator* Interface

Interface Member	Description
Current property	Gets the current element from the collection
MoveNext method	Advances the enumerator to the next element of the collection
Reset method	Sets the enumerator to its initial position, logically before the first element of the collection

By implementing this relatively simple interface, an object can enable itself to be bound to another object that expects to get an *IEnumerator* object. In the Visual Basic 6.0 world, you might bind a combo box or a list box to a recordset from a database. In the .NET world, you can bind anything from an array to an XML stream to a combo box or a list box.

To expose an enumerator and add support for the *For Each* construct, the *IEnumerable* interface must be implemented. *IEnumerable* has a single method, which is listed in Table 8-2.

Table 8-2 Members of the *IEnumerable* Interface

Interface Member	Description
GetEnumerable method	Returns an instance of the *IEnumerator* interface

Listing 8-1 shows the code-behind file for a simple page. In addition to the normal page-derived class, you'll see another class, named *MyEnumerator*. This class implements both the *IEnumerator* and the *IEnumerable* interfaces.

```
Using System;
using System.Collections;
using System.ComponentModel;
using System.Data;
using System.Drawing;
using System.Web;
using System.Web.SessionState;
using System.Web.UI;
using System.Web.UI.WebControls;
using System.Web.UI.HtmlControls;

namespace Chapter08_IEnumerator
{
    public class MyEnumerator : IEnumerator,IEnumerable
    {
        private int what;
        private int whatMax;
        public MyEnumerator()
        {
            what=0;
            whatMax=10;
        }
```

Listing 8-1 The code-behind file for a page that demonstrates the use of the *IEnumerator* interface

(continued)

Listing 8-1 *continued*

```csharp
        // IEnumeratable method...
        public IEnumerator GetEnumerator()
        {
            return this;
        }
        // IEnumerator properties and methods
        public object Current
        {
            get
            {
                return what.ToString();
            }
        }
        public bool MoveNext()
        {
            if ( what<whatMax)
            {
                what++;
                return true;
            }
            else
            {
                return false;
            }
        }
        public void Reset()
        {
            what=0;
        }
    }
    /// <summary>
    /// Summary description for WebForm1.
    /// </summary>
    public class WebForm1 : System.Web.UI.Page
    {
        protected System.Web.UI.WebControls.ListBox ListBox1;

        public WebForm1()
        {
            Page.Init += new System.EventHandler(Page_Init);
        }
```

```
private void Page_Load(object sender, System.EventArgs e)
{
    // Set the data source to a new instance
    // of MyEnumerator
    ListBox1.DataSource=new MyEnumerator();
    ListBox1.DataBind();
}

private void Page_Init(object sender, EventArgs e)
{
    //
    // CODEGEN: This call is required by the
    // ASP.NET Web Form Designer.
    //
    InitializeComponent();
}

#region Web Form Designer generated code
/// <summary>
/// Required method for Designer support - do not modify
/// the contents of this method with the code editor.
/// </summary>
private void InitializeComponent()
{
    this.Load += new System.EventHandler(this.Page_Load);
}
#endregion
    }
}
```

The *MyEnumerator* class in Listing 8-1 is a simple enumerator that provides the strings with values between *1* and *10*. Two private variables control how the class works. The variable *what* controls the current value, and the variable *whatMax* controls the maximum value.

The *Current* property, part of the *IEnumerator* interface, makes use of the fact that all types can be boxed and calls the *ToString* method on *what*. The *MoveNext* method of the *IEnumerator* interface increments the value of *what* unless it is greater than or equal to *whatMax*. The return value from *MoveNext* is a *bool* indicating whether there is a next value. The final element of the *IEnumerator* interface is the *Reset* method. In this example, the *Reset* method sets *what* to *0*. Implementing *IEnumerable* is easy. The *GetEnumerator* method simply returns *this* (in Visual Basic .NET, the value would be *Me*) because the same object that implements *IEnumerable* implements *IEnumerator*.

The code-behind class for the page itself is similar to examples in earlier chapters; the difference is in the *Page_Load* method. The page itself has a list box, named *ListBox1*. On page load, I make the following two method calls:

```
private void Page_Load(object sender, System.EventArgs e)
{
    // Set the data source to a new instance
    // of MyEnumerator
    ListBox1.DataSource=new MyEnumerator();
    ListBox1.DataBind();
)
```

First I set the *DataSource* property to a new instance of *MyEnumerator*. This works because *MyEnumerator* implements *IEnumerable*. It's also possible to pass an object that implements *ICollection*. Calling *DataBind* actually populates the list box control with the values from the data source.

Figure 8-1 shows the page with the data-bound values displayed in the list box.

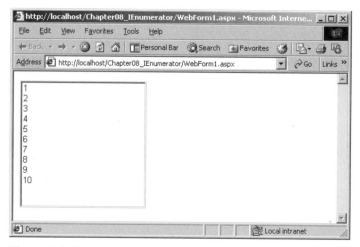

Figure 8-1 A list box populated with the *MyEnumerator* class as its data source

This is a trivial use of the power of the *IEnumerator* and *IEnumerable* interfaces. In the real world, such a simple requirement could be easily met using a loop to add items to the list box. You could also populate an array and bind to that within the *Page_Load* method like this:

```
private void Page_Load(object sender, System.EventArgs e)
{
    System.Collections.ArrayList al;
    al=new System.Collections.ArrayList();
```

```
al.Add("One");
al.Add("Two");
al.Add("Three");
ListBox1.DataSource=al;
ListBox1.DataBind();
}
```

But there certainly are real-world scenarios in which you need to bind to something other than a simple array or a traditional database. These interfaces mean that your data source is limited only by your imagination.

Introducing ADO.NET

Moving from ASP to ASP.NET can be done in a way that will allow the ASP programmer to continue to feel comfortable. You can ignore code-behind files and continue operating in an ASP way, if you want. You'll give up many of the advantages of ASP.NET, but if you want to adopt the new technology with little pain, you can do so, as long as you're willing to learn a little about the Visual Basic .NET changes.

Moving from ADO to ADO.NET is different than moving from ASP to ASP.NET. Although ADO.NET has much of the same functionality as ADO, it's really a different technology. Using ADO.NET requires learning several new namespaces, and there are a few things (*very* few things) that you just can't do with ADO.NET that you could do quite well using ADO. Fortunately, most developers—and virtually all ASP.NET developers—don't need the ADO functionality that isn't easy to duplicate in ADO.NET. First, let's take a look at ADO.

ADO Overview

ADO is made up of three primary objects: *Connection*, *Command*, and *Recordset*. The *Connection* object is used to open a channel between the program and a data source. *Connection* allows you to set the connection string as well as handle transactions and set the type of cursor. ADO supports server-side and client-side servers as well as many other cursor properties designed to control the visibility of modified records and so on.

The *Command* object is used to execute queries. These queries can be arbitrary SQL strings, or possibly stored procedures. The *Command* object supports parameters, and this support helps with passing values that might be troublesome if they were passed as part of an arbitrary SQL string. For example, consider the following SQL string:

```
SELECT * FROM Titles WHERE Title='What's Up Doc?'
```

This string will fail because the apostrophe in the title will be seen as the end of the string, and the rest of the title will be rejected as invalid syntax. Using parameters on the *Command* object allows such a string to be handled.

The *Recordset* object is used to get data from the data source and to navigate through the recordset. Depending on the type of cursor, the recordset can be navigated both forward and backward and can provide properties such as the record count.

One core weakness of ADO is the level of complexity that's involved with selecting the correct cursor location, cursor type, and other similar details. For example, how do you know whether to use a client-side or a server-side cursor? What type of locking do you want? Should other users see changes you make to the recordset before you commit the changes? Although ADO offers flexibility, for the majority of users, especially ASP users, ADO is tough to master and use correctly.

Differences Between ADO and ADO.NET

After seeing what ADO.NET has to offer, programmers accustomed to using ADO invariably respond, "But there are *so many* classes!" It's true. If you browse the .NET Framework, the *System.Data* namespace and all the namespaces under it are chock-full of classes and enumerations. Part of the problem is that the classes are divided into three distinct groups. One group of classes is designed for ODBC data sources, one group is designed for OLE DB data sources, and the other is designed specifically to take advantage of Microsoft SQL Server. These groups of classes are similar, but not identical. Figure 8-2 shows the class structure in ADO.NET.

> **Note**   At the time of this writing, the ODBC classes are expected to be available as an add-on component to the .NET Framework. It's not clear whether it will continue to be an add-on or will become part of the .NET Framework itself. If you want to download the ODBC .NET data provider, check out *http://www.microsoft.com/downloads/*.

One problem that ADO programmers might notice is the lack of server-side cursor support. This lack of support isn't a mistake; rather, it's a design decision. Two primary objects will allow you to navigate records. The first is the *DataSet* object, an in-memory cache of records that you can visit in any direction, similar to an ADO static cursor. The second object you can use to get at data in ADO.NET is *DataReader*. The *DataReader* object is a highly optimized, read-only, forward-only firehose that allows you to read through records sequentially, from front to back.

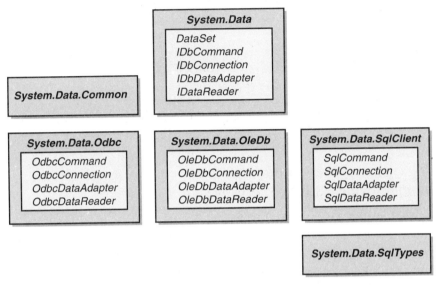

Figure 8-2 The class hierarchy of ADO.NET

For example, one of the most common Web application tasks is displaying the results of a query. In the vast majority of Web applications, none of the records returned will be updated. The read-only, forward-only *DataReader* object is perfect for this type of application.

The *DataAdapter* object acts as a bridge between a *DataSet* object and a data source for retrieving and saving data. The *Fill* method of *DataAdapter* (or *SqlDataAdapter* for SQL Server data sources) fills the *DataSet* object with the requested data from a data source. The *Update* method changes the data in the data source to match that in *DataSet*. The nature of ASP.NET applications doesn't lend itself to using this model. For example, data is often displayed when a page is initially visited, and changes are applied when the page is posted back. In such situations, allowing a single data object to handle transport to and from the data source is of little benefit.

The biggest constraint that ADO has to work with is the limitations imposed by ADO's use of COM. The most significant of these limitations is the limited number of data types supported. If an ADO recordset needed to contain an object, it had to be somehow marshaled as one of the COM data types. ADO.NET uses XML as its data transport, and so ADO.NET can take advantage of the way XML data can be self-describing. In addition, and important for corporate developers, transporting ADO recordsets through firewalls is problematic since most firewalls are configured to prevent COM marshaling. ADO.NET can pass results though firewalls because it's a text protocol that can take advantage of commonly open ports.

Speaking of the ADO recordset object, where is the ADO.NET recordset equivalent? In ADO, the recordset is the "Swiss army knife" of the database developer. Need to get records? Use a recordset. Need to delete records? Use a recordset. Need to add records? You get the idea. The recordset is used in all these situations.

The closest ADO.NET equivalent to an ADO recordset is the *DataSet* object. Using *DataSet*, you can add and update records. The *DataSet* object keeps track of the state of each record. Is the record inserted? Has the record been modified? Has the record been deleted? Unlike ADO, where navigating within the recordset commits changes to the record you navigate away from, the ADO.NET *DataSet* object is designed to allow you to make all the changes you want to (all the time, with no connection to the data source) and then commit them when you're finished.

The new model of disconnected data access works very well in the ASP.NET world. Forget about all you could do with an ADO recordset for a while, and take a look at the ADO.NET way of getting data. It's a little different, but it can greatly enhance the performance and scalability of your application.

Using ADO.NET from ASP.NET

Many of the most exciting advances in using data inside ASP.NET involve the additional server-side controls that can be used in Web Forms. I'll introduce these controls in Chapter 9. For now, I'll show you how to connect to a data source, how to select data, how to insert data, and how to update data using both SQL statements and stored procedures.

Selecting Data

Listing 8-2 shows the code-behind file for a sample that selects data from the Northwind database in SQL Server. The select query is shown here:

```
SELECT CustomerID,CompanyName,ContactName
FROM Customers WHERE ContactTitle='Owner'
```

When the data is retrieved, it's displayed on a page in an HTML table.

```
Imports System.Data
Imports System.Data.OleDb

Public Class WebForm1
    Inherits System.Web.UI.Page
    Public dr As System.Data.OleDb.OleDbDataReader

#Region " Web Form Designer Generated Code "

    'This call is required by the Web Form Designer.
    <System.Diagnostics.DebuggerStepThrough()> _
    Private Sub InitializeComponent()

    End Sub

    Private Sub Page_Init(ByVal sender As System.Object, _
      ByVal e As System.EventArgs) Handles MyBase.Init
        'CODEGEN: This method call is required by the Web Form Designer
        'Do not modify it using the code editor.
        InitializeComponent()
    End Sub

#End Region

    Private Sub Page_Load(ByVal sender As System.Object, _
      ByVal e As System.EventArgs) Handles MyBase.Load
        'Put user code to initialize the page here
        Dim cn As System.Data.OleDb.OleDbConnection
        Dim cmd As System.Data.OleDb.OleDbCommand

        cn = New OleDbConnection( _
          "Provider=SQLOLEDB;Data Source=localhost;" + _
          "Integrated Security=SSPI;Initial Catalog=Northwind")
        cn.Open()
        cmd = New OleDbCommand( _
          "SELECT CustomerID,CompanyName,ContactName " + _
          "FROM Customers WHERE ContactTitle='Owner'")
        cmd.Connection = cn
        dr = cmd.ExecuteReader(CommandBehavior.CloseConnection)
    End Sub

    Private Sub Page_Unload(ByVal sender As System.Object, _
      ByVal e As System.EventArgs) Handles MyBase.Unload
        dr.Close()
    End Sub
End Class
```

Listing 8-2 SimpleSelect.aspx.vb, the code-behind file used to display the results of a simple query

> **Note**   This example and additional examples in this chapter have the
> connection string embedded within the code-behind file. The connection
> strings use *Integrated Security=SSPI* rather than sending a user name and
> password. You will need to give the user whose context the page will be
> running under rights to the database. That user could be the end user if
> you're using impersonation or the Internet Information Services (IIS) user
> (*IUSR_<machinename>*). Another alternative is to use the *appSettings* sec-
> tion of *Web.config*, which was discussed in Chapter 4.

Listing 8-3 shows the page that displays the results of the select query. The
CustomerID, *CompanyName*, and *ContactName* are displayed in a simple HTML
table.

```
<%@ Page Language="vb" AutoEventWireup="false"
Codebehind="SimpleSelect.aspx.vb"
Inherits="Chapter08_SimpleData.WebForm1"
debug="true"%>
<!DOCTYPE HTML PUBLIC "-//W3C//DTD HTML 4.0 Transitional//EN">
<HTML>
    <HEAD>
        <title></title>
        <meta name="GENERATOR"
          content="Microsoft Visual Studio.NET 7.0">
        <meta name="CODE_LANGUAGE"
          content="Visual Basic 7.0">
        <meta name="vs_defaultClientScript" content="JavaScript">
        <meta name="vs_targetSchema"
          content="http://schemas.microsoft.com/intellisense/ie5">
    </HEAD>
    <body>
        <form id="Form1" method="post" runat="server">
            <P>
                <FONT face="Verdana" size="4">
                <STRONG>Select Data Example
                </STRONG></FONT>
            </P>
            <P>
                <table width="600">
                    <tr bgcolor="#ffff66">
                        <td>
                            CustomerID
```

Listing 8-3 SimpleSelect.aspx, displaying data using an OleDbDataReader created in
Listing 8-2, SimpleSelect.aspx.vb

```
            </td>
            <td>
                Company Name
            </td>
            <td>
                Contact/Owner
            </td>
        </tr>
    <%
    while dr.Read()
    %>
        <tr bgcolor="#ffffd7">
            <td>
                <%=dr.GetString(0)%>
            </td>
            <td>
                <%=dr.GetString(1)%>
            </td>
            <td>
                <%=dr.GetString(2)%>
            </td>
        </tr>
    <%
    end while
    %>
        </table>
    </P>
    </form>
</body>
</HTML>
```

Note   Within Listing 8-3, the individual records are written in separate table rows. This is *not* the way to display data in ASP.NET. We'll examine the more advanced ways to display data in ASP.NET in Chapter 9.

Figure 8-3 shows the page generated by running the code shown in Listing 8-3 and the code-behind file shown in Listing 8-2.

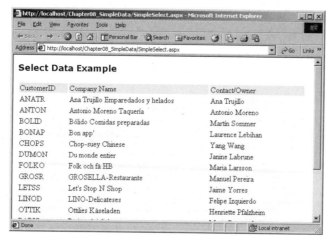

Figure 8-3 Results returned from running the code in Listings 8-2 and 8-3

The bulk of the work of getting the data is performed in the *Page_Load* method shown in Listing 8-2. Using locally created *OleDbConnection* and *OleDbCommand* objects and a public *OleDbDataReader* object, I execute a simple query against the SQL Server Northwind database. This example is in Visual Basic .NET, but the same .NET Framework objects would be used in other .NET languages.

> **Tip** Early versions of the .NET Framework used a different namespace for the non–SQL Server data access classes. Examples in other books or on Web sites that use System.ado won't work with the released version of the .NET Framework.

The process of accessing data using ADO.NET isn't terribly different from what you're used to in ADO. First an *OleDbConnection* object is created. (Note that unlike ADO used in Visual Basic Scripting Edition (VBScript), *Set* is not used when assigning a new instance to your variable.) When the *OleDbCommand* object is created, I pass a SQL string to the constructor. This SQL string will be executed later. I set the *Connection* property of the *OleDbCommand* object to the *OleDbConnection* object created a few lines above, and finally get an *OleDbDataReader* object by calling the *ExecuteReader* method of the *OleDbCommand* object, as follows:

```
dr = cmd.ExecuteReader(CommandBehavior.CloseConnection)
```

The parameter passed to *ExecuteReader* is one of five *CommandBehavior* values that can be combined as bitwise values. The values in the *CommandBehavior* enumeration are listed in Table 8-3.

Table 8-3 The *CommandBehavior* Enumeration

Value	Description
CloseConnection	When the command is executed, the associated connection object is closed when the *DataReader* object is closed.
KeyInfo	The query returns column and primary key information. The query is executed without locking any of the selected rows. When used, the .NET provider for SQL Server appends a FOR BROWSE clause to the statement.
SchemaOnly	The query returns only schema information.
SequentialAccess	Results are read sequentially to the column level, allowing the application to read large binary values using *GetChars* or *GetBytes*.
SingleResult	The query returns a single result.
SingleRow	The query is expected to return a single row. Some .NET data providers might use this information to optimize the operation of the query. Note that in many cases, using a stored procedure with output parameters will result in better performance for singleton queries.

CommandBehavior.CloseConnection is the perfect parameter to pass in this situation because the *OleDbConnection* object is created using a local parameter. When *Page_Unload* is called, closing *dr* will close the connection it was using. There are other convenient ways of working around closing the connection—for example, making the *OleDbConnection* object a public class variable. In other situations—for example, when a class method returns a data reader—it might not be as easy to get the connection closed without sending *CommandBehavior.CloseConnection* to *ExecuteReader*. To give a concrete example, say you have an *Customer* object that exposes a method *GetCustomer* that returns a data reader. Having that method call *ExecuteReader* with *CommandBehavior.CloseConnection* means that the connection, allocated and opened in *GetCustomer*, will be closed when the data reader is closed, even though you have no access to the connection object that *GetCustomer* created.

Creating Action Queries

Insert, update, and delete operations in SQL are sometimes called *action queries,* meaning that they perform some action rather than returning data. Within the ADO.NET world, they're also known as *nonqueries*. The code to execute these nonqueries is similar to the code required to execute the select query shown in Listing 8-2. Listing 8-4 shows the code-behind file SimpleExecuteNonQuery.aspx.vb, used to create a simple ASP.NET form containing three buttons: Insert, Update, and Delete.

```
Imports System.Data
Imports System.Data.OleDb

Public Class SimpleExecuteNonQuery
    Inherits System.Web.UI.Page
    Protected WithEvents Insert As System.Web.UI.WebControls.Button
    Protected WithEvents Update As System.Web.UI.WebControls.Button
    Protected WithEvents Delete As System.Web.UI.WebControls.Button
    Protected WithEvents Label1 As System.Web.UI.WebControls.Label

#Region " Web Form Designer Generated Code "

    'This call is required by the Web Form Designer.
    <System.Diagnostics.DebuggerStepThrough()> _
    Private Sub InitializeComponent()

    End Sub

    Private Sub Page_Init(ByVal sender As System.Object, _
      ByVal e As System.EventArgs) Handles MyBase.Init
        'CODEGEN: This method call is required by the Web Form Designer
        'Do not modify it using the code editor.
        InitializeComponent()
    End Sub

#End Region

    Private Sub Page_Load(ByVal sender As System.Object, _
      ByVal e As System.EventArgs) Handles MyBase.Load
        'Put user code to initialize the page here
    End Sub

    Private Sub Insert_Click(ByVal sender As System.Object, _
      ByVal e As System.EventArgs) Handles Insert.Click
        Dim cn As OleDb.OleDbConnection
        Dim cmd As OleDb.OleDbCommand
        cn = New OleDbConnection("Provider=SQLOLEDB;" + _
          "Data Source=localhost;Integrated Security=SSPI;" + _
          "Initial Catalog=Northwind")
        cn.Open()
        cmd = New OleDbCommand("INSERT INTO " + _
            "Territories(TerritoryID,TerritoryDescription,RegionID) " + _
            " VALUES('08724', 'Brick', 3)")
        cmd.Connection = cn
        Try
            cmd.ExecuteNonQuery()
```

Listing 8-4 SimpleExecuteNonQuery.aspx.vb, executing insert, update, and delete commands

```
            Catch dbe As System.Data.OleDb.OleDbException
                Label1.Text = "Exception while Inserting Record!  " + _
                    dbe.ToString()
            End Try

        End Sub

        Private Sub Update_Click(ByVal sender As System.Object, _
            ByVal e As System.EventArgs) Handles Update.Click
            Dim cn As OleDb.OleDbConnection
            Dim cmd As OleDb.OleDbCommand
            cn = New OleDbConnection("Provider=SQLOLEDB;" + _
                "Data Source=localhost;Integrated Security=SSPI;" + _
                "Initial Catalog=Northwind")
            cn.Open()
            cmd = New OleDbCommand("UPDATE Territories " + _
                "SET TerritoryDescription='Brick Township' " + _
                " WHERE TerritoryID='08724'")
            cmd.Connection = cn
            Try
                cmd.ExecuteNonQuery()
            Catch dbe As System.Data.OleDb.OleDbException
                Label1.Text = "Exception while Updating Record!  " + _
                    dbe.ToString()
            End Try

        End Sub

        Private Sub Delete_Click(ByVal sender As System.Object, _
            ByVal e As System.EventArgs) Handles Delete.Click
            Dim cn As OleDb'.OleDbConnection
            Dim cmd As OleDb.OleDbCommand
            cn = New OleDbConnection("Provider=SQLOLEDB;" + _
                "Data Source=localhost;Integrated Security=SSPI;" + _
                "Initial Catalog=Northwind")
            cn.Open()
            cmd = New OleDbCommand("DELETE FROM Territories " + _
                " WHERE TerritoryID='08724'")
            cmd.Connection = cn
            Try
                cmd.ExecuteNonQuery()
            Catch dbe As System.Data.OleDb.OleDbException
                Label1.Text = "Exception while Deleting Record!  " + _
                    dbe.ToString()
            End Try

        End Sub
End Class
```

The event handlers for all three buttons—Insert, Update, and Delete—are virtually identical, except for the SQL code passed to the constructor of the *OleDbCommand* object. One thing that was added over and above the select query example is exception handling, as shown here:

```
Try
    cmd.ExecuteNonQuery()
Catch dbe As System.Data.OleDb.OleDbException
    Label1.Text = "Exception while Inserting Record!  " + _
        dbe.ToString()
End Try
```

One fairly common mishap that can occur when you're inserting data is duplicate data. In this example, if you click the Insert button and then click it again before you have deleted the record by clicking the Delete button, you'll get an error. Rather than returning the standard unhandled exception error, clicking Insert when the record already exists in the database will instead give you the result seen in Figure 8-4.

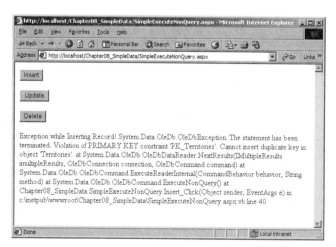

Figure 8-4 The exception information displayed by SimpleExecuteNonQuery.aspx when you insert a record that already exists

For most applications, you'd want to display only some of this information, and the *OleDbException* object has many different properties to allow you to get at individual elements of the error information.

> **Tip**   One way to slightly improve the layout of the displayed error information is to replace the carriage return characters (which are interpreted as white space within an HTML document) with *
* tags. Changing this line
>
> ```
> dbe.ToString()
> ```
>
> to this
>
> ```
> dbe.ToString().Replace(Chr(13), "<BR>")
> ```
>
> will result in a somewhat cleaner display.

Using Stored Procedures

Most relational database systems allow you to run stored procedures. Stored procedures are blocks of SQL code that are called much like functions are called in normal procedural languages. Stored procedures are parsed and validated when they're saved, and the query plan for a stored procedure is also calculated only once. These two features alone are enough to justify using stored procedures.

In addition, stored procedures can be created to return results in an efficient format. For example, if you're retrieving a single record, you could write a query that returns the single record as a recordset, or you could write a stored procedure that returns the required fields using output parameters. Retrieving even a recordset with only a single record can involve significant overhead. When a recordset is returned, not only is the data returned, but also data *about* the data (also called *metadata*) is returned. Using output parameters can be significantly more efficient.

There are other reasons to use stored procedures—for example, performing some complex data-related function as close to the data as possible. For data manipulation that would require multiple SQL statements, a stored procedure will likely be much more efficient. If you're bringing a lot of data to the client machine and filtering out data locally, you have a perfect candidate for using stored procedures. I'm most familiar with the version of Transact SQL included with Microsoft SQL Server, which isn't designed as a procedural language. However, it *does* offer many of the constructs, such as IF and WHILE, that will make a procedural programmer happy. Still, the power of stored procedures comes from their use of the set-oriented, nonprocedural SQL language.

In another scenario, you might want to grant rights to only some columns in a particular table. One way to do this is to give no rights to the table but execute rights to a stored procedure that will access the data in a safe way.

Tip Another alternative (beyond the scope of this book) is to create a SQL Server *view* with just the table columns you want to give users access to. Then you can give the users no rights to the underlying table but whatever rights are required to the view.

Executing stored procedures using ADO.NET is similar to executing normal SQL statements. In almost all cases, you'll be passing parameters to your stored procedures. Few stored procedures are useful without any parameters, although the first example we'll look at next doesn't accept any parameters.

The following SimpleSPSelect example calls a simple stored procedure named "Ten Most Expensive Products" that requires no parameters and returns a set of records. The records are read into a *DataReader* object and then displayed exactly as with the select query executed in SimpleSelect.aspx.vb shown in Listing 8-3. SimpleSPSelect.aspx is shown in Listing 8-5, and the code-behind file, SimpleSPSelect.aspx.cs, is shown in Listing 8-6.

```
<%@ Page language="c#"
Codebehind="SimpleSPSelect.aspx.cs"
AutoEventWireup="false"
Inherits="Chapter08_SimpleSPSelect.WebForm1" %>
<!DOCTYPE HTML PUBLIC "-//W3C//DTD HTML 4.0 Transitional//EN" >
<HTML>
    <HEAD>
        <meta name="GENERATOR" Content="Microsoft Visual Studio 7.0">
        <meta name="CODE_LANGUAGE" Content="C#">
        <meta name="vs_defaultClientScript"
          content="JavaScript (ECMAScript)">
        <meta name="vs_targetSchema"
          content="http://schemas.microsoft.com/intellisense/ie5">
    </HEAD>
    <body>
        <form id="Form1" method="post" runat="server">
            <TABLE WIDTH="300" BORDER="0" CELLSPACING="1" CELLPADDING="1">
                <TR bgcolor="#ffff66">
```

Listing 8-5 SimpleSPSelect.aspx, showing how to display the results from the "Ten Most Expensive Products" stored procedure from the Northwind database

```
            <TD>
                Product
            </TD>
            <TD>
                Unit Price
            </TD>
        </TR>
        <%
        while ( dr.Read() )
        {
        %>
        <TR bgcolor="#ffffc3">
            <TD>
                <%=dr.GetString(0)%>
            </TD>
            <TD align="right">
                <%=dr.GetDecimal(1).ToString("C")%>
            </TD>
        </TR>
        <%
        }
        %>
        <TR>
            <TD colspan="2" align="middle">
                <asp:Label
                    id="Label1"
                    runat="server">
                </asp:Label>
            </TD>
        </TR>
    </TABLE>
  </form>
 </body>
</HTML>
```

```
using System;
using System.Collections;
using System.ComponentModel;
using System.Data;
using System.Data.SqlClient;
using System.Drawing;
using System.Web;
using System.Web.SessionState;
using System.Web.UI;
using System.Web.UI.WebControls;
using System.Web.UI.HtmlControls;
```

Listing 8-6 SimpleSPSelect.aspx.cs, showing how to call a stored procedure from ASP.NET

(continued)

Listing 8-6   *continued*

```
namespace Chapter08_SimpleSPSelect
{
    /// <summary>
    /// Summary description for WebForm1
    /// </summary>
    public class WebForm1 : System.Web.UI.Page
    {
        protected System.Web.UI.WebControls.Label Label1;
        protected System.Data.SqlClient.SqlDataReader dr;
        public WebForm1()
        {
            Page.Init += new System.EventHandler(Page_Init);
        }

        private void Page_Load(object sender, System.EventArgs e)
        {
            // Put user code to initialize the page here
            System.Data.SqlClient.SqlConnection cn;
            System.Data.SqlClient.SqlCommand cmd;
            cn=new SqlConnection("server=localhost;" +
                "Integrated Security=SSPI;Initial Catalog=Northwind");
            cmd=new SqlCommand("Ten Most Expensive Products",cn);
            cmd.CommandType=CommandType.StoredProcedure;
            try
            {
                cn.Open();
                dr=cmd.ExecuteReader(CommandBehavior.CloseConnection);
            }
            catch (System.Data.SqlClient.SqlException sqle)
            {
                Label1.Text=sqle.ToString().Replace("\n","<BR>");
            }

        }
        private void Page_Unload(object sender, EventArgs e)
        {
            dr.Close();  // Which will also close the connection
        }


        private void Page_Init(object sender, EventArgs e)
        {
            //
            // CODEGEN: This call is required by the
            // ASP.NET Web Form Designer.
            //
            InitializeComponent();
        }
```

```
        #region Web Form Designer generated code
        /// <summary>
        /// Required method for Designer support - do not modify
        /// the contents of this method with the code editor.
        /// </summary>
        private void InitializeComponent()
        {
            this.Load += new System.EventHandler(this.Page_Load);
            this.Unload += new System.EventHandler(this.Page_Unload);
        }
        #endregion
    }
}
```

Figure 8-5 shows the page returned when SimpleSPSelect is executed.

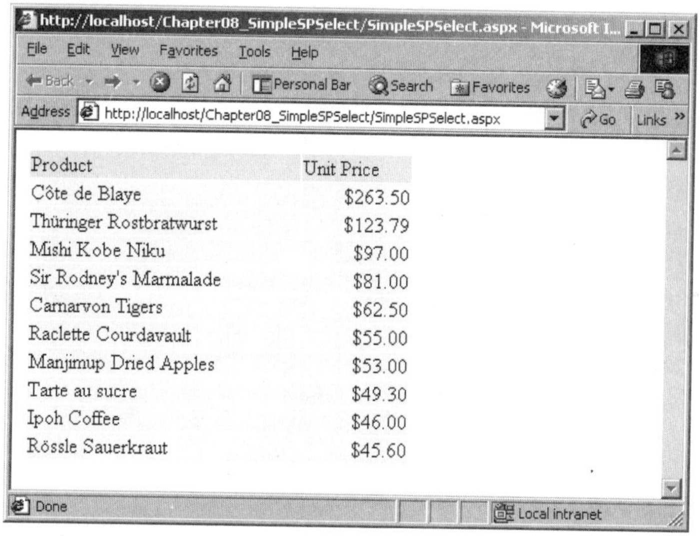

Figure 8-5 Results from SimpleSPSelect.aspx, showing the most expensive products, returned from a stored procedure

The following two lines in the code-behind file, *SimpleSPSelect.aspx.cs* in Listing 8-6, set up the stored procedure call:

```
cmd=new SqlCommand("Ten Most Expensive Products",cn);
cmd.CommandType=CommandType.StoredProcedure;
```

Rather than a SQL statement, I pass in the name of the stored procedure to the constructor for *SqlCommand*. I next set the *CommandType* property for the command to *CommandType.StoredProcedure*. Recall from examples earlier in the chapter that when executing SQL commands, I didn't set *CommandType*, because the default *CommandType* was correct. From this point, calling the *ExecuteReader* method on the *SqlCommand* object and storing the returned *SqlDataReader* object is similar to what you've seen in previous examples.

> **Note**   Careful observers will notice that the examples earlier in the chapter use *OleDbConnection* and similarly *OleDb*-prefixed classes to access data. The stored procedure examples use *SqlConnection* and similarly *Sql*-prefixed classes. We'll look more closely at the differences between these classes and where each should be used in the next section "*SqlClient* vs. *OleDb* Classes."

In Listing 8-5, I once again used some ASP-like methods to display data in a table:

```
<TD>
    <%=dr.GetString(0)%>
</TD>
<TD align="right">
    <%=dr.GetDecimal(1).ToString("C")%>
</TD>
```

Using *GetString* with an ordinal (a 0-based number representing the relative column number in the result set) is something you've seen before. The second table cell contains *dr.GetDecimal(1).ToString("C")*. What this does is to first get the 1's column data (the second column) as a decimal and convert it to a string, using *ToString*. The *ToString* method is passed a format string, in this case, "C", which means that the value is formatted as currency.

One more bit of code might require some explanation, although it's totally unrelated to calling stored procedures. The *InitializeComponent* method has one line that I've added, shown here:

```
private void InitializeComponent()
{
    this.Load += new System.EventHandler(this.Page_Load);
    // I added this
    this.Unload += new System.EventHandler(this.Page_Unload);
}
```

The added line uses the += operator to add the *Page_Unload* method as an event handler for the *Unload* event on this form. Visual Basic .NET uses a *Handles MyBase.Unload* syntax appended to the method declaration to allow a method to handle one of the events in the page's life cycle. This is just one of the many areas in which C# and Visual Basic .NET differ.

The examples of stored procedures in the Northwind database don't adequately demonstrate inserting, updating, and deleting rows, so I created a couple of stored procedures of my own. The first is named *spSaveTerritory*, and the second is named *spDeleteTerritory*. A script to create both is shown in Listing 8-7.

```
USE Northwind
SET QUOTED_IDENTIFIER OFF
GO
SET ANSI_NULLS OFF
GO

CREATE PROCEDURE spDeleteTerritory
    @TerritoryID nvarchar(20)
AS
SET NOCOUNT ON
    DELETE FROM Territories WHERE TerritoryID=@TerritoryID
GO
SET QUOTED_IDENTIFIER OFF
GO
SET ANSI_NULLS ON
GO


SET QUOTED_IDENTIFIER OFF
GO
SET ANSI_NULLS OFF
GO


CREATE PROCEDURE spSaveTerritory
    @TerritoryID nvarchar(20),
    @TerritoryDescription nvarchar(128),
    @RegionID int
AS
SET NOCOUNT ON
    DECLARE @Existing nvarchar(20)

SELECT @Existing=TerritoryID
FROM Territories
WHERE TerritoryID=@TerritoryID

    IF IsNull(@Existing,'')<>@TerritoryID -- Then, INSERT
    BEGIN
        INSERT INTO
            Territories(TerritoryID,
            TerritoryDescription,RegionID)
            VALUES(@TerritoryID, @TerritoryDescription,@RegionID)
        return(1)
    END
```

Listing 8-7 Stored procedures to save or delete a territory in the Northwind database

(continued)

Listing 8-7 *continued*

```
    ELSE
    BEGIN
        UPDATE Territories SET
            TerritoryDescription=@TerritoryDescription,
            RegionID=@RegionID
        WHERE TerritoryID=@TerritoryID
        return(0)
    END
GO
SET QUOTED_IDENTIFIER OFF
GO
SET ANSI_NULLS ON
GO
```

Neither of these stored procedures is terribly difficult to understand, so I won't describe them in detail here. The *spSaveTerritory* stored procedure will either insert or update a territory, using the *TerritoryID* as the key to determine whether the territory is already present.

Calling either of these stored procedures requires setting up parameters. Parameter objects have a number of properties, the most important of which are listed in Table 8-4.

Table 8-4 Parameter Object Properties

Property	Description
DbType	The type of the parameter, specific to the .NET data provider.
Direction	One of an enumerated type, can be *Input* (the default), *Output*, *InputOutput*, or *ReturnValue*. There can be a single *ReturnValue* for any stored procedure, and for SQL Server, the *ReturnValue* is always an *int*.
ParameterName	The name of the parameter. Note that unlike in ADO, the default (and as far as I can tell, the *only* behavior) is the requirement that parameter names *exactly* match the name of the parameter within the SQL code or stored procedure.
Size	The size, in bytes, of the data within the parameter. If this property is omitted, oversize strings are truncated at the maximum value. If *Size* is specified and the size exceeds the allowed size for the parameter, an exception occurs.
SqlDbType	The SQL type, linked to *DbType*. If one changes, the other will change appropriately. Generally, you should set only one property or the other.
Value	Gets or sets the value of the parameter. For *Input* or *InputOutput* parameters, it's important to set the *Value* property before executing the command.

Listing 8-8 shows the code-behind file SimpleSPActionQueries.aspx.cs. This code creates the appropriate parameters to call the *spSaveTerritory* and *spDeleteTerritory* stored procedures.

```
using System;
using System.Collections;
using System.ComponentModel;
using System.Data;
using System.Data.SqlClient;
using System.Drawing;
using System.Web;
using System.Web.SessionState;
using System.Web.UI;
using System.Web.UI.WebControls;
using System.Web.UI.HtmlControls;

namespace SimpleSPActionQueries
{
    /// <summary>
    /// Summary description for WebForm1.
    /// </summary>
    public class WebForm1 : System.Web.UI.Page
    {
        protected System.Web.UI.WebControls.Button Save;
        protected System.Web.UI.WebControls.Button Delete;
        protected System.Web.UI.WebControls.Label Label1;

        public WebForm1()
        {
            Page.Init += new System.EventHandler(Page_Init);
        }

        private void Page_Load(object sender, System.EventArgs e)
        {
            // Put user code to initialize the page here
        }

        private void Page_Init(object sender, EventArgs e)
        {
            //
            // CODEGEN: This call is required by the
            // ASP.NET Web Form Designer.
            //
            InitializeComponent();
        }
```

Listing 8-8 SimpleSPActionQueries.aspx.cs code-behind file demonstrating how to call a stored procedure with parameters

Listing 8-8 *continued*

```
#region Web Form Designer generated code
/// <summary>
/// Required method for Designer support - do not modify
/// the contents of this method with the code editor.
/// </summary>
private void InitializeComponent()
{

    this.Save.Click += new System.EventHandler(this.Save_Click);
    this.Delete.Click += new System.EventHandler(this.Delete_Click);
    this.Load += new System.EventHandler(this.Page_Load);


}
#endregion

private void Save_Click(object sender, System.EventArgs e)
{
    System.Data.SqlClient.SqlConnection cn;
    System.Data.SqlClient.SqlCommand cmd;
    System.Data.SqlClient.SqlParameter prm;

    cn=new SqlConnection("server=localhost;" +
        "Integrated Security=SSPI;Initial Catalog=Northwind");
    cmd=new SqlCommand("spSaveTerritory",cn);
    cmd.CommandType=CommandType.StoredProcedure;

    prm=new System.Data.SqlClient.SqlParameter("@ReturnValue",3);
    prm.Direction=ParameterDirection.ReturnValue;
    cmd.Parameters.Add(prm);

    cmd.Parameters.Add("@TerritoryID","08724");
    cmd.Parameters.Add("@TerritoryDescription","Brick");
    cmd.Parameters.Add("@RegionID",3);
    try
    {
        cn.Open();
        cmd.ExecuteNonQuery();
        Label1.Text="Returned " +
            cmd.Parameters["@ReturnValue"].Value.ToString();
    }
    catch ( System.Data.SqlClient.SqlException sqle )
    {
        Label1.Text=sqle.ToString().Replace("\n","<BR>");
    }
    finally
    {
        cn.Close();
    }
}
```

```
private void Delete_Click(object sender, System.EventArgs e)
{
    System.Data.SqlClient.SqlConnection cn;
    System.Data.SqlClient.SqlCommand cmd;

    cn=new SqlConnection("server=localhost;" +
        "Integrated Security=SSPI;Initial Catalog=Northwind");
    cmd=new SqlCommand("spDeleteTerritory",cn);
    cmd.CommandType=CommandType.StoredProcedure;

    cmd.Parameters.Add("@TerritoryID","08724");
    try
    {
        cn.Open();
        cmd.ExecuteNonQuery();
        Label1.Text="Delete Successful";
    }
    catch ( System.Data.SqlClient.SqlException sqle )
    {
        Label1.Text=sqle.ToString().Replace("\n","<BR>");
    }
    finally
    {
        cn.Close();
    }
}
```

The *Save_Click* method calls the *spSaveTerritory* stored procedure, and the *Delete_Click* method calls the *spDeleteTerritory* stored procedure. Both stored procedures use parameters, so I'll discuss only the *Save_Click* method.

Save_Click first creates a *SqlConnection* object and a *SqlCommand* object, as in previous examples. Next it creates the parameters.

Parameters can be created in a number of ways. There are six overloads of the constructor for *SqlParameter*. The IntelliSense within Visual Studio .NET and the .NET Framework documentation explain all the variations in some detail. Each of the constructor overloads contains some combination of arguments to allow you to create a parameter in a convenient way. Just as important, if you create a parameter and you need to set additional properties on it, you can do so. For example, to create the parameter to handle the return value from the stored procedure, I use the following code:

```
prm=new System.Data.SqlClient.SqlParameter("@ReturnValue",3);
prm.Direction=ParameterDirection.ReturnValue;
cmd.Parameters.Add(prm);
```

As it happens, no convenient constructor would cleanly allow me to specify the name of the parameter, *@ReturnValue* in this example; the actual value, *3*; and the direction of the parameter, *ParameterDirection.ReturnValue*. I selected the next most convenient constructor, and from there set the *Direction* property, since the default was not correct in this case. Notice that I don't set a data type in this example, nor in any other examples in this chapter. Because the .NET Framework can identify the type of the value passed in, it's not required that the type be explicitly declared. Once the parameter is constructed, I call *Add* on the *Parameters* collection of the *SqlCommand* object.

The remaining parameters are added using the follow code:

```
cmd.Parameters.Add("@TerritoryID","08724");
cmd.Parameters.Add("@TerritoryDescription","Brick");
cmd.Parameters.Add("@RegionID",3);
```

The *SqlParameter* constructor shown earlier added the *@ReturnValue* parameter to the *Parameters* collection. In this code, I call the *Add* method of the *Parameters* collection with the parameter name and parameter value for the remaining three parameters.

> **Note**   Remember that unlike in ADO, in ADO.NET the name of the parameter must match *exactly* the name in the stored procedure. In the case of SQL Server stored procedures, this includes the leading at symbol (@) required for variables. In ADO, the names of the parameters didn't matter, by default. The order in which parameters were added to the *Parameters* collection determined which parameter object referred to which parameter, and the parameter name was used only to retrieve output parameters.

Once all the parameters are set, I call *ExecuteNonQuery* on the *SqlCommand* object. After successful execution, I retrieve the return code, as shown here:

```
Label1.Text="Returned " +
    cmd.Parameters["@ReturnValue"].Value.ToString();
```

I access the correct parameter by indexing into the *Parameters* collection using the name of the parameter I want to retrieve. Note that the following syntax is incorrect:

```
Label1.Text="Returned " +
    cmd.Parameters["@ReturnValue"].ToString();
```

This code would return the literal "*@ReturnValue*" rather than the value—a *1* if the record is inserted, and a *0* if the record is updated. In many areas of the .NET Framework, qualifying an object with .*Value* will probably return the value you're after, rather than some representation of the name of the object.

I use the *finally* section of the exception handling structure to ensure that the connection is closed. In a *try/catch/finally* block, the code in the *try* block is executed in its entirety, or up to the point where the exception occurs. The *catch* block is executed if the exception is the correct type (as specified in the predicate of the *catch* block), and the *finally* block is *always* executed, making it an ideal place to clean up expensive resources, such as database connections.

SqlClient vs. *OleDb* Classes

The examples at the beginning of this chapter used a set of classes in the *OleDb* namespace to access data, and the stored procedure examples used classes in the *SqlClient* namespace. What's the difference? Plenty.

The *OleDb* classes are the more generic of the classes. You can hit any OLE DB data source, including Microsoft SQL Server, using these classes. They offer acceptable performance. It's difficult to split out database-only performance from the overall performance gains in ASP.NET over ASP.

The *SqlClient* classes parallel, for the most part, the *OleDb* classes, but are for use exclusively with Microsoft SQL Server. The *SqlDataReader* class uses SQL Server's native data-transfer format to read data directly from the database connection. I haven't done speed testing comparing the *OleDb* classes with the *SqlClient* classes, but in general, the *SqlClient* classes seem to perform better.

So how do you decide which family of classes to use? First, if you always use Microsoft SQL Server 7.0 or later as a back-end database, your choice is easy: use the *SqlClient* classes. The *SqlClient* classes, because they go through fewer layers, will virtually always outperform the *OleDb* classes.

If, on the other hand, you sometimes use Oracle or Jet (Microsoft Access) databases, you must use the *OleDb* classes, at least for any non-Microsoft SQL Server data sources. Although you might expect that any database access using any OLE DB data source would be possible, that's not the case. Specifically, the *OleDb* classes *do not* support access to the OLE DB provider for Open Database Connectivity (ODBC). However, there is a separate ODBC .NET data provider (mentioned earlier in this chapter) in early beta testing as I'm writing this chapter.

What About a Wrapper Class?

My natural inclination when presented with a situation like the choice between *OleDb* and *SqlClient* classes is to write a wrapper class to allow my program to decide at runtime which of the sets of classes to use. There are several problems to be overcome if you want to do this. First, the .NET Framework doesn't support multiple inheritance. Just as important, both the *OleDb* and *SqlClient* classes are sealed, meaning that you can't inherit from them.

An alternative would be to use *composition,* creating a class that will potentially contain an instance of either of the appropriate classes, and then decide at runtime which class to use. One problem with this solution is that the data types supported by each class are not exactly the same. In virtually all cases, it's possible to map the types to a standard set of types.

A second problem is that there are *lots* of classes to wrap up in a standard set of classes. The sets of classes are mostly identical, but not exactly. For example, *OleDbCommand* has a *Dispose* method, and *SqlCommand* does not. While the differences are small, wrapping them all up would take some time.

Generating XML from Data

One feature of the .NET Framework that expands the collection of data sources is the XML classes. Listing 8-9 shows the code required to create an XML file based on the results of query to a database. This code queries the Northwind database for all the information in the *Territories* table and then outputs the information as XML to a file named Territories.xml.

```
using System;
using System.Collections;
using System.ComponentModel;
using System.IO;
using System.Data;
using System.Data.SqlClient;
using System.Drawing;
using System.Web;
using System.Web.SessionState;
using System.Web.UI;
using System.Web.UI.WebControls;
using System.Web.UI.HtmlControls;
```

Listing 8-9 SimpleXML.FileSave.aspx.cs, used to write an XML file from the Territories table in the Northwind database

```
namespace SimpleXML
{
    /// <summary>
    /// Summary description for WebForm1.
    /// </summary>
    public class WebForm1 : System.Web.UI.Page
    {
        public string xmlStr;
        public WebForm1()
        {
            Page.Init += new System.EventHandler(Page_Init);
        }

        private void Page_Load(object sender, System.EventArgs e)
        {
            // Put user code to initialize the page here
            System.Data.SqlClient.SqlConnection cn;
            System.Data.SqlClient.SqlDataAdapter da;
            System.Data.DataSet ds;
            System.IO.StreamWriter sr;

            cn=new SqlConnection("server=localhost;" +
                "Integrated Security=SSPI;Initial Catalog=Northwind");
            da=new SqlDataAdapter("SELECT * FROM Territories",cn);
            try
            {
                cn.Open();
                ds = new System.Data.DataSet();
                da.Fill(ds,"Territories");
                xmlStr=ds.GetXml();

                FileStream fs = new FileStream(
                    "territories.xml", FileMode.OpenOrCreate);
                fs.SetLength(0);

                sr=new StreamWriter(fs);
                sr.Write(xmlStr);
                sr.Close();
            }
            catch ( System.Exception sqle )
            {
                sqle.ToString().Replace("\n","<BR>");
            }
            finally
            {
                cn.Close();
            }
        }
```

(continued)

Listing 8-9   *continued*

```
        private void Page_Init(object sender, EventArgs e)
        {
            //
            // CODEGEN: This call is required by the
            // ASP.NET Web Form Designer.
            //
            InitializeComponent();
        }

        #region Web Form Designer generated code
        /// <summary>
        /// Required method for Designer support - do not modify
        /// the contents of this method with the code editor.
        /// </summary>
        private void InitializeComponent()
        {
            this.Load += new System.EventHandler(this.Page_Load);

        }
        #endregion
    }
}
```

All the work of this page is done in the *Page_Load* method. The *SqlDataSet* object provides a *GetXml* method that returns a string containing the XML for the data in the data set. To create a *SqlDataSet* object, I use the *SqlDataAdapter* class that acts as a bridge between the underlying SQL Server database and a *SqlDataSet*. The *Fill* method of the *SqlDataAdapter* actually fills the *SqlDataSet*.

Once I have a *SqlDataSet*, I call *GetXml* and save the returned value in a string variable named *xmlStr*. Notice that I've added the *System.IO* namespace to the *using* clauses. ASP.NET applications don't normally use this namespace; however, it's required to write files. The *FileStream* class provides access to files. After the *FileStream* object is created for the XML file, I create a new *StreamWriter* object, passing in the *FileStream* object. If you're looking through the class hierarchy, you might be tempted to use the *TextWriter* class, but you can't, because *TextWriter* is an abstract class that can't be directly instantiated. I call the *Write* method on the *StreamWriter* object and pass in the XML string. Once the *Write* method completes, I close the *StreamWriter* object. The *finally* clause closes the database connection.

The XML file will be written relative to the System32 directory if the path passed in isn't an absolute path. This is a bit of a surprise, but when you think about it, it makes sense that the current working directory of the ASP.NET process is the System32 directory.

Figure 8-6 shows the Territories XML file displayed in Internet Explorer.

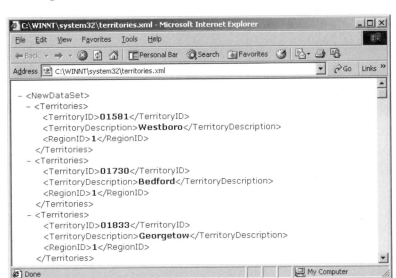

Figure 8-6 The Territories table from Northwind saved in an XML file by
SimpleXML.FileSave.aspx.cs

The ability to read and write XML data using the .NET Framework classes
opens up a whole new world of data access. The .NET Framework has some
limitations to the databases it can support, in part because of the more limited
support for ODBC and the fact that very few ODBC data sources have been tested
with the ODBC .NET data provider. Because XML is quickly becoming the data
language of choice, even if you can't directly access a given data source through
.NET, it's likely that data transfers into and out of the .NET Framework using XML
can allow your .NET application to interoperate with virtually any database.

Conclusion

Data access within ASP.NET is a big step up from data access in ASP. The
ADO.NET model is more completely thought out, and although it's more complex, it provides an ideal environment for the Web developer. The *DataReader*
classes provide fast, scalable access to data and are appropriate for virtually all
Web data access. Richer, somewhat less scalable classes are also available for times
when you need them. The lack of a cursor library will be a difficult transition

for some developers. However, most developers never really understood the implications of cursor location, and often made less than perfect choices anyway. This is just a brief introduction to using ADO.NET within ASP.NET. ADO.NET is a large topic, and certainly several books will be written about it.

In Chapter 9, we'll look at making use of all that ASP.NET has to offer for data access within Web Forms. ASP.NET offers a number of server controls that make displaying data easier than you've ever dreamed.

9

Data and ASP.NET Forms

If the only changes to the way ASP.NET developers handled data were the changes to ADO.NET, most ASP developers wouldn't be tremendously impressed. Fortunately, ASP.NET brings compelling changes to data handling that are visible in the context of ASP.NET forms. ASP.NET forms provide developers with additional assistance with one-way, read-only data binding.

As with much of the magic offered by ASP.NET, server-side controls are at the heart of the data handling improvements. The "Swiss army knife" of Microsoft Visual Basic 6.0 developers is the *data grid*. A data grid is a component that displays data in a tabular form, with rows and columns of data, and looks somewhat like a spreadsheet. For better or worse, a data grid drives many Visual Basic 6.0 user interfaces. ASP.NET doesn't disappoint in maintaining this approach, providing a data grid that takes full advantage of the data binding in ASP.NET. While providing much of the functionality of a traditional data-bound grid, the ASP.NET data grid acts much like a Web interface, making it somewhat less convenient for the user but consistent with the relatively efficient use of bandwidth that Web applications are known for.

In addition, there are other server controls that are somewhat less convenient to use but much more flexible. These controls allow the developer to create a template for the user interface and let the framework handle navigating the recordset. To fully understand the improvements involved with ASP.NET, let's first review how ASP handled access to data.

Accessing Data Using ASP Forms

You might have noticed a certain fairly consistent pattern when accessing data in Active Server Pages (ASP). This pattern is similar to the examples in Chapter 8.

First a recordset is created, and then code something like the following is written within the ASP file:

```
<%
    while rs.EOF <> True
%>
        <TR bgcolor="#ffffc3">
            <TD>
                <%=rs("Name")%>
            </TD>
            <TD align="right">
                <%=rs("Cost")%>
            </TD>
        </TR>
<%
    rs.MoveNext
    Wend
%>
```

This kind of code poses a couple of possible problems. First and foremost, the HTML code developed by the user interface designer is all mixed up with the code developed by the database designer. If the same person is doing both jobs, as is common on smaller sites, this overlap isn't a great handicap. However, when the application design task is divided between interface designers using HTML and database designers using Microsoft Visual Basic Scripting Edition (VBScript), difficulties often result. For example, during the development of a large application, it's possible that the user interface and the database design can be in flux at the same time. A source code tracking tool can help minimize this conflict, but such a tool could delay one developer while the other is doing work on a single file with both types of code inside.

A second problem is just plain silly, but I've caused it myself more times than I care to count. During the initial development of a large project, perhaps once a week, rather than following the pattern shown earlier, I write code something like this:

```
<%
    while rs.EOF <> True
%>
        <TR bgcolor="#ffffc3">
            <TD>
                <%=rs("Name")%>
            </TD>
            <TD align="right">
                <%=rs("Cost")%>
            </TD>
        </TR>
<%
    Wend
%>
```

The difference between this snippet of code and the previous one is subtle and will be obvious only when you run the page: it is, of course, the lack of code to move to the next record. This one missing line means that the page will never actually be displayed, because the predicate of the *while* statement (*rs.EOF <> True*) will always be *True* and so the program will loop—at least until you stop Internet Information Services (IIS) or until the page times out.

ADO.NET eliminates the problem of forgetting the record navigation statement by having the *Read* method of a *DataReader* object also navigate to the next record and then return a code indicating whether the navigation was successful. Thus, the ASP.NET example from Chapter 8 (using C#) is as follows:

```
<%
while ( dr.Read() )
{
%>
    <TR bgcolor="#fffffc3">
        <TD>
            <%=dr.GetString(0)%>
        </TD>
        <TD align="right">
            <%=dr.GetDecimal(1).ToString("C")%>
        </TD>
    </TR>
<%
}
%>
```

In this ASP.NET example, *dr.Read* actually reads the next record and navigates through the *DataReader* at the same time. This change alone would save me one or two reboots a week.

> **Tip**   In the preceding code snippet, I use the efficient *GetString* method of the *DataReader*. There are many different *Get* methods to obtain the variable types supported. An alternative is to use syntax such as *dr["FieldName"]* or *dr.GetBoolean(dr.GetOrdinal("BoolFieldName"))*. The problem with the *dr["FieldName"]* syntax is that the returned value is an object and so must be cast to the correct type. In this example, I know the field ordinals already, and so by calling *GetString*, I save a field name lookup.

Accessing Data Using ASP.NET Forms

In this chapter and in Chapter 10, we'll work through an example involving a system to distribute golfing articles. I do a great deal of work for the Golf Society of the U.S. and its publication, *Player* magazine. One of the things that we have long wanted to do is find additional ways to provide content to our syndication partners. Currently, if our partners want our articles, they link to a virtual directory on our Web site. The virtual directories look like the syndication partner's Web site, but if the partner changes the look and feel of their site, we need to change our site as well.

One solution to this problem is to use an XML Web service. (XML Web services are discussed in more detail in Chapter 10.) This way, syndication partners can use any Simple Object Access Protocol (SOAP)–compliant client to connect to the XML Web service and then request articles at their convenience. Once the XML Web service is in place, several other types of services could be provided. For example, many syndication partners might want to report on the latest golf tournament scores. An XML Web service is the perfect way to provide that content in a way that can be massaged by the syndication partners.

To support such an XML Web service, in this chapter we'll use a small database named GolfArticles. In addition to the articles, the GolfArticles database will contain customer information that will indicate whether the user has access to the article in question. The database can be found on the companion CD.

The *DataGrid* Server Control

The ASP.NET *DataGrid* server control is a reasonably flexible control that allows you to create grids to display, edit, and delete rows of data. Figure 9-1 shows a simple grid for displaying some of the *Customer* table data.

In addition to the data columns (*CustomerID*, *CompanyName*, *UserName*, *Password*, and *DateEntered*), there are two additional columns. The first column contains an Edit link for each row, and the second column contains a Delete link for each row. In a traditional Visual Basic 6.0 data-bound grid, you'd generally just navigate to the row in question and type away. The Edit and Delete links are used to place a single row in edit mode and delete a single row. When you click on the Edit link in one of the rows, the data grid changes the row to edit mode, as shown in Figure 9-2.

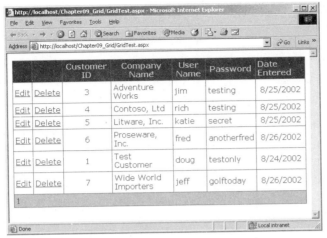

Figure 9-1 The page produced by GridTest.aspx, showing a simple ASP.NET data grid

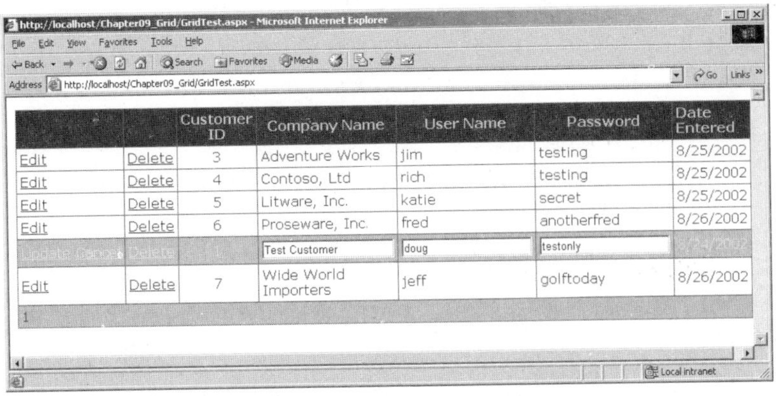

Figure 9-2 GridTest.aspx, showing a row in edit mode

You can now make changes to all the bound column entries in this row, except the *CustomerID* and *DateEntered* columns, which I've declared as read-only.

Still less than satisfying, visually, in this example are the Edit, Delete, Update, and Cancel links. Let's look at this page in design mode in Visual Studio .NET, and see what we can do to improve it it. Figure 9-3 shows GridTest.aspx in Visual Studio .NET.

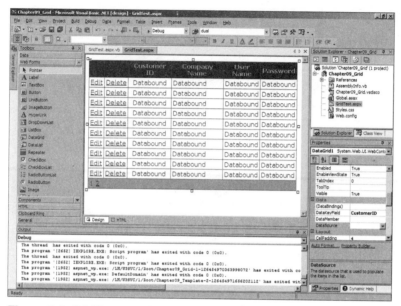

Figure 9-3 GridTest.aspx in design mode in Visual Studio .NET

Modifying a Data Grid Using the Visual Studio .NET Designer

The *DataGrid* server control has literally hundreds of properties, some of which are visible in the Properties window in the lower right in Figure 9-3. You can certainly adjust these properties using just the Properties window. However, several tools are available that can help you modify the look and feel of the data grid. If you right-click on the data grid in the designer, you'll see a shortcut menu containing a number of options; the two most interesting options are Auto Format and Property Builder.

Figure 9-4 shows the Auto Format dialog box. The Auto Format dialog box allows the developer to change literally dozens of options by selecting one of the predefined color schemes. The *ItemStyle*, *AlternatingItemStyle*, and *EditItemStyle* properties each include many settings to control color, fonts, borders and cascading style sheets. Selecting a scheme changes all these styles at once.

The other significant tool to assist the developer in creating a data grid is the Property Builder, shown in Figure 9-5. The Property Builder dialog box can be used to create individual columns, customizing the header text, the data field that will be used to fill the column, and the format of the header or items columns. I used this dialog box to center the text in all headers and in the Customer ID data column.

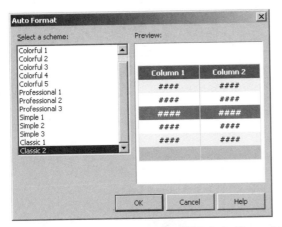

Figure 9-4 The Visual Studio .NET Auto Format dialog box

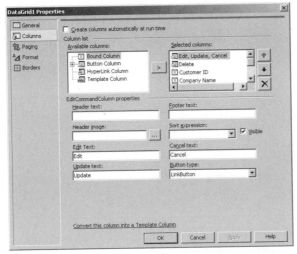

Figure 9-5 The Visual Studio .NET Property Builder for data grid components

It's not obvious from this dialog box how to replace the Edit, Update, and Cancel links with images. The less than obvious solution is to include an image link in the Edit Text box of the Property Builder dialog box. For example, changing the Edit link to *<IMG SRC=Edit.jpg>* replaces the text in the Edit column with an image named Edit.jpg. The resulting page is shown in Figure 9-6. The images could be displayed without borders by setting *Border=0* in the *<IMG>* tag. Any other enhancements allowed by HTML images can also be added by modifying the *<IMG>* tag.

> **Tip** An advantage of using the Property Builder to add the *<IMG>* tags to the *EditText* attribute and the rest of the text attributes is that the Property Builder will properly escape the characters not allowed in attributes. For instance, *<IMG SRC=Edit.jpg>* will be replaced by *<IMG SRC=Edit..JPG>*.

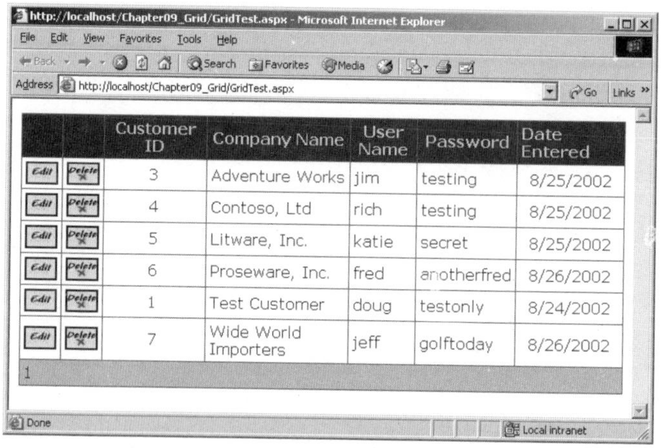

Figure 9-6 GridText.aspx, with images replacing the text links

> **Note** The small images added to Figure 9-6 are intended simply as working examples to demonstrate that you *can* add images to data grids. If you're no better than me at creating artistic images, do what I do: hire a skilled graphic designer to create the images you use in your production applications.

The bar on the left side of the Property Builder dialog box includes a Paging option. Figure 9-7 shows that section of the dialog box with the paging options that can be set for the data grid.

On this page, you can specify how and whether paging will function. You can allow paging or allow custom paging, and you can specify whether page numbers should be used to allow page selection or whether you want to show previous and next links to allow users to navigate one page at a time. You can also set the number of records allowed. If you elect to allow paging and don't request custom paging, the *DataGrid* control takes care of most of the dirty work of paging.

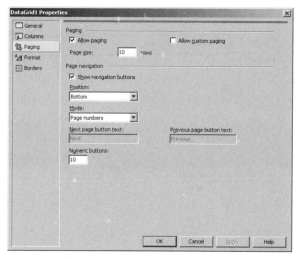

Figure 9-7 The Paging section of the Visual Studio .NET Property Builder dialog box

The final GridText.aspx file is shown in Listing 9-1.

```
<%@ Page Language="vb" AutoEventWireup="false"
Codebehind="GridTest.aspx.vb"
Inherits="Chapter09_Grid.WebForm1"%>
<!DOCTYPE HTML PUBLIC "-//W3C//DTD HTML 4.0 Transitional//EN">
<HTML>
    <HEAD>
        <title></title>
        <meta content="Microsoft Visual Studio.NET 7.0" name="GENERATOR">
        <meta content="Visual Basic 7.0" name="CODE_LANGUAGE">
        <meta content="JavaScript" name="vs_defaultClientScript">
        <meta content="http://schemas.microsoft.com/intellisense/ie5"
            name="vs_targetSchema">
    </HEAD>
    <body>
        <form id="Form1" method="post" runat="server">
            <asp:datagrid id="DataGrid1"
                runat="server"
                Font-Names="Verdana,Arial"
                AllowPaging="True"
                BorderStyle="None"
                BorderWidth="1px"
                BorderColor="#3366CC"
                BackColor="White"
                CellPadding="4"
                AllowSorting="True"
                OnDeleteCommand="OnDelete"
```

Listing 9-1 GridTest.aspx, the source file describing the data grid shown in Figure 9-6

(continued)

Listing 9-1   *continued*

```
                    DataKeyField="CustomerID"
                    OnUpdateCommand="OnUpdate"
                    OnEditCommand="OnEdit"
                    AutoGenerateColumns="False"
                    OnCancelCommand="OnCancel">
                    <FooterStyle
                        ForeColor="#003399"
                        BackColor="#99CCCC">
                    </FooterStyle>
                    <HeaderStyle Font-Bold="True"
                        ForeColor="#CCCCFF"
                        BackColor="#003399">
                    </HeaderStyle>
                    <PagerStyle NextPageText="Next"
                        PrevPageText="Previous"
                        HorizontalAlign="Left"
                        ForeColor="#003399"
                        BackColor="#99CCCC"
                        Mode="NumericPages">
                    </PagerStyle>
                    <SelectedItemStyle Font-Bold="True"
                        ForeColor="#CCFF99"
                        BackColor="#009999">
                    </SelectedItemStyle>
                    <EditItemStyle ForeColor="Yellow"
                        BackColor="#99CCCC">
                    </EditItemStyle>
                    <ItemStyle ForeColor="#003399"
                        BackColor="White">
                    </ItemStyle>
                    <Columns>
                        <asp:EditCommandColumn
                            ButtonType="LinkButton"
                            UpdateText="&lt;img src=Update.jpg&gt;"
                            CancelText="&lt;img src=Cancel.jpg&gt;"
                            EditText="&lt;IMG src=Edit.jpg&gt;">
                        </asp:EditCommandColumn>
                        <asp:ButtonColumn
                            Text="&lt;IMG SRC=Delete.JPG&gt;"
                            CommandName="Delete">
                            <HeaderStyle HorizontalAlign="Center">
                            </HeaderStyle>
                        </asp:ButtonColumn>
                        <asp:BoundColumn
                            DataField="CustomerID"
                            ReadOnly="True"
                            HeaderText="Customer ID">
```

```
                        <HeaderStyle HorizontalAlign="Center">
                        </HeaderStyle>
                        <ItemStyle HorizontalAlign="Center">
                        </ItemStyle>
                    </asp:BoundColumn>
                    <asp:BoundColumn
                        DataField="CompanyName"
                        HeaderText="Company Name">
                        <HeaderStyle HorizontalAlign="Center">
                        </HeaderStyle>
                    </asp:BoundColumn>
                    <asp:BoundColumn
                        DataField="UserName"
                        HeaderText="User Name">
                        <HeaderStyle HorizontalAlign="Center">
                        </HeaderStyle>
                        <ItemStyle Width="60px">
                        </ItemStyle>
                    </asp:BoundColumn>
                    <asp:BoundColumn
                        DataField="Password"
                        HeaderText="Password">
                        <HeaderStyle HorizontalAlign="Center">
                        </HeaderStyle>
                    </asp:BoundColumn>
                </Columns>
            </asp:datagrid>
        </form>
    </body>
</HTML>
```

Every element configured in the Auto Format and Property Builder dialog boxes is present in the resulting .aspx code. For example, the following lines create the Customer ID column in the data grid:

```
<asp:BoundColumn
    DataField="CustomerID"
    ReadOnly="True"
    HeaderText="Customer ID">
    <HeaderStyle HorizontalAlign="Center">
    </HeaderStyle>
    <ItemStyle HorizontalAlign="Center">
    </ItemStyle>
</asp:BoundColumn>
```

Attributes of the *<asp:BoundColumn>* tag control the appearance of the column. The *DataField* attribute, which is the name of the data field in the data source of the grid, controls which field is in the column. The *HeaderText* attribute allows me to label the column in a more user-friendly way. The Customer ID column is read-only, as indicated by the *ReadOnly="True"* attribute/value pair. *HeaderStyle* and *ItemStyle* tags control the appearance of the header and the individual items. Dozens of attributes can be configured for each of these styles; see the MSDN documentation for details.

There's no easy, point-and-click way within Visual Studio .NET to set the event handlers used to control the behavior when the Edit, Update, Delete, and Cancel links or images are clicked. The required code is located in the *<asp:datagrid>* tag, as shown in the last three attributes in the following code snippet:

```
<asp:datagrid id="DataGrid1"
    Runat="server"
    Font-Names="Verdana,Arial"
    AllowPaging="True"
    BorderStyle="None"
    BorderWidth="1px"
    BorderColor="#3366CC"
    BackColor="White"
    CellPadding="4"
    AllowSorting="True"
    AutoGenerateColumns="False"
    DataKeyField="CustomerID"
    OnDeleteCommand="OnDelete"
    OnUpdateCommand="OnUpdate"
    OnEditCommand="OnEdit"
    OnCancelCommand="OnCancel">
```

This tag contains two other important attributes: *AutoGenerateColumns* and *DataKeyField*. If *AutoGenerateColumns* is *True*, the grid will automatically create columns based on the *DataSource* property of the *DataGrid* control. This is almost never a good idea, since the default value for the *HeaderText* property will be the column name. For example, although Microsoft SQL Server 6.5 and later allow you to use column names with spaces, such as "Company Name", using field names with spaces causes all sorts of minor problems when you're working with such tables. Using a column name of "CompanyName" is better for internal SQL Server work. The *DataKeyField* attribute is used to control the unique column in the table being displayed by the *DataGrid* control. When this attribute is set, it's more convenient to refer to the record being edited or deleted in the event handlers.

Modifying a Data Grid Using Visual Basic .NET

Listing 9-2 shows the code-behind file for GridTest.aspx, named GridTest.aspx.vb. This code handles binding to the GolfArticles database as well as updating and deleting records.

```
Imports System.Data
Imports System.Data.SqlClient

Public Class WebForm1
    Inherits System.Web.UI.Page
    Protected WithEvents DataGrid1 _
      As System.Web.UI.WebControls.DataGrid
    Protected cn As System.Data.SqlClient.SqlConnection
    Protected da As System.Data.SqlClient.SqlDataAdapter

#Region " Web Form Designer Generated Code "

    'This call is required by the Web Form Designer.
    <System.Diagnostics.DebuggerStepThrough()> _
    Private Sub InitializeComponent()

    End Sub

    Private Sub Page_Init(ByVal sender As System.Object, _
    ByVal e As System.EventArgs) Handles MyBase.Init
        'CODEGEN: This method call is required
        'by the Web Form Designer
        'Do not modify it using the code editor.
        InitializeComponent()
    End Sub

#End Region

    Private Sub Page_Load(ByVal sender As System.Object, _
    ByVal e As System.EventArgs) Handles MyBase.Load
        'Put user code to initialize the page here
        If Me.IsPostBack <> True Then
            doDataBind()
        End If
    End Sub

    Protected Overridable Sub OnDelete( _
    ByVal Sender As Object, ByVal e As DataGridCommandEventArgs)
        Dim dr As DataRow
        Dim item As String
        Dim cmd As SqlCommand
        Me.cn = New SqlConnection("server=localhost;" + _
          "Integrated Security=SSPI;Initial Catalog=GolfArticles")
        Try
            Me.cn.Open()
            item = e.Item.Cells(2).Text
```

Listing 9-2 GridText.aspx.vb, the code-behind file for GridTest.aspx   *(continued)*

Listing 9-2 *continued*

```
            cmd = New SqlCommand( _
                "Delete FROM Customer WHERE CustomerID=" + item, cn)
            cmd.ExecuteNonQuery()
        Catch eDelete As Exception
            ' Should handle error
        Finally
            cn.Close()
        End Try
        doDataBind()
    End Sub

    Protected Overridable Sub OnEdit(ByVal sender As Object, _
    ByVal e As DataGridCommandEventArgs)
        DataGrid1.EditItemIndex = e.Item.ItemIndex
        doDataBind()
    End Sub

    Protected Overridable Sub OnUpdate( _
    ByVal sender As Object, _
    ByVal e As DataGridCommandEventArgs)
        Dim UserName As String
        Dim password As String
        Dim companyName As String
        Dim CustomerID As String

        companyName = Request.Form.Item(1).ToString()
        UserName = Request.Form.Item(2).ToString()
        password = Request.Form.Item(3).ToString()

        Dim cmd As SqlCommand
        Me.cn = New SqlConnection("server=localhost;" + _
          "Integrated Security=SSPI;Initial Catalog=GolfArticles")
        Try
            Me.cn.Open()
            CustomerID = e.Item.Cells(2).Text

            cmd = New SqlCommand( _
              "UPDATE Customer SET CompanyName='" + _
              companyName + _
              "', UserName='" + UserName + _
              "', Password='" + password + _
              "' WHERE CustomerID=" + CustomerID, cn)
            cmd.ExecuteNonQuery()
        Catch eUpdate As Exception
            ' Should handle error
```

```
    Finally
        cn.Close()
    End Try
    DataGrid1.EditItemIndex = -1

    doDataBind()
End Sub

Protected Overridable Sub OnCancel( _
ByVal sender As Object, _
ByVal e As DataGridCommandEventArgs)
    DataGrid1.EditItemIndex = -1
    doDataBind()
End Sub

' Centralized method to do data binding, when required.
Protected Sub doDataBind()
    Dim ds As DataSet
    Dim bc As BoundColumn
    Me.cn = New SqlConnection("server=localhost;" + _
        "Integrated Security=SSPI;Initial Catalog=GolfArticles")
    Me.cn.Open()
    Me.da = New SqlDataAdapter( _
    "Select * from Customer ORDER BY CompanyName", cn)
    ds = New DataSet("Customers")
    da.Fill(ds, "Customers")
    Me.DataGrid1.DataSource = _
        ds.Tables("Customers").DefaultView
    bc = New BoundColumn()
    bc.DataField = "DateEntered"
    bc.HeaderText = "Date Entered"
    bc.ReadOnly = True
    bc.ItemStyle.HorizontalAlign = HorizontalAlign.Center
    bc.DataFormatString = "{0:d}"
    Me.DataGrid1.Columns.Add(bc)
    Me.DataGrid1.DataBind()

    End Sub
End Class
```

The *Page_Load* event handler is a simple method. When the page is loaded, if this is the first time the page is being loaded (meaning that this is *not* a postback), the page calls the *doDataBind* method of the class, located toward the end of Listing 9-2. Much of the code in *doDataBind* is involved in the creating of a data source and setting the data source of the *DataGrid* control. The careful observer will notice in Figure 9-7 and Listing 9-1 that the Date Entered column is not created in GridTest.aspx. The *doDataBind* method shows how the additional column appears, as follows:

```
bc = New BoundColumn()
bc.DataField = "DateEntered"
bc.HeaderText = "Date Entered"
bc.ReadOnly = True
bc.ItemStyle.HorizontalAlign = HorizontalAlign.Center
bc.DataFormatString = "{0:d}"
Me.DataGrid1.Columns.Add(bc)
Me.DataGrid1.DataBind()
```

In this code section, I first create a new instance of a *BoundColumn* object. I set several properties, the most interesting of which is *DataFormatString*. By default, date fields will be displayed in the form *mm/dd/yyyy hh:mm:ss XM*. In many cases, display of the date with the time down to the second is overkill. In this example, I use a format string of *{0:d}*. The *0* refers to the first and only value passed into the format string—the date. The *d* after the colon tells the .NET Framework that the date should be displayed in short date format: *mm/dd/yyyy*. The *BoundColumn* object is one of several different column types that can be added to a *DataGrid* control. When programmatically adding the new column, I also set the *ReadOnly* property to *True* because the *DateEntered* field isn't designed to be modified. The complete list of column types is shown in Table 9-1.

Table 9-1 Data Grid Column Types

Column Type	Description
BoundColumn	Displays a column bound to a field in the *DataSource* property of the *DataGrid* control.
ButtonColumn	Displays a command button for each item in the column. This column type allows you to add a column of custom buttons, such as an Add button.
EditCommandColumn	Displays a column that contains a column like the Edit or Delete column in the previous examples in this chapter.
HyperLinkColumn	Displays the contents of each item in the column as a hyperlink. This column type could be used to link to more information about a particular row, for example.
TemplateColumn	Displays each item in a column following a specified template. This column type allows a great deal of customization of grid appearance.

Once the column object is created and the required properties are set, the next step is to add the column to the *Columns* collection of the *DataGrid* object, using the *Add* method.

The final step in *doDataBind* is actually calling the *DataBind* method of the *DataGrid* object. There's also a *DataBind* method on the page itself, and if there were more than a single data-bound control, that method would be called rather than the method on the *DataGrid* object. It's critical that when the page is first loaded (and when *IsPostBack* is false within the *Page_Load* event) and whenever the data source changes, the data-bound controls are re-bound. This binding is *not* a task that the . NET Framework or Visual Studio .NET will do for you automatically. You *must* explicitly bind the data.

> **Note**   I'm not using the Visual Studio .NET tools to visually generate the data sources and connections. There are several advantages to using Visual Studio .NET, including the creation of fully type-safe datasets. The disadvantage is that some of the code generated is quite bizarre. For example, you might see dozens of lines of SQL code created by Visual Studio .NET that are cut off arbitrarily at the right margin, with the rest of the SQL code concatenated on subsequent lines, meaning that you can see lines with column names or SQL keywords split in half. The resulting string that Visual Studio. NET creates contains valid SQL statements when concatenated together, but they're impossible to understand or maintain. The examples in the balance of this book won't use the visual tools to create data sources and connections. I find the amount of extra effort minimal compared with the need to subsequently continue updating the code using the visual designer.

The code-behind page contains event handlers for each of the action buttons. *OnDelete*, the event handler for the Delete button, is shown here:

```
Protected Overridable Sub OnDelete( _
ByVal Sender As Object, ByVal e As DataGridCommandEventArgs)
    Dim dr As DataRow

    Dim item As String
    Dim cmd As SqlCommand
    Me.cn = New SqlConnection("server=localhost;" + _
      "Integrated Security=SSPI;Initial Catalog=GolfArticles")
    Try
        Me.cn.Open()
        item = e.Item.Cells(2).Text
        cmd = New SqlCommand( _
          "Delete FROM Customer WHERE CustomerID=" + item, cn)
        cmd.ExecuteNonQuery()
```

(continued)

```
Catch eDelete As Exception
    ' Should handle error
Finally
    cn.Close()
End Try
doDataBind()

End Sub
```

Note that ASP.NET data binding is read-only data binding. To make changes to data will require that you write a reasonable amount of code in the code-behind file.

The first order of business is to get a connection established, just as we did in the Chapter 8 examples. Next a *SqlCommand* object is created, passing in a SQL statement. In this case, I need to delete the currently selected row in the data grid. A *DataGridCommandEventArgs* object is passed in to *OnDelete* in the *e* parameter, that object has a property named *Item*, and *Item* has a collection named *Cells*. *Cells* is a zero-based collection of *TableCell* objects that contains an element for each cell in the selected row. Using this information, I can get the *CustomerID* field for the selected row, which is in the third column, and thus referenced as *e.Item.Cells(2)*. I use this value to create the SQL delete statement passed to the *SqlCommand* object.

> **Tip**   In real-world examples, it might be better to design objects to cre-
> ate connections for classes like this that have several different methods that
> each need to obtain connections. Thus, a class might have a *GetConnection*
> method that returns a *SqlConnection* or *OleDbConnection* object, as appro-
> priate. Taking this concept a step further, it's certainly reasonable in a larger
> system to isolate all data access classes into a data access layer (DAL). In
> the COM world, the DAL was often located on a different machine from IIS.
> In ASP.NET, there's less reason to do this, and in general, although I would
> move toward creating a separate DAL in a larger system, I would be reluc-
> tant to partition it off onto a separate machine or set of machines. Learning
> how to handle the ASP.NET DAL is an evolving art, and no clear "best prac-
> tices" have emerged.

Once the *SqlCommand* object is set up, I call the *ExecuteNonQuery* method (indicating that the command won't return any records). Finally, I call *doDataBind* because I want the page to get the latest view of the data. This is important because if, for example, I was doing an update, I might change the field that the grid is sorted on, thus changing the location in the grid. The *OnUpdate* event procedure follows a pattern similar to *OnDelete*, passing a SQL update command into the *SqlCommand* constructor rather than the SQL delete command in *OnDelete*.

> **Note**   I could have just as easily used the *OleDbConnection* and *OleDbCommand* objects and their related objects. Because I'm working with SQL Server data, using the objects in the *SqlClient* namespace is more appropriate.

The remaining two event handlers, *OnEdit* and *OnCancel*, are quite different from the *OnDelete* and *OnUpdate* handlers. *OnEdit* is a short event handler, as shown here:

```
Protected Overridable Sub OnEdit(ByVal sender As Object, _
ByVal e As DataGridCommandEventArgs)
    DataGrid1.EditItemIndex = e.Item.ItemIndex
    doDataBind()
End Sub
```

Here I set the *EditItemIndex* property of the *DataGrid* object to the *ItemIndex* property of the *Item* property of the *DataGridCommandEventArgs* object passed into the event handler. Finally, I call *doDataBind*. *OnCancel* is designed to cancel edit mode, and the event handler is identical, except that *EditItemIndex* is set to −1, to indicate that no item is currently selected. *OnUpdate* also sets *EditItemIndex* to −1 when it has finished the update so that no row will be displayed in edit mode after an update.

> **Note**   There's one problem with the code in *OnUpdate*. Can you see it? When I create the SQL string for the update command, I properly enclose strings passed into the UPDATE statement in single quotation marks. But what happens if one of the strings has a single quotation mark embedded in it—for example, as in a company name such as "O'Reilly's Golf"? These internal single quotation marks will cause an error because SQL Server will think that the company name ends after the first "O" and won't be able to parse the rest. One solution would be to replace each single quotation mark character with two single quotation marks, which SQL Server interprets as a single quote character embedded within the string. A better solution is to use parameters; the next example will use a stored procedure and parameters.

The *Repeater* Server Control

The *DataGrid* control is certainly a convenient control to use for displaying the results of a search or displaying simple records. However, *DataGrid* has some deficiencies as an editing tool. First and foremost, notice the difference in the overall width of the data grids shown in Figure 9-1 and Figure 9-2. This difference is a bit of a problem when you're working with the number of fields in the example *DataGrid*, but it would be a far worse problem if there were many more fields.

The second deficiency is the lack of easy control over how the editing takes place. One solution to this problem is to use *TemplateColumn* objects to describe what the column should look like when it's being viewed and when it's being edited. Using a *TemplateColumn* object and setting the *EditItemTemplate* property is a reasonable approach when perhaps only one or two columns in a record are to be edited.

The *Customer* table that we've been working with contains both of these deficiencies. First, the *Customer* table includes date columns and an e-mail column. These columns require special validation—in the case of the *ContractEnds* field, a check for a valid date, and in the case of the *ContactEMail* field, a check for a plausible e-mail address. Next, the *Customer* table has quite a few more columns than could be conveniently displayed one per column across the page. Listing 9-3 shows the SQL statement to create the full *Customer* table.

```
CREATE TABLE [dbo].[Customer] (
    [CustomerID] [int] IDENTITY (1, 1) NOT NULL ,
    [CompanyName] [nvarchar] (50) NOT NULL ,
    [Address] [nvarchar] (50) NULL ,
    [City] [nvarchar] (50) NULL ,
    [State] [nvarchar] (10) NULL ,
    [PostalCode] [nvarchar] (20) NULL ,
    [ContactFirstName] [nvarchar] (50) NULL ,
    [ContactLastName] [nvarchar] (50) NULL ,
    [ContactEMail] [nvarchar] (128) NULL ,
    [ContractEnds] [datetime] NOT NULL ,
    [ContractLevel] [int] NOT NULL ,
    [UserName] [nvarchar] (50) NULL ,
    [Password] [nvarchar] (50) NULL ,
    [DateEntered] [datetime] NOT NULL ,
    [DateModified] [datetime] NULL
) ON [PRIMARY]
```

Listing 9-3 SQL statement to create the *Customer* table

Even if I let the database maintain the *DateEntered* and *DateModified* fields, there are still a lot of fields to maintain. Just viewing the fields from a grid would be problematic. Fortunately, other alternatives are available. Figure 9-8 shows a different representation created using a different server control, the *Repeater* control.

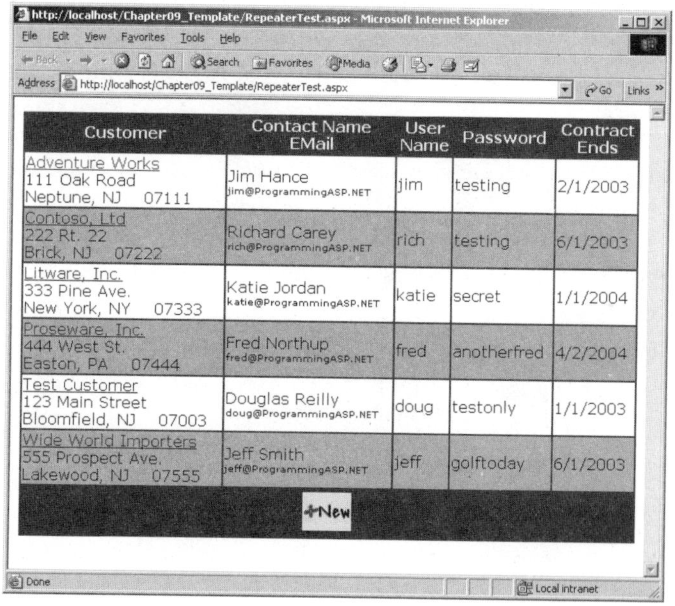

Figure 9-8 A different way to look at the *Customer* table data, using a *Repeater* control

There's clearly a great deal more information available on this listing page than in the example shown in Figure 9-1. Every bit of maintainable information (all the columns in the table, except the automatically maintained date fields) is visible in this view. I've modified the font of the e-mail addresses, since the example addresses tended to be much longer than the actual contact names displayed just above in the same column. The first and second columns contain many different fields, displayed in a convenient way. For example, the *CompanyName* and its associated address information is formatted exactly as you would normally want to see it. While this flexibility comes at the expense of a little more work than the *DataGrid* control, the advantage is that you have total control over the appearance. Just as important, if you work with HTML interface designers, they might be a bit more comfortable with the *Repeater* control than the *DataGrid* control.

Repeater Control Basics

The *Repeater* control acts in many ways like the *DataGrid* control, but it gives you greater flexibility at the individual column level. There are no restrictions on how many or how few columns you display, and technically, you don't have to use a tabular view at all. The information displayed for each record bound to the *Repeater* control could be presented without any formatting or could be formatted using only *
* and *<P>* tags. Most examples of the *Repeater* control, including the example shown here, do in fact use HTML tables to display their data. The *Repeater* control doesn't offer some of the conveniences of the *DataGrid* control, such as paging. *Repeater* does offer some assistance with events raised within the control; however, I won't make use of that support in this example.

> **Tip** The *DataList* control is similar to the *Repeater* control. The *DataList* control adds a neat feature: the ability to render multicolumn representations of data. You can set the *RepeatColumns*, *RepeatDirection*, and *Repeat-Layout* properties to control how multiple columns are displayed. The *RepeatLayout* property controls whether the control renders the data in tables or by using a flow layout without tables.

The *Repeater* control supports five templates. Each of the templates specifies how a certain portion of the data fed to the *Repeater* control should be formatted. The templates are described in Table 9-2.

Like *DataGrid*, the *Repeater* control also has a *DataSource* property. It's important to set this property and ensure that it can be read, because without data, the *Repeater* code won't be rendered.

> **Tip** Although doing so is not required, it's often helpful to create the *Repeater* control initially with only the *HeaderTemplate*, *ItemTemplate*, and *FooterTemplate* templates defined. Once you're satisfied with the display, especially *ItemTemplate*, you can copy the *ItemTemplate* rendering code into the *AlternatingItemTemplate*. Otherwise, you'll have to debug both *ItemTemplate* and *AlternateItemTemplate* at the same time, making changes in both simultaneously, which can be prone to errors.

Table 9-2 Templates Supported by the *Repeater* Control

Template	Description
ItemTemplate	Elements that are rendered once for each element in the data source. Both Web server controls and HTML server controls can be added to this template.
AlternatingItemTemplate	If specified, every other item is rendered using this template rather than *ItemTemplate*. This template can be used, for example, to obtain a gray bar effect, with every other item using one of two color schemes. (Figure 9-8 uses *AlternatingItemTemplate* to render one row on a white background, the next on a light blue background.)
HeaderTemplate	Rendered once, this template often contains code to render the start of a table and the header of a table. Note that because the closing element of the table will not be part of this tag, designing a *Repeater* control requires using the HTML view in Visual Studio .NET.
FooterTemplate	The bookend for the other side of the *Repeater* control. Tags opened but not closed in *HeaderTemplate* should be closed here.
SeparatorTemplate	This template is used to render some text between items. If, for example, the *Repeater* control will be used to render some complex HTML between each row, placing that complex code in *SeparatorTemplate* means that it will appear only once.

The code for RepeaterTest.aspx is shown in Listing 9-4.

```
<%@ Page language="c#"
Codebehind="RepeaterTest.aspx.cs"
AutoEventWireup="false"
Inherits="Chapter09_Template.WebForm1" %>
<!DOCTYPE HTML PUBLIC "-//W3C//DTD HTML 4.0 Transitional//EN" >
<HTML>
    <HEAD>
        <meta name="GENERATOR" Content="Microsoft Visual Studio 7.0">
        <meta name="CODE_LANGUAGE" Content="C#">
        <meta name="vs_defaultClientScript"
            content="JavaScript (ECMAScript)">
        <meta name="vs_targetSchema"
            content="http://schemas.microsoft.com/intellisense/ie5">
    </HEAD>\
```

Listing 9-4 RepeaterTest.aspx, showing a more complicated view of the *Customer* table

(continued)

Listing 9-4 *continued*

```
<body>
<form id="Form1" method="post" runat="server">
    <asp:Repeater id="Repeater1" runat="server">
        <HeaderTemplate>
            <table width="640" bgcolor="#0033ff">
                <tr bgcolor="#0033ff">
                    <td align="center">
                        <font
                            face="Verdana,Arial"
                            color="#ffff99">
                            <b>Customer</b>
                        </font>
                    </td>
                    <td align="center">
                        <font
                            face="Verdana,Arial"
                            color="#ffff99">
                            <b>Contact Name
                            <br>
                            EMail</b></font>
                    </td>
                    <td align="center">
                        <font
                            face="Verdana,Arial"
                            color="#ffff99">
                            <b>User
                            <BR>
                            Name</b></font>
                    </td>
                    <td align="center">
                        <font
                            face="Verdana,Arial"
                            color="#ffff99">
                            <b>Password</b>
                        </font>
                    </td>
                    <td align="center">
                        <font
                            face="Verdana,Arial"
                            color="#ffff99">
                            <b>Contract
                            <br>
                            Ends</b></font>
                    </td>
                </tr>
```

```
</HeaderTemplate>
<ItemTemplate>
    <tr bgcolor="#ffffff" width="200">
        <td>
            <font face="Verdana,Arial">
                <a href='EditCustomer.aspx?CustomerID=
                    <%# DataBinder.Eval(Container.DataItem,
                    "CustomerID") %>'>
                    <%# DataBinder.Eval(Container.DataItem,
                    "CompanyName") %>
                </a>
                <br>
                <%# DataBinder.Eval(Container.DataItem,
                "Address") %>
                <br>
                <%# DataBinder.Eval(Container.DataItem,
                "City") %>,
                <%# DataBinder.Eval(Container.DataItem,
                "State") %>
                  
                <%# DataBinder.Eval(Container.DataItem,
                "PostalCode") %>
            </font>
        </td>
        <td>
            <font face="Verdana,Arial">
                <%# DataBinder.Eval(Container.DataItem,
                "ContactFirstName") %>
                <%# DataBinder.Eval(Container.DataItem,
                "ContactLastName") %>
                <br>
                <font size="1">
                    <%# DataBinder.Eval(Container.DataItem,
                    "ContactEMail") %>
                </font></font>
        </td>
        <td>
            <font face="Verdana,Arial">
                <%# DataBinder.Eval(Container.DataItem,
                "UserName") %>
            </font>
        </td>
        <td>
            <font face="Verdana,Arial">
                <%# DataBinder.Eval(Container.DataItem,
                "Password") %>
            </font>
        </td>
```

(continued)

Listing 9-4   *continued*

```
                    <td>
                        <font face="Verdana,Arial">
                            <%# DataBinder.Eval(Container.DataItem,
                            "ContractEnds","{0:d}") %>
                        </font>
                    </td>
                </tr>
            </ItemTemplate>
            <AlternatingItemTemplate>
                <tr bgcolor="#66ccff">
                    <td>
                        <font face="Verdana,Arial">
                            <a href='EditCustomer.aspx?CustomerID=
                                <%# DataBinder.Eval(Container.DataItem,
                                "CustomerID") %>'>
                                <%# DataBinder.Eval(Container.DataItem,
                                "CompanyName") %>
                            </a>
                            <br>
                            <%# DataBinder.Eval(Container.DataItem,
                            "Address") %>
                            <br>
                            <%# DataBinder.Eval(Container.DataItem,
                            "City") %>,
                            <%# DataBinder.Eval(Container.DataItem,
                            "State") %>
                              
                            <%# DataBinder.Eval(Container.DataItem,
                            "PostalCode") %>
                        </font>
                    </td>
                    <td>
                        <font face="Verdana,Arial">
                            <%# DataBinder.Eval(Container.DataItem,
                            "ContactFirstName") %>
                            <%# DataBinder.Eval(Container.DataItem,
                            "ContactLastName") %>
                            <br>
                            <font size="1">
                                <%# DataBinder.Eval(Container.DataItem,
                                "ContactEMail") %>
                            </font></font>
                    </td>
                    <td>
                        <font face="Verdana,Arial">
                            <%# DataBinder.Eval(Container.DataItem,
                            "UserName") %>
                        </font>
                    </td>
```

```
                <td>
                    <font face="Verdana,Arial">
                        <%# DataBinder.Eval(Container.DataItem,
                        "Password") %>
                    </font>
                </td>
                <td>
                    <font face="Verdana,Arial">
                        <%# DataBinder.Eval(Container.DataItem,
                        "ContractEnds","{0:d}") %>
                    </font>
                </td>
            </tr>
        </AlternatingItemTemplate>
        <FooterTemplate>
            <tr>
                <td colspan=5 align=center>
                    <a href="EditCustomer.aspx?CustomerID=0">
                    <img src="AddNew.jpg"
                    Alt="Add New"></a>
                </td>
            </tr>
            </table>
        </FooterTemplate>
    </asp:Repeater>
    <p>
    </p>
    <asp:Label id="Label1" runat="server"></asp:Label>
    </form>
    </body>
</HTML>
```

Caution   Because the *Repeater* control allows you to specify incomplete HTML within individual elements such as a *<TABLE>* start tag without a nearby, properly nested end tag, you may not be able to display a page with a *Repeater* control in the Visual Studio .NET Design view. Because of the way that the *Repeater* control renders when run, the resulting HTML will be correct. You can edit pages with a *Repeater* control in HTML view. The error messages that appear when you try to switch to Design view will not always make it obvious what the problem is.

The code in RepeaterTest.aspx is fairly simple HTML interspersed with ASP.NET tags. Different in this example is the method used to bind data to the *Repeater* control. All data is bound using the *Eval* method of the *DataBinder* class. All data binding is done within the <%# %> delimiters.

> **Note**   The <%# %> delimiters are used only for data binding. The expression inside these delimiters is evaluated whenever *DataBind* is called. This syntax is different from the ASP syntax for displaying the contents of a variable—for example, <%=foo%>. The <%= %> delimiters are still supported, but they're not used in data binding.

The *Eval* method has two overloads, both of which are used in this example. The syntax for the first overload is shown here:

```
[Visual Basic.NET]
Overloads Public Shared Function Eval( _
    ByVal container As Object, _
    ByVal expression As String _
) As Object
[C#]
public static object Eval(
    object container,
    string expression
);
```

The *container* parameter is the object reference that the expression is evaluated against. In all the uses of *Eval* in Listing 9-4, *container* is *Container.DataItem*. This refers back to the *DataSource* property of the *Repeater* control. The second parameter, *expression*, is the field name, as it appears in the data source. Spelling does count, and the syntax for the expression can be more complex if instead of a *DataReader* object you're using a *DataSet* object. For example, the syntax could be *Tables[0].DefaultView.[0].CompanyName* rather than simply *CompanyName*, as *DataSet* objects can refer to multiple tables.

The second overload to the *Eval* method is as follows, with an additional string:

```
[Visual Basic.NET]
Overloads Public Shared Function Eval( _
    ByVal container As Object, _
    ByVal expression As String, _
    ByVal format As String _
) As String
```

```
[C#]
public static string Eval(
    object container,
    string expression,
    string format
);
```

The additional parameter, *format*, is a standard .NET Framework format string. For example, the following code snippet, from Listing 9-4, will use the *DataSource* property of the containing *Repeater* control, get the *ContractEnds* field, and format it as a date:

```
<%# DataBinder.Eval(Container.DataItem,
"ContractEnds","{0:d}") %>
```

The MSDN documentation contains complete documentation on format strings.

Listing 9-4 uses all of the templates described in Table 9-2 except *SeparatorTemplate*. *ItemTemplate* and *AlternatingItemTemplate* are identical, except for the background color on the *<tr>* tags. *HeaderTemplate* contains the start tag of the HTML table element as well as a row of headers. *FooterTemplate* contains the row that holds the image to allow you to add a new record, as well as the HTML table end tag. RepeaterTest.aspx includes several HTML anchor tags to link to another form, named EditCustomer.aspx. More on that form later in this chapter, in the section "Creating Data Entry Pages."

> **Tip**   One problem I noticed initially in RepeaterTest.aspx was that Visual Studio .NET was reformatting my code in a way that caused problems. For example, an extra space was appearing between the first name and the last name. The culprit was the addition of an unwanted line break between the binding code for the first name and the last name that was somehow causing an additional space in the output. The solution is to choose Options on the Tools menu, and in the Options dialog box, navigate to Text Editor and then HTML/XML and Format. Then clear the Apply Automatic Formatting: When Saving Document and When Switching From Design To HTML/XML View check boxes. This is the first project I've worked on in which the automatic formatting caused me any pain, but I'll leave it off for now, just to be safe. There are a number of settings that can make the text editor easier to use that you should investigate in the Options dialog box.

RepeaterTest.aspx also has a code-behind file, named RepeaterTest.aspx.cs, shown in Listing 9-5.

```csharp
using System;
using System.Collections;
using System.ComponentModel;
using System.Data;
using System.Data.SqlClient;
using System.Drawing;
using System.Web;
using System.Web.SessionState;
using System.Web.UI;
using System.Web.UI.WebControls;
using System.Web.UI.HtmlControls;

namespace Chapter09_Template
{
    /// <summary>
    /// Summary description for WebForm1.
    /// </summary>
    public class WebForm1 : System.Web.UI.Page
    {
        protected System.Web.UI.WebControls.Repeater Repeater1;
        protected System.Web.UI.WebControls.Label Label1;
        protected System.Data.SqlClient.SqlCommand cmd;

        public WebForm1()
        {
            Page.Init += new System.EventHandler(Page_Init);
        }

        private void Page_Load(object sender, System.EventArgs e)
        {
            SqlConnection cn = new SqlConnection("server=localhost;" +
                "Integrated Security=SSPI;Initial Catalog=GolfArticles");
            SqlCommand cmd;
            cmd=new SqlCommand(
                "Select * from Customer Order By CompanyName",cn);
            try
            {
                cn.Open();
                Repeater1.DataSource=
                    cmd.ExecuteReader(
                    CommandBehavior.CloseConnection);

                this.DataBind();
            }
```

Listing 9-5 RepeaterTest.aspx.cs, the code-behind file for the *Repeater* class test page

```
            catch (System.Exception eLoad)
            {
                Label1.Text=eLoad.Message;
            }
        }

        private void Page_Init(object sender, EventArgs e)
        {
            //
            // CODEGEN: This call is required by the
            // ASP.NET Web Form Designer.
            //
            InitializeComponent();
        }


        #region Web Form Designer generated code
        /// <summary>
        /// Required method for Designer support - do not modify
        /// the contents of this method with the code editor.
        /// </summary>
        private void InitializeComponent()
        {
            this.Load += new System.EventHandler(this.Page_Load);

        }
        #endregion
    }
}
```

RepeaterTest.aspx.cs has a single method that contains code critical to the operation of the *Repeater* control. In the *Page_Load* method, the following lines are most important:

```
cn.Open();
Repeater1.DataSource=
    cmd.ExecuteReader(
    CommandBehavior.CloseConnection);

this.DataBind();
```

First I open the previously created connection object. Next I set the *DataSource* property of the *Repeater* object to the return value from the *ExecuteReader* method of the *SqlCommand* object. *ExecuteReader* returns a *DataReader* object, and because I specify *CommandBehavior.CloseConnection*, the connection will be closed when the data reader is closed. Finally, I call *DataBind*. Once again, without this call, the data won't be bound, and nothing will be displayed in the *Repeater* control. And again, this code won't be added by the .NET Framework, nor by Visual Studio .NET. Whenever bound data doesn't appear, checking to see that *DataBind* is actually called (and called at the correct level) is critical.

Using Caching to Improve Performance and Scalability

One feature of ASP.NET that can improve the performance and scalability of applications displaying dynamic data is *output caching*. Say that you add the following line to an aspx page:

```
<%@ OutputCache Duration="20" VaryByParam="None" %>
```

When the page is requested, rather than actually running the underlying code, the page is served up directly from the ASP.NET cache. For pages that are expensive to generate but that don't change frequently, output caching can provide a huge performance benefit.

In the example *OutputCache* directive above, when the page is requested for the first time, the .NET Framework will run whatever code is required to generate the page. Anyone rerunning the page within the next 20 seconds (as specified by the *Duration* attribute) will get the cached copy rather than a copy created by rerunning the underlying code. The first client to request the page after the 20 seconds have expired will get a newly created copy of the page.

Often, a page will be called with one or more parameters, and the parameters might change the content that is displayed. For that common scenario, the *VaryByParam* attribute allows you to specify a semicolon-delimited list of parameters, or "*" for all parameters. When parameters or "*" is specified for *VaryByParam*, a separate copy of the page is cached for each set of parameters specified—or for each set of all parameters, if "*" is specified.

The same logic can be used to cache a fragment of a page. The *OutputCache* directive is also available for user controls.

ASP.NET caching works only with ASP.NET Premium edition installed on the server.

Creating Data Entry Pages

Although RepeaterTest.aspx provides a more convenient listing of the customers in the *Customer* table, it does nothing to allow editing of that data. I did, however, make the customer name and the Add New button in RepeaterTest.aspx hyperlinks. Remember the links to EditCustomer.aspx I mentioned in the previous section? Clicking on these links will take you to the page shown in Figure 9-9.

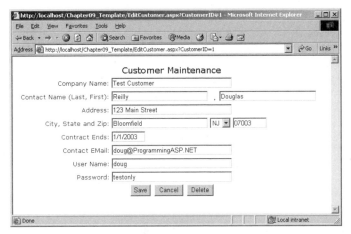

Figure 9-9 The Customer Maintenance page, EditCustomer.aspx, which allows you to edit customer records selected from RepeaterTest.aspx

The page shown in Figure 9-9 will allow you to edit or delete the current customer. It's not designed to enable you to navigate from customer record to customer record, as you might do in a traditional Microsoft Access or Visual Basic 6.0 application. However, using a limited amount of code, it does offer quite a bit of functionality. For example, let's say I changed the *ContractEnds* date to 1/32/2003, and removed the at sign (@) from the *ContactEmail* address. Figure 9-10 shows the result.

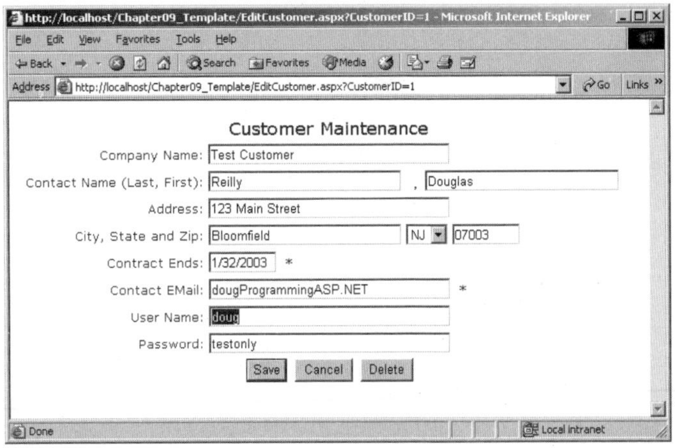

Figure 9-10 The Customer Maintenance page, showing invalid input for *ContractEnds* and *ContactEmail*

As you can see, the page displays asterisks next to the two fields that contain validation errors. The date is clearly invalid, and the e-mail address isn't valid, since there isn't an @. One thing that is important to note is that this validation took place on the client, and even if the client didn't have JavaScript working on their machine, the server-side part of the validation would have caught the errors. Also significant is that fact that each of the fields on the page is linked to at least one validation control. The State drop-down list is connected to a database table of states, located in the same GolfArticles database as the *Customer* table.

Creating the User Interface

Listing 9-6 shows EditCustomer.aspx, the file that created the pages shown in Figures 9-9 and 9-10.

```
<%@ Page Debug="true"
language="c#"
Codebehind="EditCustomer.aspx.cs"
AutoEventWireup="false"
Inherits="Chapter09_Template.EditCustomer" %>
<!DOCTYPE HTML PUBLIC "-//W3C//DTD HTML 4.0 Transitional//EN" >
<HTML>
    <HEAD>
        <META http-equiv=Content-Type
            content="text/html; charset=windows-1252">
        <meta content="Microsoft Visual Studio 7.0" name=GENERATOR>
        <meta content=C# name=CODE_LANGUAGE>
        <meta content="JavaScript (ECMAScript)"
            name=vs_defaultClientScript>
        <meta content=http://schemas.microsoft.com/intellisense/ie5
            name=vs_targetSchema>
    </HEAD>
<body>
<form id=EditCustomer method=post runat="server">
<table width=640>
    <tr>
        <td colspan=2 align=middle>
        <p><font face=Verdana,Arial
        color=#3300ff size=4>
        Customer Maintenance
        </font></p>
        </td>
    </tr>
    <tr>
        <td width="30%" align=right>
        <font face="Verdana,Arial" size=2 color="#3300ff">
        Company Name:
        </font>
        </td>
```

Listing 9-6 EditCustomer.aspx, the file used to create the Customer Maintenance page shown in Figures 9-9 and 9-10

```
        <td>
        <asp:TextBox
            id=CompanyName
            runat="server"
            MaxLength="50"
            Width="250px"
            ></asp:TextBox>
        <asp:RequiredFieldValidator
            id=RequiredFieldValidator2
            runat="server"
            ControlToValidate="CompanyName"
            ErrorMessage="*">
        </asp:RequiredFieldValidator>
        </td>
    </tr>
    <tr>
        <td width="30%" align=right>
        <font face="Verdana,Arial" size=2 color="#3300ff">
        Contact Name (Last, First):
        </font>
        </td>
        <td>
        <asp:TextBox
            id="ContactLastName"
            runat="server"
            MaxLength="50"
            Width="200px"
            ></asp:TextBox>
        <asp:RequiredFieldValidator
            id="Requiredfieldvalidator7"
            runat="server"
            ControlToValidate="ContactLastName"
            ErrorMessage="*">
        </asp:RequiredFieldValidator>, 
        <asp:TextBox
            id="ContactFirstName"
            runat="server"
            MaxLength="50"
            Width="200px"
            ></asp:TextBox>
        <asp:RequiredFieldValidator
            id="Requiredfieldvalidator8"
            runat="server"
            ControlToValidate="ContactFirstName"
            ErrorMessage="*">
        </asp:RequiredFieldValidator>
        </td>
    </tr>
```

(continued)

Listing 9-6 *continued*

```
<tr>
    <td width="30%" align=right>
    <font face="Verdana,Arial" size=2 color="#3300ff">
    Address:
    </font>
    </td>
    <td>
    <asp:TextBox
        id="Address"
        runat="server"
        MaxLength="50"
        Width="250px"
        ></asp:TextBox>
    <asp:RequiredFieldValidator
        id=RequiredFieldValidator3
        runat="server"
        ControlToValidate="Address"
        ErrorMessage="*">
    </asp:RequiredFieldValidator>
    </td>
</tr>
<tr>
    <td width="30%" align=right>
    <font face="Verdana,Arial" size=2 color="#3300ff">
    City, State and Zip:
    </font>
    </td>
    <td>
    <asp:TextBox
        id="City"
        runat="server"
        MaxLength="50"
        Width="200px"
        ></asp:TextBox>
    <asp:DropDownList
        id=ddlState
        runat="server">
    </asp:DropDownList>
    <asp:TextBox
        id="PostalCode"
        runat="server"
        MaxLength="10"
        Width="70px"
        ></asp:TextBox>
    <asp:RequiredFieldValidator
        id=RequiredFieldValidator4
        runat="server"
```

```
                Display="Dynamic"
                ControlToValidate="City"
                ErrorMessage="*">
        </asp:RequiredFieldValidator>
        <asp:RequiredFieldValidator
            id=RequiredFieldValidator5
            runat="server"
            Display="Dynamic"
            ControlToValidate="PostalCode"
            ErrorMessage="*">
        </asp:RequiredFieldValidator>
        <asp:RegularExpressionValidator
            id=RegularExpressionValidator1
            runat="server"
            ControlToValidate="PostalCode"
            ErrorMessage="*"
            ValidationExpression="\d{5}(-\d{4})?">
        </asp:RegularExpressionValidator>
        </td>
    </tr>
    <tr>
        <td width="30%" align=right>
        <font face="Verdana,Arial" size=2 color="#3300ff">
        Contract Ends:
        </font>
        </td>
        <td>
        <asp:TextBox
            id="ContractEnds"
            runat="server"
            MaxLength="10"
            Width="70px"
            ></asp:TextBox>
        <asp:RequiredFieldValidator
            id=RequiredFieldValidator1
            runat="server"
            ErrorMessage="*"
            ControlToValidate="ContractEnds"
            Display="Dynamic">
        </asp:RequiredFieldValidator>
        <asp:CompareValidator
            ID=CompareValidator1
            Runat=server
            ErrorMessage="*"
            Type=Date
            Display=Dynamic
            ControlToValidate="ContractEnds"
            Operator="DataTypeCheck">
```

(continued)

Listing 9-6 *continued*

```
        </asp:CompareValidator>
        </td>
    </tr>
    <tr>
        <td width="30%" align=right>
        <font face="Verdana,Arial" size=2 color="#3300ff">
        Contact EMail:
        </font>
        </td>
        <td>
        <asp:TextBox
            id="ContactEmail"
            runat="server"
            MaxLength="50"
            Width="250px"
            ></asp:TextBox>
        <asp:RequiredFieldValidator
            id="Requiredfieldvalidator6"
            runat="server"
            ControlToValidate="ContactEMail"
            ErrorMessage="*"
            Display="Dynamic">
        </asp:RequiredFieldValidator>
        <asp:RegularExpressionValidator
            id=RegularExpressionValidator2
            runat="server"
            Display="Dynamic"
            ControlToValidate="ContactEmail"
            ErrorMessage="*"
            ValidationExpression=
            "\w+([-+.]\w+)*@\w+([-.]\w+)*\.\w+([-.]\w+)*">
        </asp:RegularExpressionValidator>
        </td>
    </tr>
    <tr>
        <td width="30%" align=right>
        <font face="Verdana,Arial" size=2 color="#3300ff">
        User Name:
        </font>
        </td>
        <td>
        <asp:TextBox
            id="UserName"
            runat="server"
            MaxLength="50"
            Width="250px"
            ></asp:TextBox>
```

```
        <asp:RequiredFieldValidator
            id="Requiredfieldvalidator9"
            runat="server"
            ControlToValidate="UserName"
            ErrorMessage="*">
        </asp:RequiredFieldValidator>
        </td>
    </tr>
    <tr>
        <td width="30%" align=right>
        <font face="Verdana,Arial" size=2 color="#3300ff">
        Password:
        </font>
        </td>
        <td>
        <asp:TextBox
            id="Password"
            runat="server"
            MaxLength="50"
            Width="250px"
            ></asp:TextBox>
        <asp:RequiredFieldValidator
            id="Requiredfieldvalidator10"
            runat="server"
            ControlToValidate="Password"
            ErrorMessage="*">
        </asp:RequiredFieldValidator>
        </td>
    </tr>
    <tr>
        <td colspan=2 align=middle>
        <asp:Button id=BtnSave
            runat="server"
            Text="Save">
        </asp:Button> 
        <asp:Button id=BtnCancel
            runat="server"
            Text="Cancel"
            CausesValidation="False" >
        </asp:Button> 
        <asp:Button id=btnDelete
            runat="server"
            Text="Delete"
            Visible="False"
            CausesValidation="False">
        </asp:Button>
        </td>
    </tr>
```

(continued)

Listing 9-6 *continued*

```
</table>
<asp:Label id=Label1 runat="server"
    ForeColor="Red"
    Font-Names="Verdana,Arial">
</asp:Label></form>

</body>
</HTML>
```

The general structure of EditCustomers.aspx is an HTML table, with two columns. The left column contains the field names, and the right column contains the controls that allow the fields to be entered and edited.

Each of the fields, except the State drop-down list, is hooked up to a *RequiredFieldValidator* control. *RequiredFieldValidator*, as you recall, is one of the simpler validator controls. The only attributes set for most of the *RequiredFieldValidator* controls are *ControlToValidate*, each set to a different control, and *ErrorMessage*, in this case, an asterisk. Some of the *RequiredFieldValidator* controls—for example the control associated with the *ContractEnds* text box—also have the *Display* attribute set to *Dynamic*. Recall from Chapter 5 that validators not set to *Display=Dynamic* take up space even when they're not being fired. When you have multiple validators on a single control, having those validators set to *Display=Dynamic* indicates that validators that aren't signaled won't take up space, meaning that when you have two validators on a field, no matter which one is signaled, the error message will begin at the same location.

Several of the controls have *RegularExpressionValidator* controls associated with them. For example, the *PostalCode* text box uses the following *RegularExpressionValidator* declaration:

```
<asp:RegularExpressionValidator
    id=RegularExpressionValidator1
    runat="server"
    ControlToValidate="PostalCode"
    ErrorMessage="*"
    ValidationExpression="\d{5}(-\d{4})?">
</asp:RegularExpressionValidator>
```

The *ValidationExpression* attribute indicates that there must be five digits, optionally followed by a hyphen and four other digits. There's also a *RegularExpressionValidator* control associated with the *ContactEmail* field, and that *ValidationExpression* attribute is even more complex. Again, the MSDN documentation covers the regular expression syntax fairly completely.

Why Doesn't EditCustomers.aspx Use Data Binding?

In Listing 9-6, you'll see a number of text box controls, including the
CompanyName text box control, shown here:

```
<asp:TextBox
    id=CompanyName
    runat="server"
    MaxLength="50"
    Width="250px"
    ></asp:TextBox>
```

What seems to be missing is any code to bind data to the controls. This
isn't an accident, and ends up being an interesting design decision. When
I first began this page, I *did* use data binding to set the text value for the
control. This approach worked, but it left me with a couple of problems,
some obvious, some less so.

First, having the binding taking place declaratively places details of
how the data is bound in the .aspx file. This isn't a showstopper, and in
fact RepeaterTest.aspx does have the binding code intermixed within the
user interface code. The *DataGrid* object shown in the GridTest.aspx example provides some middle ground, in that you actually declare the name
of the field to be bound in each column, but you don't have the <%# %>
tags that bind code in the .aspx file.

The more compelling problem is what happens when you try to bind
to the *DataReader* object and find that there's no data. How might that
happen? Several ways. First, the *CustomerID* property is passed in as a
parameter in the URL. A user could bookmark the page, capturing the
CustomerID value as well. If the user visits the page again and the *CustomerID*
value is no longer valid, the error will occur. I might also get to this page
without a valid *CustomerID* when I try to add a customer. The +New link
at the bottom of the page in Figure 9-8 links to EditCustomer.aspx with a
CustomerID of 0, indicating that I want to add a new record. Manually setting
the text box controls within the code-behind file works well, and because
data binding is read-only anyway, there already needs to be code to handle
saving updates that deals with each text box in any event.

The final type of validator is the *CompareValidator* control. The *ContractEnds* field is a date. Although I can't be sure exactly when the date will be—in the past or in the future—I do know that it *must* be a valid date. The *CompareValidator* control is the answer to this problem, with a particular set of attributes specified, as follows:

```
<asp:CompareValidator
    ID=CompareValidator1
    Runat=server
    ErrorMessage="*"
    Type=Date
    Display=Dynamic
    ControlToValidate="ContractEnds"
    Operator="DataTypeCheck">
</asp:CompareValidator>
```

The significant attributes here are *Type=Date*, which indicates that the field should contain a date; *ControlToValidate="ContractEnds"*, which points to the control that should contain the date; and *Operator="DataTypeCheck"*, which tells the .NET Framework that I'm just checking that the correct data type has been entered.

Finally, several button controls appear toward the bottom of the page. One problem with validator controls is what to do when you just want to get out of the page. For example, when you click the Cancel button, you certainly don't want to force the user to enter valid information in each of the fields containing validators. The answer is to set the *CausesValidation* attribute of the Cancel button to *False*. This will disable client and server validation, allowing your server-side button click handler to do what it needs to do. In this example, the server-side button handler for the Cancel button will simply redirect the user back to the RepeaterTest.aspx page.

Processing Data Entry

The code-behind file for EditCustomer.aspx, EditCustomer.aspx.cs, is shown in Listing 9-7.

```
using System;
using System.Collections;
using System.ComponentModel;
using System.Data;
using System.Drawing;
using System.Web;
using System.Web.SessionState;
using System.Web.UI;
using System.Web.UI.WebControls;
using System.Web.UI.HtmlControls;
```

Listing 9-7 EditCustomer.aspx.cs, the code-behind file for the Customer Maintenance page

```
namespace Chapter09_Template
{
    /// <summary>
    /// Summary description for EditCustomer.
    /// </summary>
    public class EditCustomer : System.Web.UI.Page
    {
        protected DropDownList ddlState;
        protected TextBox CompanyName;
        protected TextBox Address;
        protected TextBox City;
        protected TextBox PostalCode;
        protected Label Label1;
        protected TextBox ContractEnds;
        protected RequiredFieldValidator RequiredFieldValidator1;
        protected CompareValidator CompareValidator1;
        protected RequiredFieldValidator RequiredFieldValidator2;
        protected RequiredFieldValidator RequiredFieldValidator3;
        protected RequiredFieldValidator RequiredFieldValidator4;
        protected RequiredFieldValidator RequiredFieldValidator5;
        protected RegularExpressionValidator RegularExpressionValidator1;
        protected TextBox ContactEmail;
        protected RequiredFieldValidator Requiredfieldvalidator6;
        protected RegularExpressionValidator RegularExpressionValidator2;
        protected TextBox ContactLastName;
        protected RequiredFieldValidator Requiredfieldvalidator7;
        protected TextBox ContactFirstName;
        protected TextBox UserName;
        protected TextBox Password;
        protected RequiredFieldValidator Requiredfieldvalidator8;
        protected RequiredFieldValidator Requiredfieldvalidator9;
        protected RequiredFieldValidator Requiredfieldvalidator10;
        protected Button BtnSave;
        protected Button BtnCancel;
        protected Button btnDelete;
        protected SqlDataReader dr;

        public int CustomerID
        {
            get { return (int)ViewState["CustomerID"]; }
            set { ViewState["CustomerID"]=value; }
        }
        public EditCustomer()
        {
            Page.Init += new System.EventHandler(Page_Init);
        }
```

(continued)

Listing 9-7 *continued*

```
private void doDataBind()
{
    System.Data.SqlClient.SqlConnection cn;
    System.Data.SqlClient.SqlConnection cnState;
    System.Data.SqlClient.SqlCommand cmd;
    System.Data.SqlClient.SqlCommand cmdState;
    cn=new System.Data.SqlClient.SqlConnection(
        "server=localhost;" +
        "Integrated Security=SSPI;Initial Catalog=GolfArticles");
    cnState=new System.Data.SqlClient.SqlConnection(
        "server=localhost;" +
        "Integrated Security=SSPI;Initial Catalog=GolfArticles");
    cmd=new System.Data.SqlClient.SqlCommand(
        "spSelectCustomer",cn);
    cmd.CommandType=CommandType.StoredProcedure;
    cmd.Parameters.Add("@CustomerID",
        Request.QueryString["CustomerID"]);
    cmdState=new System.Data.SqlClient.SqlCommand(
        "SELECT StateAbbreviation FROM " +
        "States ORDER BY StateAbbreviation",
        cnState);
    try
    {
        cn.Open();
        dr=cmd.ExecuteReader(
            CommandBehavior.CloseConnection);
        cnState.Open();
        ddlState.DataTextField="StateAbbreviation";
        ddlState.DataSource=cmdState.ExecuteReader(
            CommandBehavior.CloseConnection);
        if ( dr.Read() )
        {
            this.DataBind();
            ddlState.SelectedIndex=ddlState.Items.IndexOf(
                ddlState.Items.FindByText(dr.GetString(4)));
            CompanyName.Text=(string)dr["CompanyName"];
            Address.Text=(string)dr["Address"];
            City.Text=(string)dr["City"];
            PostalCode.Text=(string)dr["PostalCode"];
            ContractEnds.Text=
                ((DateTime)dr["ContractEnds"]).ToShortDateString();
            ContactEmail.Text=(string)dr["ContactEmail"];
            ContactFirstName.Text=(string)dr["ContactFirstName"];
            ContactLastName.Text=(string)dr["ContactLastName"];
            UserName.Text=(string)dr["UserName"];
            Password.Text=(string)dr["Password"];
```

```
                // Close data reader, and thus connection.
                dr.Close();
            }
            else
            {
                this.DataBind();
            }
        }
        catch ( System.Exception eLoad)
        {
            // Handle it...
            Label1.Text=eLoad.Message;
            btnDelete.Visible=false;
        }


    }

    private void Page_Load(object sender, System.EventArgs e)
    {
        // Put user code to initialize the page here

        if ( !(this.IsPostBack) )
        {
            CustomerID=System.Convert.ToInt32(
                (string)Request["CustomerID"]);
            doDataBind();
        }
        if ( CustomerID!=0 )
        {
            btnDelete.Visible=true;
        }
        else
        {
            btnDelete.Visible=false;
        }


    }
    private void Page_Init(object sender, EventArgs e)
    {
        //
        // CODEGEN: This call is required by the
        // ASP.NET Web Form Designer.
        //
        InitializeComponent();
    }
```

(continued)

Listing 9-7 *continued*

```csharp
#region Web Form Designer generated code
/// <summary>
/// Required method for Designer support - do not modify
/// the contents of this method with the code editor.
/// </summary>
private void InitializeComponent()
{
    this.BtnSave.Click +=
        new System.EventHandler(this.BtnSave_Click);
    this.BtnCancel.Click +=
        new System.EventHandler(this.BtnCancel_Click);
    this.btnDelete.Click +=
        new System.EventHandler(this.btnDelete_Click);
    this.Load +=
        new System.EventHandler(this.Page_Load);

}
#endregion

private void BtnCancel_Click(object sender, System.EventArgs e)
{
    Response.Redirect("RepeaterTest.aspx");
}

private void BtnSave_Click(object sender, System.EventArgs e)
{
    System.Data.SqlClient.SqlConnection cn;
    System.Data.SqlClient.SqlCommand cmd;
    System.Data.SqlClient.SqlParameter prm;
    if ( this.IsValid )
    {
        cn=new System.Data.SqlClient.SqlConnection(
            "server=localhost;" +
            "Integrated Security=SSPI;Initial Catalog=GolfArticles");
        cmd=new System.Data.SqlClient.SqlCommand(
            "spSaveCustomer",cn);
        cmd.CommandType=CommandType.StoredProcedure;

        try
        {
            prm=new System.Data.SqlClient.SqlParameter(
                "@ReturnValue",0);
            prm.Direction=ParameterDirection.ReturnValue;
            cmd.Parameters.Add(prm);
            cmd.Parameters.Add("@CustomerID",CustomerID);
            cmd.Parameters.Add("@CompanyName",CompanyName.Text);
```

```
cmd.Parameters.Add("@Address",Address.Text);
cmd.Parameters.Add("@City",City.Text);
cmd.Parameters.Add("@State",
    ddlState.SelectedItem.Text);
cmd.Parameters.Add("@PostalCode",PostalCode.Text);
cmd.Parameters.Add("@ContractEnds",
    System.DateTime.Parse(
    ContractEnds.Text));
cmd.Parameters.Add("@ContactFirstName",
    ContactFirstName.Text);
cmd.Parameters.Add("@ContactLastName",
    ContactLastName.Text);
cmd.Parameters.Add("@ContactEMail",
    ContactEmail.Text);
cmd.Parameters.Add("@UserName",UserName.Text);
cmd.Parameters.Add("@Password",Password.Text);

cn.Open();

cmd.ExecuteNonQuery();
int prmNum;
prmNum=cmd.Parameters.IndexOf("@ReturnValue");
if ( Convert.ToInt64(
    cmd.Parameters[prmNum].Value)!=0 )
{
    Label1.Text="Customer " +
        cmd.Parameters["@ReturnValue"].Value.ToString()+
        " Saved!";
    CustomerID=Convert.ToInt32(
        cmd.Parameters["@ReturnValue"].Value);
    // Put a friendlier name on button
    this.BtnCancel.Text="Close";
}
}
catch ( System.Exception eSave )
{
    Label1.Text=eSave.Message;
}
finally
{
    cn.Close();
}
}

}
```

(continued)

Listing 9-7 *continued*

```csharp
        private void btnDelete_Click(object sender, System.EventArgs e)
        {
            System.Data.SqlClient.SqlConnection cn;
            System.Data.SqlClient.SqlCommand cmd;
            if ( CustomerID!=0 )
            {
                cn=new System.Data.SqlClient.SqlConnection(
                  "server=localhost;" +
                  "Integrated Security=SSPI;Initial Catalog=GolfArticles");
                cmd=new SqlCommand("spDeleteCustomer",cn);
                cmd.CommandType=CommandType.StoredProcedure;

                try
                {
                    cmd.Parameters.Add("@CustomerID",CustomerID);
                    cn.Open();
                    cmd.ExecuteNonQuery();
                    // Put a friendlier name on button.
                    this.BtnCancel.Text="Close";
                    // Display confirmation...
                    Label1.Text="Customer " +
                        CustomerID + " Deleted!";
                    // No customer anymore...
                    CustomerID=0;
                    doDataBind();
                    btnDelete.Visible=true;
                }
                catch ( System.Exception eDelete )
                {
                    Label1.Text=eDelete.Message;
                }
                finally
                {
                    cn.Close();
                }


            }
        }
    }
}
```

Toward the top of Listing 9-7, I declare a property named *CustomerID* that is persisted as part of the *ViewState*. I could have used a hidden field on the form, as I would have done in ASP, but using *ViewState* here is more convenient.

The next interesting part of EditCustomer.aspx.cs is the *doDataBind* method. First I create two connection objects and two command objects. I actually use results from both command objects at the same time, and so I need two separate connection objects. Note once again that I'm using *SqlConnection* objects because I'm connecting to Microsoft SQL Server.

Once the connections are set up, I create the command objects. For the main connection to the *Customer* table, I set up the command to call a stored procedure, *spSelectCustomer*, and for the connection to the *State* table, I set up the command to call a standard SQL select statement. After opening both connection objects and calling *ExecuteReader* on the main command object used for the *Customer* table (named *cmd* in the code), I do the following:

```
ddlState.DataTextField="StateAbbreviation";
ddlState.DataSource=cmdState.ExecuteReader(
    CommandBehavior.CloseConnection);
```

The *DataTextField* property tells the State drop-down list, *ddlState*, that the field to use as the displayable text is the *StateAbbreviation* field. The *States* table has a *StateID*_field, a *StateAbbreviation* field, and a *StateName* field. The drop-down list component also has a *DataValueField* property, so I could have set these properties to different values. If I did, the rendered *<OPTION>* tags would have the *DataValueField* property as the *Value* attribute of the *<OPTION>* tag for each item, and the *DataTextField* property between the start *<OPTION>* tag and the end *</OPTION>* tag. Because screen real estate is limited in this example, I'm only displaying the state abbreviation, using it for both the text and the value.

The following code sets the selected index on the State drop-down list.

```
if ( dr.Read() )
{
    this.DataBind();
    ddlState.SelectedIndex=ddlState.Items.IndexOf(
        ddlState.Items.FindByText(dr.GetString(4)));
```

If *dr.Read* returns *true*, I call *DataBind* and then set the selected index on the *ddlState* drop-down list. The selected index should be set so that the value in the drop-down list is the value already in the *Customer* table for this customer. This looks a bit tortured, and certainly does seem to be more code than should be required, but it does work.

Tip   None of the code following the call to *dr.Read* would work without that call. Unlike an ActiveX Data Objects (ADO) recordset, which points to the first record in the dataset upon being opened, the *DataReader* object in ADO.NET points just before the first record, and the *Read* method must be called to make the first record, if any, available. I've spent an hour once or twice trying to get data when the *DataReader* object hasn't been read. It didn't fail, it simply didn't have anything to display.

After setting the selected index for the State drop-down list, the code sets the *Text* property of the *CompanyName* text box to the *CompanyName* field of *dr*, the *DataReader* object that contains the customer record I'm trying to display. I must cast the value to a string, since the returned value is an object.

```
CompanyName.Text=(string)dr["CompanyName"];
```

> **Note**   The casting syntax used here will look familiar to C and C++ pro-
> grammers, but it might look a little strange to Visual Basic programmers. In
> Visual Basic .NET, the same task can be accomplished by calling the *CType*
> function—for example, *CompanyName.Text = CType(dr("CompanyName"),
> String)*.

After setting the *CompanyName* text box, the code continues with a number of similar lines of code, each setting one of the text boxes displayed on the EditCustomer.aspx page. The line to set the *ContractEnds* text box is a little different, since the underlying type is a *DateTime* object rather than a string, as follows:

```
ContractEnds.Text=
    ((DateTime)dr["ContractEnds"]).ToShortDateString();
```

In this case, I'm casting the returned object to a *DateTime* object, and then calling the *ToShortDateString* method on the resulting *DateTime* object.

If I can't read the record I'm looking for (*dr.Read* returns *false*), I still call *DataBind*—in this case, to ensure that the State drop-down list is populated. If an exception occurs, I set *Label1* to the *Message* property of the resulting exception, and make the Delete button invisible. There's no sense in deleting what might not be there. The Save button is still active because, in theory, the user can still enter all the required information and attempt the save.

Because all the code involved with filling in the text boxes is located in *doDataBind*, the *Page_Load* method is fairly straightforward, as shown here:

```
if ( !(this.IsPostBack) )
{
    CustomerID=System.Convert.ToInt32(
        (string)Request["CustomerID"]);
    doDataBind();
}
if ( CustomerID!=0 )
{
    btnDelete.Visible=true;
}
```

```
else
{
    btnDelete.Visible=false;
}
```

If this is *not* a postback, meaning this is the first time the user is visiting the page, I set the *CustomerID* property from the value in the *Request* object, and call *doDataBind* to actually fill in the drop-down list and the text boxes. If the *CustomerID* property is nonzero, I make the Delete button visible; otherwise, I make it invisible. That's all there is to *Page_Load*.

The *BtnCancel_Click* event handler is a single line, redirecting the user to the RepeaterTest.aspx page—the page that in the normal course of events is the one that got me to EditCustomer.aspx. The event handlers for the Save and Delete buttons are more complicated. We'll examine the details of the more complicated event handler, *BtnSave_Click*, here. You can then explore *btnDelete_Click* on your own.

Once I establish the connection, I set up the command object to execute a stored procedure, *spSaveCustomer*. I next add a return value parameter by creating a *SqlParameter* object and setting the required properties. Additional parameters are appended to the *Parameters* collection, with the most interesting parameter addition being for *ContractEnds*, a date field, as follows:

```
cmd.Parameters.Add("@ContractEnds",
    System.DateTime.Parse(ContractEnds.Text));
```

Because I know that *ContractEnds* is a *DateTime* object, I parse the date using the *System.DateTime.Parse* method. In most cases, I'd put this specific code in an exception handler, since an exception could be thrown. I'm reasonably comfortable that an exception won't be thrown here, since I wouldn't get here unless the validator accepted the date entered. After all the parameters are set, I open the connection and call *ExecuteNonQuery* on the command object. After the command is executed, I check the return value, which is set to the *CustomerID*, either the one passed in, in the case of a saved record, or the new *CustomerID*, if this is a new record.

> **Note**   As with ADO, any command that executes a query that returns records—for example, a record returning stored procedure called using the *ExecuteReader* method of the *SqlCommand* object—will *not* allow you to retrieve return codes or output parameters until the object getting the records—for example, the *DataReader* object—is closed.

I let the stored procedure tell me whether it's a new record, as indicated by the code for *spSaveCustomer* shown in Listing 9-8.

```
CREATE PROCEDURE spSaveCustomer
    @CustomerID int,
    @CompanyName nvarchar(50),
    @Address nvarchar(50),
    @City nvarchar(50),
    @State nvarchar(10),
    @PostalCode nvarchar(20),
    @ContractEnds datetime,
    @ContactFirstName nvarchar(50),
    @ContactLastName nvarchar(50),
    @ContactEMail nvarchar(128),
    @UserName nvarchar(50),
    @Password nvarchar(50)
AS
SET NOCOUNT ON
DECLARE @Ret int
    SELECT @Ret=CustomerID FROM Customer WHERE CustomerID=@CustomerID
    IF IsNull(@Ret,0)=0
    BEGIN
        INSERT INTO Customer(
            CompanyName ,
            Address ,
            City ,
            State ,
            PostalCode ,
            ContractEnds ,
            ContactFirstName ,
            ContactLastName ,
            ContactEMail ,
            UserName ,
            [Password] )
        VALUES(
            @CompanyName ,
            @Address ,
            @City ,
            @State ,
            @PostalCode ,
            @ContractEnds ,
            @ContactFirstName ,
            @ContactLastName ,
            @ContactEMail ,
            @UserName ,
            @Password )
```

Listing 9-8 The *spSaveCustomer* stored procedure used to save a row in the *Customer* table

```
            -- Be careful about triggers and @@Identity
        SET @Ret=@@Identity
    END
    ELSE
    BEGIN
        UPDATE Customer SET
            CompanyName=@CompanyName ,
            Address=@Address ,
            City=@City ,
            State=@State ,
            PostalCode=@PostalCode ,
            ContractEnds=@ContractEnds ,
            ContactFirstName=@ContactFirstName ,
            ContactLastName=@ContactLastName ,
            ContactEMail=@ContactEMail ,
            UserName=@UserName ,
            [Password]=@Password ,
            -- Set modified date conveniently
            DateModified=GetDate()
        WHERE
            CustomerID=@Ret
    END
    IF @@Error=0
    BEGIN
        Return(@Ret)
    END
    ELSE
    BEGIN
        Return(0)
    END
```

The stored procedure shown in Listing 9-8 is reasonably straightforward. Rather than having two separate stored procedures, one for an insert and one for an update, *spSaveCustomer* decides at runtime whether an *INSERT* or an *UPDATE* is appropriate. If this is a new customer, I insert the new record and return the *@@IDENTITY* value, which will be the last value inserted.

> **Tip**   If you're using SQL Server 2000, you can use *IDENT_CURRENT* or *SCOPE_IDENTITY*, which might be better under some circumstances. The *@@IDENTITY* value can be misleading if the table in which you've just inserted a record has a trigger that inserts a record in another table with an identity column.

If the save succeeds, I change the *Label1 Text* property to reflect that, and change the caption of the Cancel button to *Close*, reflecting that the change has already taken place and that exiting the page now won't discard any changes.

Within the *InitializeComponent* method, Visual Studio .NET writes the code to add event handlers for the buttons. When you're in the designer, double-clicking the button will add the code to add a *Click* handler and display the newly created method in the code editor.

A couple of minor enhancements would be appropriate for this application if it were being developed in a production environment. A *ValidationSummary* control would allow you to more clearly state what the problem is with each of the fields. You could also use client-side code to display a confirming message box when the user clicks the Delete button. Of course, additional error handling and even error and event logging would also be helpful in a production system.

Conclusion

Of all the areas of ASP.NET, data access is the area that provides perhaps the most ways to perform a given task. The examples presented in this chapter have used many of the objects within ADO.NET, but by virtue of the breadth of ADO.NET, I haven't explored every nook and cranny. ADO.NET could be the topic of a book all by itself, and extensive documentation for it is available on MSDN.

The choice of objects is also shaped by what works for me. I've used a *DataSet* object when I needed to retrieve the XML representing a set of data, because that object supports the *GetXml* method. Normally, the *DataReader* object has what I need for the kind of applications I write, and so many examples use that object. The *DataReader* object is fast and efficient, and since virtually all Web data access is designed to display data that can arrive in a one-direction, firehose manner, I think use of *DataReader* objects will become standard practice. Time will tell.

In Chapter 10, I'll expand on the example introduced here. The next step toward realizing the dream of distributing content to syndication partners (customers) is to create an XML Web service. This is the other major kind of ASP.NET application. Creating and consuming XML Web services will become a large part of working on the expanding Internet and will also allow applications within the enterprise to work and play well together.

10

XML Web Services

ASP.NET applications will change the way Web developers create Web applications. XML Web services, on the other hand, will change the way Web applications share information and disperse functionality. Distributed COM (DCOM) was one of many different attempts at allowing program functionality to be distributed throughout a network and yet remain available to all interested systems. DCOM was built on top of the remote procedure call (RPC) architecture. DCOM was *far* easier to use than RPC, but it retained several of the shortcomings of RPC.

The first of these shortcomings was that both RPC and DCOM were much better suited for intranet use than Internet use. It's uncommon for the ports required by RPC and DCOM to be opened in a corporate firewall. Before the Internet boom, the inability to use resources distributed across the public Internet wasn't a significant problem, but this limitation has become a significant burden in recent years.

The second shortcoming was the impact that using RPC or DCOM had on the application. With DCOM, the impact was much less than with raw RPC, but nonetheless, serious program and architectural changes needed to be made to exploit either technology. DCOM also had the burden of being a superset of COM, and although using COM in Microsoft Visual Basic is much easier than using COM in some other languages (notably, C++), it's still not easy to use. Add to that the extra plumbing required to keep components properly registered, and you can see that DCOM isn't the ideal solution.

An additional burden that DCOM had to carry was the fact that it wasn't platform neutral. DCOM was basically a Microsoft Windows–only option, and so, the dizzying array of Windows versions makes maintaining a significant DCOM system quite a task.

> **Note**   COM Internet Services (CIS) is one option that allows DCOM users to use the HTTP port and establish an HTTP-based handshake. Although using CIS eliminates the firewall problem, it does nothing to change the fact that DCOM is still platform specific.

Fortunately for ASP.NET developers, there is a new solution to this old problem of spreading around the functionality an application might require. As you'll see in this chapter, XML Web services provide a standard way of exposing parts of an application to be shared across process boundaries and, more important, across machine boundaries. Using standard protocols and data formats, XML Web services allow machines across the Internet or intranets to communicate.

Standards for XML Web Services

There aren't many technologies that developers on all platforms and using all languages can agree on. Two technologies that have gained virtually universal acceptance are XML and HTTP. Both protocols take a "simple is better" approach to what they do.

XML is rapidly becoming the lingua franca of data. Although not all standards bodies have caught up, and certainly quite a few non-XML formats are widely used, most of those standards (such as HL7, mentioned in Chapter 8) had arrived before XML caught on. New standards for virtually any industry will almost certainly use XML, with a specialized grammar.

HTTP is ubiquitous. It's present on any computer of any sort that uses a Web browser—which by now includes just about any device of any consequence, even some cell phones. Significantly, because browsers need to have the ports used by HTTP open, most corporate firewalls have the ports open required for regular HTTP as well as secured HTTP using the Secure Sockets Layer (SSL) protocol (HTTPS).

Putting XML and HTTP together seems like a natural. A new protocol based on XML and HTTP named the Simple Object Access Protocol (SOAP) was first proposed to the World Wide Web Consortium (W3C) in 1999. SOAP uses XML over HTTP to conveniently send a request and get back a response. Because XML and HTTP are standards, the applications that supply or consume XML Web services can be created in any language and can run on whatever platform is most convenient.

In addition to XML and HTTP, several other protocols can be used in conjunction with SOAP: Web Services Description Language (WSDL); Universal Description, Discovery, and Integration (UDDI); and Discovery. WSDL was developed by Microsoft, IBM, and others. WSDL is an XML *schema* that describes the methods and parameters of a Web service. An XML schema is grammar that describes a set of tags to be used within an XML document. Given an XML schema, it's possible to determine exactly what data is contained in a conforming XML document—and of course, you can also validate an XML document.

UDDI is a platform-independent, open framework for describing services, discovering businesses, and integrating services on the Web. UDDI was proposed by IBM and Microsoft. You can learn more about UDDI at *http://www.uddi.org*.

Discovery is a Microsoft-sponsored proprietary protocol for XML Web services discovery. Discovery uses a .disco file to locate and interrogate XML Web services. A .disco file is a simple XML document that contains links to other resources that describe the XML Web service, as shown here:

```xml
<?xml version="1.0" encoding="utf-8"?>
<discovery xmlns:xsi="http://www.w3.org/2001/XMLSchema-instance"
    xmlns:xsd="http://www.w3.org/2001/XMLSchema"
    xmlns="http://schemas.xmlsoap.org/disco/">
    <contractRef
        ref="http://localhost/Chapter10_SimpleService/Simple.asmx?wsdl"
        docRef="http://localhost/Chapter10_SimpleService/Simple.asmx"
        xmlns="http://schemas.xmlsoap.org/disco/scl/" />
    <soap address="http://localhost/Chapter10_SimpleService/Simple.asmx"
        xmlns:q1="http://tempuri.org/" binding="q1:SimpleSoap"
        xmlns="http://schemas.xmlsoap.org/disco/soap/" />
</discovery>
```

This example specifies that the service description can be obtained at *http://localhost/Chapter10_SimpleService/Simple.asmx?wsdl*.

SOAP has been around since 1999, but there haven't been huge numbers of developers using it to create SOAP applications. For the most part, this lack of popularity is because creating SOAP-compliant applications isn't easy. Creating a SOAP application is simpler than creating a DCOM application, but it's still not simple. Part of the problem for Windows developers is that there was a lengthy calm before the .NET storm in terms of development tools for developers on the Windows platform. For example, Microsoft Visual InterDev 6.0 gives a copyright date of 1997–98—before SOAP was even proposed. Microsoft has released a number of SOAP toolkits; however, these toolkits haven't met with the same level of acceptance.

Creating a Simple XML Web Service

You probably won't be surprised to discover that Microsoft Visual Studio .NET provides powerful tools to help you create XML Web services. The ease of creating XML Web services is nothing short of amazing, as you'll see.

XML Web services reside in a folder that's also a virtual directory in Internet Information Services (IIS). XML Web services can have the same security settings as traditional Web folders, although you must be careful to ensure that XML Web services that are accessed by other programs have some way to allow an application to pass in credentials rather than being routed to a login screen.

XML Web services are exposed in the .NET Framework as files with an .asmx extension. This extension, like the .aspx and .ascx extensions, is registered with IIS and handled specially rather than being dumped directly to the browser, as an HTML file might be. An .asmx file might contain actual code, but it will more likely contain just a pointer to the code, as in this example:

```
<%@ WebService Language="vb"
Codebehind="Simple.asmx.vb"
Class="Chapter10_SimpleService.Simple" %>
```

This *WebService* directive is similar to the *Page* directive used for .aspx files. *Language* refers to the language used in the code. *Codebehind* is once again used only by Visual Studio .NET and similar designers. The *Class* attribute specifies the name of the class. In addition to the class name—in this example, *Chapter10_SimpleService.Simple*—I could specify the assembly name in the *Class* attribute. Because the assembly name is *Chapter10_SimpleService*, I'd use a *WebService* directive like this to specify the assembly:

```
<%@ WebService Language="vb"
Codebehind="Simple.asmx.vb"
Class="Chapter10_SimpleService.Simple,Chapter10_SimpleService"
%>
```

Without explicitly specifying the assembly, ASP.NET will search through the assemblies in the bin folder below where the .asmx file resides until it finds the correct assembly the first time the XML Web service is accessed. This search can be a performance hit, and if you have a bin folder with lots of assemblies, the time to search them all can be nontrivial.

In Visual Studio .NET, you'll likely never see the code in the .asmx file. Visual Studio .NET by default has you create the code required in a code-behind file. In this example, the code would be located in Simple.asmx.vb.

As with all Visual Studio projects, the first step in creating a new XML Web service is to create a new project. Figure 10-1 shows the dialog box that appears, with a Visual Basic .NET XML Web service application selected.

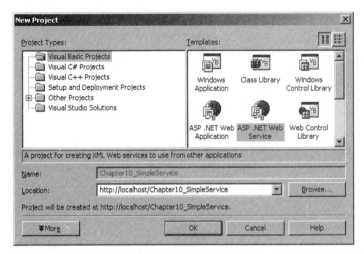

Figure 10-1 The New Project dialog box in Visual Studio .NET, showing how to create a new XML Web service in Visual Basic .NET

Expanding and Testing the XML Web Service

After you create the new project, you'll have a base XML Web service. Visual Studio .NET places comments in a file that, when uncommented, will provide a simple "Hello World" XML Web service. I modified that service slightly; the resulting code-behind file is shown in Listing 10-1.

```
Imports System.Web.Services

Public Class Simple
    Inherits System.Web.Services.WebService

#Region " Web Services Designer Generated Code "

    Public Sub New().
        MyBase.New()

        'This call is required by the Web Services Designer.
        InitializeComponent()

        'Add your own initialization code after the
        'InitializeComponent() call

    End Sub


    'Required by the Web Services Designer
    Private components As System.ComponentModel.Container
```

Listing 10-1 Simple.asmx.vb, a simple, multilanguage "Hello World" XML Web service

(continued)

```
'NOTE: The following procedure is required by the
'Web Services Designer
'It can be modified using the Web Services Designer.
'Do not modify it using the code editor.
<System.Diagnostics.DebuggerStepThrough()> _
Private Sub InitializeComponent()
    components = New System.ComponentModel.Container()
End Sub

Protected Overloads Overrides Sub Dispose(ByVal disposing As Boolean)
    'CODEGEN: This procedure is required by the Web Services Designer
    'Do not modify it using the code editor.
    If disposing Then
        If Not (components Is Nothing) Then
            components.Dispose()
        End If
    End If
    MyBase.Dispose(disposing)
End Sub

#End Region

<WebMethod()> _
Public Function HelloWorld( _
ByVal Language As String) As String
    Select Case Language
        Case "Norwegian"
            HelloWorld = "God dag Verden"
        Case "Spanish"
            HelloWorld = "Hola Mundo"
        Case "German"
            HelloWorld = "Hallo Welt"
        Case Else
            HelloWorld = "Hello World"
    End Select
End Function

End Class
```

The *Simple* class inherits *System.Web.Services.WebService*. The *WebService* class provides many members; most are inherited from ancestor objects. Among the most important is an *HttpContext* object named *Current*. Using the *Current* object, it's possible to determine whether tracing is enabled, for example, by using code such as this:

```
HttpContext.Current.Trace.IsEnabled;
```

The *WebService* class also exposes a property that returns a *Session* object. The *Session* object can store and retrieve values that are specific to the single user session. Session state must also be enabled, as described in Table 10-1 on page 342.

> **Tip**   Although ASP.NET session state can be accessed across multiple Web servers in a cluster, using session state will limit the scalability of the application. Once you scale out to multiple Web servers, any access to the session state will require a call across machine boundaries. This is a *very* expensive operation, and something that can often be avoided with other ASP.NET features. Using session state in an XML Web service is almost always a bad idea.

Another interesting property of the *WebService* class is *User*. The *User* property is most useful in the case of XML Web services used within an organization that has Windows 2000 Active Directory in place and uses Windows authentication. There are more common ways to handle authentication, and I'll introduce these in the section "Security Options" later in this chapter

The *Server* property of the *WebService* class returns an *HttpServerUtility* object that can be used to get the machine name and get or set the script timeout, as well as provide various path mappings. The *Execute* and *Transfer* methods familiar to IIS 5.0 users are also exposed on the *Server* property.

The XML Web service in Listing 10-1 has the following *HelloWorld* function:

```
<WebMethod()> _
Public Function HelloWorld( _
ByVal Language As String) As String
    Select Case Language
        Case "Norwegian"
            HelloWorld = "God dag Verden"
        Case "Spanish"
            HelloWorld = "Hola Mundo"
        Case "German"
            HelloWorld = "Hallo Welt"
        Case Else
            HelloWorld = "Hello World"
    End Select
End Function
```

The most interesting part of this function is just how simple it is. Using a *Select/Case* statement, I select the correct translation and return that value from the function. The only hint that this function is something out of the ordinary is the *<WebMethod()>* attribute. (The same attribute in a C# module would be declared as *[WebMethod()]*.) This version of *HelloWorld* is somewhat international, requesting a string parameter, named *Language*, and returning "Hello World" in the language selected (if the language selected is Norwegian, Spanish, German; failing that, the string is returned in English).*

One of the historical difficulties with testing an XML Web service—or any similar service, for that matter—is the need to create a client framework to actually exercise the service. Fortunately, XML Web services provide an easy way to test themselves. Run the XML Web service shown in Listing 10-1, and a page like the one shown in Figure 10-2 will appear.

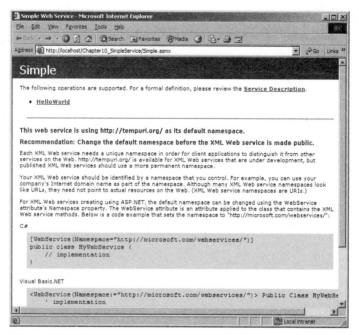

Figure 10-2 The page returned when the *Simple* XML Web service is run in Visual Studio .NET

This page contains a link to the one-and-only exposed method offered in this class: *HelloWorld*. Clicking this link displays a page such as the one shown in Figure 10-3.

The single parameter, *Language*, can be entered in the text box above the Invoke button. If you didn't remember that *Language* was a string, you could refer to the SOAP request detailed on the same page, and you'd know that it's expecting a string. If you enter "Spanish" in the Language text box and click Invoke, a page such as the one shown in Figure 10-4 will appear.

---

* I'd like to thank Bente and Jorge Mindyk for providing the Norwegian and Spanish translations, and Kathy Cox for the German translation. The Norwegian translation is literally "Good Day World," which Bente assures me is more likely what a Norwegian would say.

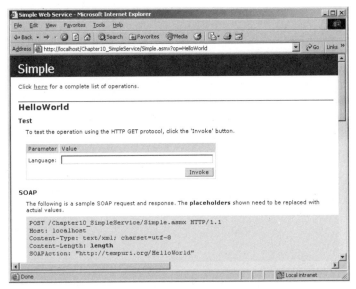

Figure 10-3 The page that lets you test the *HelloWorld* method for the *Simple* XML Web service

Figure 10-4 The results returned by a call to the *HelloWorld* method with "Spanish"

In Figure 10-4, notice that the URL in the Address bar is nothing more than a path to the .asmx file, along with the parameter, passed exactly as it would be to an ASP.NET Web Forms page.

Notice in Figure 10-2 the warning that the XML Web service is using *http://tempuri.org* as its namespace. This is the default namespace Visual Studio .NET uses for XML Web services. This namespace is fine for testing XML Web services, but a real XML Web service should point to a different namespace. To change the namespace used by the XML Web service, you need to add a line such as this immediately before the class declaration:

```
<WebService(Namespace:="http://ProgrammingASP.NET/webservices/")>
```

The URL doesn't have to be anything specific, nor does it actually need to exist.

Using *WebMethod* Attribute Properties

The *WebMethod* attribute accepts six properties to control how the XML Web service operates. These properties are described in Table 10-1.

Table 10-1 Properties of the *WebMethod* Attribute

Property	Description

BufferResponse	Enables buffering of responses from the XML Web service. The default value is *true*, and this is almost always the best setting. If set to *false*, the response from the XML Web service will be sent to the requesting client in 16-KB blocks. The syntax for setting this parameter is shown here:
	`[Visual Basic.NET]`
	`<WebMethod(BufferResponse:=False)>`
	`[C#]`
	`[WebMethod(BufferResponse=false)]`

CacheDuration	Enables caching of the results for an XML Web service method. ASP.NET will cache the results for each unique parameter set. The value of this property specifies how long, in seconds, ASP.NET will cache the results. The default value is *0*, meaning that nothing is cached. This property often should be set, especially if the number of unique sets of parameters is limited and the underlying response will likely not change frequently. The syntax for setting this property is shown here:
	`[Visual Basic.NET]`
	`<WebMethod(CacheDuration:=60)>`
	`[C#]`
	`[WebMethod(CacheDuration=60)]`

Description	Supplies a description for an XML Web service method that will appear on the Service help page. The syntax for setting this property is shown here:
	`[Visual Basic.NET]`
	`<WebMethod(Description:="Text")>`
	`[C#]`
	`[WebMethod(Description="Text")]`

EnableSession	Enables session state for an XML Web service method. Once enabled, the XML Web service can access the session state directly from *HttpContext.Current.Session* or with *WebService.Session*. The syntax for setting this property is shown here:
	`[Visual Basic.NET]`
	`<WebMethod(EnableSession:=True)>`
	`[C#]`
	`[WebMethod(EnableSession=true)]`

Property	Description
MessageName	Enables the XML Web service to uniquely identify overloaded methods using an alias. The default value for *MessageName* is the method name. The most obvious use for this property is with overloaded methods. The syntax for setting this property is shown here:

```
[Visual Basic.NET]
<WebMethod(MessageName:="AddDouble")>
[C#]
[WebMethod(MessageName="AddDouble")]
```

TransactionOption	Enables the XML Web services method to participate as the root object of a transaction. You can set the value to any of the *TransactionOption* enumerations, but in fact, only two behaviors are possible for XML Web services: either the XML Web service can't participate in a transaction (*Disabled*, *NotSupported*, or *Supported*), or it creates a new transaction (*Required*, *RequiresNew*). The default value is *TransactionOption.Disabled*. To enable transaction support, you must add a reference to System.EnterpriseServices.dll. The syntax for setting this property is shown here:

```
[Visual Studio.NET]
<WebMethod(TransactionOption:=
    TransactionOption.RequiresNew)>
[C#]
[WebMethod(TransactionOption=
    TransactionOption.RequiresNew)]
```

As an example of using the *WebMethod* attribute properties, I could modify *HelloWorld* as follows:

```
<WebMethod(CacheDuration:=600)> _
Public Function HelloWorld( _
ByVal Language As String) As String
' And so on...
```

Because the response to the *HelloWorld* request is unlikely to change, caching the response for 600 seconds (10 minutes) isn't at all unreasonable. When *HelloWorld* is called with "Spanish" as the parameter for the first time, the value will be cached. For all other requests within the next 10 minutes, *HelloWorld* won't actually be run; instead, the caching system in ASP.NET will supply the same response as the first request.

Consuming a Simple XML Web Service

Writing an XML Web service is a wonderful accomplishment, but using it is even better. There are several ways to consume an XML Web service. The easiest way is to use Visual Studio and add a Web reference to the service. (Command-line purists should refer to the next section, "XML Web Services and Command-Line Tools.")

The first step in this process is to create a new Web application, with a new Web Forms page. In the Solution Explorer window, right-click the project name, and choose Add Web Reference from the shortcut menu. The Add Web Reference dialog box will appear. In the Add Web Reference dialog box, you can manually enter the address of the XML Web service or use UDDI to search for an XML Web service. This dialog box also has a link to display the XML Web services on the local Web server. Figure 10-5 shows the Add Web Reference dialog box with the *Simple* XML Web service selected. The documentation for *Simple* is shown in the left pane.

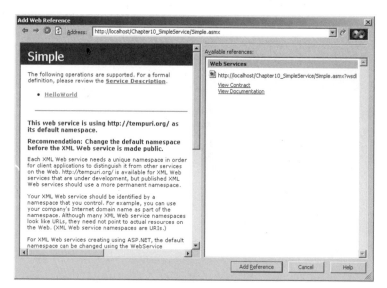

Figure 10-5 The Add Web Reference dialog box in Visual Studio .NET, pointing to the *Simple* XML Web service

Once you click the Add Reference button in the Add Web Reference dialog box, Solution Explorer will contain an additional node, named Web References. Figure 10-6 shows the Web References node expanded.

Figure 10-6 Solution Explorer, showing the newly added Web reference to the *Simple* service

One bit of confusion exists with the default behavior of the Add Web Reference dialog box. Notice that the name of the Web reference in the Solution Explorer is *localhost*. I happened to refer to the XML Web service using a URL that contained *localhost*. I can almost guarantee that's *not* what you'd expect the Web reference to be named. If you're like me, you'll initially presume that *localhost* refers to the server the service resides on and that *Simple* is the object you want to create. In reality, *localhost* refers to the namespace, and *Simple* is in fact the object you want to create. Most times, you will rename *localhost* something more meaningful. Therefore, I've renamed the namespace from *localhost* to *HelloWorld*, which I'll use for the rest of this example.

> **Tip**   My initial thought after I added the Web reference using the URL *http://localhost/Chapter10_SimpleService/Simple.asmx* was, "Darn, I should've used the machine's full name in the URL, not *localhost*." My concern was that I wouldn't be able to test the page using the XML Web service from my workstation, *Dual,* because the XML Web service was on my test machine, *Test933*. Referring to *localhost* from *Dual* wouldn't work, however, because *Dual* doesn't have the XML Web service installed, nor does it have the .NET Framework. Of course, testing from *Dual* worked just fine. The reason, obvious in retrospect, is that the XML Web service was being resolved on the Web server, *not* on the client workstation. Thus, *localhost* was resolved properly on the server, because relative to the Web server, the XML Web service was located on the *localhost*. In the real world, an XML Web service is used to expose functionality over the Internet. If you want to expose functionality that will be used on the same machine, using an XML Web service would not be very efficient, because the overhead incurred in calling an XML Web service.

Now that the Web reference has been added, I can reference the XML Web service as if it were any other class. How does this magic work? When you look at the directory on the Web server where the test page with the added Web reference is located, you'll see a new directory, named Web References. Within that directory is another directory, named HelloWorld, the name of the namespace for the Web reference. In that directory, you'll find a C# file with code similar to the code in Listing 10-2. On my system, this file is named Reference.cs.

```
//-------------------------------------------------------------------------
// <autogenerated>
//     This code was generated by a tool.
//     Runtime Version: 1.0.3307.0
//
//     Changes to this file may cause incorrect
//     behavior and will be lost if
//     the code is regenerated.
// </autogenerated>
//-------------------------------------------------------------------------

//
// This source code was auto-generated by Microsoft.VSDesigner,
// Version 1.0.3307.0.
//
namespace Chapter10_TestSimpleService.HelloWorld {
    using System.Diagnostics;
    using System.Xml.Serialization;
    using System;
    using System.Web.Services.Protocols;
    using System.Web.Services;


    /// <remarks/>
    [System.Diagnostics.DebuggerStepThroughAttribute()]
    [System.ComponentModel.DesignerCategoryAttribute("code")]
    [System.Web.Services.WebServiceBindingAttribute(
      Name="SimpleSoap", Namespace="http://tempuri.org/")]
    public class Simple :
      System.Web.Services.Protocols.SoapHttpClientProtocol {

        /// <remarks/>
        public Simple() {
            this.Url =
              "http://localhost/Chapter10_SimpleService/Simple.asmx";
        }
```

Listing 10-2 Reference.cs, the proxy code to allow consumption of the *Simple* XML Web service

```
/// <remarks/>
[System.Web.Services.Protocols.SoapDocumentMethodAttribute(
  "http://tempuri.org/HelloWorld",
  RequestNamespace="http://tempuri.org/",
  ResponseNamespace="http://tempuri.org/",
  Use=System.Web.Services.Description.SoapBindingUse.Literal,
  ParameterStyle=
  System.Web.Services.Protocols.SoapParameterStyle.Wrapped)]
public string HelloWorld(string Language) {
    object[] results = this.Invoke("HelloWorld", new object[] {
                Language});
    return ((string)(results[0]));
}


/// <remarks/>
public System.IAsyncResult BeginHelloWorld(
  string Language, System.AsyncCallback callback,
  object asyncState) {
    return this.BeginInvoke("HelloWorld", new object[] {
                Language}, callback, asyncState);
}


/// <remarks/>
public string EndHelloWorld(System.IAsyncResult asyncResult) {
    object[] results = this.EndInvoke(asyncResult);
    return ((string)(results[0]));
}
    }
}
```

Listing 10-2 is a C# file that represents a *proxy class*. (A proxy class acts like the real class but is really just a stand-in.) This proxy file happens to be a C# file because the test project I used to generate it is a C# project. Fortunately, there's no problem with using an XML Web service created with Visual Basic .NET inside a Web Forms page created using C#. As you can see, the code in this *Simple* class doesn't do any of the work of interpreting the string sent as a parameter and returning the strings based on the parameter passed in. Ignoring the complex attributes preceding the proxy class's *HelloWorld* function, the function itself is quite simple, as shown here:

```
public string HelloWorld(string Language) {
    object[] results = this.Invoke("HelloWorld", new object[] {
        Language});
    return ((string)(results[0]));
}
```

The *Invoke* method is called, and the return value is an array of objects. In this example, the first element of the array of objects is returned, cast as a *string*.

You might think the code in Listing 10-2 is a little complex (with things like *BeginInvoke*, asynchronous callbacks, and so on). Programmers familiar with RPC will recognize just how compact and relatively simple the code is. There's no need to understand this code fully; however if you're interested in learning more, you can look at the *System.Web.Services.Protocols.SoapHttpClientProtocol* class in the MSDN documentation. This proxy class descends from *SoapHttpClientProtocol*. The code in Listing 10-2 is automatically generated, and as such it should not be directly modified. If the XML Web service changes, the proxy code must be re-generated.

To use the *Simple* XML Web service, I've created a page, shown in Figure 10-7. This page initially displays "—Pick Language—" in the drop-down list box. You can select a language from the drop-down list, and the *SelectedIndexChanged* event handler will change the text of the label to "Hello World" in that language. What's actually happening here is that the page is posted back to the Web server and I then call the *Simple* XML Web service from the page. If I set the *CacheDuration* property of the *WebMethod* attribute to *600*, the XML Web service might run or the requested value might be returned from the cache. It's transparent to the consumer of the XML Web service.

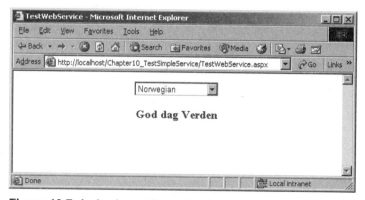

Figure 10-7 A simple test form showing the XML Web service being accessed from a Web Forms page

The TestWebService.aspx file that created the page in Figure 10-7 is shown in Listing 10-3. To make the drop-down list post back to the server, the *AutoPostBack* attribute is set to *True*. I've added *<asp:ListItem>* tags for the language selections, but I could just as easily have used the *Add* method of the *DropDownList1* object in the code-behind file.

```
<%@ Page language="c#"
Codebehind="TestWebService.aspx.cs"
AutoEventWireup="false"
Inherits="Chapter10_TestSimpleService.TestWebService" %>
<!DOCTYPE HTML PUBLIC "-//W3C//DTD HTML 4.0 Transitional//EN" >
<HTML>
    <HEAD>
        <meta name="GENERATOR" content="Microsoft Visual Studio 7.0">
        <meta name="CODE_LANGUAGE" content="C#" >
        <meta name="vs_defaultClientScript" content="JavaScript">
        <meta name="vs_targetSchema"
            content="http://schemas.microsoft.com/intellisense/ie5">
    </HEAD>
    <body>
        <form id="TestWebService" method="post" runat="server">
            <p align="center">
                <asp:DropDownList
                id="DropDownList1"
                runat="server"
                AutoPostBack="True">
                    <asp:ListItem Value="-- Pick Language --">
                    --Pick Language --</asp:ListItem>
                    <asp:ListItem Value="Spanish">
                    Spanish</asp:ListItem>
                    <asp:ListItem Value="Norwegian">
                    Norwegian</asp:ListItem>
                    <asp:ListItem Value="German">
                    German</asp:ListItem>
                    <asp:ListItem Value="English">
                    English</asp:ListItem>
                </asp:DropDownList></p>
            <p align="center">
                <asp:Label id="Label1" runat="server"
                Font-Size="Medium"
                Font-Bold="True"
                ForeColor="Red">
                </asp:Label></p>
        </form>
    </body>
</HTML>
```

Listing 10-3 TestWebService.aspx, a Web Forms page used to test the *Simple* XML Web service

The code-behind file for TestWebService.aspx is shown in Listing 10-4.

```
using System;
using System.Collections;
using System.ComponentModel;
using System.Data;
using System.Drawing;
using System.Web;
using System.Web.SessionState;
using System.Web.UI;
using System.Web.UI.WebControls;
using System.Web.UI.HtmlControls;

namespace Chapter10_TestSimpleService
{
    /// <summary>
    /// Summary description for WebForm1.
    /// </summary>
    public class TestWebService : System.Web.UI.Page
    {
        protected System.Web.UI.WebControls.DropDownList DropDownList1;

        protected System.Web.UI.WebControls.Label Label1;

        private void Page_Load(object sender, System.EventArgs e)
        {
            // Put user code to initialize the page here.
        }

        #region Web Form Designer generated code
        override protected void OnInit(EventArgs e)
        {
            //
            // CODEGEN: This call is required by the ASP.NET
            // Web Form Designer.
            //
            InitalizeComponent();
            base.OnInit(e);
        }
```

Listing 10-4 The code-behind file TestWebService.aspx.cs, used to consume the *Simple* XML Web service

```
/// <summary>
/// Required method for Designer support - do not modify
/// the contents of this method with the code editor.
/// </summary>
private void InitializeComponent()
{
    this.DropDownList1.SelectedIndexChanged +=
        new System.EventHandler(
        this.DropDownList1_SelectedIndexChanged);
    this.Load += new System.EventHandler(this.Page_Load);


}
#endregion

private void DropDownList1_SelectedIndexChanged
(object sender, System.EventArgs e)
{
    HelloWorld.Simple Hello;
    Hello=new HelloWorld.Simple();

    Label1.Text=Hello.HelloWorld(DropDownList1.SelectedItem.Text);
}
}
}
```

The three lines of the *DropDownList1_SelectedIndexChanged* handler are deceptively simple. First, I declare an object of type *Simple*. Next, I create the *Simple* object. Because I added the Web reference to this project, it will *not* try to instantiate the real *Simple* class, but rather, the proxy class shown in Listing 10-2. Finally, I set the *Label1.Text* property to the string returned from a call to the *HelloWorld* method.

What's really happening behind the scenes is quite a bit more interesting. The proxy class is calling to the XML Web service (which could be anywhere, on any accessible server). On getting a response, the string is retrieved from the object array that is returned, and the page is then refreshed with the label set to the text from the *HelloWorld* method.

XML Web Services and Command-Line Tools

As mentioned, many users will prefer adding a Web reference within Visual Studio. For those interested in the details of what's actually going on, however, the WSDL command-line tool (Wsdl.exe) will generate the proxy code for you explicitly. The command-line options for WSDL are described in Table 10-2.

Table 10-2 WSDL Command-Line Help

Command or Option	Description
wsdl.exe	Utility to generate code for XML Web service clients and XML Web services using ASP.NET from WSDL contract files, XSD schemas, and .discomap discovery documents. This tool can be used in conjunction with disco.exe. wsdl.exe <options> <url or path> <url or path> ...
<url or path>	A URL or path to a WSDL contract, an XSD schema or .discomap document.
/nologo	Suppresses the banner.
/language:<language>	The language to use for the generated proxy class. Choose from 'CS', 'VB', or 'JS' or provide a fully qualified name for a class implementing *System.CodeDom.Compiler.CodeDomProvider*. The default is 'CS' (CSharp). The short form is '/l:'.
/server	Generate an abstract class for an XML Web service implementation using ASP.NET based on the contracts. The default is to generate client proxy classes.
/namespace:<namespace>	The namespace for the generated proxy or template. The default namespace is the global namespace. The short form is '/n:'.
/out:<fileName>	The filename for the generated proxy code. The default name is derived from the service name. The short form is '/o:'.
/protocol:<protocol>	Override the default protocol to implement. Choose from 'SOAP', 'HttpGet', or 'HttpPost' or a custom protocol as specified in the configuration file.
/username:<username> /password:<password> /domain:<domain>	The credentials to use when the connecting to a server that requires authentication. The short forms are '/u:', '/p:', and '/d:'.
/proxy:<url>	The URL of the proxy server to use for HTTP requests. The default is to use the system proxy setting.
/proxyusername:<username> /proxypassword:<password> /proxydomain:<domain>	The credentials to use when the connecting to a proxy server that requires authentication. The short forms are '/pu:', '/pp:', and '/pd:'.

Command or Option	Description
/appsettingurlkey:\<key>	The configuration key to use in the code generation to read the default value for the *Url* property. The default is to not read from the config file. The short form is '/urlkey:'.
/appsettingbaseurl:\<baseurl>	The base URL to use when calculating the *url* fragment. The *appsettingurlkey* option must also be specified. The *url* fragment is the result of calculating the relative URL from the *appsettingbaseurl* to the URL in the WSDL document. The short form is 'baseurl:'.

Many of these options aren't required for normal use, but you'll generally specify at least the language and the URL of the service. For example, to generate a proxy class for the *Simple* XML Web service, I'd use the WSDL command-line tool to create a proxy class. The command is shown here:

```
C:\>wsdl.exe
    /l:VB
    http://localhost/Chapter10_SimpleService/Simple.asmx
    /n:HelloWorld.Simple
```

After this command is run, you'll need to compile the resulting Visual Basic .NET source into a DLL. The minimum command to perform this operation is shown here:

```
C:\>vbc.exe simple.vb
    /target:library
    /reference:System.dll
    /reference:System.Web.Services.dll
    /reference:System.Xml.dll
    /out:Simple.dll
```

Once the DLL is built, you can place it in the bin folder of the project you want to reference the XML Web service from and add the DLL to the *Imports* or *using* statements at the beginning of the code file.

Once Simple.dll is compiled, I created a virtual directory named TestCommandLineTools to test it. In the TestCommandLineTools folder, I created a bin folder and moved the Simple.dll created using the vbc command above into that folder. Finally, I created a simple page to ensure that I could access the XML Web service through the manually created DLL. That TestCommandLineTools.aspx file is shown in Listing 10-5.

```
<%@ Page language="C#" %>
<%@ Import Namespace="HelloWorld.Simple" %>

<html>
    <script language="C#" runat=server>
    public void Page_Load(object sender,EventArgs e)
    {
        Simple Hello=new Simple();
        Response.Write(Hello.HelloWorld("Spanish"));
    }
    </script>

<body>

</body>
</html>
```

Listing 10-5 TestCommandLineTools.aspx, a page to test using the *Simple* XML Web service.code-behind file

This page, when run, displays the Spanish version of "Hello World", "Hola Mundo".

This approach is markedly less convenient than using Visual Studio. On the other hand, it will work on a machine with nothing more than the .NET Framework and Notepad installed. In addition, the process must be repeated whenever a change takes place that affects the interface exposed by the XML Web service. Visual Studio .NET provides a more convenient Update Web Reference option.

> **Tip**   As of the build of the .NET Framework used to test this example, many of the command-line utilities seem to be spread around in a variety of directories, none of which appear in the path by default. If you're planning to use these command-line utilities, you should find the most commonly used utilities and add the directories they reside in to your path. Note that some utilities are in directories that include the build number, so you should be sure to change your path when you change versions.

A Real-World XML Web Service: Article Distribution

The *Simple* XML Web service example is certainly interesting technically, but perhaps less satisfying in other respects. What might you want to do in the real world with an XML Web service? One possibility is to allow the sharing of content between content providers and syndication partners. As I've mentioned, I do some work for the Golf Society of the U.S. In addition to the Internet content that's displayed on their own Web page, they also have a syndication arm that allows syndication partners to link their sites to the Golf Society site. This means that the Golf Society site includes dozens of virtual directories, each with the look and feel of a different syndication partner. Until now, there's been no other good way to share content. Fortunately, XML Web services offer an alternative.

Imagine an XML Web service that has access to a database of articles, indexed by author and initial publication date. The XML Web service could then dole out the appropriate content to the syndication partners, with only minimal HTML markup. The syndication partners could access the XML Web service and place the content on their pages, ideally with style sheets or font tags that would make the Golf Society content fit right in.

The following steps are required to develop such an XML Web service:

- Review security options.

- Create and test the XML Web service.

- Create a Web Application project to consume the XML Web service.

Security Options

Creating an XML Web service to distribute articles is similar to our earlier XML Web service example, but with a couple of important differences. First, if we're creating an XML Web service as part of a business, we might want to validate the user. Two sets of options are available for securing an XML Web service. The first set consists of built-in IIS security options. These options have the advantage of not requiring an additional user database, but for Internet applications, creating a domain user record for each customer probably isn't ideal. The second set of options allows for custom authentication, including the following possibilities:

- Accept user name and password as a parameter to your method calls.

- Provide a *Login* method that must be called before any other methods. You can then use cookies to verify that the requester has been authenticated.

■   Use SOAP headers or the SOAP body to store credentials.

■   Create a custom HTTP header to hold credentials.

Of these custom authentication options, the first is the most straightforward, and the least likely to fail based on client configuration problems. One subtle problem with passing credentials to the method call is that caching based on passed parameters will likely be less effective. This example will accept user name and password information as parameters to method calls. This information will then be checked against user name and password information stored in a database.

The Customer table in the GolfArticles database has *UserName* and *Password* fields that would work for this XML Web service example. The simple stored procedure shown in Listing 10-6 can be used to validate the user by selecting all the fields based on the *UserName* and *Password* parameters. Obvious extensions to this stored procedure would include setting some logging information and perhaps verifying that the article requested is dated within the contract period.

```
CREATE PROCEDURE spSelectCustomerByUsername
    @UserName nvarchar(128),
    @Password nvarchar(128)
AS
SET NOCOUNT ON
SELECT CustomerID, CompanyName, Address, City, State, PostalCode,
       ContactFirstName, ContactLastName, ContactEMail,
       ContractEnds, ContractLevel,
       UserName, [Password], DateEntered, DateModified
FROM dbo.Customer
WHERE UserName=@UserName AND [Password]=@Password
```

Listing 10-6 Stored procedure to retrieve customer information based on the *UserName* and *Password* parameters

Creating and Testing the XML Web Service

The XML Web service that will retrieve the articles from the GolfArticles database is named *GetGolfArticle*. The code for this XML Web service is contained in GetGolfArticle.asmx.vb, shown in Listing 10-7.

```
Option Strict On
Option Explicit On

Imports System.Web.Services
Imports System.Data.SqlClient


Public Class GetGolfArticle
    Inherits System.Web.Services.WebService

#Region " Web Services Designer Generated Code "

    Public Sub New()
        MyBase.New()

        'This call is required by the Web Services Designer.
        InitializeComponent()

        'Add your own initialization code after the
        'InitializeComponent() call

    End Sub

    'Required by the Web Services Designer
    Private components As System.ComponentModel.Container

    'NOTE: The following procedure is required by the
    'Web Services Designer
    'It can be modified using the Web Services Designer.
    'Do not modify it using the code editor.
    <System.Diagnostics.DebuggerStepThrough()> _
    Private Sub InitializeComponent()
        components = New System.ComponentModel.Container()
    End Sub

    Protected Overloads Overrides Sub Dispose( _
    ByVal disposing As Boolean)
        'CODEGEN: This procedure is required by the Web Services Designer
        'Do not modify it using the code editor.
        If disposing Then
            If Not (components Is Nothing) Then
                components.Dispose()
            End If
        End If
        MyBase.Dispose(disposing)
    End Sub

#End Region
```

Listing 10-7 GetGolfArticle.asmx.vb, the source for an XML Web service to distribute golf articles   *(continued)*

Listing 10-7 *continued*

```vb
<WebMethod(CacheDuration:=3600)> _
Public Function GetArticle(ByRef ArticleDate As String, _
ByVal Author As String, ByVal UserName As String, _
ByVal Password As String) As String
    Dim cn As SqlConnection
    Dim cmd As SqlCommand
    Dim dr As SqlDataReader
    Dim userDr As SqlDataReader
    Dim dt As Date

    If Me.ValidateUser(UserName, Password, userDr) = False Then
        GetArticle = "Sorry, User Information passed is invalid."
        Exit Function
    End If
    ' If the user IS valid, we might want to record
    '    that they were here...Left as an exercize for the
    '    reader
    Try
        cn = Me.GetConnection()
        cmd = New SqlCommand("spSelectArticle", cn)
        cmd.CommandType = CommandType.StoredProcedure
        cmd.Parameters.Add("@Author", Author)
        Try
            dt = Date.Parse(ArticleDate)
            cmd.Parameters.Add("@ArticleDate", dt)
        Catch edt As Exception
            ' Ignore...This is an "expected" exception.
        Finally
            dr = cmd.ExecuteReader()
            dr.Read()
            GetArticle = CType(dr("ArticleText"), String)
            ArticleDate = _
                CType(dr("ArticleDate"), Date).ToShortDateString()
        End Try
    Catch e As Exception
        GetArticle = "An exception occured " + _
        "retrieving the requested article: " + _
        e.Message
    Finally
        If cn.State = ConnectionState.Open Then
            cn.Close()
        End If
    End Try
End Function
Protected Function GetConnection() As SqlConnection
    GetConnection = New SqlConnection("server=localhost;" + _
        "Integrated Security=SSPI;Initial Catalog=GolfArticles")
```

```
        GetConnection.Open()
    End Function

    Protected Function ValidateUser(ByVal UserName As String, _
    ByVal Password As String, ByRef dr As SqlDataReader) _
    As Boolean
        Dim cn As SqlConnection
        Dim cmd As SqlCommand
        cn = GetConnection()
        Try
            cmd = New SqlCommand("spSelectCustomerByUsername", cn)
            cmd.CommandType = CommandType.StoredProcedure
            cmd.Parameters.Add("@UserName", UserName)
            cmd.Parameters.Add("@Password", Password)
            dr = cmd.ExecuteReader(CommandBehavior.CloseConnection)
            ' dr.Read will return true if data exists.
            ValidateUser = dr.Read()
        Catch e As Exception
            ValidateUser = False
        End Try
    End Function
End Class
```

The single exposed method of the *GetGolfArticle* XML Web service is *GetArticle*. This method accepts four parameters, *ArticleDate, Author, UserName,* and *Password.* The first, *ArticleDate,* is declared as a *String* rather than a *Date.* Declaring the date as a *String* allows the service to accept invalid dates as input and behave in some reasonable way. The *ArticleDate* parameter is a *ByRef* parameter because I might want to modify the date.

The stored procedure called to actually retrieve the article from the database can accept either a valid date or a *null*; the default value is *null.* When the date passed to the stored procedure is *null,* the stored procedure gets the most recent article by the specified author. The stored procedure, *spSelectArticle,* is shown in Listing 10-8.

> **Note** The *CacheDuration* property for the *GetArticle* method is set to 60 minutes. Articles aren't frequently updated, so they could be cached for up to an hour. Setting *CacheDuration* has the side effect of not recognizing username or password changes to disallow access to the service for up to an hour. If the username or password for a customer is changed, both the old and the new username and password will be recognized for the period of the *CacheDuration.* If the username and password change frequently, set *CacheDuration* to a smaller number or don't use it at all.

```
CREATE PROCEDURE spSelectArticle
    @Author nvarchar(50),
    @ArticleDate datetime = null
AS
SET NOCOUNT ON

    -- If NULL passed in, then
    IF IsNull(@ArticleDate,'19000101')='19000101'
    BEGIN
        SET @ArticleDate=GetDate()
    END

    SELECT TOP 1 ArticleDate, Author, ArticleText FROM Article
        WHERE Author=@Author AND ArticleDate<=@ArticleDate
        ORDER BY ArticleDate DESC
```

Listing 10-8 Stored procedure to select article by date or the most recent article

Inside the *GetArticle* method, the first thing I do is call the *ValidateUser* method. *ValidateUser* calls the stored procedure shown in Listing 10-5, and returns a *Boolean*. One of the parameters passed to *ValidateUser* is a *ByRef* parameter of type *SqlDataReader*. In a more realistic example, it's possible that some additional action would take place for a specific customer, and so returning the *SqlDataReader* as a *ByRef* parameter could be useful.

Once the user is validated, I create the required *SqlConnection* and *SqlCommand* objects. The connection is returned from a *protected* method named *GetConnection*. As soon as the connection and command are set up, I add parameters to the command object, as shown in this code fragment:

```
cmd.Parameters.Add("@Author", Author)
Try
    dt = Date.Parse(ArticleDate)
    cmd.Parameters.Add("@ArticleDate", dt)
Catch edt As Exception
    ' Ignore. This is an "expected" exception.
Finally
    dr = cmd.ExecuteReader()
    dr.Read()
    GetArticle = CType(dr("ArticleText"), String)
    ArticleDate = _
        CType(dr("ArticleDate"), Date).ToShortDateString()
End Try
```

The first parameter, *@Author*, is a required stored procedure parameter. The *@ArticleDate* stored procedure parameter is added within a *Try/Catch/Finally* block, because it's possible that the *ArticleDate* parameter passed to the *GetArticle* method could be invalid. If the parameter is invalid, I simply ignore it, and continue in the *Finally* block to call *ExecuteReader* on the *SqlDataReader* object. *Read* is called on the returned *SqlDataReader* object, the return value is set to the *ArticleText* parameter returned in *SqlDataReader,* and the *ArticleDate* parameter of *GetArticle* is set to the *ArticleDate* parameter returned in *SqlDataReader,* cast as a *Date* and then formatted as a short string. A *Try/Catch* block surrounds the code fragment shown here, and so if the *SqlDataReader* object doesn't contain any results, the return string will be set to a default value.

Testing this XML Web service as presented isn't as easy as testing the earlier *Simple* example. The *ByRef* parameter passed to *GetArticle* means that you can't use an HTTP *Get* method, and so you can't test the XML Web service by executing the page, as was shown in Figure 10-3. I was able to test the code by changing the *ByRef* parameter to a *ByVal* parameter temporarily.

Consuming the XML Web Service

The next step is to create a new project to test the *GetArticle* XML Web Service—again, a C# Web application. And again, calling the Visual Basic .NET XML Web service from a C# program is no problem. I added a Web reference to the *GetGolfArticle* service, exactly as shown in Figure 10-5. I renamed the namespace that appeared in Solution Explorer from *localhost* to *GolfArticle.*

To simulate a real page, I created a Web Forms page with a navigation area on the left and a main content area on the right, using a standard HTML table. I added some static content on the navigation menu, and placed a label in the main content area, and I applied some colors and fonts in both areas of the Web Forms page. The code for GetArticleTest.aspx is shown in Listing 10-9.

```
<%@ Page language="c#"
Codebehind="GetArticleTest.aspx.cs"
AutoEventWireup="false"
Inherits="Chapter10_TestArticleService.GetArticleTest" %>
<!DOCTYPE HTML PUBLIC "-//W3C//DTD HTML 4.0 Transitional//EN" >
<HTML>
    <HEAD>
        <meta name="GENERATOR" Content="Microsoft Visual Studio 7.0">
        <meta name="CODE_LANGUAGE" Content="C#">
        <meta name="vs_defaultClientScript" content="JavaScript">
        <meta name="vs_targetSchema"
            content="http://schemas.microsoft.com/intellisense/ie5">
    </HEAD>
```

Listing 10-9 GetArticleTest.aspx, the user interface part of a form that uses the *GetGolfArticle* XML Web service

(continued)

Listing 10-9 *continued*

```
    <body >
    <form id="GetArticleTest" method="post" runat="server">
        <table width="640">
            <tr>                    <td width=30%  bgcolor="#333399" valign=top>
                <font face="Verdana, Arial" color="#ffff33"><b>
                This is the normal side navigation text. The
                article text to the right is retrieved from the
                Web Service.</b><br>
                This is the article for
                <asp:Label id=Label2 runat="server"></asp:Label>
                </font>
                </td>
                <td>
                <asp:Label id="Label1"
                    runat="server"
                    Font-Names="Verdana,Arial"
                    ForeColor="Blue"></asp:Label>
                </td>
            </tr>
        </table>
    </form>
    </body>
</HTML>
```

All the real work of this page (a modest amount of work) is done in the code-behind file, GetArticleTest.aspx.cs, shown in Listing 10-10.

```
using System;
using System.Collections;
using System.ComponentModel;
using System.Data;
using System.Drawing;
using System.Web;
using System.Web.SessionState;
using System.Web.UI;
using System.Web.UI.WebControls;
using System.Web.UI.HtmlControls;

namespace Chapter10_TestArticleService
{
    /// <summary>
    /// Summary description for WebForm1
    /// </summary>
    public class WebForm1 : System.Web.UI.Page
```

Listing 10-10 GetArticleTest.aspx.cs, the code-behind file used to display text from the *GetGolfArticle* XML Web service

```
    {
        protected System.Web.UI.WebControls.Label Label2;

        protected System.Web.UI.WebControls.Label Label1;

        private void Page_Load(object sender, System.EventArgs e)
        {
            // Put user code to initialize the page here.
            string strDate;
            string strRet;
            strDate="";
            GolfArticle.GetGolfArticle Article;
            Article=new GolfArticle.GetGolfArticle();
            strRet=Article.GetArticle(
                ref strDate,"Ragone, Nick",
                "Doug","Testonly");
            Label1.Text=strRet;
            Label2.Text=strDate;
        }


        #region Web Form Designer generated code
        override protected void OnInit(EventArgs e)
        {
            //
            // CODEGEN: This call is required by the
            // ASP.NET Web Form Designer.
            //
            InitializeComponent();
            base.OnInit(e);
        }


        /// <summary>
        /// Required method for Designer support - do not modify
        /// the contents of this method with the code editor.
        /// </summary>
        private void InitializeComponent()
        {
            this.Load += new System.EventHandler(this.Page_Load);
        }
        #endregion
    }
}
```

By now, most of this code should look familiar, but one part of the listing, shown here, might not be obvious:

```
strRet=Article.GetArticle(
    ref strDate,"Ragone, Nick",
    "Doug","Testonly");
```

When calling a method in C# that expects what Visual Basic .NET calls a *ByRef* parameter, the parameter must be prefixed by the keyword *ref*. C# methods can also use *out* modifiers. The *out* modifier indicates that the parameter can be modified but will not be used in any way before being set by the method the *out* parameter is passed to. Specifying *ref* means that the parameter will be modified and that the parameter passed in to the method will be used in the method, and thus must be initialized in the calling routine.

Note that the call to *GetArticle* hard-codes the *UserName* and *Password* parameters. In this case the user name is "Doug", with a password of "Testonly". If you pass an incorrect user name and password, *GetArticle* returns a message saying that the user information is invalid. When you run this test, GetArticleTest.aspx displays the page shown in Figure 10-8.

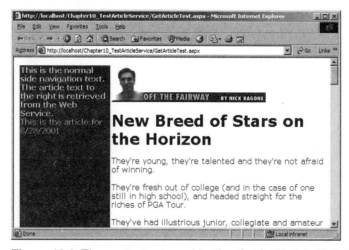

Figure 10-8 The content returned by the *GetGolfArticle* XML Web service

The actual article text stored in the database has little in the way of HTML directives beyond simple paragraph breaks and an *<H1>* tag for the title. The GetArticleTest.aspx page controls the color and face of the font. In the real world, this type of design moves us closer to separating content from presentation, the holy grail of Web site designers everywhere.

Possible Enhancements

Returning more than a single value from an XML Web Service can cause some difficulty, as our experience with a *ByRef* parameter demonstrates. In other scenarios, a larger number of values need to be returned.

Publishing articles by means of an XML Web service is useful, but there are certainly some additional methods that could be exposed to make using the

GetGolfArticle XML Web service easier. With a method to publish a catalog of authors as well as a method to retrieve the dates of all articles, a user of this syndicated content could dynamically create pages that show all the authors, with a drill-down list that would allow users to view the existing dates and possibly titles. This XML Web service wouldn't need to be protected by a user name and password—allowing noncustomers to discover what articles are present might even be desirable. For example, a simple XML Web service method to return all articles, ordered by *ArticleDate*, is shown here:

```
<WebMethod(CacheDuration:=3600)> _
Public Function GetArticleList() As DataSet
    Dim cn As SqlConnection
    Dim da As SqlDataAdapter
    Dim ds As DataSet
    cn = GetConnection()

    Try
        da = New SqlDataAdapter( _
            "SELECT * FROM Article ORDER BY ArticleDate", cn)
        ds = New DataSet()
        da.Fill(ds, "Article")
        GetArticleList = ds
    Catch e As Exception

    Finally
        cn.Close()
    End Try
End Function
```

In this example, the *GetArticleList* method returns a *DataSet* object rather than a *DataReader* object or any of the other objects that can contain multiple records. Why a *DataSet?* When data moves across a machine or process boundary, it's said to be *marshaled*. The data must somehow be converted from the internal type to a format that can be sent across a wire. In the case of XML Web services, the wire format is XML, and so the object must in some way be convertible to text.

The *GetArticleList* method returns a *DataSet* object, because *DataSet* can be marshaled by ASP.NET. All of the other alternatives (such as *SqlDataReader*) *can't* be marshaled by an XML Web service. All the standard types, such as *int* and *double, Enum* types, classes and structs, *XmlNode* objects, and *DataSet* objects can be marshaled by ASP.NET. Arrays of the supported types can also be marshaled. Although not every object can be marshaled by an XML Web service, the types that can be marshaled are much richer than those available to DCOM objects, without using custom marshaling.

Conclusion

HTML changed how we work in ways the originators of the format couldn't have imagined. In a similar way, it's almost inevitable that XML Web services will change how we work in unimagined ways. No longer will each corporate intranet be an island, isolated from all the data and processes that exist beyond its walls. With XML Web services, work can be partitioned in almost any way that makes sense, without regard to the operating system or tools used to create the XML Web service.

Most important to those of us who develop applications for the Microsoft .NET Framework, Visual Studio .NET makes creating and using XML Web services easier than we could have imagined. When I was developing the outline for this book, I predicted that this chapter especially would be a challenge. My expectations were framed by my experience using some of the predecessor technologies, such as RPC and DCOM. But surprisingly, all the examples presented in this chapter were relatively easy to produce.

This book has laid the foundation for your explorations with the .NET Framework in general, and with ASP.NET in particular. ASP.NET is *the* way for Web developers to create scalable, dynamic Web applications. From Web Forms through XML Web services, ASP.NET presents tremendous opportunities for developers in the know. I hope I've helped you become such a developer.

Appendix A

Configuring ASP.NET Applications in IIS

One of the most confusing aspects of working with ASP.NET is properly configuring the security of your Web application. Security configuration can be critical to the life of the application and even to the life of a business. Unfortunately, a large part of how an ASP.NET Web application is configured might have nothing to do with ASP.NET and everything to do with Internet Information Services (IIS).

In this appendix, I'm going to walk you through setting up your ASP.NET applications in IIS. The most important point to remember is that ASP.NET doesn't operate in total isolation from IIS. As you'll see, in some cases—most notably, authentication—ASP.NET and IIS must be configured in tandem to allow you to get the most out of both ASP.NET and IIS.

ASP.NET User Authentication

ASP.NET allows you to configure one of three types of user authentication: *forms authentication, Passport authentication,* and *Windows authentication.* Forms authentication is the type of security used by virtually all Internet applications. Using forms authentication, you can do pretty much whatever you want in terms of determining who is and isn't an authorized user. You can also determine which pages require security. In addition, whenever a user gets to a page that requires authentication, the user is transparently redirected to a specified login page. The login page can use whatever source of information it wants to authenticate the user. Once authenticated, the user can be redirected to the page originally requested. The process of authenticating a user via a custom form is much cleaner using ASP.NET forms authentication than it has traditionally been in ASP.

With Passport authentication, a Passport server determines who is an authorized user. The Passport software development kit (SDK) will allow you to begin development using Passport, but there's also specific Passport authentication support within the .NET Framework to support this type of authentication. The Passport SDK is available for download from *http://msdn.microsoft.com/downloads/*.

Windows authentication piggybacks on top of the authentication capabilities in IIS. Although the implementation of authentication in IIS hasn't changed significantly with the most recent releases of IIS, ASP.NET actually uses this authentication in a slightly different way, which has resulted in some confusion. In the next section, we'll step through the creation of a new Web application in IIS to help clarify this process.

While you're developing Web applications using Visual Studio .NET, you don't have to worry, for the most part, about configuring your applications in IIS. Visual Studio .NET makes most of the decisions for you, and it does most of the configuration the way you'd want to. Configuring ASP.NET to use Windows authentication is one notable exception. However, when you're moving to a production server, you might be on your own, faced with the IIS configuration dialog boxes for the first time. Never fear!

Creating a New Virtual Directory in IIS

When you need to create a new Web application on a Windows 2000 Web server, the first thing to do is to create the folder in which the application will be located. This sounds obvious and simple, but the location of the folder you create can have implications for the ease of maintaining your application later.

Whenever possible, the *physical* layout of your application should mimic the *logical* layout. If you have an application named AppB that should inherit most of its settings from AppA, creating AppB logically under AppA makes a lot of sense. To make that relationship clear, it also makes sense for the folder in which AppB resides to be a subdirectory of AppA. *IIS doesn't require this arrangement, however!* When searching through the logical folders that exist at a higher level than a given application for configuration settings, IIS uses the logical hierarchy, not the physical hierarchy. Using a set of applications in which the logical and physical hierarchies match is much easier.

For this example, we'll create a folder named AppendixA in C:\Inetpub\wwwroot. After the folder is created, open the Internet Information Services console by double-clicking Internet Services Manager in Administrative Tools. Internet Information Services is shown in Figure A-1.

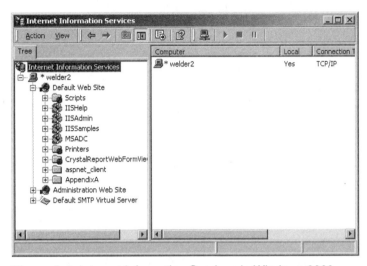

Figure A-1 Internet Information Services in Windows 2000

As you can see in the left pane of Internet Information Services, the folder we added, AppendixA, is displayed as a normal folder under Default Web Site. Above AppendixA you can see folders with various icons. The icon next to IISHelp and others indicates that these folders are set up as virtual directories.

If you right-click on AppendixA and choose Properties from the shortcut menu, the Properties dialog box will appear, as shown in Figure A-2.

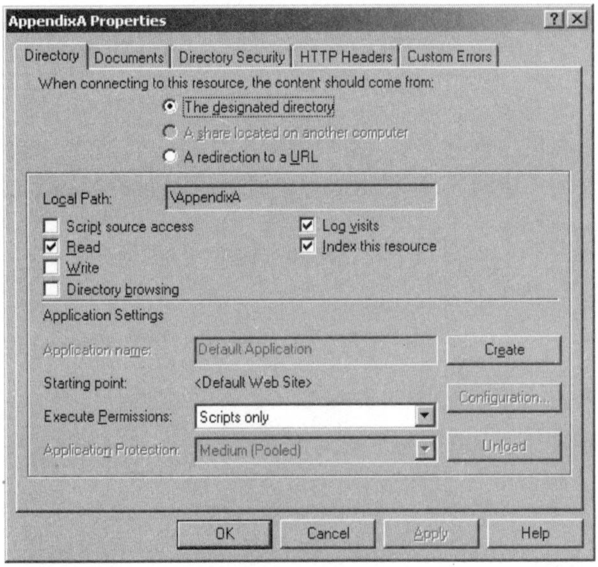

Figure A-2 The Properties dialog box in Internet Information Services for the AppendixA folder that isn't a virtual directory

Figure A-2 shows the Properties dialog box as it appears for a directory that isn't set up as a virtual directory. To make this folder a virtual directory for IIS, click the Create button on the Directory tab. The settings on the tab will be modified as shown in Figure A-3.

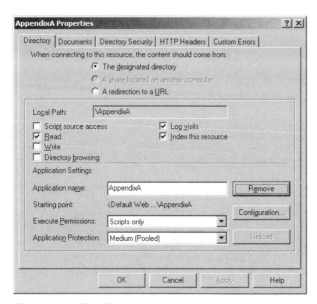

Figure A-3 The Properties dialog box in Internet Information Services for the AppendixA folder after it has been made a virtual directory

Several of these settings can be configured to customize the behavior of your Web application. You might want to clear the Read check box because in general, users shouldn't have to actually read files in the folder in the traditional sense. The exception, when Read must be set, is when you're allowing a default document—that is, a document that will be called if only the virtual folder is specified. (More on default documents later in this appendix.) The Execute Permissions drop-down list enables you to specify the type of operations that can occur. You'd set Execute Permissions to None only when you're running applications that have just HTML content, without any ASP.NET pages. Setting Execute Permissions to Scripts Only allows the application to execute scripts—files with extensions such as .asp and .aspx. This is commonly the setting for your ASP.NET application directories. The last setting in the Execute Permissions drop-down list is Scripts And Executables, which allows the application to execute scripts and executable files.

> **Note**   Visual Studio stores executable files in a subfolder named bin. You might think that the bin folder should have Execute Permissions set to Scripts And Executables because the DLLs used by ASP.NET pages are located there, but that's not the correct setting. In practice, when you call an .aspx page, you're not really directly calling any of the DLLs, so it makes sense, from the standpoint of IIS, that you don't need to have Execute permission in the bin folder.

The Documents tab of the Properties dialog box is shown in Figure A-4.

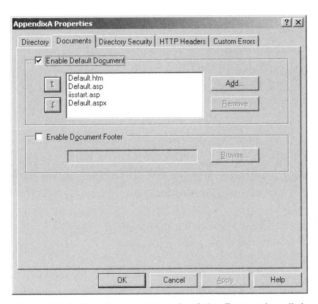

Figure A-4 The Documents tab of the Properties dialog box

If you have a default document set on the Documents tab and one of the default documents exists, when a user goes to a folder and specifies only the folder name (for example, http://localhost/AppendixA/), that document will be shown. In practice, you often need to set the default document only in the root of the Web site. Remember, if you want to use a default document, the folder must have Read selected on the Directory tab of the Properties dialog box. Selecting the Enable Document Footer check box on the Documents tab allows you to specify the name of a file containing an HTML fragment (not an entire document) that will be included as a footer for documents displayed in this folder.

The Directory Security tab of the Properties dialog box is shown in Figure A-5.

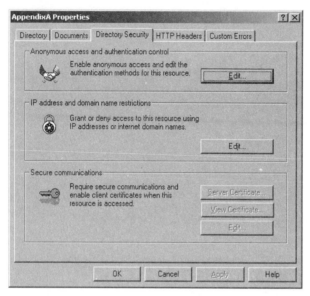

Figure A-5 The Directory Security tab of the Properties dialog box

The Anonymous Access And Authentication Control section of this tab allows you to control how users are authenticated in your virtual directory. Clicking this Edit button displays the Authentication Methods dialog box, shown in Figure A-6.

Figure A-6 The Authentication Methods dialog box

There are a few options available here, but basically, this dialog box allows you to do two things: you can either allow anonymous access to the virtual directory or require users to be Windows users.

All Windows operations are in fact controlled by security, and all actions must take place in the context of some user. So when we specify that anonymous users are allowed by selecting the Anonymous Access checkbox, what user account is used? Clicking Edit in the Anonymous Access section of the Authentication Methods dialog box will display the Anonymous User Account dialog box that will allow you to select the account under whose context anonymous users will work. By default, this account is named *IUSR_<machine name>*. This account needs to have permissions for the folders containing documents that anonymous users will have access to.

If your ASP.NET application plans to use Windows authentication, you *must* clear the Anonymous Access check box. If you don't do this, all users will be allowed access to your application without authentication taking place. One reason you might use Windows authentication is to enable the application to get the identity of the user. When Windows authentication is set correctly in IIS (that is, Anonymous Access is disabled) and in ASP.NET, you'll be able to get the domain name of the user in *Context.User.Identity.Name*.

> **Caution**   If you don't properly set Windows authentication in both IIS *and* ASP.NET, *Context.User.Identity.Name* won't return the value you expect. You might get the name of the anonymous user or even no user if both IIS and the Web.config file for a virtual directory don't agree. This is a *very* common problem seen on the newsgroups throughout the Betas for ASP.NET. Similar problems existed in ASP; however, ASP.NET has some configuration settings that might lull you into thinking that ASP.NET is controlling authentication all by itself. That's not the case. ASP.NET provides more support for the existing IIS authentication methods, but it doesn't override them.

The Authenticated Access section of the Authentication Methods dialog box contains three check boxes: Basic Authentication, Digest Authentication For Windows Domain Servers, and Integrated Windows Authentication. Selecting Basic Authentication sends the user name and password in essentially clear text from the client to the server. (The credentials are encoded but not encrypted.)

The Digest Authentication For Windows Domain Servers option addresses many of the weaknesses of Basic Authentication, with a couple of restrictions.

The Windows 2000 server must be in a domain, and all user accounts must be configured to have the Save Password As Encrypted Clear Text option enabled. Strictly speaking, Internet Explorer 5.0 or later isn't required, but browser support for Digest authentication isn't universal.

If the Integrated Windows Authentication option, formerly known as NT LAN Manager or NTLM and Windows NT Challenge/Response authentication, is selected, the browser attempts to use the current user's credentials from a domain login. If that fails, a login prompt appears. This isn't a very attractive login prompt, and the developer has no control over it.

Remember, as long as you disable Anonymous Access, any of these authenticated access methods will allow your application to determine the user name for any page requested.

The IP Address And Domain Name Restrictions section of the Directory Security tab of the Properties dialog box (Figure A-5) contains an Edit button that allows you to control IP address and domain name restrictions. These sorts of restrictions are seldom used, but they can be effective in some intranet applications by allowing you to specify a subnet mask to control IP addresses allowed or disallowed into the application. The Server Certificate, View Certificate, and Edit buttons in the Secure Communications section of the Directory Security tab can be used to set up a security certificate to allow Secure Sockets Layer (SSL) communications. The MSDN documentation (especially the IIS Resource Kit) contains much more information on these options.

The last two tabs in the Properties dialog box, HTTP Headers and Custom Errors, aren't terribly interesting. As their names suggest, they allow you to control HTTP headers and custom errors. By configuring the Custom Errors tab, you can set up error handling pages for any of the standard HTTP errors—such as a 400 error, "resource not found."

The Configuration button on the Directory tab of the AppendixA Properties dialog box (Figure A-3) allows you to control certain aspects of the application as well as troubleshoot problems with an ASP.NET installation. When you click Configuration, the Application Configuration dialog box appears, as shown in Figure A-7.

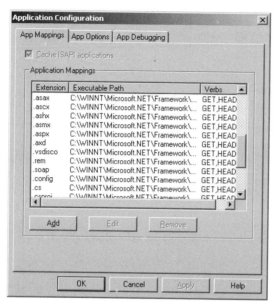

Figure A-7 The Application Configuration dialog box

I've scrolled down in the list of application mappings so that you can see the extensions used by ASP.NET. In this dialog box, you can add or edit the executable path associated with each file extension.

Topics such as application mappings and verbs might seem somewhat obscure, but the Application Configuration dialog box can help you track down some odd problems. In several instances, people using ASP or ASP.NET applications have reported that when they execute an .asp or .aspx page, they get the source code in their browser rather than the HTML that should be rendered by the page. The root of this problem is often found in the Application Configuration dialog box. If the mapping between extensions and executable paths breaks, either through a botched installation or some gremlin, you can correct that problem using this dialog box.

The other two tabs in the Application Configuration dialog box, App Options and App Debugging, contain settings used mostly by ASP applications.

Appendix B

What You Need to Know About HTML to Use This Book

ASP.NET applications are similar to traditional applications in many ways. If you're creating a simple form that will add a patient to a database, for example, the application will have three parts:

■ The *database logic* saves the record.

■ The *validation logic* ensures that the record being added is valid.

■ The *user interface layer* allows the user to interact with the database and the validation logic.

To a large extent, the database logic in an ASP.NET application is exactly the same as that in a traditional application. The validation logic is similar as well, although there's the complication of client-side JavaScript working together with server-side validation written in Visual Basic .NET or C#. (I discuss this topic in Chapter 7.) The user interface layer, however, is really quite different. Traditional applications provide a mechanism for creating widgets on screen. Often the widgets are designed in advance using a screen designer, and the metalanguage that describes the exact layout is a mystery to most programmers. ASP.NET applications are different. Hypertext Markup Language (HTML) is used as the metalanguage. HTML is a language that describes how various text and widgets should be displayed on the browser screen.

> **Note** Keep in mind that this appendix is only the briefest introduction to HTML. Check your favorite bookstore to find more information about this topic.

HTML Tags

HTML consists of *tags*—special directives that let the browser know how you want elements on the page to display. HTML tags are enclosed within angle brackets (< >). For example, at the very beginning and the very end of an HTML page, you would have the *<HTML>* and *</HTML>* tags, respectively. By convention, tags that require a start tag and an end tag (as the *<HTML>* tag does) are identical except for the leading slash (/) in the end tag. Within the *<HTML></HTML>* tags, every HTML page should have *<HEAD></HEAD>* tags and *<BODY></BODY>* tags. The *<HEAD></HEAD>* tags can contain *<META>* tags, which can offer hints of what the page will be displaying. (*<META>* tags are useful for automated tools that roam the Web looking for pages to include in search engine results.) The *<TITLE></TITLE>* tags mark the beginning and end of the title of the page. This title will appear in the browser's title bar.

> **Note**   Although most people capitalize the text in HTML tags, HTML isn't case sensitive. This is one of many contrasts between HTML and the newer, but related by heritage, Extensible Markup Language (XML), which is case sensitive.

With the exception of the *<META>* tag, all the tags mentioned so far are always used in pairs, with a start and an end tag. Some tags don't require an end tag. The most common is the line break tag, *
*. With some tags, the end tag is optional. For example, some folks don't use the end tag for the paragraph tags, *<P></P>*.

HTML Links

HTML allows you to create *links*, also known as *hyperlinks*, within your pages. A link enables you to jump from one page to another. These links are marked by *<A></A>* tags. For example, to create a link on a page that will enable you to jump to a page named test.aspx, you would use code like this:

```
To get to test.aspx, <A HREF="test.aspx">Click Here</A>
```

The Click Here link would appear on most browsers as underlined text, although you can control and modify exactly what links look like. Generally, changing what a link looks like isn't a good idea. Users have grown to expect that underlined words and phrases allow them to jump to another page, so working against that expectation can lead to frustration and confusion. The <A> tag is unusual in that it can be used as a link, as in the example here, or as an anchor that defines a named section of a document. If the name of an anchor is appended to a URL, the browser will jump to the anchor of that name. If the <A> tag has an *HREF* attribute, it is a link. If the <A> tag has a *NAME* attribute but not an *HREF*, it is an anchor. If both *NAME* and *HREF* attributes are present, the tag is both an anchor and a link.

If you wanted to jump to another page but also pass in an argument that could be used inside the page, you could use the following code:

```
To get to test.aspx, <A HREF="test.aspx?arg=1">Click Here</A>
```

To pass multiple arguments to a page, the same syntax is used, but with an ampersand between arguments, like this:

```
To get to test.aspx,
<A HREF="test.aspx?arg1=1&arg2=2">Click Here</A>
```

HTML Widgets

HTML provides text boxes, drop-down lists, list boxes, check boxes, and radio buttons. Although ASP.NET uses slight variations on these widgets, understanding how the base HTML widgets are used is helpful. To get an idea, take a look at Listing B-1.

```
<HTML>
<HEAD>
<TITLE>Example HTML Widget Page</TITLE>
</HEAD>
<BODY>

What follows is a form.  <B><I>This text is outside the form.</I></B>

<FORM action="appendixb.htm">

This is a text box.  The <I>value</I> attribute means that there is a
default value for this text box:
<INPUT type="text" id=text1 name=text1 value="Hello HTML"><BR>

This is a text box that displays "*" for each character,
commonly used as a password entry box:
<INPUT type="password" id=password1 name=password1><BR>
```

Listing B-1 HTML listing showing the use of common HTML widgets   *(continued)*

Listing B-1   *continued*

```
This is a text area.  I have set the rows to 2, and the columns to 20:
<TEXTAREA rows=2 cols=20 id=textarea1 name=textarea1>
</TEXTAREA><BR>

This is a check box:<INPUT type="checkbox" id=checkbox1 name=checkbox1><BR>

This is a group of radio buttons:<BR>
<INPUT type="radio" id=radio1 name=radiotest>Yes?<BR>
<INPUT type="radio" id=radio2 name=radiotest>No?<BR>

This is a drop-down list:<SELECT id=select1 name=select1>
<OPTION>Option 1</OPTION>
<OPTION>Option 2</OPTION>
<OPTION>Option 3</OPTION>
<OPTION>Option 4</OPTION>
</SELECT><BR>

This is a list box.  This is a multi-select list box, because the "multiple"
directive is inside the &lt;SELECT&gt; tag.
<SELECT size=3 id=select2 name=select2 multiple>
<OPTION>Option 1</OPTION>
<OPTION>Option 2</OPTION>
<OPTION>Option 3</OPTION>
<OPTION>Option 4</OPTION>

<INPUT type="submit" value="This is a Submit button" id=submit1 name=submit1>

</FORM>
</BODY>
</HTML>
```

Notice first the general structure of this simple HTML page. Surrounding everything are the start and end *<HTML></HTML>* tags. Inside the *<HTML></HTML>* tags are *<HEAD></HEAD>* tags, which contain *<TITLE></TITLE>* tags. Next are the *<BODY></BODY>* tags, which contain the HTML code that will drive the browser's display.

In the text at the top of the *<BODY>* section, I've used *<I></I>* and *<B></B>* tags to create italic and boldface text. Notice that the end tags for the italic and boldface text are properly nested. Although current browsers generally will accept HTML code in which the start and end tags of such blocks aren't nested, it's a good idea to properly nest your tags.

All the widgets are contained within *<FORM></FORM>* tags. HTML widgets outside a form are of no value and generally won't do what you want them to do. A *<FORM>* tag can also contain an attribute describing what *action* to take when the form is submitted as well as a *method* attribute to specify how the information from the form is transmitted to the server. The method attribute can be one of two values, *Post* or *Get*. The *Get* method is the default; however, *Get* is deprecated in HTML 4 because of internationalization problems. The *Post* method is a two-step method (transparent to you, as the developer of the page) that sends all the information entered in a form to a standard location, where the server reads it. The *Get* method appends the form contents to the URL as arguments. For example, if a form has a single text box, *name*, that contains the value "Doug", and if the form is using the *Get* method and the action is a page named test.aspx, this is the resulting URL that will next appear in the browser's location window (barring any processing error):

```
http://<host>/<directory>/test.aspx?name=Doug
```

So which method is best to use—*Post* or *Get*? As is often the case, there's no simple answer. For small forms with little data being passed back and forth, *Get* can be more efficient. For larger forms, some servers will break if the URL is too long, and so it's often best to use *Post*. In addition, if you're sending a password back from the form, you should use *Post* so that the password won't appear in the URL as plain text.

Each widget is fairly self-explanatory once you've seen the code in Listing B-1 and then the resulting browser screen, shown in Figure B-1. For the text box, I've provided a default value for the control. In virtually all cases, the *value* attribute in an HTML control determines either what is initially displayed or what is returned when the widget is selected and the form is submitted. The ASP.NET controls use a more Visual Basic–like structure, so the *Text* property of a control maps to the HTML *value* attribute. Some users may not like the fact that the ASP.NET objects have properties with different names than the HTML attributes they are mapped to, but Visual Basic programmers should feel comfortable with the ASP.NET objects.

Also, in the description of the list box, I wanted to display the text "<SELECT>". Rather than using that literal, I used *<SELECT>*. If I'd used less than and greater than symbols (< or >), *<SELECT>* would have been interpreted as the beginning of a list box, which isn't what I wanted.

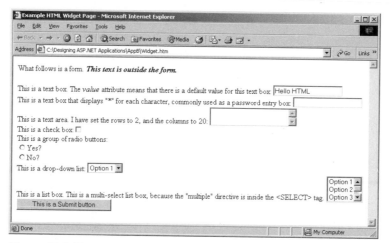

Figure B-1 The results of displaying the HTML from Listing B-1 in Microsoft Internet Explorer

Many more character entity references that enable you to display special characters within the HTML stream are available. One of the more common character entity references is * *, which creates a nonbreaking space. This reference can be useful if you want to force some text to be displayed on a single line without a line break—for example, the first and last name in a proper name such as "George Washington". You can test for where line breaks might occur, but for a variety of reasons, the breaks might not occur on one browser in exactly the same place as on other browsers. For example, the fonts selected by one browser on one machine might not exactly match what another browser on another machine selects.

HTML Tables

One of the maddening things about HTML is just how flexible it can be and how forgiving many browsers are about sloppy HTML. The flip side of that flexibility is that other browsers are *not* so flexible, and so code that's not exactly correct might perform well in one browser yet produce nothing in another. One area in which it's easy to misuse HTML is with HTML tables.

If you use Microsoft Word, you might be familiar with the powerful table features. I've never done any serious work in the financial areas most often associated with tables, but I've used tables extensively to properly format many different types of documents, including some of the text for this book. Tables can be useful when you're using variable-pitch fonts and trying to get more than a single column to align. "But wait," you say, "I don't need to do that in my ASP.NET application." Well, I think you might.

As you've seen, the underlying metalanguage used to describe the user interface in an ASP.NET application is different from what you'd expect in a standard Visual Basic application. In addition, the underlying assumptions about what you can do and what the metalanguage was designed to convey are also quite different. In a Visual Basic application, you might drop a widget in a particular location and expect that it will always appear exactly there on any machine that runs the application. HTML is different. Remember, HTML was designed as a *markup* language that basically gave hints to the browser as to the location of various text and widgets. The browser was free to render these components as best it could, using widgets native to the underlying operating system to render an approximation of what you laid out. Unlike in Visual Basic, there's no convenient way in HTML to use absolute positioning to exactly locate a text box at, say, 1 inch below and 2 inches to the right of the upper left of the screen. Dynamic HTML (DHTML) and style sheets offer greater control over positioning, but not all browsers in use today support all the same DHTML syntax; even where the syntax is compatible, the results are often not identical across different browsers.

Look again at Figure B-1. Even though the underlying HTML text might be formatted in a particular way, with indentation and line breaks to allow the listing to appear correctly in this book, the browser simply ignores all formatting I implicitly add with indenting and line breaks, and uses only those directives it understands—in this example, *
* tags.

What if I wanted the form to line up more like what appears in Figure B-2? In this case, all the text is conveniently aligned on the left, and all the widgets are lined up on the right.

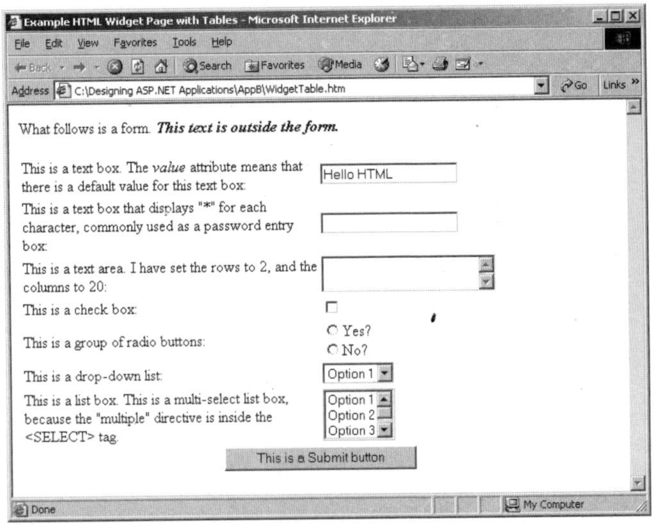

Figure B-2 The results of displaying the HTML from Listing B-2 in Internet Explorer, using a table to format the form

Listing B-2 shows how this alignment was accomplished, but in short, the answer is *HTML tables*. The *<TABLE>* tag marks the beginning of an HTML table. In Figure B-2, it's not obvious that a table was used because no table border is showing. (Many attributes can control the display of tables, and I encourage you to look at a book dedicated to HTML for more information on this subject.)

```
<HTML>
<HEAD>
<TITLE>Example HTML Widget Page with Tables</TITLE>
</HEAD>
<BODY>

What follows is a form. <B><I>This text is outside the form.</I></B>

<FORM action="appendixb.htm">
<TABLE width=100%>
<TR>
    <TD width=50%>
    This is a text box.  The <I>value</I> attribute means that there is a
    default value for this text box:
    </TD>
    <TD>
    <INPUT type="text" id=text1 name=text1 value="Hello HTML"><BR>
    </TD>
</TR>
<TR>
    <TD>
    This is a text box that displays "*" for each character,
    commonly used as a password entry box:
    </TD>
    <TD>
    <INPUT type="password" id=password1 name=password1><BR>
    </TD>
</TR>
<TR>
    <TD>
    This is a text area.  I have set the rows to 2, and the columns to 20:
    </TD>
    <TD>
    <TEXTAREA rows=2 cols=20 id=textarea1 name=textarea1>
    </TEXTAREA><BR>
    </TD>
</TR>
<TR>
    <TD>
    This is a check box:
    </TD>
```

Listing B-2 HTML listing showing the use of common HTML widgets and HTML tables

```
    <TD>
    <INPUT type="checkbox" id=checkbox1 name=checkbox1><BR>
    </TD>
</TR>
<TR>
    <TD>
    This is a group of radio buttons:
    </TD>
    <TD>
    <INPUT type="radio" id=radio1 name=radiotest>Yes?<BR>
    <INPUT type="radio" id=radio2 name=radiotest>No?<BR>
    </TD>
</TR>
<TR>
    <TD>
    This is a drop-down list:
    </TD>
    <TD>    <SELECT id=select1 name=select1>
    <OPTION>Option 1</OPTION>
    <OPTION>Option 2</OPTION>
    <OPTION>Option 3</OPTION>
    <OPTION>Option 4</OPTION>
    </SELECT><BR>
    </TD>
</TR>
<TR>
    <TD>
    This is a list box.
    This is a multi-select list box, because the "multiple"
    directive is inside the &lt;SELECT&gt; tag.
    </TD>
    <TD>    <SELECT size=3 id=select2 name=select2 multiple>
    <OPTION>Option 1</OPTION>
    <OPTION>Option 2</OPTION>
    <OPTION>Option 3</OPTION>
    <OPTION>Option 4</OPTION>
    </TD>
</TR>
<TR align=center>
    <TD colspan=2>
    <INPUT type="submit" value="This is a Submit button"
        id=submit1 name=submit1>
    </TD>
</TR>
</TABLE>
</FORM>
</BODY>
</HTML>
```

Each row of the table is enclosed within *<TR></TR>* tags. These table row tags have additional attributes to control the background color, alignment, and other properties. Within each row, *<TD></TD>* tags control the individual columns of the row. To align the widgets in the second column starting in the middle of the page, I set the *width* attribute of the *<TD>* tag to *50%*, meaning that the first column will take up 50 percent of the table, and because the table has only two columns, the second column will take up 50 percent of the table as well.

The last row of the table is different: it will contain only the single Submit button. To center this button in the table, I use another special attribute of the *<TD>* tag, the *colspan* attribute. In this case, I specify that the first column of this row will span two columns, meaning that it will take up the entire row. Using *colspan* and the related *<TR>* attribute *rowspan*, complex formatting can be accomplished in a way that retains the browser independence that's the hallmark of a good Web application. In addition, the *align* attribute of the *<TR>* tag is set to *center*, meaning that the contents of the row will appear centered. The *<CENTER></CENTER>*tags also enable centering, but the *align* attribute of the table row or column can be more convenient.

One problem with HTML tables is that if you omit an end tag or perhaps nest the tags improperly, the results vary depending on the browser in use. Internet Explorer will generally render the table correctly, albeit more slowly than a correctly formed HTML table. Netscape Navigator 4 and earlier might not display the table. Thus, while tables are almost essential to properly laying out the user interface for your ASP.NET application, they can be a source of some difficulties.

Note   Other techniques are available for tricking HTML into laying out a document or form exactly as you want. One common way is to use invisible images sized to force text, graphics, and widgets to appear exactly where you want them to be. This approach isn't something I've found especially useful. In addition, in some examples in this book, I don't use tables to pretty up the display if the result is to obscure the underlying program logic. That said, in the real world, virtually every page I create has a specific structure that involves the extensive use of tables.

Index

Send feedback about this index to *mspindex@microsoft.com*.

Special Characters

& (ampersand), 80, 379
<> (angle brackets), 1, 192, 378
* (asterisk), 119
@ (at symbol), 272
\ (backslash), 225
^ (caret), 135
{} (curly braces), 57, 135
- (hyphen), 135
( ) (parentheses), 57
+ (plus sign), 80
"" (quotation marks), 86, 225
' (single quotation mark), 297
/ (slash), 1, 378
/// (slashes), 198
[] (square brackets), 135
<% and %> (tags), 15, 116, 306
~ (tilde), 180
_ (underscore), 135

A

<A></A> tags, 378
action attribute, 110, 381
action queries, 257–61
Active Server Pages. *See* Microsoft Active Server Pages
ADO. *See* Microsoft ActiveX Data Objects
ADO.NET. *See* Microsoft ADO.NET
alert function, JavaScript, 215
<allow> tags 95
ampersand (&), 80, 379
anchors, HTML, 379
AndAlso operator, 55–56
angle brackets (<>), 1, 192, 378
animations, 2
anonymous access settings, 372–74
application development, 65–108
  application files and directories, 75–76 (*see also* directories)
  ASP and ASP.NET file names, 67
  ASP example, 65–66
  ASP.NET development model, 71–72
  C# example, 66–69
  case sensitivity and, 68
  configuring applications (*see* configuration; Web.config files)

application development, *continued*
  creating Web pages, 76–81
  environment (*see* Microsoft Visual Studio .NET)
  history of (*see* application development history)
  HTTP handlers and HTTP modules, 84
  Page directive, 67–68
  separating coding of presentation and content, 10, 18–19, 164, 186, 280
  Visual Basic .NET example, 69–70
  Visual Studio .NET IDE for, 72–74
  XML Web services, 81–84
application development history, 1–20
  ASP and, 11–19
  ASP.NET and, 19–20
  CGI and, 3–7
  dynamic content and, 2–3
  HTML and, 1–2
  ISAPI and, 7–11
application directory, 75–76, 93
applications
  ASP.NET Web Applications (*see* ASP.NET Web Applications)
  configuring, in IIS, 367–75
  configuring, with Web.config files (*see* Web.config files)
  console, 5
  developing (*see* application development)
  dynamic, 2–3
  identity settings, 99
  .NET Framework support, 23
  partitioning, 215, 240, 241–42 (*see also* client-side scripting)
  parts of traditional, 377
  service, 5, 81
  Web Forms (*see* Web Forms)
  Windows Forms, 23
  XML Web service consumer, 344–54, 361–64
  XML Web services (*see* XML Web services)
Application Service Providers, 13
appSettings section, 87, 254
arrays, 41, 56, 58–59
ascx extension, 172, 173
asmx extension, 336
ASP. *See* Microsoft Active Server Pages

387

W

X

Z

About the Author

Ever since he convinced his wife to spend what seemed like far too much money on an Atari 800, Douglas J. Reilly has loved to play with computers. For many years before that, he made a living repairing photocopiers and early personal computers. But after a while, the software seemed to be more fun than the hardware.

Doug is the owner of Access Microsystems Inc., a small consulting firm that develops software using Microsoft Visual C++, Borland Delphi, Microsoft Access, and the Microsoft .NET Framework. He has created applications to electronically test job applicants, track retailer's inventory, and repair damaged databases. Currently he is working on a variety of healthcare applications for the St. Barnabas Health Care System as well as applications for the golf and leisure industry for Golf Society of the U.S., both in New Jersey. In addition to developing software, Doug has published articles in *Dr. Dobb's Journal* and *Software Development*, and he wrote a column in the *Pervasive Software Developer's Journal*. He has also published another book with Microsoft Press, *Inside Server-Based Applications* (2000).

Doug lives with his wife, Jean, and their two children, Tim and Erin. When not programming, he enjoys music, reading, and bicycle riding, although book writing and other concerns have conspired against serious riding this year. Maybe next year.

Doug can be reached by e-mail at *doug@ProgrammingASP.NET*.

The manuscript for this book was prepared and galleyed using Microsoft Word 2002. Pages were composed by Microsoft Press using Adobe PageMaker 6.52 for Windows, with text in Garamond and display type in Helvetica Condensed. Composed pages were delivered to the printer as electronic prepress files.

Cover Designer: Methodologie, Inc.
Interior Graphic Designer: James D. Kramer
Principal Compositor: Carl Diltz
Interior Artist: Joel Panchot
Principal Copy Editor: Cheryl Penner
Indexer: Shane-Armstrong Information Systems

Go beyond
knowing how Visual Basic works to learning how to write professional-level Microsoft .NET code.

Microsoft

CODING TECHNIQUES FOR MICROSOFT
VISUAL BASIC .NET

Microsoft
.net

John Connell

U.S.A. **$59.99**
Canada $86.99
ISBN: 0-7356-1254-4

Most books about Visual Basic use abstract snippets of code to illustrate the language's syntax, data structures, and controls. But even if you know the language, it's sometimes difficult to see how to put these elements together to write a complete program. This practical handbook of software construction covers the vital details about the latest version—Microsoft® Visual Basic® .NET, with its integrated development environment (IDE), complete support for XML, and ASP.NET Web-development functionality, including Web Forms and XML Web services. Whether you're a beginner or a self-taught programmer, a professional looking for a refresher in coding techniques, or a programmer coming from another language, this is the Visual Basic book for you.

Microsoft®
microsoft.com/mspress

Get a **Free**
e-mail newsletter, updates,
special offers, links to related books,
and more when you

register on line!

Register your Microsoft Press® title on our Web site and you'll get a FREE subscription to our e-mail newsletter, *Microsoft Press Book Connections.* You'll find out about newly released and upcoming books and learning tools, online events, software downloads, special offers and coupons for Microsoft Press customers, and information about major Microsoft® product releases. You can also read useful additional information about all the titles we publish, such as detailed book descriptions, tables of contents and indexes, sample chapters, links to related books and book series, author biographies, and reviews by other customers.

Registration is easy. Just visit this Web page and fill in your information:

http://www.microsoft.com/mspress/register

Microsoft®

- -

MICROSOFT LICENSE AGREEMENT
Book Companion CD

IMPORTANT—READ CAREFULLY: This Microsoft End-User License Agreement ("EULA") is a legal agreement between you (either an individual or an entity) and Microsoft Corporation for the Microsoft product identified above, which includes computer software and may include associated media, printed materials, and "online" or electronic documentation ("SOFTWARE PRODUCT"). Any component included within the SOFTWARE PRODUCT that is accompanied by a separate End-User License Agreement shall be governed by such agreement and not the terms set forth below. By installing, copying, or otherwise using the SOFTWARE PRODUCT, you agree to be bound by the terms of this EULA. If you do not agree to the terms of this EULA, you are not authorized to install, copy, or otherwise use the SOFTWARE PRODUCT; you may, however, return the SOFTWARE PRODUCT, along with all printed materials and other items that form a part of the Microsoft product that includes the SOFTWARE PRODUCT, to the place you obtained them for a full refund.

SOFTWARE PRODUCT LICENSE

The SOFTWARE PRODUCT is protected by United States copyright laws and international copyright treaties, as well as other intellectual property laws and treaties. The SOFTWARE PRODUCT is licensed, not sold.

1. **GRANT OF LICENSE.** This EULA grants you the following rights:

    a. **Software Product.** You may install and use one copy of the SOFTWARE PRODUCT on a single computer. The primary user of the computer on which the SOFTWARE PRODUCT is installed may make a second copy for his or her exclusive use on a portable computer.

    b. **Storage/Network Use.** You may also store or install a copy of the SOFTWARE PRODUCT on a storage device, such as a network server, used only to install or run the SOFTWARE PRODUCT on your other computers over an internal network; however, you must acquire and dedicate a license for each separate computer on which the SOFTWARE PRODUCT is installed or run from the storage device. A license for the SOFTWARE PRODUCT may not be shared or used concurrently on different computers.

    c. **License Pak.** If you have acquired this EULA in a Microsoft License Pak, you may make the number of additional copies of the computer software portion of the SOFTWARE PRODUCT authorized on the printed copy of this EULA, and you may use each copy in the manner specified above. You are also entitled to make a corresponding number of secondary copies for portable computer use as specified above.

    d. **Sample Code.** Solely with respect to portions, if any, of the SOFTWARE PRODUCT that are identified within the SOFTWARE PRODUCT as sample code (the "SAMPLE CODE"):

    i. **Use and Modification.** Microsoft grants you the right to use and modify the source code version of the SAMPLE CODE, *provided* you comply with subsection (d)(iii) below. You may not distribute the SAMPLE CODE, or any modified version of the SAMPLE CODE, in source code form.

    ii. **Redistributable Files.** Provided you comply with subsection (d)(iii) below, Microsoft grants you a nonexclusive, royalty-free right to reproduce and distribute the object code version of the SAMPLE CODE and of any modified SAMPLE CODE, other than SAMPLE CODE, or any modified version thereof, designated as not redistributable in the Readme file that forms a part of the SOFTWARE PRODUCT (the "Non-Redistributable Sample Code"). All SAMPLE CODE other than the Non-Redistributable Sample Code is collectively referred to as the "REDISTRIBUTABLES."

    iii. **Redistribution Requirements.** If you redistribute the REDISTRIBUTABLES, you agree to: (i) distribute the REDISTRIBUTABLES in object code form only in conjunction with and as a part of your software application product; (ii) not use Microsoft's name, logo, or trademarks to market your software application product; (iii) include a valid copyright notice on your software application product; (iv) indemnify, hold harmless, and defend Microsoft from and against any claims or lawsuits, including attorney's fees, that arise or result from the use or distribution of your software application product; and (v) not permit further distribution of the REDISTRIBUTABLES by your end user. Contact Microsoft for the applicable royalties due and other licensing terms for all other uses and/or distribution of the REDISTRIBUTABLES.

2. **DESCRIPTION OF OTHER RIGHTS AND LIMITATIONS.**

    - **Limitations on Reverse Engineering, Decompilation, and Disassembly.** You may not reverse engineer, decompile, or disassemble the SOFTWARE PRODUCT, except and only to the extent that such activity is expressly permitted by applicable law notwithstanding this limitation.

    - **Separation of Components.** The SOFTWARE PRODUCT is licensed as a single product. Its component parts may not be separated for use on more than one computer.

    - **Rental.** You may not rent, lease, or lend the SOFTWARE PRODUCT.

    - **Support Services.** Microsoft may, but is not obligated to, provide you with support services related to the SOFTWARE PRODUCT ("Support Services"). Use of Support Services is governed by the Microsoft policies and programs described in the user manual, in "online" documentation, and/or in other Microsoft-provided materials. Any supplemental software code provided to you as part of the Support Services shall be considered part of the SOFTWARE PRODUCT and subject to the terms and conditions of this EULA. With respect to technical information you provide to Microsoft as part of the Support Services, Microsoft may use such information for its business purposes, including for product support and development. Microsoft will not utilize such technical information in a form that personally identifies you.

- **Software Transfer.** You may permanently transfer all of your rights under this EULA, provided you retain no copies, you transfer all of the SOFTWARE PRODUCT (including all component parts, the media and printed materials, any upgrades, this EULA, and, if applicable, the Certificate of Authenticity), **and** the recipient agrees to the terms of this EULA.

- **Termination.** Without prejudice to any other rights, Microsoft may terminate this EULA if you fail to comply with the terms and conditions of this EULA. In such event, you must destroy all copies of the SOFTWARE PRODUCT and all of its component parts.

3. **COPYRIGHT.** All title and copyrights in and to the SOFTWARE PRODUCT (including but not limited to any images, photographs, animations, video, audio, music, text, SAMPLE CODE, REDISTRIBUTABLES, and "applets" incorporated into the SOFTWARE PRODUCT) and any copies of the SOFTWARE PRODUCT are owned by Microsoft or its suppliers. The SOFTWARE PRODUCT is protected by copyright laws and international treaty provisions. Therefore, you must treat the SOFTWARE PRODUCT like any other copyrighted material **except** that you may install the SOFTWARE PRODUCT on a single computer provided you keep the original solely for backup or archival purposes. You may not copy the printed materials accompanying the SOFTWARE PRODUCT.

4. **U.S. GOVERNMENT RESTRICTED RIGHTS.** The SOFTWARE PRODUCT and documentation are provided with RESTRICTED RIGHTS. Use, duplication, or disclosure by the Government is subject to restrictions as set forth in subparagraph (c)(1)(ii) of the Rights in Technical Data and Computer Software clause at DFARS 252.227-7013 or subparagraphs (c)(1) and (2) of the Commercial Computer Software—Restricted Rights at 48 CFR 52.227-19, as applicable. Manufacturer is Microsoft Corporation/One Microsoft Way/Redmond, WA 98052-6399.

5. **EXPORT RESTRICTIONS.** You agree that you will not export or re-export the SOFTWARE PRODUCT, any part thereof, or any process or service that is the direct product of the SOFTWARE PRODUCT (the foregoing collectively referred to as the "Restricted Components"), to any country, person, entity, or end user subject to U.S. export restrictions. You specifically agree not to export or re-export any of the Restricted Components (i) to any country to which the U.S. has embargoed or restricted the export of goods or services, which currently include, but are not necessarily limited to, Cuba, Iran, Iraq, Libya, North Korea, Sudan, and Syria, or to any national of any such country, wherever located, who intends to transmit or transport the Restricted Components back to such country; (ii) to any end user who you know or have reason to know will utilize the Restricted Components in the design, development, or production of nuclear, chemical, or biological weapons; or (iii) to any end user who has been prohibited from participating in U.S. export transactions by any federal agency of the U.S. government. You warrant and represent that neither the BXA nor any other U.S. federal agency has suspended, revoked, or denied your export privileges.

DISCLAIMER OF WARRANTY

NO WARRANTIES OR CONDITIONS. MICROSOFT EXPRESSLY DISCLAIMS ANY WARRANTY OR CONDITION FOR THE SOFTWARE PRODUCT. THE SOFTWARE PRODUCT AND ANY RELATED DOCUMENTATION ARE PROVIDED "AS IS" WITHOUT WARRANTY OR CONDITION OF ANY KIND, EITHER EXPRESS OR IMPLIED, INCLUDING, WITHOUT LIMITATION, THE IMPLIED WARRANTIES OF MERCHANTABILITY, FITNESS FOR A PARTICULAR PURPOSE, OR NONINFRINGEMENT. THE ENTIRE RISK ARISING OUT OF USE OR PERFORMANCE OF THE SOFTWARE PRODUCT REMAINS WITH YOU.

LIMITATION OF LIABILITY. TO THE MAXIMUM EXTENT PERMITTED BY APPLICABLE LAW, IN NO EVENT SHALL MICROSOFT OR ITS SUPPLIERS BE LIABLE FOR ANY SPECIAL, INCIDENTAL, INDIRECT, OR CONSEQUENTIAL DAMAGES WHATSOEVER (INCLUDING, WITHOUT LIMITATION, DAMAGES FOR LOSS OF BUSINESS PROFITS, BUSINESS INTERRUPTION, LOSS OF BUSINESS INFORMATION, OR ANY OTHER PECUNIARY LOSS) ARISING OUT OF THE USE OF OR INABILITY TO USE THE SOFTWARE PRODUCT OR THE PROVISION OF OR FAILURE TO PROVIDE SUPPORT SERVICES, EVEN IF MICROSOFT HAS BEEN ADVISED OF THE POSSIBILITY OF SUCH DAMAGES. IN ANY CASE, MICROSOFT'S ENTIRE LIABILITY UNDER ANY PROVISION OF THIS EULA SHALL BE LIMITED TO THE GREATER OF THE AMOUNT ACTUALLY PAID BY YOU FOR THE SOFTWARE PRODUCT OR US$5.00; PROVIDED, HOWEVER, IF YOU HAVE ENTERED INTO A MICROSOFT SUPPORT SERVICES AGREEMENT, MICROSOFT'S ENTIRE LIABILITY REGARDING SUPPORT SERVICES SHALL BE GOVERNED BY THE TERMS OF THAT AGREEMENT. BECAUSE SOME STATES AND JURISDICTIONS DO NOT ALLOW THE EXCLUSION OR LIMITATION OF LIABILITY, THE ABOVE LIMITATION MAY NOT APPLY TO YOU.

MISCELLANEOUS

This EULA is governed by the laws of the State of Washington USA, except and only to the extent that applicable law mandates governing law of a different jurisdiction.

Should you have any questions concerning this EULA, or if you desire to contact Microsoft for any reason, please contact the Microsoft subsidiary serving your country, or write: Microsoft Sales Information Center/One Microsoft Way/Redmond, WA 98052-6399.